Teaching about Asian Pacific Americans

Critical Perspectives on Asian Pacific Americans Series

Critical Perspectives on Asian Pacific Americans aims to educate and inform readers regarding the Asian Pacific American experience and to critically examine key social, economic, psychological, cultural, and political issues. The series presents books that are theoretically engaging, comparative, and multidisciplinary, and works that reflect the contemporary concerns that are of critical importance to understanding and empowering Asian Pacific Americans.

Books in the Series:
1. Diana Ting Liu Wu, *Asian Pacific Americans in the Workplace* (1997)
2. Juanita Tamayo Lott, *Asian Americans: From Racial Category to Multiple Identities* (1998)
3. Jun Xing, *Asian America Through the Lens: History, Representations, and Identity* (1998)
4. Pyong Gap Min and Rose Kim, editors, *Struggle for Ethnic Identity: Narratives by Asian American Professionals* (1999)
5. Wendy Ho, *In Her Mother's House: The Politics of Asian American Mother-Daughter Writing* (1999)
6. Deborah Woo, *Glass Ceilings and Asian Americans* (2000)
7. Patricia Wong Hall and Victor Hwang, editors, *Anti-Asian Violence in North America: Asian American and Asian Canadian Reflections on Hate, Healing and Resistance* (2001)
8. Pyong Gap Min and Jung Ha Kim, editors, *Religions in Asian America: Building Faith Communities* (2002)
9. Pyong Gap Min, editor, *The Second Generation: Ethnic Identity among Asian Americans* (2002)
10. Susie Lan Cassel, editor, *The Chinese in America: A History from the Gold Mountain to the New Millenium* (2002)
11. Sucheng Chan, editor, *Remapping Asian American History* (2003)
12. Monica Chiu, *Filthy Fictions: Asian American Literature by Women* (2004)
13. Him Mark Lai, *Becoming Chinese American: A History of Communities and Institutions* (2004)
14. Daniel F. Detzner, *Elder Voices: Southeast Asian Families in the United States* (2004)
15. Edith Chen and Glenn Omatsu, editors, *Teaching about Asian Pacific Americans: Effectiveness Activities, Strategies, and Assignments for Classrooms and Communities* (2006)

Teaching about Asian Pacific Americans

Effective Activities, Strategies, and Assignments for Classrooms and Communities

Edited by
Edith Wen-Chu Chen
and
Glenn Omatsu

ROWMAN & LITTLEFIELD PUBLISHERS, INC.
Lanham • Boulder • New York • Toronto • Oxford

ROWMAN & LITTLEFIELD PUBLISHERS, INC.

Published in the United States of America
by Rowman & Littlefield Publishers, Inc.
A wholly owned subsidiary of The Rowman & Littlefield Publishing Group, Inc.
4501 Forbes Boulevard, Suite 200, Lanham, Maryland 20706
www.rowmanlittlefield.com

P.O. Box 317, Oxford OX2 9RU, UK

British Library Cataloguing in Publication Information Available

Library of Congress Cataloging-in-Publication Data

Teaching about Asian Pacific Americans : effective activities, strategies, and assignments for classrooms and communities / Edith Wen-Chu Chen and Glenn Omatsu, editors.
    p.   cm. — (Critical perspectives on Asian Pacific Americans series)
  Includes bibliographical references and indes.
  ISBN-13: 978-0-7425-5337-8 (alk. paper)
  ISBN-10: 0-7425-5337-X (alk. paper)
  ISBN-13: 978-0-7425-5338-5 (pbk. : alk. paper)
  ISBN-10: 0-7425-5338-8 (pbk. : alk. paper)
  1. Asian Americans—Study and teaching. 2. Pacific Islander Americans—Study and teaching. 3. Asian Americans—Politics and government. 4. Pacific Islander Americans—Politics and government. 5. Asian Americans—Social conditions. 6. Pacific Islander Americans—Social Conditions. I. Chen, Edith Wen-Chu, 1966– II. Omatsu, Glenn. III. Series.
  E184.A75T43 2006
  973'.0495—dc22

2005057649

Printed in the United States of America

♾™ The paper used in this publication meets the minimum requirements of American National Standard for Information Sciences—Permanence of Paper for Printed Library Materials, ANSI/NISO Z39.48-1992.

To my first teachers, my parents Flora Huang-Chung Hsia Chen and Mo-Shing Chen;
my sister Eunice Shin Chen, who is always there for me in ways big and small;
and my little niece Elle with whom I am joyfully learning about life all over again.

— Edith Wen-Chu Chen

Contents

Acknowledgments

We would like to extend our appreciation to the many people and institutions that made this book a reality. First, we would like to thank Timothy Fong, the series editor who believed in the book from the very beginning and has continued to provide his unwavering support to this project. This book owes much to Glenn Omatsu, brilliant teacher, well-known community activist, and formerly the long-time associate editor of *Amerasia Journal*, the nation's oldest research journal in Asian American studies. I could not think of a better co-editor for this book. He represents the very best in Asian American studies and continues to serve as an inspiration to us all. I'd also like to acknowledge Teresa Kay Williams-León who has been a dear friend, mentor, colleague, and one of my former teachers. It was as a student in her classroom that I was first introduced to interactive teaching techniques, which are the basis for how I currently approach teaching. I am forever indebted to Shirley Hune, my graduate school mentor, who continues to share with me her gems of wisdom and guidance. Others who have provided invaluable input, feedback, and/or moral support to this project are Gilda Ochoa, Estela Ballon, Kimberly Nettles, Daniel Malpica, Karen Umemoto, Brian Niiya, Dennis Arguelles, Claudia Fajardo-Lira, Benjamin Kudo, Eunai Shrake, Juana Mora, Ayanna Yonemura, Enrique del a Cruz, Mary Kao, Anna Gonzalez, Russell Leong, and Don Nakanishi.

We would like to acknowledge Jessica Gribble, Jenn Nemec, and Rowman & Littlefield Publishers, Inc., who saw this book to its fruition. Heartfelt thanks also goes to Malcolm Kao who patiently and beautifully typeset and re-typeset (many times) the contents of the book.

Cal State University, Northridge Probationary Faculty Support Grant, CSUN College of Humanities, and the CSUN Asian American Studies department provided time or funds to offset costs associated with the production of the book. We also would like to express our gratitude to Elizabeth Say and Gordon Nakagawa for seeing the value of this project and for their commitment to supporting faculty and teaching. Thanks also to Janaki Bowerman, Reyna Kennedy, Molly Nguyen, Janet Wong, and Stephanie Nguyen for their administrative and technical assistance. We would also like to recognize Darryl Mar, the artist who gave us permission to use his powerful artwork as the cover. This image is one section of his mural that poignantly captures the historical struggles of different Asian American groups, now hanging at the Cross-Cultural Center, at the University of California, Irvine.

This book would not have been possible without the contributing authors. It was a pleasure to work, collaborate, and learn from them.

Finally, we would like to honor the many students, faculty, staff, community people, and allies who continue to fight for social justice and a better world.

Introduction

Edith Wen-Chu Chen and Glenn Omatsu

The lesson plans in this book were inspired by the editors' combined experience of teaching, research, community activism, and dedication to anti-racist struggles. The legitimization of Asian American Studies as an academic discipline has led to the publication of research and policy reports and creative writings. Despite the plethora of scholarship, many of the significant findings and critical ideas have failed to captivate most college and high school students or the general public.

At the K-12 level, the little attention given to Asian Pacific Americans is usually framed in terms of "celebrating differences," while failing to address issues of racism, institutional inequality, privilege, and power. Two notable exceptions are the excellent teaching anthologies *Beyond Heroes and Holidays: A Practical Guide to K-12 Anti-Racist, Multicultural Education, and Staff Development* and *Resistance in Paradise: Rethinking 100 Years of U.S. Involvement in the Carribean and the Pacific*.[1] At the college level, Professor Lane Ryo Hirabayashi compiled *Teaching Asian America: Diversity and the Problem of Community* to help faculty grapple with pedagogical challenges in Asian American Studies.[2]

Our book shares important scholarship, research, and community-based work in the form of engaging, student-oriented teaching activities. The word "students" is used broadly here to include high school and college students as well as community workshop participants. Overall, the lesson plans encourage students to integrate and apply their own experiences, strengths, and/or perspectives with the course material.

Who Should Use This Book?

Teaching about Asian Pacific Americans was created for educators and other practitioners who want to use interactive activities, assignments, and strategies in their classrooms or workshops. Experts in the field of Asian American Studies will find powerful, innovative teaching activities that help convey established as well as new areas of knowledge. Those with less knowledge about Asian Pacific Americans will also find this book helpful, for each chapter provides background information on an issue that impacts Asian Pacific Americans.

Additionally, this book is not limited to only those in Asian American Studies but is also intended as a resource for those teaching classes relating to race and diversity who wish to include issues pertaining to Asian Pacific Americans in their curriculum. Diversity in the United States is often framed in terms of black-white relations or majority-minority relations, leaving out the experiences of Asian Pacific Americans.[3] While the book centers on the experiences of Asian Pacific Americans, users will find activities that make comparisons with other people of color as well as covering general issues dealing with power, privilege, and identity. Hence, anyone working in the field of race, ethnicity, and diversity will find this book a valuable resource.

Implementing Liberatory Pedagogy

Asian American Studies and Ethnic Studies are grounded in a tradition of seeing students as resources and valuable sources of knowledge. Interactive teaching activities provide an opportunity for students to contribute their knowledge in a way that cannot happen in a lecture style of teaching. While there is a growing awareness that teaching about multiple systems of domination are important, many educators find it challenging to teach these complex topics in an engaging, thoughtful, and productive way.[4] Similarly, although many have critiqued the hierarchical nature of traditional forms of teaching and advocated for more of a student-centered approach, instructors are often left on their own to figure out just how to do this in an effective way.[5] Sometimes activities can be productive, but other times they can lead to out-of-control discussions with some students feeling intense anger and/or shame. In short, just because an activity is interactive does not necessarily make it "liberatory."

This book is based on the ideas of liberatory pedagogy but implements the approach with tested strategies and activities. An important feature of this book is that all the chapters follow a basic format to facilitate the user's understanding and implementation. Each lesson plan contains a set of objectives, background information on the topic, a step-by-step guide for implementing the activity, as well as tips on how to deal with possible student responses. Some chapters also include extra features—personal profiles, historical notes, and community-based reports—to enhance the user's understanding of the lesson. Finally, each chapter ends with reference notes or a recommended resource list. Each list is a careful selection of no more than three helpful resources, keeping in mind the time limitations facing most educators.

Asian Americans, Pacific Islanders, and Asian Pacific Americans

This book consists of lesson plans on Asian Americans with unfortunately only a handful relating to the experiences of Pacific Islanders. The terms "Asian Americans," "Pacific Islanders," and "Asian Pacific Americans" need to be understood as political constructions and not biological categories. The late historian and activist Yuji Ichioka coined the term Asian American in the late 1960s to emphasize self-definition, critical consciousness and social engagement, similar to the political terms "Black" and "Chicano."[6] Eventually, the U.S. government adopted these terms—along with later terms, "Pacific Islanders" and "Asian Pacific Americans"—but redefined them as racial classifications based on biology, geography, and culture. In reality, the designation Asian American includes more than thirty ethnic groups, most with different languages and cultures, while the classification Pacific Islander encompasses more than forty ethnic groups. In this book, the editors and contributors use the terms Asian American, Pacific Islander, and Asian Pacific Americans as political constructions. Thus, Asian American and Pacific Islander communities are not racial groupings but rather political communities constantly forming and reforming through struggles based on solidarity, such as movements against racism.

Organization of the Book

The book is divided into four parts. Part I, "Definitions, Concepts, and Issues," covers some of the core research-based and community-driven issues in Asian American Studies. These topics include immigration, the experience of separation and loss for immigrants and refugees, the cost of assimilation, the model minority thesis, labor struggles, globalization, and representations in media. Other topics not often covered in many classes include Filipino American history, sexuality, transnationalism, non-verbal counseling techniques, and the nuances of collectivism and individualism as applied to Asian Pacific Americans.

Part II devotes a special section to war, colonialism, and imperialism given the recent post-9/11 events and the U.S. invasion and occupation of Iraq. Although these are recent events, imperialism and colonialism are not new to Asian Americans and Pacific Islanders as seen in the chapter discussing the U.S. military conquest and occupation of Hawai'i and the Philippines. Equally important are the struggles to seek justice as discussed in the chapter on Japanese American redress and reparations, which also have implications for other communities of color.

Part III, "Community Building, Learning, and Organizing," focuses on what students and teachers can learn from the community, whether from their classroom communities or from off-campus neighborhoods. These lesson plans cover student leadership training and field trips and also show how to organize students around community projects, conduct oral histories with elderly and other Asian Pacific Americans, and build bridges with other communities of color.

Part IV, "Critical Thinking Teaching Strategies," provides teachers and practitioners with strategies that address different components of critical thinking. The lesson plans address the complex topic of privilege, power, and "Whiteness." Other chapters provide tools for helping students to find meaning in events, to problem-solve, and to engage in original thinking.

Finally, the last section (part V) provides web resources on teaching strategies and topics impacting Asian Americans and Pacific Islanders.

Although this book covers a range of issues that impact Asian Pacific Americans, it is by no means comprehensive. We hope that it serves as a resource and inspiration for educators for creating their own lesson plans.

Notes

1. American Friends Service Committee and Office of Curriculum Support, School District of Philadelphia, *Resistance in Paradise: Rethinking 100 Years of U.S. Involvement in the Carribean and the Pacific* (Philadelphia: American Friends Service Committee and School District of Philadelphia, 1998); and Enid Lee, Deborah Menkart, and Margo Okazawa-Rey, eds., *Beyond Heroes and Holidays: A Practical Guide to K-12 Anti-Racist, Multicultural Education, and Staff Development* (Washington, D.C.: Network of Educators, 1998).

2. Lane Ryo Hirabayashi, *Teaching Asian America: Diversity and the Problem of Community* (Lanham, MD: Rowman and Littlefield, 1998).

3. Shirley Hune, "Rethinking Race: Paradigms and Policy Formation," *Amerasia Journal* 21:1 & 2 (1995): 29-40.

4. Maxine Baca Zinn and Bonnie Thorton Dill, "Theorizing Difference from Multiracial Feminism," *Feminist Studies* 22 (Summer 1996): 321-31.

5. Paulo Freire, *Pedagogy of the Oppressed* (New York: Continuum Press, 1993); bell hooks, *Teaching to Transgress: Education as the Practice of Freedom* (New York: Routledge Press, 1994); Carmen Luke and Jennifer Gore, eds., *Feminisms and Critical Pedagogy* (New York: Routledge, 1992).

6. Yuji Ichioka, "A Historian by Happenstance," *Amerasia Journal* 26:1 (2000): 32-53.

Part I

Definitions, Concepts, and Issues

Chapter 1

Vietnamese Boat People:
Separation and Loss

Mariam Beevi Lam, James Lam,
Michael Matsuda, and Diep Tran
Orange County Asian & Pacific Islander Community Alliance

According to the 2000 Census, Vietnamese Americans make up the fourth largest Asian American population, following Chinese Americans, Filipino Americans, and Asian Indian Americans. Most Vietnamese who came to the United States after 1975 were *refugees*, not *immigrants*. Unlike immigrants who have some choice in leaving their countries, refugees have little choice but to leave their country in order to survive. This lesson plan on Vietnamese "boat people" helps high school and college students understand the difference between refugees and immigrants, and also enables students to understand the experiences of *separation and loss* connected to the lives of Vietnamese Americans and their families. This lesson plan can also be used by social service agencies and community-based organizations for training purposes, for example, in the context of developing understanding among co-workers, or between employer and employees.

This lesson plan is adapted from the first of ten lesson plans in *Vietnamese Americans: Lessons in American History*, a first-of-its-kind, comprehensive curriculum and teaching guide on the Vietnamese American experience for secondary education developed by OCAPICA and community partners. For more information about *Lessons in American History*, contact Diep Tran, Orange County Asian and Pacific Islander Community Alliance, 12900 Garden Grove Blvd., Suite 214A, Garden Grove, CA 92843, telephone (714) 636-9095, e-mail ndtt@ocapica.org.

Objectives

- To develop students' understanding of separation and loss in the context of the Vietnamese "boat people" experience.
- To develop students' understanding of the difference between refugees and immigrants in the United States.

Time

- One hour

Number of Participants

- Five to fifty persons

Materials Needed

- Background information on boat people is included with this lesson plan (see excerpts from the monograph *Straddling Two Social Worlds: The Experience of Vietnamese Refugee Children in the United States* by Min Zhou and Carl L. Bankston III).

Background

The Vietnam War caused more than 58,000 American and approximately three million Vietnamese casualties. After the fall of Saigon in 1975, thousands of Vietnamese began fleeing their country in fear of persecution by the new Vietnamese Communist government. The phrase "boat people" came into common use as a result of the flood of refugees casting off from Vietnam in overcrowded, leaky boats beginning in the 1970s and early 1980s. Between 1978 and 1981, more than one million Vietnamese ventured across the South China Sea for freedom and safety, and it is estimated that half of those who attempted the trip died due to hunger, thirst, disease, and assault at the hands of pirates. These boat people gave up their homes, friends, and essentially their lives for a better life abroad. Read the excerpt from "Straddling Two Social Worlds: The Experience of Vietnamese Refugee Children in the United States" for an overview of the historical and social context of the Vietnamese refugee experience.

Suggested Procedures

This lesson plan will enhance students' understanding of the concept "separation and loss" in the context of the Vietnamese American refugee experience. Remind them that America has a long history as a destination point for refugees. Give students the example of the Mayflower pilgrims as the most famous "boat people;" however, it is important to note to students that the arrival of such earlier European groups to America resulted in the displacement of Native Americans, who also experienced "loss" and "separation" as a result of war, persecution, and forced removal from indigenous lands.

1. Ask the students to name other refugee groups or countries of origin from which refugees have emigrated and permanently resettled in the United States. For example, the twelve largest source countries for refugees (comprising 98 percent of arrivals in 1999) who permanently settle in the United States are: Yugoslavia (former), Cuba, Soviet Union (former), Vietnam, Somalia, Liberia, Sudan, Iraq, Ethiopia, Iran, Haiti, and Sierra Leone. Discuss reasons why these countries have the most refugees abroad, for example: civil wars, political unrest, land disputes, and conflicts, etc.

2. Write the word "separation" on the board and have the students brainstorm what the word means to them. Write all their ideas on the board and briefly discuss. Words should reflect wide interpretations of separation.

3. Ask students to take out a piece of paper and write down the ten most important things in their lives in no particular order. The list could include people, pets, objects—anything.

4. Now tell them to eliminate two items on their list. Tell them to choose carefully because they will never see or touch these things again. Give them a few seconds to do this.

5. Now have them eliminate two more items. Again, tell them that they will never be able to see the items again. Some students might protest but encourage them to continue.

6. Eliminate two more items and continue until there are only two items left. Now have them cross out the last two items.

Assessment/Closure

1. This activity will be difficult because students will have to choose among siblings, parents, and other important aspects in their lives. Some may refuse to go on. Tell them that these are the decisions that the Vietnamese boat people and nearly all refugees have made in order to survive. Immigrants, on the other hand, come to another country with "paperwork," and they usually have time and discretion to choose what they want to carry.

2. Ask students how they felt during the process. Remind them that this, of course, was not real. Tell them that these are decisions that the Vietnamese boat people and nearly all refugees have made in order to survive. Remind them that separation for refugees is often of the harshest kind—parents separated from their children, siblings separated from each other, and people separated from their homes and country.

3. Conclude by having students write about their feelings regarding this activity and whether or not they have developed new insight into the plight of the boat people.

Straddling Two Social Worlds:
The Experiences of Vietnamese Refugee Children in the United States

Min Zhou and Carl L. Bankston, III

(Excerpted with permission from the authors from the monograph of the same title, ERIC Clearinghouse on Urban Education, New York, 2000).

The story of Vietnamese Americans is one of very rapid growth. In the early 1970s, there were fewer than 15,000 Vietnamese in the United States. After the fall of Saigon in 1975, Vietnamese became of one of the largest refugee groups, and, thus, increasingly visible in the American ethnic mosaic. By 1990, the group numbered over 615,000, a forty-fold increase in just fifteen years; and even this figure understates the true size of the Vietnamese-origin population, since it excludes no fewer than 200,000 Sino-Vietnamese (ethnic Chinese), who arrived in the United States as part of the larger refugee outflow from Southeast Asia.[1]

Unlike most other immigrant groups in American history, most Vietnamese arrived as refugees. As a group, they were uprooted from their homeland under frequently violent and traumatic circumstances. This history has caused members of the parent generation to face special difficulties of adjustment to the new land. These difficulties affect the children as well. The parents' low socioeconomic status makes it hard for the children to succeed, even though both parents and children desperately want to get ahead. The environment in which the children find themselves further limits their chances: too many live in neighborhoods that are poor and socially isolated, where local schools do not function well and the streets are beset by gang violence and drugs. To all these difficulties are added the generic problems of second-generation acculturation, aggravated by the troubles associated with coming of age in an era far more materialistic and individualistic than encountered by immigrant children in years gone by. Often, they find themselves straddling two social worlds. At home or within their ethnic community, they hear that they must work hard and do well in school in order to move up; on the street they often learn a different lesson, that of rebellion against authority and rejection of the goals of achievement. Like other immigrant children, this bicultural conflict defines the experience of Vietnamese children in growing up in America.

The sudden emergence of Vietnamese and other Southeast Asians on the American scene was primarily the result of U.S. military involvement in Southeast Asia. In the post-World War II period, the development of the Communist bloc dominated by the former Soviet Union, the Communist takeover in China, the direct confrontation with Communist troops in the Korean War, and the threat of the Communist "domino" effect prompted a U.S. foreign policy to "contain" Communism, pushing Americans into Southeast Asia.

The Vietnam War

In 1954, the French army was defeated by Ho Chi Minh's Viet Minh Front forces, and Vietnam was divided into two countries: the Democratic Republic of Vietnam (North Vietnam), headed by Ho Chi Minh, and the Republic of Vietnam (South Vietnam), headed by Ngo Dinh Diem. In response, the United States, acting on the primary foreign policy objective of containing international Communism, became increasingly dedicated to the preservation of Diem's anti-

Additional Reading

Communist government in South Vietnam. However, Diem, born of a Catholic family and relying heavily upon Vietnamese Catholics and Catholic refugees from the North for his suppression of Communist infiltration in the South, began to lose his popularity. In a country where Buddhism dominated, Diem's favoritism toward Catholics created strong resentment, which opened up opportunities for the North Vietnamese-supported insurgents. These insurgents organized themselves as the National Liberation Front, known as the Viet Cong (Vietnamese guerrilla fighters who opposed the South Vietnamese government). In 1963, a military coup overthrew Diem. This coup apparently took place with the knowledge and consent of the American Embassy. The new leaders of South Vietnam proved less able to maintain control than Diem. By 1965, with the South Vietnamese government on the verge of collapse, President Lyndon B. Johnson sent ground troops to South Vietnam. By the early 1970s, American political leaders began to realize that a quick military victory was extremely unlikely, that the American public was divided over the war, and that continuing a war that was increasingly unpopular would mean committing American soldiers to an indefinite future. At the Paris Peace Talks in 1973, the United States agreed on a timetable for withdrawing American soldiers fighting in Vietnam, and turned the war over to the South Vietnamese army with the support of American funding and continued training. It turned out that the South Vietnamese government was no better prepared to defend itself than it had been in 1965. In April 1975, Saigon, the capital of South Vietnam, fell to North Vietnamese troops. Vietnam was unified under the Hanoi government, and Saigon was renamed Ho Chi Minh City.

The war caused over 58,000 American and about three million Vietnamese casualties. It also left nightmares, depression, and posttraumatic stress disorders that continue to affect Americans and Vietnamese Americans, as well as hundreds and thousands of refugees. In a 1987 study, August and Gianola find that many Vietnamese Americans suffer from war-related stress similar to that of American soldiers who had served in Vietnam.[2]

The Refugee Exodus

Vietnamese refugees fled their country in several significant waves. The first wave surged at the fall of Saigon in 1975. This group was made up primarily of South Vietnamese government officials, U.S.-related personnel, and members of the Vietnamese elite. The second wave, which became known as the crisis of the boat people, hit the American shore in the late 1970s. A large proportion of the boat people were Sino-Vietnamese. The third wave occurred in the early 1980s. This group consisted of the boat people as well as those leaving Vietnam under the U.S. Orderly Departure program. In late 1989, a distinct group—Amerasian children and their families—entered in large numbers under the U.S. Homecoming Act. Then, in the early 1990s, another large group reached the American shore under the U.S. Humanitarian Operation Program. The Vietnamese refugee flight subsided in the mid-1990s. Since then, the arrival of the Vietnamese has become part of the regular family-sponsored immigration.

Before 1977, 130,000 refugees who had fled Vietnam were allowed to settle in the United States on parole status granted by the U.S. government. Those in this initial wave of refugees were mostly members of the elite and the middle class who either had access to the evacuation arranged by the American military or could afford their own means of flight. After the initial airlift of Vietnamese to the United States in 1975, thousands of additional refugees fled Vietnam by boat over the next three years. The phrase "boat people" came into common usage as a result of the flood of refugees casting off from Vietnam in overcrowded, leaky boats at the end of the 1970s and the beginning of the 1980s. By 1979, an estimated 400,000 refugees, known as the second wave of flight, escaped Vietnam in boats to Thailand, Malaysia, Indonesia, and Singapore.[3] This mass exodus was disproportionately made up of ethnic minorities, particularly the Sino-Vietnamese, who fled Vietnam after China became involved in Vietnam's war with Cambodia.[4] According to most reports, almost half the boat people perished at sea. The remaining half ended up in camps in other countries in Southeast Asia.[5] Nevertheless, the refugee exodus continued throughout the 1980s.

It seems relatively easy for most Americans to understand why many South Vietnamese fled their country in the early days after the fall of Saigon. But it is more difficult to grasp why the refugees kept fleeing for so many years after the Vietnam War ended, especially considering that the Hanoi government did not plunge the South into a bloodbath as so many had once feared. Several factors account for the lengthy flow of refugees from Vietnam. First, political repression continued to make life difficult for those individuals who were detained at or released from reeducation camps as well as for their family members.

Second, economic hardships, exacerbated by natural disasters and poor harvests in the years following the war, created a widespread sense of hopelessness. Third, incessant warfare with neighboring countries further drained Vietnam's resources for capital investment and development. These severely adversarial conditions, triggering the second and third exodus of Vietnamese "boat people" in the late 1970s and early 1980s, continued to send thousands of refugees off on the rugged journey to a better life.

Once the early refugee waves established communities in the United States, the new informal and officially unrecognized ties between America and Vietnam provided an impetus for a continuing outward flow. Upon resettlement in the United States and other Western countries, many Vietnamese refugees rebuilt overseas networks with families and friends. Letters frequently moved between the receiving countries and Vietnam, providing relatives in the homeland with an in-depth knowledge of the changing refugee policies and procedures of resettlement countries.

After peaking in 1982, the influx of refugees slowed somewhat, but it rose sharply between the years 1988 and 1992. From 1990 onward, political prisoners constituted the largest category of Vietnamese refugees admitted to the United States. Some former South Vietnamese civilian and military officials had been imprisoned in reeducation camps in Vietnam since 1975, and many of those who had been released from camps were marginal members of a society that discriminated against them and their families in employment, housing, and education. In 1989, the United States and the Socialist Republic of Vietnam agreed that current and former detainees in reeducation camps would be allowed to leave for the United States.

Since the mid-1990s, immigration from Vietnam has begun to assume a different shape. Though a substantial proportion continues to be admitted as refugees, an increasing number have been entering the United States as family-sponsored immigrants, a flow that will probably grow in years to come. As the refugee influx ebbs, family reunification can be expected to dominate Vietnamese immigration into the next century.

Vietnamese Americans are a newly established ethnic population, but they are also a very fast growing population as a result of their continuing immigration. By 1996, over 700,000 refugees from Vietnam had arrived in the United States. The history of exile and hardship has left marks. Many Vietnamese parents pressure their children to excel in school and to enter professional fields such as science, medicine, or engineering because these parents continue to feel the insecurities of the past and to view education as the only ticket to a better life. "My mom and dad have been through so much in their lives," one young woman said, "that now they don't want me to take any chances at all."

There is also a significantly large number of Vietnamese children who do not experience similar parental pressures because their mothers and fathers were left behind in Vietnam. Unaccompanied minors and children with relatives other than parents came to the United States without family direction. Even when the children later reunited with parents and family members, normative parent-child relations proved difficult because of the lengthy and severe family disruptions resulting from warfare and the chaotic situation in Vietnam. Forsyth and Bankston, for example, discuss the case of a young Vietnamese man who had been separated from both parents for over a decade before being reunited with mother and father in the United States.[6] Relations proved impossible to reconstruct and the young man began a career of juvenile delinquency that ultimately ended in a murder conviction. Along similar lines, McClements-Hammond find that unaccompanied Vietnamese minors suffer significantly more mental health problems than children living with their families.[7] Disrupted family patterns, as a consequence of uprooting and resettlement rather than divorce, became a problem for many Vietnamese arriving in the United States.

Transition: The Refugee Camps

Between exile from Vietnam and entry into American society, many Vietnamese refugees stayed in refugee camps. The camps put strains on family relations in some respects, strengthened those relations in others, and began a process of changes in families that would continue in the United States.[8] Researchers observe that the camps often had a disintegrative effect on families, since family members were left behind or lost; thus, the process of fleeing Vietnam and staying in refugee camps broke up many families.[9] However, connections among family members also helped many Vietnamese endure the stresses of camp life. In an important study of Vietnamese American family life, astutely observed extended family ties were more important to Vietnamese in America than they had been in Vietnam.[10] Much of the increase in interdependence of cousins, in-laws, and other extended family members, even unrelated persons, began to strengthen in the camps.

Government Policies and the Beginning of Vietnamese America

U.S. refugee policies have something of an ad hoc character, developed as a series of responses to unforeseen and changing policies. When President Gerald R. Ford authorized the entry of 130,000 refugees from the three countries of Indochina (Vietnam, Cambodia, and Laos), 125,000 of whom were Vietnamese, into the United States on April 18, 1975, he was reacting to the victory of Communist forces in those countries with a one-time action. But the refugee exodus showed no sign of slowing down. The resettlement continued as a result of the lobbying of concerned American citizens and organizations, and the refugee crisis of 1979 and 1980 created pressure for a new refugee policy. The Refugee Act of 1980 became the most comprehensive piece of refugee legislation in U.S. history. In place of the "seventh preference category" established in 1965, which admitted refugees as part of the total number of immigrants allowed into the United States, the Refugee Act provided for an annual number of admissions for refugees, which was designated independent of the number of immigrants admitted and was to be established each year by the president in consultation with Congress. This act, then, became a policy of refugee resettlement, reflecting a continuing process, rather than a mere reaction to specific emergency events.

Those who work with Vietnamese youth will frequently hear them say that their parents came to the United States as "ODPs." Sometimes the young people themselves do not know the meaning of these initials. The Orderly Departure Program (ODP) was created in late May 1979 as an agreement between the United Nations High Commission for Refugees and the Hanoi government as a tentative solution to worldwide attention attracted by the boat people. The ODP allowed those interviewed and approved for resettlement in America by U.S. officials in Vietnam to leave by plane with their Vietnamese passports. This group was made up mostly of former South Vietnamese soldiers, who had been in prison or reeducation camps, and their families. By 1989, 165,000 Vietnamese had been admitted to the United States under the Orderly Departure Program and by the mid-1990s the number had grown to over 200,000.

Since 1990, political prisoners and their families have constituted the largest category of Vietnamese refugees admitted to the United States. Some former South Vietnamese civilian and military officials had been imprisoned in reeducation camps in Vietnam since 1975, and many of those who had been released from camps into Vietnamese society were marginal members of a society that discriminated against them and their families in employment, housing, and education. The arrival of the political prisoners contributed to the continuing importance of home country politics in many Vietnamese American communities. Although younger generations are beginning to question the ideological conformity of their elders, many first-generation Vietnamese are deeply anti-Communist in their attitudes. The result of the "circle the wagons" mentality fostered by this history is that older Vietnamese can be suspicious of rebels or unconventional individuals within their own ethnic group. In March 1999, for example, a Vietnamese video shop owner in the Little Saigon community of Westminster, California, was threatened by thousands of angry protestors when the shop owner hung a flag of unified Vietnam and a portrait of Ho Chi Minh on his wall.[11] The heightened pressure for conformity tends to subject Vietnamese American children to more intense social controls than those experienced by other American children. At the same time, these social controls can drive rebellious children into intense reactions against adult expectations.

Exit, Limbo, and New Life in America

The fact that the Vietnamese generally arrived in the United States as refugees means that they came under the guidance of government or voluntary agencies. Unlike most immigrants, who are sponsored either by close families or by U.S. employers and can make decisions about where to settle in the United States, refugees are often sponsored by the government or by voluntary agencies of the receiving country and cannot choose their places of resettlement. In the case of the Vietnamese and other Southeast Asian refugees who did not have established ethnic communities in the United States to assist them, the U.S. government-sponsored voluntary resettlement agencies, known as VOLAGs, usually made the decision about their settlement location.[12]

Vietnamese refugees have endured severe living conditions. However, over the course of a decade or so of adjustment, they have made progress in assimilating into American society. Even with a continuously large refugee influx, 1990 Census data show a number of quite striking improvements over the pattern observed ten years earlier. In the ten-year period between 1980 and 1990, the percentage of Vietnamese who did not speak English very well had decreased from 42 percent to 34 percent. The proportion of college graduates among adults age twenty-five and over was 17 percent, up from 13 percent. The poverty rate stood at 24 percent, down from 35 percent in 1980. Despite significant improvements, the Vietnamese still lagged behind their American counterparts economically; substantially more Vietnamese families than average American families are still struggling below the poverty line.

The epic narrative of flight from Vietnam and resettlement in America has become a central shared memory of the Vietnamese American population. Those who personally survived these events and who are old enough to remember them continue to be haunted by them. Those who arrived under the auspices of the Orderly Departure Program or the Humanitarian Operation may be free of these kinds of horrific experiences, but they must still deal with memories of loved ones left behind and with the loss of the world of early childhood. Those who stayed in refugee camps experienced the extreme anxiety and insecurity of their families.

U.S.-born Vietnamese children and those who arrived in the United States as infants have no clear personal memory of life in Vietnam, of the flight from the ancestral land, or of life in refugee camps. But they are still deeply affected by family histories and quasi-mythical accounts of life in the host country. Older generations pass on stories of the struggle to reach the new country. Even when the children dismiss these stories as remnants of a bygone era, the trials of the parents continue to influence their understanding of family history. The question of conformity to parental cultures or rebellion against them is faced by most young people with immigrant parents. But for Vietnamese youth, the fact that their parents are not simply immigrants, but refugees, adds a unique dimension to their outlook on life. Since they are political refugees, as well as people struggling to make lives in a new society, adult Vietnamese Americans can be deeply suspicious of nonconformity within their own ethnic group.

Notes

1. R. G. Rumbaut, "Vietnamese, Laotian, and Cambodian Americans," in *Asian Americans: Contemporary Trends and Issues*, ed. P. G. Min (Thousand Oaks, CA: Sage, 1995).

2. L. R. August and B. A. Gianola, "Symptoms of War Trauma Induced Psychiatric Disorders: Southeast Asian Refugees and Vietnam Veterans," *International Migration Review* 21:3 (1987): 820-32.

3. N. Caplan, J. K. Whitmore, and M. H. Choy, *The Boat People and Achievement in America: A Study of Family Life, Hard Work, and Cultural Values* (Ann Arbor: University of Michigan Press, 1989); T. V. Tran, "Sponsorship and Employment Status among Indochinese Refugees in the United States," *International Migration Review* 25:3 (1991): 536-50.

4. N. Chanda, *Brother Enemy: A History of Indochina Since the Fall of Saigon* (San Diego: Harcourt, Brace, Jovanovich, 1986).

5. Caplan et al., *The Boat People*; Tran, "Sponsorship and Employment Status"; K. B Chan and D. Loveridge, "Refugees in Transit: Vietnamese in a Refugee Camp in Hong Kong," *International Migration Review* 21:3 (1987): 745-59.

Additional Reading

6. C. F. Forsyth and C. L. Bankston, "Mitigation in a Capital Murder Case with a Vietnamese Defendant: The Interpretation of Social Context," *Journal of Applied Sociology* 14 (1997): 147-165.

7. R. B. McClements-Hammond, "Effects of Separation on Vietnamese Unaccompanied Minors: Assessment through the Use of the Kinetic Family Drawing Test, Hopkins Symptom Checklist-25, and the Vietnamese Depression Scale," Ph.D. dissertation, Rutgers, the State University of New Jersey, 1993.

8. M. Zhou and C. L. Bankston, *Growing Up American: How Vietnamese Children Adapt to Life in the United States* (New York: Russell Sage Foundation, 1998).

9. H. A. Williams, "Families in Refugee Camps," *Human Organization* 49:2 (1990): 100-107.

10. N. Kibria, *Family Tightrope: The Changing Lives of Vietnamese Americans* (Princeton: Princeton University Press, 1993).

11. D. Foote, "The Siege of Little Saigon." *Newsweek,* 1 March 1999, 34.

12. C. M. Lanphier, "Dilemmas of Decentralization: Refugee Sponsorship and Service in Canada and the United States," in *The Southeast Asian Environment*, ed. D. R. Webster (Ottowa: University of Ottowa Press, 1983); D. Montero, *Vietnamese Americans: Patterns of Resettlement and Socioeconomic Adaptation in the United States* (Washington, D.C.: Economic Policy Institute, 1979).

Additional Reading

Huy Tran:
A Vietnamese American Refugee's Story

Orange County Asian and Pacific Islander Community Alliance

The following is an excerpt from an oral history of Huy Tran, a world history teacher at Orangeview Junior High School in Anaheim, California, conducted by high school students participating in the 2000 Summer Leadership Academy at the Anaheim Union High School District. Tran immigrated to the United States in 1984 at the age of fourteen. The oral history is an account of his life in Vietnam, his escape from Vietnam, his one-year stay at an Indonesian refugee camp, and his initial experiences as a Vietnamese American immigrant. In the following passage, Tran recalls the struggles on the boat as he and other "boat people" fled Vietnam.

I was thirteen at the time. I remember that night being very cold, windy, and dark. November was in a stormy season. And many of those who wanted to escape tried to avoid November. But the opportunity came and we had to take it. . . . We got on this boat, which was thirteen meters long and two-and-a-half meters wide. I remember the boat just jammed with people. There were ninety-five of us. We sat just knee to chin. . . . We spent the next four days and three nights at sea. It was hot and stuffy, and it smelled really bad—many people had to relieve themselves right there where they sat. . . . And I remember being extremely thirsty and hot. All we had to eat was rice. Each person would get half a bowl a day with some salt. Just to make it a little easier to swallow the food, you also get a half a cup of water. . . . After the second day, our little boat engine died and we were just drifting. . . . I remember there was a Norwegian cruise ship that passed right by our fishing boat and we could see the people in it. The people on the cruise ship just watched us for about fifteen minutes and then they just took off. Of course, we begged for food and help, but it didn't work.

Chapter 2

Feast of Resistance:

Asian American History Through Food

Tony Osumi

The Feast of Resistance was created to make learning Asian American history fun. It uses food to convey the Asian American experience. Moments in history are symbolized through food items like grape juice, salmon, and nectarines. By highlighting Asian American struggles for social justice, participants are encouraged to find inspiration and connections to their own lives. As an alternative to traditional educational methods, the exercise taps into a variety of learning styles and can help build a sense of community among participants. This lesson plan introduces readers to several ways the Feast of Resistance has been used by college professors, high school teachers, community groups, and social service agencies.

Objectives

- To challenge current approaches to teaching history by promoting more interactive and inclusive methods.
- To help participants find inspiration from earlier Asian immigrants and movements for social justice.
- To promote positive group and classroom dynamics through sharing of food and personal stories.
- To take Asian American Studies into the community by sharing it with multigenerational audiences and those unable to take traditional college classes.

Time

- One to two hours depending on the number of people

Number of Participants

- Five to thirty persons

Materials Needed

- Tea
- Bamboo shoots (canned)
- Sugar cane (canned or fresh)
- Pineapple (canned or fresh)
- Sugar beets or canned or fresh red beets
- Salmon (canned or cooked)
- Bing cherries (canned, frozen, or fresh)
- Nectarines
- Fruit salad (canned or fresh with a variety of fruits)
- Grape juice
- Grapes
- Raisins
- Shrimp (canned, shrimp chips, cooked)
- Donuts

Background

The Feast of Resistance began as an idea to take Asian American Studies off campus and into the community. It was developed as a way to share Asian American history with audiences who never get the opportunity to take Asian American classes. This includes not just youth but parents, seniors, and new immigrants. Instead of using traditional readings and lectures, food was chosen for its familiarity and ability to bring people together in a relaxed atmosphere—the very opposite of many classrooms. Lowering classroom stress and building a sense of community set the stage for student teamwork and future action. People at ease and enjoying themselves are also more likely to learn and retain new information. Viewed in this way, the Feast of Resistance shouldn't be seen as a one time exercise, but part of a larger process that builds group dynamics and challenges traditional educational methods that emphasize fear and individualism.

Sharing Asian American history with others is a responsibility. But equally important are what themes and experiences we choose to emphasize. Will we focus on issues facing the voiceless or the powerful? Will history hide the contributions of grassroots movements, or will it become a tool to critique and challenge current injustices?

One issue facing Asian Americans is the model minority stereotype. Yet, the Asian American experience is full of resistance and struggle. Asian American pioneers had dreams of not only improving their own lives but radically transform society with values based on justice, equality, and dignity. Naming the activity the Feast of Resistance encourages us to embrace this mission and keep us rooted in lives dedicated for social change.

There is no one right way to conduct a Feast of Resistance. It can be used in a variety of formats from large and small potluck gatherings, group workshops, and classroom presentations. It could even lay the groundwork for a uniquely Asian American holiday—a new tradition created from the rich experiences of Asians in America.[1]

Because the Feast of Resistance is flexible, included are three approaches to get teachers started that can be used individually or in combination. The following foods are only starting points. Take the initiative to modify and add foods relevant to your audience, geographical location, and current issues.

Foods and Descriptions

Hot tea, bamboo shoots, and **mushrooms**: Early Chinese mining, railroad, and agricultural workers stayed healthier than their White counterparts because of their diet. Because Chinese workers boiled their water to make hot tea and ate more vegetables like bamboo shoots and mushrooms, they didn't fall victim to water-borne diseases or scurvy. These foods were probably some of the last foods eaten by striking Chinese railroad workers who wanted pay equity with White workers and improved working conditions before their food supplies were cut off by Central Pacific railroad contractor, Charles Crocker. Isolated in the California Sierra Mountains, a week of malnutrition and an armed company posse forced workers back to work.

Sugarcane and **pineapple**: Hawai'i's first plantation workers were Native Hawaiians. But foreign diseases killed hundreds of thousands of Hawaiians between 1778 and 1853 when the population dropped from 300,000 to 71,000.[2] This led plantation owners to import Asian labor. But the working conditions were harsh. Serving sugarcane and pineapple reminds us of the Chinese, Japanese, Korean, and Pilipino workers who organized numerous strikes during the late 1800s and first half of the 1900s. When their grievances were ignored, sometimes out of frustration and anger, workers set strategic "cane fires" in the fields. This can be symbolized by serving the sugar cane flambéed.

Grape juice, grapes, and **raisins**: Often overlooked when we think of the United Farm Workers (UFW), Pilipino workers initiated the 1965 Grape Boycott. As members of the Agricultural Workers Organizing Committee (AWOC), Pilipino grape workers struck for better wages and working conditions in Delano, California. Joined later by the National Farm Workers' Association (NFWA) and Cesar Chavez, later renamed UFW, then went on to lead a five-year grape boycott before winning numerous union contracts.

Presenting grape juice, grapes, and raisins recognizes the first-generation Manongs' courage to take on the powerful agri-business growers. By not drinking or eating these foods, we honor the strike, Pilipino labor leaders like Philip Vera Cruz and Larry Itliong, and farmworkers like Paolo Agbayani who died from a heart attack while picketing in 1967. The UFW retirement home, Agbayani Village is named after him and was built by 2,000 volunteers, including many Asian American activists and youths. Grape products also remind us to support today's farmworkers and their current struggles against poverty wages and pesticides.

Sugar beets (or canned or fresh red beets): This root crop represents the interethnic solidarity between Japanese and Mexican farmworkers who formed the Japanese-Mexican Labor Association (JMLA) and led the victorious 1903 Oxnard Sugar Beet Strike. When Samuel Gompers, president of the American Federation of Labor agreed to charter the new union only if they excluded Chinese and Japanese members, union secretary, J. M. Larraras sent back a letter of protest stating that his "union would refuse any kind of charter except one which would wipe out race prejudice."[3]

Fruit salad: Any bowl of fruit salad is full of Asian American history. Farms and orchards in western states like California were built on the backs of early Asian immigrants. In 1860, 45,000 Chinese helped transition California from wheat to fruit orchards, a move that would have been delayed twenty-five years without their help. By 1910, Japanese farmers in California produced half of the state's agricultural products, and their ingenuity turned once ignored desert "waste land" into some of the state's richest farm lands.[4] Successive waves of Korean, Asian Indian, and Pilipino workers continued turning California into an agricultural giant. Oranges, strawberries, melons, peaches, cherries, nuts, grapes, and many vegetables all owe their development and growth to Asian American labor and know-how.

As Asian American women immigrated in greater numbers beginning in the early 1900s, they often worked a double shift—one in the fields and another at home. The additional responsibility of cooking, cleaning, and raising children fell on mothers and daughters. With control over home life, women played a leading role in maintaining and passing on food culture.

Nectarines: In 1920, agricultural entrepreneurs Charles Ho Kim and Hyong-sun Kim started the Kim Brothers Company in California. It was Kim Hyong-sun and an employee named Anderson who invented the nectarine by crossing a peach and a plum.[5]

Bing cherries: This fruit is named after the Chinese American orchard foreman, Ah Bing, who first cared for the modified cherry trees in Oregon. During the anti-Chinese violence of the early 1880s, Bing and other workers lived in the orchard owner's home for safety. After living in America for over thirty-five years, Bing returned to China around 1889 to visit his family, but because of the Chinese Exclusion Act, was never able to return.[6]

Salmon: Large numbers of Asian Americans worked in salmon canneries in San Francisco, Washington, and Alaska after harvesting crops as migrant workers. Salmon also introduces us to unions such as the multiracial CIO Alaskan Cannery Workers Union Local 5 that held meetings in Spanish, Chinese, Japanese, and Pilipino and to labor activists like Communist Party USA member Karl Yoneda.

Shrimp: During the late 1970s, a second wave of Vietnamese and ethnic Chinese from Vietnam immigrated and found jobs in fishing communities, especially along the Gulf Coast of Texas. Serving simple shrimp dishes like shrimp cocktail or inexpensive shrimp chips reminds us of the anti-Asian violence, boat burnings, and harassment Vietnamese fishermen endured by the Ku Klux Klan and competing White fishermen.

Donuts: In Southern California, Cambodian immigrants own up to 80 percent of the independent donut shops.[7] Helping to open up this niche economy was the health consciousness of consumers in the 1980s when donut consumption dropped making ownership more affordable. As new immigrants arrive, word of mouth and financial assistance within the community makes new and previously owned stores available. Including donuts in the Feast of Resistance represents these strong community ties and the long hours of work that donut shops require.

Suggested Procedures and Discussion

Feast of Resistance as a Potluck

The Feast of Resistance makes an effective potluck for classroom, community, and home gatherings.[8] Like a typical potluck, people are asked to bring dishes with special meaning for them. This can take a variety of directions. Dishes can remind them of a childhood memory, a loved one, a dish that brings them pride, or any other reason. The following dishes are examples brought to previous Feasts of Resistance:

- Cranberry Topped Turkey and Chicken was invented when a Vietnamese family celebrated their first Thanksgiving in America. They knew cranberries were traditional, but they didn't know how to serve them. What they did was pour them over the turkey. It tasted so good, they now sometimes serve baked chicken in the same way.

- Pancit, the Pilipino noodle dish, was brought to one Feast of Resistance by a Chinese and Pilipino woman. Since she had grown up more within a Chinese cultural background, the pancit represented her desire to explore more of her Pilipino background.
- Kimchi Fried Rice was important to a second-generation Korean American woman because it was one of the first things she taught herself to cook while growing up in a working-class home. It reminded her of her mother's struggle as a single parent and her own self-reliance.
- The pink cardboard boxes bakeries use to wrap up cakes and cookies had special meaning for one Chinese American student. Bringing a variety of Chinese pastries, he said that the pink box reminded him of his grandfather and their monthly visits to Chinatown together.

Along with all the personal dishes brought by participants, a presentation of the core Feast of Resistance foods discussed earlier should be included. These foods can be small symbolic amounts displayed on a large platter or center table area or in dishes prepared in amounts large enough for everyone to enjoy. Preparing extra food is especially important if a large number of young people or college students attend. Many have limited cooking experience and inadequate cooking facilities.

Before eating, allow everyone who brought a dish to speak about its significance to their life. Question prompts include: "What is the dish?" "Where did it come from?" "How do you make it?" "Why did you bring it?" "How do they draw strength from it?" When possible, have individuals or the group find connections between personal foods and the larger Asian American experience. For example, have students reflect on how a dish, its ingredients or its preparation may fit into Asian American history. When working with non-Asian students, similar questions can help students place their food into a larger context as well.

Historical movements are made up of personal stories. No matter how small, it's these collective experiences that form social change. Helping students re-see the world and the political nature inherent in their everyday lives leads them to understand how their actions make a difference and to look for creative approaches to organize others.

It is possible that someone may feel shy or self-conscious because they didn't bring anything or their dish didn't turn out the way they wanted. People should still speak about a special dish even if they didn't bring one. If needed, remind everyone that the stories behind the food are what are most important, not how well they taste.

Seeing and tasting unfamiliar foods can create a variety of student responses. Building an inclusive classroom community and reviewing guidelines on respect and courtesy beforehand can prepare students to remain open-minded. It may also help to have students reflect on family foods and discuss how these dishes are enjoyed and to think about how foods from different cultures may seem strange to those unfamiliar with them.

Taking Feast of Resistance to the Community

The first public presentation of the Feast of Resistance captured the idea of college students taking their education back to the community. In 1995, students from UCLA's Asian American Studies Center Student/Community Projects 199 Independent Study Class organized a Feast of Resistance for SNAPY, the Service Network for Asian Pacific Youth.[9] During SNAPY's annual Asian Pacific Islander History and Cultural Workshop, approximately thirty Asian Pacific youth, ages thirteen to seventeen, were treated to Spam, shrimp cocktail, sugarcane, fruit salad, and grapes. Between servings, a short history about each food was shared. The college students researched, served, and prepared all the food as well as creating a booklet for each student titled, *Feast of Resistance . . . Food For Thought*, describing the foods in further detail.

College shouldn't be the only place to experience Asian American Studies. By taking the time and effort to serve the community, a small group of college students provided a powerful example for students, teachers, and community-based organizations to follow. Each of these groups has the ability to spread Asian American Studies and raise community consciousness. College instructors can challenge themselves by planning syllabi around community service projects. Social service agencies can expand their job descriptions to include popular education and client organizing. Students, with access to campus resources, can link their education to current issues and real-life needs.

Feast of Resistance in the Classroom

Over the last several years, the Feast of Resistance has been adapted by several teachers.[10] Its most successful application is "What's in the Bag?" developed by college instructor Glenn Omatsu. It moves students from passively listening to lectures to reflecting on their knowledge of Asian American history. Forced to think beyond Asian clichés and stereotypes, the activity engages students to brainstorm foods hiding in the bag. What makes this Feast of Resistance variation excellent is how it draws student answers out, rather than putting them in. In chapter 3, authors Joseph Galura and Emily Porcincula Lawsin discuss their use of the activity in more detail. Passed on from colleague to colleague, the adaptations underscore how teachers benefit from talking with each other. Sharing ideas, problem-solving and even venting together fights off the isolation that drives teachers to frustration and leaving the profession.[11]

Like all lesson plans, teachers must adapt the Feast of Resistance to their students' needs. Instead of approaching the activity as a traditional teacher-led exercise, they should take advantage of the foods' hands-on nature. Fruits and vegetables can be grown in pots and class gardens, individual dishes can be cooked in class, and presenting one food each day can maintain student curiosity over an extended period.[12] Approaches can also be combined. One week, students can experience "What's in the Bag?" and the next they can bring in a personal dish for a class potluck.

The Feast of Resistance can raise student consciousness about educational reform. They can compare and contrast using food to teach history with more traditional methods like reading textbooks and attending lectures. They can also critique the top-down approach to classroom dynamics that leaves students as consumers of history instead of active creators and participants. While expanding student ideas of what constitutes effective teaching, they should be encouraged to create additional activities that engage others and take their knowledge into the community.

Notes

1. To view an earlier article by the author discussing the role food plays in cultural resistance and information on expanding the Feast of Resistance with additional side dishes and activities, visit www.kuidaosumi.com/TOwriting/index.html.

2. Ronald Takaki, *Pau Hana: Plantation Life and Labor in Hawaii* (Honolulu: University of Hawaii Press, 1984), 22.

3. Ronald Takaki, *Strangers from a Different Shore* (New York: Penguin, 1984), 198-200.

4. UCLA Asian American Studies Center Student/Community Projects 199 Independent Study Class, "Feast of Resistance, Food for Thought," Asian Pacific Islander Cultural and History Workshop, Booklet, May 13, 1995.

5. Korean Americans, www.publiciastate.edu/~ematibag/las325/koreanam1_s03.doc.

6. "Fact Monster from Information Please," www.factmonster.com/ipka/A09000104html.

7. Sara Bir, "Do-Nut Believe the Hype," *Metroactive Dining*, February 20, 2003, www.metroactive .com/papers/sonoma/02.20.03/donuts-0308.html.

8. Formerly named National Coalition for Redress/Reparations, NCRR is a Japanese American civil rights group. For more information, visit www.ncrr-la.org.

9. SNAPY is an umbrella network involving Asian Pacific Islander social service and youth agencies based in Los Angeles. History workshop organizers included Cindy Cheng, Ayako Hagihara, Karman Ng, and Gwendelyn Tan from UCLA Asian American Studies Center's Spring Quarter Student/Community Project 199 independent study class supervised by Meg Malpaya Thornton.

10. The Feast of Resistance has been used by instructors Glenn Omatsu, Emily Porcincula Lawsin, Joseph Galura, and Allan Aquino at California State University, Northridge, UCLA, Pasadena City College, and University of Michigan, Ann Arbor.

11. Personal conversation with Glenn Omatsu, Fall 2001.

12. Personal conversation with Emily Porcincula Lawsin, July 29, 2003.

Recommended Resources

Emma Gee et al., eds., *Counterpoint: Perspectives on Asian Americans* (Los Angeles: UCLA Asian American Studies Center, 1976).

Ronald Takaki, *Strangers from a Different Shore* (New York: Penguin, 1989).

What Is Chick Sexing?

Eiichiro Azuma

In the 1930s the U.S. poultry industry emphasized a technique called chick sexing that attracted young, second-generation Japanese Americans (Nisei) seeking job opportunities at a time of intense racism and economic hardships. From the 1940s through the 1960s, the Nisei virtually monopolized the trade of chick sexing in America.

Previously, the poultry industry had incurred heavy financial losses due to the inability to separate female and male chicks. The baby chick gives no indication—to the average eye—whether it will grow into an egg-laying hen or a worthless cock. Chick sexing was a new technique that trained workers to quickly examine and sort chicks; however, the birds could be easily killed if too much pressure was applied when examining them. Chick sexing was believed to require dexterity, small fingers, and myopic vision—a set of racial characteristics attributed to the Japanese at that time. What reinforced this racial thinking was the fact that only Japan initially offered training for this new trade. Thus, all Nisei pioneer chick sexers learned the trade in Japan before setting up their own schools in California in the late 1930s.

When World War II broke out, two Nisei chick sexing schools moved to Pennsylvania and Minnesota. In 1944, when Chicago emerged as a major destination for Japanese Americans leaving the internment camps, another school was established there. During the war, these schools assisted Nisei men and women to seek freedom from confinement and achieve a degree of economic independence.

Despite their near monopoly in the trade, few Nisei had long-term commitment to it. Chick sexing was largely seasonal work, typically running from the beginning of the year to the summer months, during which time they worked eighteen to twenty hours a day. Reflecting the rapid expansion of U.S. poultry industry during and after the war, Nisei chick sexers nevertheless received much higher wages than those in other jobs, and to young Japanese Americans wishing to re-integrate themselves as quickly as possible into mainstream society, the financial advantage was a major, if not the only, attraction. However, because there were better work opportunities as years passed, many Nisei chick sexers moved on to small business pursuits and farming ventures, while others went back to school to become professionals.

By the 1960s, chick sexing was no longer a Nisei occupation. Moreover, the new method of feather sexing made the trade less specialized. Since feather sexing required practically no skill or training, chick sexing turned into just another "immigrant trade." During the late 1960s, Korean and Mexican immigrants began to enter the occupation, driving down wages. By the following decade, chick sexing was no longer a Japanese American trade, but simply a variation of low-wage agricultural work reserved for unskilled immigrants.

Additional Reading

Chapter 3

"Pin@y Time":

Mapping the Filipino American Experience

Emily Porcincula Lawsin and Joseph A. Galura

In this chapter, we present two activities that help participants concurrently learn about history and know themselves. These activities situate the Filipino American experience within the larger spectrum of American history and Asian/Pacific Islander American Studies. The activities can be done separately or together, and by any age group. We have facilitated the activities with college students, who then adapted them to initiate conversations with K-12 youth and elders. Each activity can also be used in diversity seminars or by community organizations.

Objectives

- To locate participants' family migration patterns in an historical and geographical context.
- To encourage discussion of people's "positionality" in the world.
- To learn key facts about the Filipino Americans and enhance group dynamics by connecting the information to participants' personal histories.

Time

- Thirty minutes for each activity

Number of Participants

- Five to twenty people

Materials Needed

For "Where Are You From? Mapping Activity"

- World map (the larger the better)

- Push pins and yarn (bright colors work best, or use Post-it Notes and pens)

For "Pin@y Time" Timeline Activity

- Butcher paper (or use a long chalkboard)
- Colorful marking pens
- Post-It Notes
- Masking tape
- Filipino American history timeline (see handouts)

Background

One of our favorite phrases was coined by Mel Orpilla, a trustee of the Filipino American National Historical Society:

> *Know history, know self.*
> No history, no self.

As in many other ethnic minority cultures, the concept of time and place can be both essential and overwhelming in Filipino American communities. Asian Americans are often faced with the interrogative question of "Where Are You From?" (as in "When are you going back?"), so the Mapping Activity helps participants realize and take pride in the fact that we all come from different places in the world. Playing off the pun of "Filipino Time" (which usually means one is constantly late), our "Pin@y Time" activity helps students situate their own family history along a timeline of Filipino American history. (In this cyber-age, we use the @ symbol in "Pin@y" not for an e-mail address but as an abbreviation for "a" and "o" to connote the inclusion of "Pinoy"—Filipino American men—*and* "Pinay"—Filipino American women's experiences in history. The @ symbol also helps engage a discussion of where our communities are "at" these days, as compared to other points in history.)

We have found that the activities not only help raise awareness about different communities, they also help dispel stereotypes and ease the once-daunting process of learning history. We often follow up the activities with a variation of Tony Osumi's "Feast of Resistance" (see Chapter 2). These activities can produce interactive discussions, while participants enjoy personal stories and delicious food.

We believe that there is an important connection between knowing who you are and where you fit in with regards to your comparative cultural heritage. This is particularly true for people of Filipino descent, an ethnic group some scholars describe as "transmigrants," existing between the social and geographic landscapes of the Philippines and the United States. At the same time, many Asian Americans are often seen by mainstream Americans as perpetual "foreigners," despite the many generations who have worked tirelessly here and call America their home. Moreover, historian Fred Cordova calls Filipinos the "forgotten Asian Americans" because the general public knows so little of our history, if any at all.[1]

The earliest known record of Filipinos landing in what is now the continental United States was in the year 1587, when a Spanish galleon sent "Luzones Indios" as a landing party to scout the area of what is now known as Morro Bay, California. These "indios" were Filipino seamen and slaves who were part of Spain's galleon trade that ran from Manila to Acapulco, trading silks, silver, spices, porcelain, and other wares. Scholar Marina Espina identifies the earliest known community of Filipinos in 1765 near Barataria Bay, where "Manilamen" from the galleons jumped ship and created eight different Filipino villages in the bayous of Louisiana. The descendants of these early settlers are now in their eighth generation.

Larger waves of Filipinos—men and women—immigrated to the United States after the 1898 Spanish-American War when Spain ceded the Philippines to the United States for a mere $20 million, along with Puerto Rico, Guam, and Cuba. That same year, the United States overthrew the Hawaiian monarchy and Hawai'i also became a U.S. territory. In 1899, the Philippine-American War began, leading to many years of struggle for Philippine independence. Shortly after the Philippines became a territory of the United States, the Hawaiian Sugar Planters Association and other employers began actively recruiting agricultural workers to add to and replace the Chinese and Japanese workers who had earlier immigration restrictions placed upon them. Around the same time, teams of researchers and teachers—known as "Thomasites" because of their ship the *U.S.S. Thomas*—began traveling to the Philippines to reform the educational system. A select number of elite Filipinos then migrated to the United States as *pensionados*—government-sponsored college students, many of whom were required to return to the Philippines to help rebuild the country. Soon after, their compatriots followed, often as self-supporting students, who sought a better life in the United States. Oftentimes, many of these students would inevitably end up as migrant workers in the agricultural fields of California or the salmon canneries of Alaska while trying to finish school. Some became small business entrepreneurs, while others headed to the Midwest and East Coast to attend school and worked as boxcar porters, houseboys, busboys, chauffeurs, and factory workers. Other Filipinos were able to join the U.S. Navy, mostly relegated to steward positions, even if they had a college degree. Seen as the new source of cheap labor, Filipinos became targets of race riots and rampant discrimination, especially right before and during the Great Depression. Anti-immigration legislation was passed, along with anti-miscegenation laws, in many states. A Repatriation Act was even introduced, but only a couple thousand Filipinos chose to return to their native Philippines, forfeiting their right to ever return to the United States.

In 1934, Filipinos were reclassified from "nationals" to "aliens ineligible for citizenship." Filipino immigration to the United States was limited to a quota of only fifty per year, after the passage of the Tydings-McDuffie Act, which also promised the Philippines independence in ten years. However, due to the outbreak of World War II, the Philippines did not gain official independence until the year 1946. During this time period, only a few students, civil servants, military personnel, and merchants could immigrate. Meanwhile, earlier immigrants had children or formed extended families and raised them in both urban and rural areas.

When World War II erupted, Filipinos in the United States petitioned President Franklin D. Roosevelt to allow Filipinos to serve in the U.S. Army. Ironically, FDR approved their petition on the same day that he signed Executive Order 9066, incarcerating 120,000 Japanese Americans in U.S. concentration camps. More than 7,000 Filipinos—both Philippine-born and American-born—served in the U.S. Army's 1st and 2nd Filipino Infantry Regiments.

In 1945, the War Brides Act and the Fiancés Act temporarily waived immigration quotas and allowed military personnel to bring spouses, fiancés, and other dependents.

Families of Spanish-American War and Philippine-American War veterans, as well as those from World War II, began immigrating. This introduced a new layer of immigrants to Filipino American communities, which included nuclear families and many more women. By 1946, Filipinos became eligible for U.S. citizenship. Immigration quotas increased by small increments in 1952.

In 1965, the Immigration and Naturalization Act eliminated race-based quotas, established a preference system for immigration, and increased the number of immigrants allowed to enter the United States. Soon after, many Filipino professionals began to immigrate, including nurses, doctors, engineers, and accountants, many of whom were reunited with other family members already in the United States. When martial law was declared in the Philippines in 1972, many anti-martial law activists and students sought refuge in the United States.

According to the 2000 Census, there are now more than 2.3 million Filipinos in the United States. We constitute one of the fastest-growing communities in the country, second only to Mexican Americans. Of the Asian American population, Filipinos are the second largest group, after Chinese. Half of all Filipinos in America live on the West Coast. In California, Filipinos are the largest ethnic minority group, as San Francisco and Los Angeles were once the major ports of entry for immigration. However, few Americans know anything about Filipinos other than common stereotypes or misperceptions. Our activities seek to rectify that situation.

The "Where Are You From Mapping" activity and the "Pin@y Time" activity are both based on the following premises:

- Every participant has come to the activity from someplace else in the world;
- Filipino Americans—men and women—have made significant contributions to American labor; and
- The number of Filipinos that come to the United States and their reasons for immigrating are largely shaped by national and international policy.

We use these activities in our team-taught service-learning course at the University of Michigan, American Culture 311, "Filipino American Experience." We share academic content with college students with the intention that they will use that information to serve the community. We also share our own previously published articles outlining our philosophies on pedagogy, so that students understand our teaching strategies.[2] Student involvement in the community is a required part of the course, along with an oral history interview of a local Filipino over the age of forty. Over time, the interviews will be edited, published in a book, and presented in the community as spoken word poetry, live and recorded songs, and staged as a play. We do this because besides our first book, *Filipino Women in Detroit: 1945-1955*, virtually nothing has been published on the history of Filipinos in Michigan. Our ongoing research begins to broach this regrettable silence. Community involvement, therefore, is structured in such a way to both enhance how our students learn Filipino American history and directly benefit the community. Members of our Philippine American Community Center of Michigan are happy with our donation of historical material, not to mention the time our students take to instruct the youth there about history. This approach is similar to the ones employed by the Filipino Youth Activities' "Pinoy Teach" program in Seattle public schools and the "Pin@y Educational Partnership" out of San Francisco State University's Asian American Studies Department. We have found that multiple levels of involvement enhance students' learning. Our students remark on these interactions throughout the term, qualitatively, and in their papers, stating, for example:

> The knowledge and understanding that I gained from this interview was not anything I could have learned from reading a book or an article. Our readings for the class helped to subsidize aspects of (my interviewee's) story, but it was definitely the interview itself that solidified my understanding of the Filipino American experience.

We view the activities outlined here as stepping stones to the larger term projects. By getting the students comfortable with each other, with their own personal history, and with Filipino American history early on in the semester, they are much more confident and comfortable when interacting in the local community.

We should note that even though our class is listed as "American Culture 311: Filipino American Experience," in the Midwest we do not always get a class of only Filipino students. In fact, oftentimes, the class includes students of African, Asian, Chicano/Latino, Native American, or European descent. We have also enrolled international students from Africa and countries of Asia other than the Philippines. We find this as an asset, broadening the discussion of the activities to incorporate a truly global comparative perspective.

Suggested Procedures

We facilitated these activities in class with college students, who, in turn, facilitated the activities in the community with Filipino American youth at the local cultural center. Thus, our discussion includes what we did on campus, as well as variations—how our college students adapted the activities for multiple age groups in the community.

Exercise 1: "Where Are You From?" Mapping Activity

1. Ask students if they have ever been asked the daunting question, "Where are you from?" Discuss what the implications of such a question are in terms of racism, immigration, and national policy.
2. Ask the students to write a short essay (i.e., one to three pages, double-spaced), on their own family's migratory patterns to the United States or to their hometown. (If they are Native American, they can discuss where their family has lived.) Although this assignment can be done in class, we like to have the students write this at home, so they can ask their parents or other family members for detailed information. Sometimes we give them one week to complete this assignment so that they invest time in it and take their own history seriously.
3. On the day that the assignment is due, place a large world map at the front of the room. You can usually get a map from a bookstore or your geography department. Some classrooms already have them as part of the décor. (It's interesting to note on these maps where the United States falls—usually smack dab in the center—compared to where the Philippines or Asia falls—pushed to the far left margins. On some really old maps, the Philippines may even appear as "The Philippine Islands" rather than "The Republic of the Philippines.")

4. Have thumbtacks/push pins and different colored yarn (or small Post-It Notes) available. (If you use Post-It Notes, ask the students to write down on separate sheets the relevant places in their families' histories—for example, the ports of entry where family members immigrated, the cities they lived in, and those of relatives.)

5. The instructor should lead by example, taking a long piece of yarn (or Post-It Note) and tack it to different cities on the world map, while briefly relating your own family's migration patterns. Allow time for students to comment (i.e., "Oh, my mom is from that town too!") and encourage questions (i.e., "Why did your dad only stay in Hawai'i for three years?").

6. Then ask each student, one by one, to approach the map and do the same, tracing their own family's migration patterns. Remember to allow time for comments and questions for each student. You will find that a classroom community is established by the combination of each participant's willing self-disclosure. The intricate web of relationships that emerges on the map will probably link every continent.

7. After the activity, lead a discussion of migration and global economy because, inevitably, most of the students' families have moved from place to place to reunite with other families or because of employment opportunities. We find this a good starting point to discuss the long history of anti-immigrant legislation.

8. *Variation*: At the community center, students conducted this activity for children and adults. The students used the push pins and different colored yarn. They used an enlarged map of the Philippines and pasted it on to the world map because the 7,100 islands looked so small! They placed a large "Where Are You From?" sign above the map, with instructions in case there was no one present to lead the activity. Children and adults traced their family's journey from various points in the Philippines to Michigan, most often stopping first in Hawai'i, Los Angeles, or Seattle. A few elders even stopped to share stories of their hometown.

Exercise 2: "Pin@y Time" Timeline Activity

The campus version of the "Pin@y Time" activity is a discussion of assigned readings. The assigned text is *Filipino Women in Detroit: 1945-1955*, particularly our "Timeline of Filipino American History" and "Filipino Women in Detroit: 1945-1955."[3] For a general Asian American class, instructors can use the timeline in Sucheng Chan's book, *Asian Americans: An Interpretive History*, or Judy Yung's women-centered timeline in *Making Waves: An Anthology of Writings By and About Asian American Women*.[4] The purpose is to get participants to place themselves and their family histories onto a larger timeline so they can see the connections between their own personal histories and the textbooks.

Sometimes we introduce the activity by reading an excerpt from Emily Lawsin's poem, "On the Unveiling of the Aloha Grocery Mural, History: Our Story," which details the ironic and similar history of her husband's Japanese American family and her Filipino American family (see www.greatleap.org/aloha/alohalawsin.html). The common refrain of the poem is "This is the History That We Share." We then write that refrain boldly across the top of the timeline.

1. Tape a large piece of butcher paper to a long wall at the front of the room. If you do not have butcher paper, you could also use a long chalkboard.

2. Draw a long horizontal line across the middle of the paper/chalkboard, with arrows at both ends of the line. This will be the base of your timeline.

3. Across the top of the paper, write, "Pin@y Time: Filipino American History and Me" (or depending on your class, "Asian American History and Me").

4. Pass out stacks of Post-It Notes to each student and ask them to write down different significant moments in their family's history on as many sheets as they can. One or two students may make a comment like, "My family hasn't done anything important," to which you can answer, "Sure they have! They had you, didn't they?" This is a good time to point out that they can write anything on the Post-It Note (i.e., when they were born, when their first relative came to America, etc.). If you are into giving prizes, you can tell them that the one with the most Post-Its gets a prize, along with the one who can go the farthest back in their family history.

5. As the students are writing on their Post-It Notes, mark along the timeline five to ten significant years in Filipino/Asian American history. We like to start as far back as possible, so we often have the first mark as the year 1587, then maybe the next mark at 1765, the next mark 1882 (for the Chinese Exclusion Act), the next mark 1898, 1924 (for the anti-Asian Immigration Act), 1934, 1941, 1952, 1965, 1975, and the current year. You could also divide the line by decades or centuries. Just be sure to leave a lot of room on the timeline from 1980 to the present, because most students will have many Post-It Notes around their own birth and school years. Do not write anything next to the years on the timeline until the students tell you why the years are important.

6. When the students are finished writing, ask them what the specific dates already on the timeline represent. If they are stuck, you can remind them that this is not a quiz, and they can refer to the handout. As they tell you the answers, congratulate them and write that event next to the date on the timeline. If students are reticent, you can just go around the room in order, then they will all begin looking feverishly at the handout, trying to find corresponding dates before their name is called.

7. After you discuss why all of these dates are important, ask each student, one by one, to place their individual Post-It Notes onto the timeline, explaining to the class what each date means. Allow time for comments and questions for each student.

8. After each student has placed all of their Post-It Notes on the timeline, ask them, "What does this timeline tell us about our class?" This can lead to great discussions of immigration, family, education, labor, gender dynamics, community formation, political involvement, etc. You can also ask them what they thought of the activity. Every time we have led this exercise, more than one student comments, "I never thought my family or I was part of history until we did this."

9. *Variation*: At the community center, the college students led about a dozen Filipino American youth through the timeline activity and Tony Osumi's Feast of Resistance. This led to a good discussion of labor, while participants enjoyed the valuable commodity of food. The facilitators then fielded questions from the youth that would be incorporated into the activity. They also had chosen, in advance, five or six dates in Filipino American history that should be presented on the timeline. Each college student had written about the event on another piece of butcher paper and asked the youth to look at the year on the handout before they guessed

what the event was. Once the youth answered correctly, the college students un-veiled the explanation. They rehearsed the explanations, particularly attempting to be clear and concise with an audience that didn't have the benefit of having read all the background articles. They were also sure to include events that happened after the youth were born.

In these activities and throughout our work, it becomes very important to separate events that happened to Filipinos in the Philippines from what happened to Filipinos in America, particularly in Michigan, even if there is some overlap. That is not to say that there are no parallels, because there definitely are. It is our experience that, in the community, there is some awareness of Philippine history; however, there is a general lack of information, in both the academic and cultural community, regarding Filipino American history. We enjoy using activities like these to begin to set the stage for those Filipino American voices to be heard.

Notes

1. Fred Cordova, *Filipinos: Forgotten Asian Americans: A Pictorial History, 1763-1963* (Dubuque, Iowa: Kendall-Hunt Publishing, 1983).

2. Joseph A. Galura and Emily P. Lawsin, *Filipino Women in Detroit: 1945-1955, Oral Histories from the Filipino American Oral History Project of Michigan* (Ann Arbor: University of Michigan OSCL Press, 2002); Emily P. Lawsin, "Empowering the *Bayanihan* Spirit: Teaching Filipina/o American Studies," in *Teaching Asian America: Diversity and the Problem of Community*, ed. Lane Ryo Hirabayashi (Lanham, MD: Rowman & Littlefield Publishers, 1998), 187-197; Stella Raudenbush and Joseph A. Galura, "We Made the Road by Talking: Teaching Education 310, 'Service-Learning with Multicultural Elders' at the University of Michigan," in *Integrating Service Learning and Multicultural Education in Colleges and Universities*, ed. Carolyn R. O'Grady (Mahwah, NJ: Lawrence Erlbaum Associates, 2000), 153-167.

3. Joseph A. Galura and Emily P. Lawsin, "Filipino American History Timeline," *Filipino Women in Detroit: 1945-1955, Oral Histories from the Filipino American Oral History Project of Michigan* (Ann Arbor: University of Michigan OSCL Press, 2002), xv-xvii.

4. Sucheng Chan, *Asian Americans: An Interpretive History* (Boston: Twayne Publishers, 1991); Asian American Women United, *Making Waves: An Anthology of Writings by and about Asian American Women* (Boston: Beacon Press, 1990).

Recommended Resources

Carlos Bulosan, *America Is in the Heart: A Personal History* (Seattle: University of Washington Press, 1973).

Barbara M. Posadas, *The Filipino Americans* (Westport, CT: Greenwood Press, 1999).

Filipino American National Historical Society, *Filipino Americans: Discovering Their Past for the Future* (Seattle: FANHS, 1994), videorecording available from FANHS, www.fanhs-national.org.

Timeline of Filipino American History
Compiled by Emily P. Lawsin

1565 Spain colonizes the Philippines and begins the Manila-Acapulco Spanish Galleon Trade.

1587 October 18: First documented landing of Filipinos on what is now the continental United States; Pedro Unamuno of the galleon Nuestra Senora de Esperanza, sends "Luzon Indios" to scout out Atacadero Bay by Morro Bay, California.

1765 Earliest known Filipino American settlements, when "Manilamen" jump ship from the Spanish galleons and eventually form eight different villages in the bayous of Louisiana.

1781 In some records, Antonio Miranda Rodriguez is listed as one of the 12 founders of el Pueblo de Nuestra Senora la Reina de Los Angeles del Porciúncula (Los Angeles), but Rodriguez stayed behind in Santa Barbara with his ailing daughter.

1815 Filipinos fight with Jean Laffitte in the Battle of New Orleans.

1870 July 24: Sociedad de Beneficencia de los Hispanos Filipinos de Nueva Orleans becomes first Filipino American organization.

1882 Chinese Exclusion Act forbids immigration of Chinese laborers.

1883 Lumber mill in Port Blakely, Washington, lists "Manilla" as one of its employees.

1896 Philippine Revolution against Spain.

1897 Pact of Biak-na-bato temporarily suspends fighting between Filipinos and Spain.

1898 February: Fighting resumes in the Philippines.
May 1: U.S. Admiral Dewey sails in to Manila Bay to fight Spain.
June 12: Emilio Aguinaldo declares Philippine Independence.

August: Spanish-American War ends.
December: Treaty of Paris, Spain cedes the Philippines to the United States for $20,000,000 pending approval by the U.S. Senate. The U.S. also annexes Cuba, Puerto Rico, Guam, and Hawai'i.

1899 February 4: Philippine-American War begins with a shooting of a Filipino at San Juan Bridge. Some reports say the war lasts until 1902, locals say it lasts for ten years, killing over 1 million Filipinos.
February 6: U.S. Senate votes in favor of annexation of the Philippines.

1900 Prof. Dean C. Worcester of the University of Michigan, begins anthropological studies of the Philippines. As a Philippine Commission member, Worcester suggests a competitive exam for elite students from the Philippines to study in the United States; the first three Filipino students arrive in Ann Arbor, Michigan.
Santiago Artiaga wins a scholarship from the International Club of Manila to also study in the U.S; in 1904, he becomes the first Filipino to graduate from the University of Michigan.

1901 July 4: U.S. President William McKinley establishes Philippine civil government under appointed Philippine Commission, headed by William Howard Taft. U.S.S. Thomas sails from San Francisco to the Philippines with 600 teachers aboard.
Section 60 of the California Civil Code forbids marriages of white persons to "Negroes, Mongolians, or mulattoes."

1902   First war brides from the Philippines settle in the United States.

1903   Pensionado Program begins, sending the colonial government-sponsored students from the Philippines to the United States to study. Self-supported students follow a decade later.

1904   Filipinos begin serving as U.S. Navy stewards.
St. Louis World's Fair features 47-acre Philippine exhibit, including "Igorrotte Village," using 1100 Filipinos from the United States and the Philippines to justify colonizing the "savages" of the Philippines.

1906   Hawaiian Sugar Plantation Association begins recruiting Filipinos as contract laborers.
The Knights of Rizal, a mutual aid fraternal organization, establishes two branches in Chicago.

1907   Gentleman's Agreement restricts immigration of Japanese laborers to the United States.

1909   Payne-Aldriff tariff establishes free trade between the United States and the Philippines.

1911   Filipino Federation of Labor founded in Hawai'i.

1912   Alien Land Law passed in California, forbidding "aliens ineligible for citizenship" to own land.

1917   Jones Bill establishes bicameral legislature in the Philippines, with an American appointed Governor General as head of state.

1920   Filipino Higher Wage Movement founded in Hawai'i.
January 19: 3,000 Filipino plantation workers start a strike in Aiea, Waipahu, Ewa, and Kahuku on Oahu in Hawai'i.
Gran Oriente Filipino, mutual aid fraternal organization is founded in California.
Caballeros de Dimas Alang, mutual aid fraternal organization is founded in San Francisco, California.

1922   The Filipino Students Christian Movement, under the Committee on Friendly Relations of the YMCA, begins its 17-year run of publishing *The Filipino Student Bulletin*, a national bi-monthly newsletter about Filipinos in America.

1923   Maria Lanzar, the first Barbour Scholar from the Philippines, enters the University of Michigan and graduates in 1928 with a Ph.D. in political science; she returns to teach at the University of the Philippines.

1924   Legionarios del Trabajo, mutual aid fraternal organization is founded in California.

1925   Hilario Camino Moncado founds the Filipino Federation of America; publishes *The Filipino Nation*.

1924   Immigration Act excludes virtually all immigration of Asian laborers to the United States, except for Filipinos, who were nationals.
1600 sugar workers strike for 8 months on 23 plantations in Hawai'i. Hanapepe camp massacre on Kauai, where police attack union headquarters, killing 16 Filipinos and 4 police.

1926   June 8: Attorney General U.S. Webb rules that Filipinos should be classified as "Mongolian" and included in the California Civil code's anti-miscegenation law.

1928   Filipino farm workers are driven out of Yakima Valley, Washington.

1929   October 24: Race Riot in Exeter, California; a carnival stabbing and racial intolerance leads to a mob of 300 burning a barn at a ranch that employed Filipinos.

1930   January 19-23: Watsonville, California, Race Riots. Fermin Tobera, a 22-year-old Filipino laborer, was shot and killed by three high school youths as he lay sleeping in his bunk at labor camp near Murphy's crossing. The youths were never convicted of the killing. Tobera's body was returned to the Philippines, where on February 2, a National Day of Humiliation was held.

August: Dynamite is thrown into a labor camp of 100 sleeping Filipinos in Reedley, California. Other mob actions to drive out Filipinos occur in Imperial, Lake, and Sonoma Counties for the next few years.

1933 March 30: Roldan vs. Los Angeles County & L. E. Lampton, County Clerk. Salvador Roldan, a law student, successfully challenges anti-miscegenation laws that forbade marriages between whites and "Mongolians," arguing that Filipinos are of the "Malay" race.

April 21: the California State Assembly adds "Malay" to Section 60 and 69 of the California Civil Code. Twelve other states also had anti-miscegenation laws.

Filipinos organize the Cannery Workers & Farm Laborers Union, Local 18257 in Seattle, which in 1937 becomes Local 7 of United Cannery, Agricultural, Packing & Allied Workers of America (UCAPAWA).

1934 March 24: U.S. Tydings-McDuffie Act promises Philippines independence in 10 years and limits immigration of Filipinos to 50 per year; Philippine legislature accepts it in 1935. Independence isn't granted until 12 years due to World War II.

August 27: Filipino Labor Union leads 7,000 workers to strike against lettuce growers in Salinas, California.

1935 Repatriation Act offered to Filipinos in the United States to return to the Philippines at no cost, provided that they never return to the United States. Only 2,190 repatriated.

1939 Filipino Agricultural Laborers Association leads 6,000 asparagus workers in a strike in the San Joaquin delta.

1941 December 7: Pearl Harbor bombed, leading the United States into World War II.

December 8: Japan invades the Philippines, attacks Clark Air Field.

December 20: President Franklin D. Roosevelt signs Public Law 360, allowing Filipinos to serve in the U.S. Army.

1942 February 19: President Franklin D. Roosevelt signs Executive Order allowing for the formation of all-Filipino fighting units in the U.S. Army. On the same day, he signs Executive Order 9066, leading to the internment of 210,000 Japanese Americans from the West Coast.

March 29: People's Anti-Japanese Army (Hukbalahap or "Huks") forms in the Philippines.

April 9: the city of Bataan, in the Philippines, is captured by Japan.

1st & 2nd Filipino Infantry Regiments of the U.S. Army formed later that year in San Luis Obispo and Fort Ord, California. More than 7,000 Filipino and Filipino Americans served in these two regiments. Meanwhile, the Philippine Scouts, the Philippine Army, and the Philippine guerrillas all fall under U.S. armed forces command in World War II, creating "USAFFE," United States Armed Forces in the Far East. Second War Powers Act temporarily allows Filipinos and other alien servicemen to become naturalized U.S. citizens.

1945 August 15: World War II ends.

December 28: Public Law 271, War Brides Act, temporarily waives quota restrictions, allowing for the immigration of spouses and dependents of military service personnel.

1946   July 4: Philippine Independence. Immigration quota raised to 100 per year.

Luce-Cellar Bill allows Filipinos who arrived before 1934 to become naturalized U.S. citizens: 10,764 become citizens the next year.

Carlos Bulosan publishes the novel *America is in the Heart*, detailing the struggles of Filipinos in early 20th Century America; he dies ten years later in obscurity.

Recission Act ends Filipino servicemen's rights to citizenship and military benefits if they did not apply before the December 31 deadline.

1947   Military Bases Agreement Act allowed for more Filipinos to join the U.S. armed forces in exchange for the lease of 23 U.S. military installations there.

July 4: Filipino-American Citizens Society of Michigan forms, publishing the Filipino-American Citizens News of Michigan in 1949.

1948   California repeals anti-miscegenation law.

Victoria Manalo Draves wins two gold medals for the United States in diving, becoming the first woman to win two gold medals at the Olympics. She competes using her mother's maiden name of "Taylor," for fear of backlash towards Filipinos.

Information & Education Exchange Act passed, which leads to creation of Exchange Visitor Program (EVP) for foreign nurses.

1952   McCarran-Walter Immigration & Nationality Act allows permanent residents of the United States who were born in the Asia/Pacific Triangle to become U.S. citizens. How-

ever, those returning from the U.S. territories were screened and all "undesirable aliens" prevented from re-entering.

Filipino Women's Club of Detroit is founded.

1956   California repeals its Alien Land Laws.

1961   The Federation of Filipinos Clubhouse is opened at 9115 St. Cyril Avenue, in Detroit, Michigan.

1962   *Philippine News* begins its weekly newspaper publication in San Francisco, covering national and international news.

1965   Immigration & Nationality Act establishes a preference system, based on family reunification and occupation, eliminating "national origins" quota and raising immigration limits from the Philippines to 20,000 per year. Triggers "brain drain" of Filipino professionals from the Philippines.

Philippine President Ferdinand Marcos sends civic action unit to support the United States in Vietnam War.

September 8: Agricultural Workers Organizing Committee in Delano, led by Larry Itliong, Andy Imutan, and Philip Vera Cruz, votes to strike, beginning a 5-year boycott of grapes; Sept. 16: Cesar Chavez's National Farm Workers Association joins the strike and merges with AWOC a year later to become the United Farm Workers Organizing Committee (UFWOC).

1967   Loving v. Virginia Supreme Court decision declares anti-miscegenation laws unconstitutional.

1968   Students at San Francisco State College go on strike demanding Ethnic Studies, including members of the Philippine-American College Endeavor (PACE).

Handout

1969 Students at University of California, Berkeley, strike for Ethnic Studies, including members of the Pilipino American Alliance.

1970 January-March: "First-Quarter Storm," massive student demonstrations in Manila against Marcos and the U.S. government.

1971 August 21: Grenades are thrown on the platform of Marcos' political opponents; writ of habeas corpus suspended until January 1972.

1972 September 21: President Ferdinand Marcos declares Martial Law in the Philippines.
September 22: the National Committee for the Restoration of Civil Liberties (NCRCLP) was formed in the United States to oppose the Marcos dictatorship, followed by the Movement for a Free Philippines, Friends of the Filipino People, and the Katipunan ng Demokratikong Pilipino (KDP).

1976 Leonaro Perez and Filipina Narciso, two Filipino nurses are charged for poisoning patients at the Veterans Administration Hospital in Ann Arbor, Michigan; a nationwide justice campaign ensues, the two nurses are later acquitted.
Health Professionals Education Assistance Act reduces the number of foreign doctors, nurses, and pharmacists from immigrating to the United States.

1977 August 3: Thousands form a human chain around the International Hotel in San Francisco's Manilatown at the height of a ten-year community battle fighting the eviction of elderly Filipino and low-income residents.

1981 ILWU Cannery Union and KDP leaders Gene Viernes and Silme Domingo are gunned down in Seattle, beginning a ten-year legal investigation, charging Ferdinand and Imelda Marcos with conspiracy.

1983 Former Philippine Senator Benigno "Ninoy" Aquino, Jr., assassinated at Manila International Airport, after years of exile in the United States.

1986 After fraudulent elections, People Power Revolution overthrows the Marcos Dictatorship in the Philippines. Marcos flees to Hawai'i and Corazon Aquino becomes President of the Philippines.

1987 Pilipinos are removed from affirmative action at UCLA; the following years, Pilipinos have the lowest admit rate at the university.

1991 Mt. Pinatubo in the Philippines explodes, giving the U.S. an excuse to abandon its military sites in the Philippines, leaving behind toxic waste and environmental hazards.

1992 The last U.S. military base in the Philippines closes.

1994 Benjamin Cayetano elected in Hawai'i as the first Filipino American governor in the United States.

1997 Byron Acohido and Alex Tizon of *The Seattle Times*, become the first Filipino Americans to win the Pulitzer Prize in journalism.

1999 August 10: Joseph Santos Ileto, a Filipino American postal worker is murdered by an avowed white supremacist in the Chatsworth area of Los Angeles, California. After shooting up the North Valley Jewish Community Center, the gunman admitted he targeted Ileto because he was non-white and worked for the federal government.

2000 United States renames the post office in Chino Hills, California, in honor of the late Joseph Santos Ileto. Census records show 2.4 million Filipinos in the United States, the second largest Asian group, after Chinese Americans.

Handout

2001   The Philippine American Community Center of Michigan is opened in Southfield, Michigan, after 26 years of fundraising. It houses the Paaralang Pilipino cultural school, a reading room, and meeting space for over 50 Filipino organizations in the state of Michigan.

Chapter 4

Deconstructing the Model Minority Image:
Asian Pacific Americans, Race, Class, Gender, and Work

Edith Wen-Chu Chen

Asian Pacific Americans are often regarded as a successful minority group facing little discrimination and racial barriers. Census data has often been used to support these claims. This chapter introduces some interactive teaching activities to help students deconstruct the model minority thesis. One activity facilitates a student dialogue regarding the use of statistical data on national income across different racial groups, regions, and types of households. Another activity, using vignettes, facilitates discussion regarding the significance of Asian American women's work to the well-being of families. These activities can be used in courses in introductory Asian American Studies, contemporary Asian American issues, Asian American women, and in race and ethnicity. This exercise can also be used in diversity training seminars.

Objectives

- To help students deconstruct the image of Asian Pacific Americans as the model minority through the examination of census data.
- To sensitize students to the economic and ethnic diversity of the Asian Pacific population.
- To help students understand the role of gender in the economic and general well-being of their families.

Time

- Two forty-five minute sessions or one one-and-a-half hour session

Number of Participants

- Five to forty-five people

Materials Needed

Templates of the following are provided at the end of this chapter:

- Overheads of Census graphs
- Overhead projector
- Activity cards representing Asian Pacific households
- Handout on Asian Pacific American women, children, and work
- Outline of "Deconstructing the Model Minority Image"

Background

Much attention has been given to the success and achievements of Asian Pacific Americans. Their image as the successful or model minority is not a new one. This term originally referred to Japanese and Chinese Americans and became popular in the 1960s with magazine headlines such as "Success Story of One Minority Group in the U.S." and "Success Story: Japanese American Style." Accused of "Outwhiting the Whites," Asian Pacific Americans are perceived as the model minority.[1]

One achievement that is especially remarkable is the household income of Asian Pacific Americans, which exceeds that of all other racial ethnic groups, including whites. According to the 2000 Census, the Asian Pacific median household income was $55,525 (see figure 4.1). This income not only exceeded that of African Americans and Latinos, which were $30,436 and $33,455 respectively, but also was significantly higher than that of non-Hispanic whites, which was $45,910. The Asian Pacific median household income has exceeded that of other racial groups, including whites, for two decades. The policy implication is that Asian Pacific Americans do not need special poverty or job training programs, and that economic struggle is not an issue for them as for many African Americans and Latinos.

This kind of data has led scholars, journalists, and the general public to believe that racism is not significant in the lives of Asian Americans, and that they are relatively free of economic problems. In a poll conducted by the *Wall Street Journal* and NBC in 1992, the majority believed that Asian Americans are not discriminated against, and some even believed that Asian Americans receive too many special advantages. Some scholars have even gone further to suggest that Asians will soon merge into the white category, suggesting that race is not a disadvantage in their lives.[2]

In contrast, scholars in Asian American Studies have argued that the use of national median household income data is a poor indicator of the economic well-being of Asian Pacific Americans and racial progress. The data fails to illustrate that generally Asian Pacific households are larger and have more people working and contributing to the household income compared to whites. Also, Asian Pacific Americans tend to live in large metropolitan areas (New York, Los Angeles, San Jose, San Francisco, Honolulu, etc.) where the salaries are higher to account for the higher cost of living (see figure 4.2). Finally, the high Asian Pacific median household income hides the reality that many are living in poverty (see figure 4.3 and figure 4.4). For example, in metropolitan areas for every Asian Pacific household that makes $75,000 or more, there is almost another household living in poverty.[3]

A more accurate measure of racial equality would compare individual income data and control for regional differences, educational level, type of jobs, skills, experience, age, etc. A number of studies point out that when these factors are taken into consideration, Asian Pacific Americans earn less than whites, which suggests that they face discrimination in the workplace. For example, a *Los Angeles Times* analysis of the 1993-1997 Census data found that college-educated Asian Americans in management earned on average 38 percent less than white college graduates, despite English fluency.[4] While it is often perceived that Asian Americans excel in the fields of engineering and science, Asian American engineers and scientists are grossly underrepresented in management positions and are still underpaid compared to whites. In one in-depth study in the Phoenix and Tuscon metropolitan areas, Asian American scientists and engineers in managerial positions earned half the income of whites in similar positions.[5]

The failure to disaggregate the Asian Pacific median household income leads to a false image of a relatively homogenous group. The Asian Pacific population is composed of more than forty ethnic groups with different experiences. For example, Japanese Americans have been in the United States for several generations and are doing economically better than later arriving groups such as Vietnamese, Cambodian, Laotian, and Hmong. In addition, these Southeast Asian groups have unique circumstances associated with being refugees (see chapter 1 and "Southeast Asian Refugee Groups and the Barriers They Face," at the end of this chapter). Some federal programs have failed to consider the diversity of the Asian Pacific population, which has caused Southeast Asian organizations as well as other struggling communities to be overlooked for funding.[6]

It should also be pointed out that the history of Hawaiians shares more in common with Native Americans than Asian Americans. Native Hawaiians are distinct from Asian Americans in that they are not immigrants but are original people of the land and became Americans through illegal conquest and imperialistic practices (see chapter 11). Native Hawaiian struggles include land rights, self-sufficiency, and cultural reclamation, and many hope to achieve sovereignty similar to the status accorded to Native Americans. As with other Pacific Islanders, a large number of Native Hawaiians have reluctantly left for the "mainland," in search of better economic opportunities.

One factor that is often overlooked in discussing the economic well-being of Asian Pacific American households is the role of women. More Asian Pacific women work than in the general American population, and they work longer hours and more consistently throughout their life cycle.[7] It should also be noted that the ranks of Asian Pacific women in the workforce is as diverse as their skills, ranging from native-born and immigrants with high levels of education and professional skills to refugees with less education and marketable skills.[8]

The general image of Asian Pacific Americans as the model minority contradicts the economic realties of women, who not only face racial barriers but gender ones as well. Like men, Asian Pacific women receive lower return for comparable levels of education and may face glass ceilings, or barriers to positions of upper management. Asian Pacific women are more likely than other women of color to have a graduate education and yet are the least likely to be at senior levels of management.[9] In addition, despite their educational levels, interestingly, Asian Pacific women professors have one of the lowest tenure rates of all racial groups, male and female.[10] Asian Pacific women may have trouble being taken seriously due to the pervasive stereotype of being exotic and passive and having communication styles that do not conform to the aggressive, take-charge, top-down approach that typifies Western styles of leadership[11] (see chapter 16).

The number of Asian Pacific women working and their hours as documented in the census is likely underestimated. This is especially true for those who are working in small family businesses or in sectors that heavily rely on cheap immigrant labor. Industries such as garment manufacturing (see chapter 6) and electronics assembly often do not fully document the number of hours their employees work, especially since workers are often paid by the piece.[12] Besides working in low-wage sectors, immigrants who lack language abilities but have a small amount of capital may open small family businesses. It is well known that Koreans and other Asian immigrants are more likely to own small businesses than the general American population. However, in order for these family businesses, such as liquor stores and restaurants, to survive, they depend on the free or cheap labor of women and children. Even though the business may be registered under the husband's name, the wife and/or children are often working at the store although not as registered employees[13] (see handout).

In conclusion, when a closer examination of the data is taken into account, the success of Asian Pacific Americans is overestimated. While it is true that growing numbers are middle-class professionals, they are less likely to be in decision-making positions compared to whites with similar levels of education and skills and receive lower pay. Even more damaging is that the model minority image hides the fact that a significant portion of the Asian Pacific population is poor, with Samoans and Cambodian, Laotian, and Hmong refugees exceeding the poverty rates of African Americans and Latinos.

Suggested Procedures

Refer to the discussion outline, "Deconstructing the Model Minority Image: Asian Pacific Americans, Race, Class, and Gender and Work." Here, I discuss the steps in more detail.

Pre-Activity Discussion

Part I: Median Household Income of NH Whites, Asian Pacific Americans, African Americans, and Hispanic Origin—A Valid Measure of Success?

1. Ask students if they have ever heard of the model minority thesis. Discuss what the model minority thesis is and when it originated. Tell them that the median household income data from the census has often been used to support this thesis.
2. Show students Figure 4.1, "Median Household Income of NH whites, Asian Pacific Americans, African Americans, and Hispanic Origin." I recommend making overheads beforehand, but you can also make handouts.
3. Ask students how are Asian Americans doing compared to the other groups. Some more advanced students may want to critique the use of household income data. Ask them to hold their comments for the group discussion.
4. Ask students, "Using the data presented here, if you were going to fund a poverty program, which group would you most likely fund?" "Least likely fund?" Discuss the policy implications.
5. Ask students, "Does race appear to be an issue for Asian Pacific Americans when it comes to being economically successful, according to the data presented here?" Discuss the *Wall Street Journal* opinion poll.

Small Group Activity

Part II: What the Data Doesn't Reveal

1. To facilitate a discussion of what the data does not take into account, tell the students they will be participating in a short activity. Ask the students to form groups of four to six people. You will need to make cards beforehand. Use the template provided at the end of the chapter and make as many copies as needed on cardstock (i.e., for a class of forty, you would need to make five double-sided copies).

2. Before passing out the cards, show the students the front of a sample card. Tell students that each of them will be receiving a card, which represents an Asian Pacific household. The front of the card has the income of the household.

3. Pass the cards out to the students, so that only the front of the cards is revealed. Ask students not to look at the back of the card. Make sure that each member of the group gets a different card. While passing out the cards, ask students to look at their household income and compare it with others in their group. Students often become excited or disappointed at their incomes, some feeling very rich with a household income of $120,000 a year compared to others with much lower incomes.

4. After students have examined their own household income and have compared it with others, ask students to turn to the other side of their cards to discuss with their group the data as presented in Figure 4.1 and what it does not take into account. This should take between five to seven minutes.

5. Have students share their discussion with the rest of the class. Here, you may want to ask a group representative to offer one factor that the data from Figure 4.1 does not reveal. Usually, students raise the issue of geographical location (Figure 4.2), the number of people working in the household, and the number of people living in the household (Figure 4.3). As each group raises points, show the corresponding figures to add to their points.

6. Other factors that you may want to raise if students don't do so are the ethnic and economic diversity of the Asian Pacific population as illustrated in Figure 4.4, "Asian Americans, Pacific Islanders, Whites, African Americans, and Latinos Living in Poverty, Los Angeles, 2000." Here, you may want to discuss the diverse histories of Asian Pacific Americans (i.e., immigrant, refugee, or native-born, and the economic diversity between and within groups). In particular, the 14 percent poverty rate of the aggregate Asian Pacific population obscures the high level of poverty among Pakistani, Vietnamese, Cambodian, Hmong, and Samoan groups, which is similar to if not double that of Latinos and African Americans.

7. You may also want to mention to students that the data also does not take into account the general higher educational attainment of Asian Pacific Americans.

Small Group Discussion

Part III: The Role of Women's Work

1. Show students Figure 4.1 again. In the previous discussion critiquing median household income as a basis for explaining Asian Pacific American success, one factor that was discussed was the number of people working and living in the house-

hold. Ask the students to imagine who are these contributors? Often what is invisible when median household income data is emphasized is the contributions of women and children.

2. To facilitate a discussion on the gendered dynamics underlying paid work, give students the handout, "Asian American Women, Children, and Work." This handout focuses on the intersection of race, class, and gender and the challenges working Asian Pacific women face both inside and outside the home. Questions you may want to ask to prompt further discussion are:

    - How important is the women's work in contributing to the finances of their families? How does their work contribute to their overall families' well-being?
        - Why do you think Ann Nguyen works?
        - Why do you think Flora Huang works?
        - Why does Sumi Lee work?
    - In what way are the women's struggles similar? Different? What is the role of class in shaping their experiences?
        - What sort of struggles does Ann Nguyen face in the workplace?
        - What are the issues that Flora Huang faces in the workplace?
        - What do you think life must be like for Sumi Lee?

3. You should discuss both paid and unpaid work, including housework and childcare.

    - What is the role of children in contributing to the income of their families? In what ways are their struggles similar? Different? What is the role of class in shaping their experiences?
    - What is the role of ethnicity/race in shaping their work experiences? How are their work experiences/options interconnected with their husbands' work?
    - What is the role of gender in shaping their work experiences/options?

4. Ask participants if any of them could relate to the vignettes, whether to their own experience or someone they know. Often, this activity provides a vehicle for participants to share their own experiences with the class.

Notes

1. "Success Story of One Minority Group in the U.S.," *New York Times Magazine* (January 1966); "Success Story: Japanese American Style," *U.S. News and World Report* (December 26, 1966); "Success Story: Outwhiting the Whites," *Newsweek* (June 21, 1971).

2. Andrew Hacker, *Two Nations: Black and White, Separate, Hostile, Unequal* (New York: Charles Scribner's Sons, 1992); Douglas Massey and Nancy Denton, "Trends in Residential Segregation of Blacks, Hispanics, and Asians, 1970-1980," *American Sociological Review* 52 (1987): 802-25.

3. Paul Ong and Suzanne Hee, "Economic Diversity," in *The State of Asian Pacific America: Economic Diversity, Issues & Policies*, ed. Paul Ong (Los Angeles: LEAP Asian Pacific American Public Policy Institute and UCLA Asian American Studies Center, 1994).

4. "Asian American Finding Cracks in Glass Ceiling," *Los Angeles Times* (July 15, 1988), cited in Deborah Woo, *Glass Ceilings and Asian Americans: The New Face of Workplace Barriers* (Walnut Creek, CA: AltaMira Press, 2000).

5. Paul Wong and Richard Nagasawa, "Asian American Scientists and Engineers: Is There a Glass Ceiling for Career Advancement?" *Chinese American Forum* 6:3 (1991): 3-6; cited in Woo, *Glass Ceilings and Asian Americans*, 63.

6. Noy Thrupkaew, "The Myth of the Model Minority," *The American Prospect* 13:7 (April 8, 2002).

7. Timothy P. Fong, *The Contemporary Asian American Experience: Beyond the Model Minority*, 2nd ed. (Upper Saddle River, NJ: Prentice Hall, 2002); Keiko Yamanaka and Kent McClelland, 1994. "Earning the Model-Minority Image: Diverse Strategies of Economic Adaptation by Asian-American Women," *Ethnic and Racial Studies* 17:1 (January 1994).

8. Yamanaka and McClelland, "Earning the Model-Minority Image."

9. Fong, *The Contemporary Asian American Experience*; Yamanaka and McClelland, "Earning the Model-Minority Image"; Catylyst, "Executive Summary," *Women of Color in Corporate Management: Opportunities and Barriers* (New York: Catalyst, 1999), cited in Woo , *Glass Ceilings and Asian Americans*, 18.

10. Shirley Hune, *Asian Pacific American Women in Higher Education: Claiming Visibility and Voice*, Association of American Colleges and Universities, Program on the Status and Education of Women, 1998.

11. Julia Matsui-Estrella, "From Hawaii to Berkeley: Tracing Roots in Asian American Leadership," *Journal of Women and Religion* (1995).

12. Lora Foo, *Asian American Women: Issues, Concerns, and Responsive Human and Civil Rights Advocacy* (New York: Ford Foundation, 2002).

13. Kyeyoung Park, "Impact of New Productive Activities on the Organization of Domestic Life: A Case Study of the Korean Community," in *Frontiers of Asian American Studies*, eds. Gail Nomura, Russell Endo, Stephen H. Sumida and Russell C. Leong (Pullman, WA: Washington State University Press, 1989).

Recommended Resources

Eric Lai and Dennis Arguelles, *The New Face of Asian Pacific America: Numbers, Diversity & Change in the 21st Century* (Los Angeles: Asian Week and UCLA Asian American Studies Center, 2003).

Lora Foo, *Asian American Women: Issues, Concerns, and Responsive Human and Civil Rights Advocacy* (New York: Ford Foundation, 2002).

Deborah Woo, *Glass Ceilings and Asian Americans: The New Face of Workplace Barriers* (Walnut Creek, CA: AltaMira Press, 2000).

Deconstructing the Model Minority Image:
Asian Pacific Americans, Race, Class, Gender, and Work

I. Median Household Income of NH Whites, Asian Pacific Americans, African Americans, and Latinos—is it a valid measure of success?
    A. Class and economic implications: If you were going to fund a poverty program, which group would you most likely fund? Least likely fund?
    B. Race implications: Does race appear to be an issue for Asian Pacific Americans when it comes to income, according to these figures?

II. What the data do not reveal (pass out card activity to help facilitate student discussion)
    A. Region
    B. More people working in household contributing to household income
    C. Diversity—some Asian Pacific Americans are not doing so well
    D. Education—Asian Pacific Americans as a group have a higher education than whites

III. The role of women's work
    A. More Asian Pacific women work than all American women
        1. The number of Asian Pacific women working is probably undercounted
    B. More Asian Pacific women work longer than all American women
        1. The number of hours Asian Pacific women work is probably undercounted
    C. Challenges in the workplace
        1. Working-class women
            a. often have to work due to husband's low income is not enough to support the family
            b. are still often responsible for reproductive labor
            c. children may have to help out economically as well as with reproductive labor
        2. Women with small family businesses
            a. often their labor is undercounted; business often is registered under husband's name, and she is not an official employee
            b. they are often responsible for reproductive labor
            c. grandmothers may play an important role in terms of reproductive labor
        3. Professional women
            a. glass ceiling issues
            b. workplace culture may still privilege Western forms of leadership and communication
            c. workplace culture may still be very male-oriented

Discussion Outline

Front of Activity Cards

$45,000

$120,000

$25,000

$45,000

$55,000

$70,000

Back of Activity Cards

Number of People in
Household: 6

Number of People Working: 4

Residence: New York, NY

Number of People in
Household: 1

Number of People Working: 1

Residence: San Francisco, CA

Number of People in
Household: 4

Number of People Working: 2

Residence: Chicago, IL

Number of People in
Household: 3

Number of People Working: 2

Residence: Honolulu, HI

Number of People in
Household: 5

Number of People Working: 3

Residence: Los Angeles, CA

Number of People in
Household: 2

Number of People Working: 1

Residence: Los Angeles, CA

Activity Cards

Figure 4.1 Median Household Income of Non-Hispanic Whites, Asian Pacific Americans, African Americans, and Hispanic Origin, U.S.A., 2000

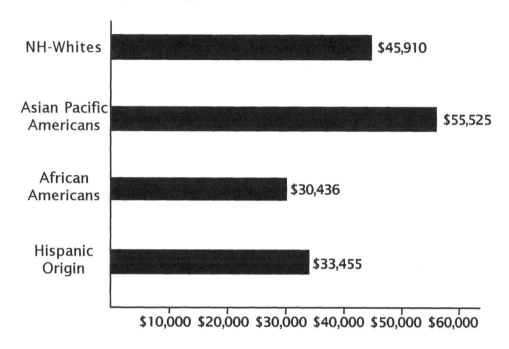

Source: U.S. Census Bureau, www.census.gov/hhes/income/histinc/h05.html.

Figure 4.2 Top 10 Places Where Asian Pacific Americans Live, 2000

  1. New York, NY
  2. Los Angeles, CA
  3. San Jose, CA
  4. San Francisco, CA
  5. Honolulu, HI
  6. San Diego, CA
  7. Chicago, IL
  8. Houston, TX
  9. Seattle, WA
 10. Fremont, CA

Source: U.S. Bureau of Census, 2000.

Overhead

Figure 4.3 Per Capita Income for Whites and Selected Asian Pacific American Ethnic Groups, Los Angeles County, 2000

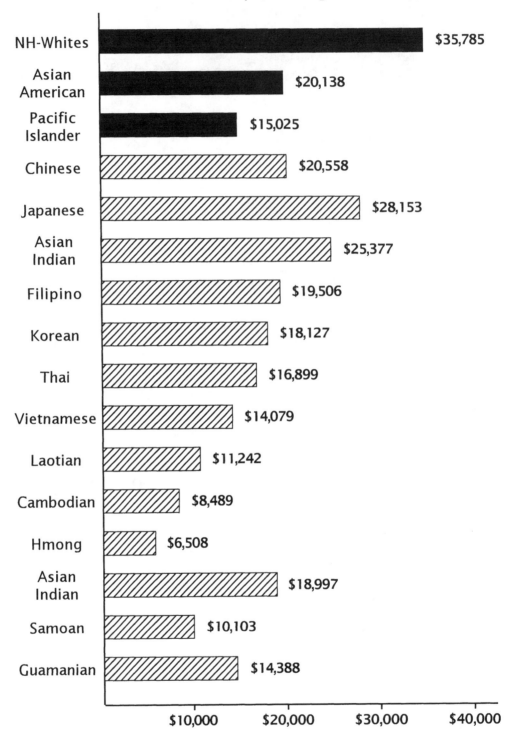

NH-Whites	$35,785
Asian American	$20,138
Pacific Islander	$15,025
Chinese	$20,558
Japanese	$28,153
Asian Indian	$25,377
Filipino	$19,506
Korean	$18,127
Thai	$16,899
Vietnamese	$14,079
Laotian	$11,242
Cambodian	$8,489
Hmong	$6,508
Asian Indian	$18,997
Samoan	$10,103
Guamanian	$14,388

Note: Figures are for the inclusive population (single race and multi-race combined) and not exclusive of Latino/Hispanic except for white, which is single race, non-Hispanic.

Source: U.S. Bureau of Census, 2000. Compiled by Kimiko Kelly, Asian Pacific American Legal Center, Los Angeles.

Overhead

Figure 4.4 Asian Americans, Pacific Islanders, Whites, African Americans, and Latinos Living in Poverty, Los Angeles County, 2000

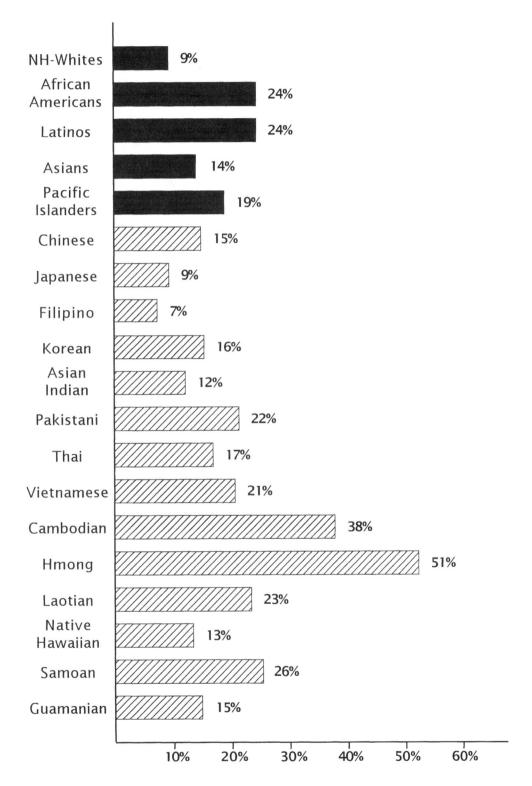

Source: U.S. Bureau of Census, 2000. Compiled by Kimiko Kelly, Asian Pacific American Legal Center, Los Angeles.

Overhead

Asian American Women, Children, and Work

Directions

For each of the women profiled, discuss how race, class, and gender impact their lives. How do their work and family life impact each other? How do your family experiences compare to these vignettes?

1. Ann Nguyen arrived in Oakland from Vietnam in 1982 with her husband and five kids. They moved into a one-bedroom apartment with Ann's sister who was already living there. Mr. Nguyen quickly found work as a dishwasher in Chinatown. Ann's sister helped her to find work in a small garment shop, making designer dresses alongside Asian and Latina immigrants. She got paid by the piece and made about two dollars an hour. She would usually work Monday through Thursday, but sometimes she would go in on Sunday when there was a rush order although she would never receive overtime pay. Breaks are allowed, but since she sews by the piece, she doesn't get paid for them. Oftentimes she takes work home with her, so that she can look after her children while she sews. The kids also help out with some of the simpler tasks of making the dresses, such as undoing a hem that Ann had sewn incorrectly or ironing a belt she had sewn.

2. Flora Huang is a Chinese immigrant who holds a Ph.D. in chemistry from the University of Texas. After receiving her Ph.D., she taught at a private college in Texas. Currently, her husband is a professor at a local university, and she works at a top pharmaceutical company as a research scientist. She is recognized by her peers for her dedication, hard work, professional integrity, and her ability to troubleshoot tough problems. After work, sometimes her co-workers would go out for drinks to socialize. Flora would go home immediately so she could spend time with her husband and her two daughters who were in high school. Also, she didn't particularly care to socialize with her American co-workers and didn't always get or appreciate their jokes. All her bosses have been male, white, and younger, some with MBA degrees and others with bachelor's degrees. She has applied for a promotion to be a project manager, but the senior management turned down her request, stating that she lacked good communication skills.

3. Sumi Lee is a forty-two-year-old Korean immigrant woman who came from Seoul to the United States in the 1980s. Back in Korea, she led a middle-class lifestyle in which her main responsibilities were taking care of the house, children, and her husband. She did not work outside the home. Her husband held a professional job. When they moved to the United States, Mr. Lee's credentials were not valid in the United States, so he and his wife opened up a liquor store in Los Angeles. The store is registered under Mr. Lee's name, although Sumi works alongside her husband everyday. The store hours are from eight a.m. to midnight Monday through Thursday, and eight a.m. to two a.m. during the weekends. They also work on holidays. They have two teenage children who help at the store after school and on the weekends. Sumi's parents came to the United States and moved in with them. Sumi's mom often helps take care of the children, while Sumi and Mr. Lee are at work.

Handout

Southeast Asian Refugee Groups and the Barriers They Face

Kimiko Kelly, Asian Pacific American Legal Center

The Asian American population as a whole often ranks above average for measures of socioeconomic status, but data separated for Asian ethnic groups reveals some of the most poverty stricken and least educated groups in the country. Southeast Asian refugee groups—including Cambodian, Hmong, Laotian, and Vietnamese—consistently rank among those most disadvantaged. Analysis of the 2000 Census reveals that nationally all four Southeast Asian refugee groups have poverty rates higher than the general population, and two groups, Cambodian and Hmong, have poverty rates higher than any racial or ethnic group. In Los Angeles County, three of these groups have the highest public assistance rates in the county.

War in Indochina

Following the United States pullout from Vietnam, communist regimes took power not only in Vietnam but shortly after also in Cambodia and in Laos. Many years of U.S. efforts to eradicate communism in Indochina created millions of refugees in the region through bombing, deploying troops, and spending millions of dollars in aid.

Since the major supply line for North Vietnamese troops ran through Laos, the United States bombed Laos massively during the war. The Hmong, an ethnic group in Laos, were recruited to fight in the CIA's secret war against Laotian communists and lost tens of thousands of their people. When the United States withdrew from the region, Hmong were left as targets for those in power. With the U.S. withdrawal, the Khmer Rouge came to power in Cambodia in 1975 and began a program to create an agrarian socialist state. In the years following, over 1.5 million Cambodians were murdered during the efforts to eradicate any opposition, initially focusing on professionals, the educated, and government officials, but ultimately encompassing Cambodians of every background.

Forced Migration

Southeast Asian refugees came to the United States involuntarily, fleeing their countries in a time of distress and unprepared for adjustment to life in the United States. Many arrived via refugee camps in Thailand or Malaysia. Those who escaped on make-shift boats endured harsh physical conditions, deaths of loved ones, and rape and robbery by pirates.

Many who arrived came from rural backgrounds and had little or no formal education. The Hmong had no written language until the 1950s and other Laotian ethnic groups arrived without any written language at all. Most Cambodians who arrived had little education since the educated and professional classes were systematically murdered by the Khmer Rouge. The backgrounds of refugees in rural farming offered few skills helpful in transitioning to life in the urban United States.

Resettlement Challenges

With few skills to offer, little or no education, and little or no ability to speak English, many began their lives in the United States dependent on public assistance. The Refugee Act of

Additional Reading

1980 required states to provide social services to refugees. This created a unique population on welfare. Southeast Asian welfare households are more likely to be larger, have two-parent families, have less formal education, and are limited English proficient. With few resources dedicated to addressing the distinct needs of this group, Southeast Asian welfare recipients are having a more difficult time exiting from welfare than other recipients.

Those who do enter the workforce find low-wage jobs with little opportunity for advancement and often work more hours than others to make ends meet. As a consequence, children may be left unattended at home, contributing to low academic achievement and juvenile delinquency. Urban ethnic enclaves have developed problems of street crime, gangs, and high incarceration rates.

In the twenty-five years since the first wave of Southeast Asian refugees arrived, limited English proficiency and low levels of education have persisted. These communities have experienced improvements over the decades but still remain among the most disadvantaged groups in society. A lack of services aimed at addressing these issues has allowed the problems of low income, public assistance use, and poverty to continue among Southeast Asians.

Who Is a Refugee?

"A refugee is a person who owing to a well-founded fear of being persecuted for reasons of race, religion, nationality, membership of a particular social group, or political opinion, is outside the country of his nationality, and is unable to or, owing to such fear, is unwilling to avail himself of the protection of that country."

—*The 1951 United Nations High Commissioner for Refugees (UNHCR) Convention Relating to the Status of Refugees*

Additional Reading

Chapter 5

Building Allies:
Linking Race, Class, Gender, and Sexuality in Asian American Studies

Gina Masequesmay

This chapter exposes students to the variegated experiences of Asian Pacific American lesbians, gays, bisexuals, transgenders, and intersexuals (LGBTI). It also addresses the general issues of gender, sexual, class, and racial oppression. This curriculum focuses on the intersections of race, class, gender, and sexuality, highlighting gender and sexual discrimination and prejudice against LGBTIs with emphasis on the unique experiences of Asian Pacific Americans. This curriculum is for college-leveled or mature participants who have some understanding of issues of oppression such as racism and sexism.

Objectives

- To sensitize students to the experiences of Asian Pacific American lesbians, gays, bisexuals, transgenders, and intersexuals (LGBTI).
- To help students connect different forms of oppression (e.g., racism, sexism, heterosexism, homophobia) and their intersections.

Time

- Introduction and ground rules (fifteen minutes)
- Terminology and stereotypes exercise and discussion (sixty minutes)
- Break (ten minutes)
- Coming out as a process and the challenges facing Asian Pacific American LGBTIs (thirty minutes)
- Role-playing and different levels of oppression (thirty minutes)
- Questions and answers (five minutes)

Number of Participants

- Maximum of twenty-five people

Materials Needed

- Transparencies (see handouts)
- Overhead projector
- Board to write down notes or ten to fourteen sheets of butcher paper to tape up on wall around the room and lots of markers (at least eight)

Background

"Injustice anywhere is a threat to justice everywhere."

Martin Luther King, Jr.

In "Homophobia, Why Bring It Up?" Barbara Smith links racism and homophobia, contending that one cannot fight one without the other.[1] For example, how can Asian Pacific Americans fight for their rights without including issues of lesbians, gays, bisexuals, transgenders, and intersexuals (LGBTIs). Smith also suggests that homophobia is one of the last forms of prejudice and discrimination that is still socially acceptable. We see this intolerance in terms of laws as well as in media, in high rates of suicides among teens (30 to 50 percent of suicides are by LGBT teens), and in everyday interactions. For example, among children and adolescents, the terms "fag" and "gay" are used to deride others and are acceptable to adults, while racial epithets are discouraged. Operating on a more innocuous level, heterosexism occurs in everyday meetings when most assume that the other person is heterosexual unless the other person "comes out" as not straight. And when they do come out, we wonder why they have to display it in our face. We do not see that our heterosexual institutions limit the possibilities of being anything else but straight. These examples from macro-policies to micro-levels of interaction suggest that issues of homophobia, heterosexism, and heteronormativity must be addressed in addition to racism, sexism, and classism. If we ignore them, then as Martin Luther King, Jr. and Barbara Smith argue, we do not really address the "matrix of domination" where different forms of oppression based on their race, class, gender, and sexuality intersect and create differential inequalities.[2]

Overcoming homophobia (the fear of and prejudice and discrimination against LGBTIs), heterosexism (the assumption that everyone is straight) and heteronormativity (the assumption that heterosexuality is normal and the institutionalization of such assumption) is one of the final frontiers concerning our mistreatment of people in this country. Nationwide efforts (e.g., safe zone projects) include sensitivity workshops to teach others about the struggles of the LGBTI community. This curriculum is one such effort. The focus here is on Asian Pacific LGBTI issues, where we can examine how race and sexuality/gender intersect. That is, how do the hierarchies of race, gender, sexuality, and class intersect in the lives of Asian Pacific LGBTIs?

The terms "lesbian" (a female homosexual), "gay" (a male homosexual), "bisexual" (a person who is attracted to either male or female), "transgender" (someone who transgresses gender boundaries in identity as transsexual, crossdresser, drag queen, drag king, or gender queer), and "intersexual" (a hermaphrodite) are Western political constructs to describe a diversity of gender and sexual experiences of people who do not conform to the traditional roles and hierarchies that Christianity and modern sciences created, that of the heterosexist binary sex-gender system.[3] According to this system, one is assigned a "sex" of male or female at birth based on one's perceived genitalia and then one is socialized to be feminine if the assigned sex is female or masculine if the assigned sex is male. From this gender socialization, one is then expected to become sexually attracted to the "opposite sex" or become heterosexual. Because this path is not the only way for someone to be gendered and sexualized, social movements of feminists and lesbians, gays, bisexuals, transgenders, and intersexuals (LGBTIs) have also emerged to offer and legitimate other ways of being. Feminists have made it more possible for women to cross strict gender norms such as women working in predominantly male occupations and women appearing with pants and shirts instead of skirts and blouses and still be seen as women (although strong and assertive women are often called "bitch" or "ballbreaker"). Similarly, the gay and lesbian movements have legitimated homosexual (and later bisexual) experiences as normal sexual experiences in our human diversity. The recent transgender revolt and emerging movement of the intersexuals further complicated the original binary sex-gender system by suggesting that sexual organs do not dictate gender identity and arguing that natural ambiguous sexual organs should not be pathologized nor "corrected" by our biased cultural lens that only sees two sexes, male and female, when nature offers much more variations.

Evidently, the heterosexist binary sex-gender system in the United States is not the only way to organize society. In India, the *hijras* are considered a third gender or sex. In pre-colonial India, the *hijras* were a revered caste of men who castrated themselves and crossdressed to become women and to take on women's roles including some marrying men. They were thought to have magical power to curse or bless people, and many functioned as advisors to the king in the court palace. When Christianity was introduced into India under British rule, the *hijras* slowly lost their status. While many Indians still believe *hijras* have magical power to curse and bless, *hijras* occupy a marginal status in India today where many resort to begging and prostitution for survival. Similarly in Hawaiian tradition, a *mahu* was considered a person of magical power, a shaman who possesses both essential qualities of male and female. *Mahus* were revered in Hawaiian culture until Christianity deviantized them along with other Hawaiian practices of free sexuality. *Mahus* and *titas* (female homosexual or masculine women) had a place in Hawaiian culture. Similarly, in pre-colonial Vietnamese tradition, hermaphrodites or intersexuals were not considered freaks of nature but special people to be sent to the palace to serve the king. Unlike our current Western binary understanding of gender and sex, other cultures have had more than two sexes or genders so that an intersexual is considered a part of nature's creation rather than an aberration. In contrast, in U.S. society, babies naturally born with ambiguous genitalia are considered "abnormal" because they are neither male nor female. In fact, doctors and parents feel the need to "correct" the ambiguity by turning the baby into a boy or a girl, conforming to this society's perceptions of only two possible sexes: male or female. Recently, there is a growing movement of intersexuals who are fighting for the rights of ambiguously sexed babies to decide how they want to live out their lives instead of letting the parents and doctors decide at birth. Similar to the gay, lesbian, and bisexual movements that are fighting for people's rights to love whom they choose, transgender and intersexual people are fighting for their rights to decide their own gender and sex identities in a society that has not been accepting of anything deviating from the heterosexist binary sex-gender thinking that is solidified by Christianity and culturally biased sciences.[4] In short, the heterosexist binary sex-gender system is restrictive of the gender and sexual diversity of our human experiences that other cultural systems allowed to exist as in the cases of the *hijras* and *mahus*. Because of Western colonialism, however, the heterosexist binary sex-gender system is the dominant view of organizing our world today. It deviantizes the experiences of alternative genders and sexualities.

Living in the United States where the heterosexist binary sex-gender system is imposed on people's lives, Asian Pacific LGBTIs must deal with this heteronormativity despite coming from traditional culture that may have allowed for sexual and gender expressions. Being both a sexual and racial minority means having to cope with both white privilege and heteronormativity. Many discuss having two types of experiences in LGBTI settings. One is being objectified as an exotic "other," and the second is being ignored as undesirable. On the Asian homefront, LGBTIs face invisibility and silence where homosexuality is often perceived as a "Western disease" or a sign of assimilation. While the ethnic community may provide a safe space to protect them from racism, it also functions in heteronormativity, and the struggles of LGBTIs as sexual and gender minorities are often painfully isolated from their struggle as racial minorities. Many feel that they have to choose between their race/ethnicity and their sexuality/gender identity. For immigrants, in particular, choosing one's sexual/gender identity often means losing the safety net against racism and cultural insensitivity from their ethnic community. To fight against racism and heteronormativity, Asian Pacific LGBTIs have created their own community and network of support. Such organizations as the Gay Asian Pacific Support Network and Lotus (a lesbian/bisexual women's group) are testaments to the need for support networks that address specific needs of sexual/gender and racial minorities.

In our curriculum, we begin with stereotypes of different social categories of people and discuss the issues of marginalization and stigmatization. Students discuss the difficulties that Asian Pacific LGBTIs encounter and the processes that create the problems for them. Students also begin to learn how marginalization not only affects Asian Pacific LGBTIs but everyone. For example, homophobia not only threatens gay men but also any man who does not look or act according to the dominant understanding of manliness. Given the desexualized image of Asian American men, we can discuss how homophobia operates within the Asian community and among mainstream LGBTIs to relegate Asian gay men to the passive positions that Asian women occupy in their relationships with non-Asians, especially white men. We thus have such terms as "Rice Queen" and "Potato Queen" to describe the prevalent interracial relationships of older gay white men with younger Asian men. The image of an Asian lesbian, on the other hand, is unthinkable given that she does not serve the interest of white men, reflecting our racist, patriarchal society. Asian lesbians indeed complain how their presence is often a shock to other lesbians who claim they never knew such a combination could exist and who do not know what to do with them. When other lesbians have an interest, it often evolves into an exoticism of Asian people. In contrast, Pacific Islanders are constructed as hypersexual instead of desexualized. As indigenous people, they were perceived as savages that needed to be civilized and desexualized in the image of the conquerors. With the stigmatization of *mahus* in Hawai'i, the only way to be "real men" is to be restrained heterosexual men. Either seen as hypersexual or hyposexual, Asian Pacific Americans are relegated to stereotypes at the interest of white men, straight or gay.

Focusing on Asian American LGBTIs, this workshop offers opportunities to draw parallels between racism and heteronormativity. For example, students can compare and contrast how racism and heteronormativity construct and marginalize racial and sexual minorities. Connecting different forms of oppression, students can further inquire how class and gender also interplay with race and sexuality. Particularly, being both sexually and racially marginalized, how do Asian American LGBTIs fare in the desirability market? How do the men's experiences differ from women's? How do transsexuals with money for operations differ in realizing their "true identity" from those without when both need lifetime hormonal injections and surgeries, surgeries that may not guarantee functionality of the constructed genitalia?

To understand the experiences of Asian Pacific LGBTIs, this workshop incorporates Gust Yep's model (see handout) to examine the different levels of oppression, from internalized homophobia or internalized racism, to hate crimes, to hostile climate, to hostile institutional policies.[5] Here, we make a distinction between negative experiences of Asian American LGBTIs at the individual versus the collective level and at the interior or internal versus the exterior or external level. Specifically, at the individual and interior level, a person could internalize racism and homophobia (he does not identify as gay, and he is in the closet) so that he only has sex with European Americans and not other Asian Pacific Americans. At the individual level and at the exterior level, a person faces racism or homophobia done by another person, such as being a victim of a hate crime. In contrast, institutional violence is racism, homophobia and heterosexism at the collective and exterior level—what we call institutional discrimination—because policies are set up to discriminate against people because of their race and/or sexual/gender identification (e.g., no health benefits for one's LGBTI partner). Distinct from institutional violence is the discursive violence experienced at the interior level but done at the collective level. An example is a person who cannot come out at the workplace even though no one explicitly makes homophobic remarks. Rather, the social climate feels heterosexist and sets LGBTIs apart from the rest of society. These four different levels of oppression come together to create a situation that we call heteronormativity, or white supremacy that privileges heterosexuality and whiteness by deviantizing or marginalizing LGBTIs and people of color. Similarly, we can discuss how gender privilege and sexism help to perpetuate patriarchy.

In summation, this handout exposes students to some of the issues that Asian Pacific LGBTIs face. The instructor need not be an expert, but rather someone who is open to the struggles of those who are multiply marginalized by our racist and heteronormative society.

Suggested Procedures

1. Facilitator welcomes students and reads the workshop agenda covering terminology and stereotypes, the coming-out process and the challenges of Asian Pacific LGBTIs, and role-playing and different levels of oppression. The facilitator provides ground-rules for discussion in workshop and asks if there are more ground-rules students want to add. The ground-rules for interaction are to be open to and respectful of others' opinions, to listen attentively, to use "I" statements, to give constructive criticism and avoid personal attacks, and to keep everything discussed confidential in this workshop. The facilitator asks students to introduce themselves and identify one item that they wish to learn by the end of the workshop. The facilitator explains the objectives of the workshop and what will be covered and not covered, based on the students' responses that are recorded on the board.

2. The facilitator introduces students to the first exercise on terminology as well as the stereotypes and images associated with LGBTIs, Asians, Asian men and Asian

women. The facilitator creates fourteen columns or boxes on the board and writes down the following words for each column: Gay, Lesbian, Bisexual, Transgender, Intersexual, Asians, Asian Women, Asian Men; Queer Asians, Asian Lesbians, Asian Gay Men, Asian Bisexuals, Asian Transgenders, Asian Intersexuals. For the categories Transgender and Intersexual, facilitator can use smaller columns since there will not be as much knowledge about these categories. The facilitator asks students to walk around and write down words or phrases associated with each of these labels and to not duplicate words/ideas written by others. They can put checks next to those words if they were also going to write them on the board. Give students about five minutes to do this. Ask students to be as exhaustive as possible. The facilitator can add words that students have not written down.

3. Go over each column, starting with gay, then lesbian, bisexual, transgender, and intersexual. Begin by clarifying what the term means (see handout on "Terminology") and then reading out the students' words. As you do this, ask students if the image is positive, neutral, or negative. Put a plus for a positive image, a minus for a negative image and a circle for a neutral idea. When you are done, ask the students what they think of the images associated with the term. The discussion should involve:
    *   How there are more negatives than positive images for LGBTIs overall.
    *   More information about gays and lesbians than the other groups, with overlapping images for some categories (e.g., gay men as transvestites).
    *   Most of the images are male-centric in that for gays it is about them not being a real man, and for lesbians it is about them not having the right man or perversely wanting to be a man. For bisexuals, the binary thinking puts them at odds with society, and hence they are confused and a dangerous liaison between the straight and LGBTI worlds. For transgenders, the binary thinking constructs them as confused and going against nature's intention. Ironically for intersexuals, the binary thinking renders them freaks of nature even though they were born naturally so.

4. Move on to the next column on Asians, then Asian men, and finally Asian women. Read out loud the students' input. For the Asians' column, ask students if any of the images refer to sexuality. Then ask the student to compare that to the Asian women and men's list. Discussion should emphasize heterosexist thinking that suggests:
    *   Asian men are asexual, while Asian women are hypersexual for the white male's fantasy. Note that Asian men were originally seen as a sexual threat to white men. Anti-immigrant legislation, white supremacy and anti-miscegenation laws from the 1880s to the early 1900s created a Chinese American bachelor society that dwindled in numbers. Along with this image of impotence to reproduce the community was the emergence of the image of Asian men as asexual. This desexualization of Asian men has not changed even as Asian American men have gained socioeconomic power.
    *   The general Asian group, on the other hand, is seen as an asexual model minority and outsider with distinct cultural norms and values.
    *   Underscore how specific the sexualization process is for each gender group versus the group as a whole.

5. Go on to the columns of Asian LGBTIs. Ask students to look at the input and give quick feedback. Frame the students' feedback in the following way:

- Given how LGBTIs are perceived and how Asians are perceived, ask students to discuss the images of Asian LGBTIs. Sexualized Asians are to fulfill the white man's fantasy. Note the similar role of Asian women and gay men as passive dolls and boys for white men.

- Whereas the desexualization of straight Asian men led to the effeminate and passive role of Asian gay men, the gay men are sexualized because they are gay. However, their role as sexual beings is to be the passive bottom for the white men. They basically play the same role as straight Asian women.

- Unlike Asian men, Asian women are (hyper)sexualized as exotic and erotic creatures. Being women, they are subservient and pampering to white men. Being that their purpose is to serve white men, this construction renders Asian lesbians invisible and inconceivable.

- Underscore the connection between the construction of these images of Asian straight and LGBTI men and women—that is, the racialization process is also a sexualized process.

- To resist objectifications, Asian gay men and women have identified themselves to be "sticky rice" (see handout on "Terminology").

- Discuss how the images of Asian bisexuals, transgenders, and intersexuals are almost non-existent in popular culture because of heterosexism, binary thinking, and the specific constructions of Asian men and women. However, introduce the terms *Mahu* and *Hijra* to discuss how in Hawaiian and Indian cultures there are roles for people who are not typical men and women.

6. Following a short break (ten minutes), summarize points from the earlier discussion on the marginalization of Asians and the stigmatization of LGBTIs. Ask students where they think the negative images of LGBTIs came from. Obvious answers would be Judeo-Christian religions. Emphasize how mainstream Christianity has deviantized LGBTIs and made such identities a stigma. Discuss how growing up in such an environment would lead to self-hate (cite suicide rate of LGBT teenagers) and denial. Introduce the terms homophobia and heterosexism if they have not come up yet.

7. To begin discussion on the coming out process, introduce the terms "in the closet" and "coming out" to show how homophobia and heterosexism could facilitate or hinder individuals from coming out. Ask students how the Asian community perceives homosexuality, bisexuality, transgenderism and intersexualism. Their points will be similar to mainstream concepts with an addition that some Asian Americans perceive homosexuality and being LGBTI as a "Western disease." Dispel this myth with the *Mahu* and *Hijra* examples. In addition, students may raise the issue that it is not so much about homophobia as it is about a taboo in discussing sex because sex is a private matter. Confirm this with the following example: in some Asian societies, men can have private male-to-male sex while remaining happily married with wives and kids. As long as the homosexual behavior is not publicized and is not interfering with maintaining a family, homosexuality is a non-issue.

8. Introduce the modified model of Cass' coming out stages (see handout) and emphasize the following points:

- Some LGBTIs can pass as straight ("in the closet") and "normal," while others cannot hide. The sissy gay men, the butch lesbians and the transgender persons have a harder time in our society than those who can pass as straight men and women.

- Coming out is not a one-time event, but a lifelong process. The stages are not linear and people may be out in one context and in the closet in another. For example, a person can be out to friends but not parents and co-workers.
- The risk of coming out is losing family support, employment, and friendship.
- The risks of not coming out are living a lie, suppressing one's desire, and avoiding closeness with other people.
- Bisexuals may first come out as homosexual before they come out as bisexual. Since biphobia exists within the gay/lesbian community, some bisexuals may have to hide their bisexuality to be accepted in the gay/lesbian community.
- The institutionalization of gender makes the everyday life of transgenders a living hell from deciding which bathroom to enter to responding to people's address of oneself as "sir" or "miss." They sometimes do not receive much support from the gay/lesbian community because they are seen as lesbians who hate their bodies or gay men who went too far with dragging.

9. Ask students to identify some of the values, norms and practices within the Asian American family that would affect the coming out process. Write down on board. Students may raise the lack of discussion about private matters in the family; the powerful pressure of filial piety, the nobility in self-sacrifice for the benefit of the family; the need to avoid family shame and promote family pride; the perception that homosexuality is a Western disease; and the perception that homosexuality or transgenderism is a manifestation of confusion, sickness, or assimilation.

10. After highlighting the specific challenges for Asian American LGBTIs, inform students that they will have a chance to better understand the issues through role-playing. Have students break into groups of three and role-play four scenarios (see handout) for five minutes. Some students can observe the interactions and give feedback to the actors. More than one group can do the same scenario. Give students time to discuss as participants and observers. Switch roles if there is more time. As a full class, ask students what they learned from the role-play. Select one group from each scenario. Emphasize the following issues from this group sharing:

- Passing is usually not an option for Asians who cannot hide their race. Some Asians LGBTIs, however, can hide their sexuality or gender identification.
- Facing racism from the larger society, Asians fall back on their family and community for support. However, if an Asian American is LGBTI and if this person's community is homophobic or heterosexist, this person will not be able to rely on the community and family for support on being LGBTI. This person will face a double burden of being racially marginalized and sexually/genderwise stigmatized.
- The family is the main source of social, emotional, financial, and psychological support. For Asian Americans, the family is even more significant in being a buffer against racism. For immigrants, the ethnic community is crucial in providing social capital. The risk of coming out to one's family would be losing all that is familiar and vital to one's well-being. Asian American LGBTIs often feel they have to choose between their sexuality/gender orientation and their race.

- In many Asian families, the son has the responsibility of carrying on the family's name. Many gay Asian men end up living double lives to fulfill their family obligations and their desire.
- Internalized racism and institutional racism have manifested in the rice queen and potato queen dynamic, where Asian men would not date other Asian men because they find them undesirable. The pairing of older, middle-class, white gay men and younger, poorer immigrant Asian men is prevalent in the gay community where people of unequal power play out their stereotypes for love and/or security.

11. Conclude the scenario discussion with Yep's model on the different levels of oppression (see handout). This is to raise awareness among students about the different forms in which racism, homophobia and heterosexism can manifest. Ask students to give an example of each from the earlier role-playing exercise. If there is time left, devote it to questions and answers.

Notes

1. Barbara Smith, "Homophobia: Why Bring It Up?" in *The Lesbian and Gay Studies Reader*, eds. Henry Abelove, Michele Aina Barale, and David M. Halperin (New York: Routledge, 1993), 99-102.

2. Patricia Hill Collins, *Black Feminist Thought: Knowledge, Consciousness, and the Politics of Empowerment* (Boston: Unwin Hyman, 1990).

3. Gayles S. Rubin, "Thinking Sex: Notes for a Radical Theory of the Politics of Sexuality," in *The Lesbian and Gay Studies Reader*, 3-44; Michel Foucault, "The Perverse Implantation," in *Forms of Desire: Sexual Orientation and the Social Constructionist Controversy*, ed. Edward Stein (New York: Routledge, 1992), 11-23; Patricia Gagne and Richard Tewksbury, "Conformity Pressures and Gender Resistance Among Transgendered Individuals," *Social Problems* 45:1 (1998): 81-101; Anne Fausto-Sterling, "How to Build a Man," in *Gender Sexuality Reader: Culture, History, Political Economy*, eds. Roger N. Lancaster and Micaelo di Leonardo (New York: Routledge, 1997), 244-248.

4. Fausto-Sterling, "How to Build a Man."

5. Gust A. Yep, "From Homophobia and Heterosexism to Heteronormativity: Toward the Development of a Model of Queer Interventions in the University Classroom," *Journal of Lesbian Studies* 6:3/4 (2002): 163-176.

Recommended Resources

David L. Eng and Alice Y. Hom, eds., *Q & A: Queer in Asian America* (Philadelphia, Temple University Press, 1999).

Kumashiro, Kevin K., ed., *Troubling Intersections of Race and Sexuality: Queer Students of Color and Anti-Oppressive Education* (New York: Harrington Park Press, 2004).

Russell C. Leong, ed., *Asian American Sexualities: Dimensions of the Gay and Lesbian Experience* (New York: Routledge, 1996).

Terminology

LGBTIQQ: An abbreviation for lesbian, gay, bisexual transgendered, intersexual, queer, and questioning (e.g., "LGBTIQQ community").

Lesbian: Term referring to a female homosexual. Popular during the 1970s and used widely by radical feminists who are "political lesbians."

Gay: Term referring to a male homosexual, although some people also use it as a non-gender-specific term to describe anyone homosexual.

Bisexual: Term describing a person whose sexual attractions are to both males and females.

Transgender (TG): Crossing over or transcending the common social assignment of gender at birth to incorporate one or more characteristics of the other sex. (Virginia Prince originally used this term as a political concept to frame the diversity of gender expression.) An umbrella term to include transsexuals, crossdressers, transvestite, drag kings, drag queens, and gender queers.

Transsexual (TS): An individual who experiences intense, persistent discomfort and feelings of inappropriateness with the sex assignment made at birth and who actively seeks to change or has changed his/her body through hormonal reassignment and/or various surgical procedures.

FTM/F2M: Abbreviation for a female-to-male transsexual.

MTF/M2F: Abbreviation for a male-to-female transsexual; sometimes called a transvestite.

Cross-dresser: A person who cross-dresses for emotional reasons. He or she may not be a transsexual or a homosexual.

Drag queen or Drag king: People who impersonate the opposite sex for entertainment purposes.

Intersexual/Intersexual: People born with ambiguous sexual organs. Hermaphrodites.

Gender Queer: A person who expresses ambiguous gender identity as a political stance.

Queer: A generic term used by Queer theorists to describe all that do not conform to the patriarchal gender-sex binary system. This includes an FTM who identifies as a straight man. Also used as a shortcut for "gay, lesbian, bisexual, transgender, and intersexual." Others use "queer" as an inclusive term for all other non-conformist gender/sexual behavior and identities.

Questioning: People who are questioning their sexual or gender identity.

Sexual Orientation: Sexual preference for emotive/erotic partners of the same, opposite, or either sex. Orientations are typically described as heterosexual, homosexual, bisexual, or asexual. (In 1973, the term "homosexual" was taken out of the DSM-IV after much protests and in-workings of activists.)

Overhead/Handout

Homosexual: A person who is sexually attracted to the same-sex, i.e., gay man and lesbian woman.

Heterosexual/Straight: A person who is sexually attracted to the opposite sex.

In the Closet: May refer to a queer person who has not yet accepted his or her own sexuality/gender identity (to be "in the closet" to one's self). Also may refer to one who chooses not to share their sexuality/gender identity with family, friends, coworkers, or society (to be "in the closet" to everyone).

MSM: Men who have sex with men. A descriptive term about behavior that doesn't impose an identity on a person.

WSW: Women who have sex with women. A descriptive term about behavior that doesn't impose an identity on a person.

Coming Out: Referring to the process by which one accepts one's own sexuality/gender identity (to "come out" to one's self). Also refers to the process by which one shares one's sexuality/gender identity with others (to "come out" to friends, etc.). This process is a continual, lifelong process for homosexual, bisexual, transgendered, and intersexual individuals.

Heterosexism: The assumption that everyone is heterosexual, and that heterosexuality is superior to homosexuality, bisexuality, transgenderism, and intersexualism. Usually used to the advantage of the group in power. Any attitude or practice—backed by an institutional power—which subordinates people because of their alternative sexual orientation and/or gender identity.

Homophobia: The irrational fear of homosexuals or homosexuality, or any behavior, belief, or attitude that can lead to discrimination, rejection, verbal assaults and/or physical violence. (Biphobia, lesbophobia, transphobia)

Rice Queen: Non-Asian men (usually white) who are into Asian men (usually younger men).

Potato Queen: Nonwhite men who are into white men.

Sticky Rice: Asian gay men who are into other Asian gay men, or Asian lesbians who are into other Asian lesbians.

Mahu: Hawaiian term referring to a group of people who are what we would today consider gay men, MTF transgenders, drag queens, and lesbians. We can think of *mahu* as a third gender or sexual category of people that in Hawaiian society had a place and role. They were revered, considered shaman, and believed to possess both male and female spirits in them. When colonialism and Christianity entered Hawaiian society, the *mahus* became a marginalized group.

Overhead/Handout

Hijra: An Indian caste of people whom we would today consider to be gay men, MTF transgenders and drag queens. They are considered a third gender. Hijras are thought to possess magical power to bless and curse people. In Indian society before colonialism, they were revered and played important roles in the king's court. After colonialism, Christianity took away the power of *hijras,* and they became outcasts in Indian society.

Overhead/Handout

Cass' Developmental Stages of the Coming Out Process

This modification of Cass' developmental stages in the coming out process emphasizes how being "in the closet" or "coming out" will vary in different contexts.

Identity confusion	• see self as member of mainstream group; • denial of inner feelings; • recognize possibility of self as homosexual or transgender; • For intersexuals, it is to learn that one was born with ambiguous genitalia that was "corrected," a decision made by doctors and parents.
Identity comparison	• sense of alienation from general society; • compare self to others, realize self is different; • inner struggle over what is true about own identity.
Identity tolerance	• begin to seek out LGBTI community; • begin to tolerate, but not accept, LGBTI identity.
Identity acceptance	• begin to immerse self in LGBTI community; • feel validated and normal as LGBTI; • accept self as LGBTI • For transsexuals, they are finding information and resources to live their lives as the other sex. • For intersexuals, they form support groups to advocate for the rights of intersexuals to decide on their own sex assignment at birth.
Identity pride	• pride in new identity; • anger at anti-homosexual, biphobic, and transphobic attitudes; • no longer hide identity as LGBI; • utilize energy from pride and anger to work for LGBI activism; • prefer to mix socially with other LGBIs; • For FTMs, they would live their life as a man; for MTFs, they would live life as a woman. TSs not undergoing surgeries would continue to hide their transitional status in public.
Identity synthesis	• at peace with self as LGBTI; • personal and public identity become one; • see value in supportive heterosexuals; • mix socially with heterosexuals and LGBTs equally comfortably; • For TSs, they have realized their dreams by living their life as the opposite sex. • Some intersexuals and transgenders may choose to live as androgynous or gender queer people who display both gender identities.

Source: V. C. Cass, "Homosexuality Identity Formation: A Theoretical Model," *Journal of Homosexuality* 4 (1979): 219-235.

Overhead/Handout

Role Playing Exercise

Scenario 1 (can reverse gender roles)

You are a closeted bisexual Asian man still having shame about your homosexual inclination. You have only come out to a few LGBTI friends whom you have met. You act and appear straight at work. One day you go out to lunch with your male co-workers. Your co-workers discuss how cute this one female staff member is from another department. Your co-workers get into a discussion about what kind of woman they want to have sex with, whom they want to marry, and who's cute and who's not. They notice you not sharing and ask for your opinion. You choose not to come out to your co-workers.

Scenario 2 (can reverse gender roles; third person can observe the interaction)

Your sister seems upset/distracted about something. You check up on her and ask her what is happening because you have been noticing that she seems withdrawn, distracted, and bothered by something. After a bit of hesitation, she confides in you that she thinks her roommate might be a lesbian. She doesn't know what to do because the Bible says it's wrong, and she doesn't know how to save her roommate. She seems distraught about how her roommate will come out to the family and will create disharmony and may be kicked out of the house. She also suspects that her roommate may have a crush on her. It turns out that your sister is trying to come out and not her roommate. It also turns out that she has a crush on her roommate, not her roommate on her. Your family is a devout Korean Christian family.

Scenario 3

Your brother has been very distant from the family since he graduated and moved away. He finally calls home after five years and says he's visiting to make an announcement. You suspect that he's gay given how he was a sissy child. Instead, your brother comes back as a woman and wants the family to refer to him as Diane instead of David. He is the only son in the family to carry on the Ho name.

Scenario 4

You have just befriended a very out gay Asian American. One day, he comes to you very upset and complains to you that he heard homophobic remarks made in class by his Asian American professor. He goes on deriding Asian patriarchy. Then, he tells you how his relationship with his lover is a lot more egalitarian. You learn that he is dating an older white man who "has a thing for Asian men." He tells you how he has an allowance every week from his lover and that his lover pays for his schooling ever since he got kicked out of his family at age sixteen for being gay. Your friend has also just learned about racial fetishism from his Asian American Studies class and is looking for your approval in his relationship with his older, white male lover, whom he has joked as his "Rice Queen Sugar Daddy."

Yep's Model on Different Levels of Oppression

Homophobia: The irrational fear of homosexuals or homosexuality, or any behavior, belief, or attitude that can lead to discrimination, rejection, verbal assaults and/or physical violence. (Related terms: biphobia, lesbophobia, transphobia)

Heterosexism: The assumption that everyone is heterosexual, and that heterosexuality is superior to homosexuality, bisexuality, transgenderism, and intersexualism. Usually used to the advantage of the group in power. Any attitude, action, or practice—backed by an institutional power—which subordinates people because of their sexual orientation or gender identification.

Modification of Yep's Grid on Types of Homophobia and Heterosexism

		Context of Experiences	
		Interior (affect, cognition, sensations)	**Exterior** (affect, cognition, sensations)
Done by:	**Individual**	**Soul Murder** Internalized Homophobia or Racism	**Hate Crime** External Homophobia or Racism
	Collective	**Social Climate** Discursive Violence	**Policies** Institutional Violence

Source: Gust A. Yep, "From Homophobia and Heterosexism to Heteronormativity: Toward the Development of a Model of Queer Interventions in the University Classroom," *Journal of Lesbian Studies* 6:3/4 (2002), 163-176.

Internet Resources: Asian Pacific LGBTI Groups

Asian Pacific Islander for Human Rights (Los Angeles), (323) 860-0876
   www.apihr.org
Asian Pacific Islander Parents and Friends of Lesbians and Gays (API PFLAG)
   www.api-pflag.org
Asian Pacific AIDS Intervention Team (Los Angeles)
   www.apaitonline.org
Asian and Pacific Islander Wellness Center (San Francisco)
   www.apiwellness.org
The Asian and Pacific Islander Lesbian and Bisexual Women and Transgender Network
   www.APLBTN.org
Gay Asian Pacific Support Network (GAPSN)
   www.gapsn.org
The Gay, Lesbian, and Straight Education Network (GLSEN)
   www.glsen.org
Lambda Legal
   www.lambdalegal.org
Queer Resources Directory
   www.qrd.org

Alan: A Female-to-Male Transsexual Straight Man

Gina Masequesmay

LGBTI experiences vary depending on a person's sexual orientation, gender identification, race, ethnicity, class, and other social characteristics, and, hence, no one story can adequately represent the range of Asian Pacific LGBTI experiences. The story of Alan (pseudonym), who was born biologically female, provides some insights into the experience of one Vietnamese American female-to-male transsexual. While this is one experience, it offers a glance into some of the struggles (e.g., coming out to self versus family; finding support; making a life for oneself) that an LGBTI person experiences. However, this is not to be read as representative of *the* Asian Pacific LGBTI experience. Instead, I hope this story will evoke questions for further discussion.

Alan, a female-to-male transsexual who identifies as a straight man, could trace his experience of feeling different when he was six. He remembered vividly playing with his brother in Vietnam: "I'm not going to be a blood sister, . . . I was going to be a blood brother." But everyone around him told him he was a girl. Despite these negations, Alan was convinced he was a boy. "I know I'm a boy; I was just in the wrong body."

When he became attracted to women, he wondered if he was gay, but a "twisted gay" because he did not identify as a woman, definitely not a lesbian. He thought he might be a sub-group within the category "gay." For Alan, everyday gendered rituals were a setback to his male identification. It became more poignant when he reached puberty.

[W]hen I was a kid, I always know I should have been a boy, so I kept thinking, if I didn't have the period then something is wrong with me physically, okay, like a defect, then it would explain why I think the way I do. But it didn't; everything was in its natural biological female course. And so that just depressed me in the sense that I'm thinking, oh, great, you know, was I crazy or mentally disturbed . . . because . . . physically . . . everything was where it supposed to be . . . that's when I thought it was a tomboyish thing and that I would grow out of it, but I didn't. There was a period where I was thinking that I must be mentally disturbed.

Having to face the body that he hated every day made life difficult at its most mundane level. Alan recalled how going to private school was a torturous experience.

[W]hen you're at home, you don't have to think so much about it, but when I was at school, that's where it distinguished between, if you're a boy or a girl . . . I always hated it. . . . I wanted to be put in a public school, you know, because I could wear pants.

Alan got his wish to wear pants when he lied about graduating from eighth grade to enroll in a public high school. Resisting hegemonic femininity was not easy, however, even at public school. Alan would get into fights for dressing and acting like a boy. At the age of seventeen, when Alan learned about transgenderism on *Donahue,* it helped to validate his feeling about himself. However, Alan was Catholic, and when he became romantically interested in his female friends, he was sure he was facing eternal damnation. Alan went through years of depression and suicidal ideations. Fortunately, constant family obligations held him back from attempting suicide. He was too busy helping out his siblings and could not find time to end his life. It was then that he met the group Ô-Môi, a support group for Vietnamese lesbian, bisexual women, and female-to-male transgenders. Alan also knew about other transgender groups, but he opted for Ô-Môi because the other groups were predominantly white. Alan did not have positive interactions with white people whom he saw as culturally insensitive to his needs. He was tired of explaining to white LGBTIs about his family obligations; he didn't have to do that with other Asian Pacific LGBTIs. Alan is now happily out to his family who is very supportive of his transitioning. His father even gave him a Vietnamese male name. He even has a Chinese-Vietnamese girl-friend whom his family approves!

Personal Profile

Chapter 6

Globalization and Transnationalism Role-Playing Activity:
Korean Immigrants and the Garment Industry

Steven Masami Ropp

I n recent years, transnationalism, a term used to describe social and cultural phenomena that take place across multiple national contexts, has gained considerable attention in Asian American Studies. However, its usage tends toward the abstract—e.g., imaginaries, identities, and literary representations. Too little attention is paid to the concrete and everyday aspects of how transnational connections are constituted through global business practices and the role that people of Asian descent play in such transactions. This role-playing activity, focusing on Korean immigrants in the garment industry in various locations in the Americas, is designed to provide a starting point for critical discussion and analysis of globalization and transnationalism. In particular, attention can be drawn to the multiple roles that people of Asian descent, on an individual and collective level, play in the contemporary "global assembly line" of garment manufacturing—as "victims," as "oppressors," as "consumers," and as "producers." This activity should be useful in Asian American Studies, Asian Studies, Latin American Studies or where race and ethnicity are being considered in international and transnational contexts.

Objectives

- To identify the different actors and competing interests that go into trade networks, commodity chains, and global markets.
- To identify the role that cultural and linguistic ties can play in establishing and maintaining transnational networks.
- To reflect on the issues of labor and politics in garment manufacturing from the perspectives of various actors: owners, governments, consumers, subcontractors, and workers.

Time

- Forty-five minutes
  - Fifteen minutes to explain and set up the activity
  - Fifteen minutes to carry out the activity
  - Fifteen minutes for discussion

Number of Participants

- Fifteen to twenty-five people

Materials

- Activity cards describing the roles and objectives of each group
- Scissors, tape, and markers for at least three groups
- Ten to fifteen sheets of colored paper
- Three rolls of yarn (medium-size, different colors)
- National flags of Brazil, Argentina, the United States, and South Korea (optional)
- Photos or images of garment manufacturing (sweatshops or otherwise) in these locales (optional)
- Props such as cardboard sewing machines, time clocks, display racks, etc. (optional)

Background

Transnationalism and its larger context of globalization are important concepts. As consumers and as citizens, we are all implicated in a global production process that puts labor and customers everywhere at the disposal of transnational and multinational corporations. However, much of that process—where and how garments are manufactured, for example—tends to be obscured by both corporations and academic jargon. Instead of attending to the global assembly line—how global capitalism shapes our lives and how we might challenge such practices—most of the discussion in Asian American Studies tends to focus on the symbolic aspects of globalization such as transnational imaginaries, literary representations, and identities as multiple, overlapping, and complex. Although the symbolic aspects are important, by focusing on the clothes that students buy and the name brands as status symbols that they so proudly display, this activity opens up the possibility for a more critical understanding of the unequal power relations characteristic of globalization. From that analysis, perhaps students can begin to challenge the inequalities of the global assembly line as embedded in the clothes they wear and the brands they idolize.

Transnationalism, a term that gained popular usage in the 1990s, refers to "the processes by which immigrants forge and sustain multi-stranded social relations that link together their societies of origin and settlement."[1] These processes are transnational because they "cross geographic, cultural and political borders."[2] While such connections across time and space are not necessarily a new phenomenon—e.g., the Chinese diaspora is centuries old—they have taken on greater significance in recent decades because of changes in production that are often referred to under the rubric of "flexible accumulation."[3] This shift, starting in the late 1960s, is characterized by the change from fixed, large-scale production tied to national contexts to subcontracting, flexible production, and the rise of multinational and transnational corporations.

For the purposes of this activity, transnationalism is but one subset, focusing on the human cultural and social dimensions, of larger changes under the rubric of globalization. Globalization, in its broadest sense, refers to changes that have taken place in finance, capital, communication and transportation technologies, political relations and cultural forms that facilitate and result from the globalization of production and the closing of distances between markets, labor, and consumers across time and space.[4] The ubiquity of global brands such as Sony or Gap is a product of and a driving force for the changes that link consumers, capital, and production across what were in a previous era relatively fixed national markets and boundaries.

The relevance of transnationalism and globalization for Asian immigrants today is that such immigrants are often able to deploy claims to identity and citizenship that are increasingly "deterritorialized." In other words, the "natural" connections between culture and place that underlie the notion of identity as fixed to one national context are increasingly challenged by the reality of multiple connections across time and space. For example, researchers show how wealthy Chinese investors from Hong Kong and Taiwan have created family and business networks that extend from California to Canada to Malaysia and China, thereby challenging the ability of any one nation-state to circumscribe the identity or citizenship of these mobile transnational families.[5]

Moving beyond the effects of immigrants to consider the impact of globalization on Asian Americans in general, a sort of false dichotomy has emerged that pits the "local" against the "global."[6] In the field of literary criticism, this is the idea that Asian American politics operates either from a cultural nationalist perspective with primarily a domestic focus, or from a diasporic perspective that is internationalist in outlook.[7] In reality, the local is increasingly subsumed by the global, and the global is constituted out of the local struggles and contexts. In terms of garment manufacturing, the fact is that local practices of production and consumption are constituted in global contexts. In other words, Nike sweatshops exploiting low-wage labor in Vietnam are an issue for Asian Americans regardless of their identity/political orientation because without doing anything they benefit from and perpetuate those practices through their patronage of Nike. As such, the particular approach that is taken in order to locate Asian Americans at the *intersection* of the local and the global is to "follow the thing" and "follow the people."[8] In this activity, the "thing" is the garment, and the "people" are Korean immigrants and Korean communities in various parts of the Americas.

Historically, garment manufacturing has had strong connections to a segregated ethnic labor market (e.g., Jewish manufacturing on the East Coast and Chinese in the San Francisco Bay Area). In recent decades, as the global assembly line in garment manufacturing emerged, Koreans have taken on an increasingly important role. As part of the post-1965 immigration, Koreans have developed a strong presence in the Los Angeles garment district, especially in manufacturing and retail. What many people do not realize is that this presence is very much transnational and global. Korean textile manufacturing and distribution networks constitute important suppliers of raw materials to Korean manufacturers and subcontractors in the United States, Central America, and South America. The manufacturers have set up operations in places such as Guatemala to take advantage of cheap labor and easier access to the U.S. market. Immigrants in Argentina and Brazil since the 1960s and 1970s have developed economic niches in garment manufacturing and distribution, in many instances, constituting a majority presence in these nations despite being a relatively recent and small minority.[9] Since the 1980s, many of those Korean Latin Americans have since moved on to the United States, in a secondary migration, but have maintained connections with Latin America and Korea with the intersection point being the garment industry in Los Angeles. These immigrants have therefore established their own ethnic and business networks that extend well beyond the borders of a single nation and provide a concrete example of the complex role that people of Asian descent play in the global assembly line of garment manufacturing today.

The garment industry is notorious for low-wage exploitation due to the nature of subcontracting, a process by which prominent clothing brands delegate out nearly all of their manufacturing to subcontractors. These subcontractors are, in turn, forced to compete on the basis of price, with razor-thin profit margins, thereby creating strong downward pressure on wages. This is the case for both domestic or international production, but in the case of international production, companies such as Nike, with the backing of the U.S. government, are able to pressure national elites desperate for job-creation to foster an even more hostile and oppressive labor environment than is possible in the United States.

Suggested Procedures

1. Introduce the concept of the "global assembly line" (i.e., sweatshops, subcontracting, corporate marketing, and third world labor). This can be accomplished through one or all of the following: 1) refer students to a website such as Sweatshop Watch (www.sweatshopwatch.org) prior to the class with a keyword/vocabulary list assignment; 2) assign an excerpt from a text such as *Behind the Label* by Bonacich and Appelbaum or *Sweatshop Warriors* by Louie that analyzes inequalities in the garment industry;[10] 3) do an interactive exercise prior to the activity. For example, have students do a quick inventory to determine where each piece of clothing came from that they are wearing. As a class, write all the countries on the board and discuss why and how the global assembly line operates and who gets paid what at each stage of the process. Essentially the idea is to begin drawing out the knowledge that the participants themselves already have of where and how profits are generated.

2. Divide up the class; the following groups are based on the recommended minimum number of fifteen participants. If there are more, try to maintain the same ratios.
   - Korea: two people
   - Argentina: two people
   - Brazil: four people
   - United States: seven people

3. Give each group their corresponding activity card (see handout) that describes the overall goal—to produce clothing—and the specific roles that are available—workers (legal and/or illegal), subcontractors, manufacturers, etc. Give the Argentina, Brazil, and U.S. groups one ball of yarn each. Give all of the sheets of paper to Korea. Have scissors, tape, and markers available for use.

4. Each group should divide itself up deciding who takes on the role of the manufacturer and who are the workers. The goal of the manufacturers is to secure raw

material and labor and to produce clothes that can then be sold to retailers. In this case the raw material—cloth, as represented by the sheets of paper—is available from the Korean textile mills, and the labor is that which is locally available and for which wages and working conditions need to be negotiated based on the skill level and legal status of the workers.

5. Instruct the participants to imagine themselves to be Korean or of Korean descent. All of the manufacturers and subcontractors should be Korean, while the workers do not necessarily have to be.

6. As the students are conducting transactions between countries, explain that they need to do so by using the yarn. For example, when manufacturers buy cloth from Korea, they should hold onto one end of the yarn and then throw the yarn to Korea in order to conduct their transaction. Upon completion, Korea should hold onto the yarn and then throw the ball back to where it came from. Using yarn to represent forms and lines of communication, students "conduct business," carrying out transactions, producing garments, and finding markets for their products. Students should continue to hold on to the yarn until the discussion at the end of this exercise.

7. Encourage the groups to take advantage of lower labor costs in other countries such as Brazil or Argentina and to sell their products in markets with higher return such as the United States. In each instance, they need to maintain hold on the yarn. As the yarn goes back and forth between groups, there will be a "web" of transactions that represents globalization in terms of communication and transportation technologies (fax, Internet, container ships, etc.) and also the nature of production and subcontracting in the global economy. The web also represents the language and cultural connections that sustain ethnic and business networks across time and space. Students must "maintain" this web throughout the activity. At the end, it will symbolize the concepts of transnationalism and globalization.

8. Encourage the students to actually use the paper to make clothes. The students usually enjoy spending time cutting out the clothes and writing brand names on the clothing. The students, without prompting, will often use the current in-style brand names such as Nike. This represents the crucial point where the participants can make the concrete connection between their experiences as consumers and the production process of the global assembly line. This will also be an important opening for discussion about what they buy, where it comes from and how it gets made. Once the groups have had a chance to produce their clothing and once the web of connections is sufficiently evident, the activity can be brought to a close.

Discussion and Debriefing

Production and the Global Assembly Line: Each group should have the opportunity to describe what happened. Students usually enjoy showing off what they made. As they do so, ask them questions based on what role that they assumed in the activity.

For manufacturers and subcontractors: Where did you get your material? How did you secure labor? How much did you pay them? Are your workers unionized?

For workers: How did you find this job? Do you speak English? What is your legal status? How much did you get paid?

Students, having been raised in a capitalist society, will probably have developed their business transactions with profit-making as the primary motive with little concern for wages and working conditions. In addition, because workers in a capitalist society do not have much of a voice, students will likely assume the outlook of the manufacturers. For this reason, it is important to hear the voice of the workers. As workers in the garment industry are most likely to be in marginal positions—hence their need to accept low wages and difficult working conditions—make sure to provide a space for the workers to voice their concerns.

Communication, Ethnicity, and Transnationalism: The web of yarn that students are holding at the end of the activity symbolically represents globalization and transnationalism. Having to hold onto the web for the duration of the activity is important in making the point about transnationalism from the standpoint of language, culture, and ethnicity. Some of the questions that can be asked to facilitate this discussion include:

- What does the network of yarn represent?
- What language were you using?
- Did you all have a common language?
- Did that make it easier to conduct business across national borders?
- How did you communicate? (fax, Internet, video-conferencing, etc.)

From these questions, the social aspects of transnationalism should become clearer. In essence, transnationalism refers to phenomena such as language, family connections, and ethnic networks that are above and beyond the boundaries of any nation-state and the cultural and economic processes that sustain connections across time and space. Make sure to draw connections between business practices and culture and ethnicity as interrelated processes. In other words, things like culture, language or family connections facilitate and overlap with business interactions and networks.

The Global Assembly Line: Finally, I usually end the discussion with some questions about the role that we all play as consumers of products created by the global assembly line. It is good to talk about where and how profits are generated and who benefits from the global assembly line in international and domestic contexts. Obviously, in addition to the corporations that make the most profits, we as consumers in the United States also benefit by having cheap and abundant clothing options. I find that students tend not to be too concerned about corporate profiteering, largely because they've been socialized into a capitalist mindset, but when they are able to make a connection between their choices as consumers and how those clothes were made, they are able to take a more critical standpoint.

Follow-up activities might include having students research examples of efforts to hold corporations responsible for their actions, such as campaigns against Nike and Gap. Other possibilities, depending on where one is located, are to have students visit areas where garments are manufactured such as the Garment District in Los Angeles. Students can also contact organizations that work on behalf of workers (see "Recommended Resources.")

Notes

1. Linda Basch, Nina Glick Schiller, and Christine Szanton-Blanc, *Nations Unbound: Transnational Projects, Postcolonial Predicaments, and Deterritorialized Nation-States* (Langhorne, PA: Gordon & Breach, 1994), 7.

2. *Ibid.*

3. Anthony Giddens, *A Runaway World* (New York: Routledge, 2000).

4. David Held and Anthony McGrew, eds., *The Global Transformations Reader: An Introduction to the Globalization Debate* (Cambridge: Polity Press, 2000).

5. Aihwa Ong and Donald Nonini, eds., *Ungrounded Empires: The Cultural Politics of Modern Chinese Transnationalism* (London: Routledge, 1997).

6. Arif Dirlik, "Asians on the Rim: Transnational Capital and Local Community in the Making of Contemporary Asian America," in *Across the Pacific: Asian Americans and Globalization* (Philadelphia: Temple University Press, 2000), 29-60.

7. Sau-ling Wong, "Denationalization Reconsidered: Asian American Cultural Criticism at a Theoretical Crossroads," *Amerasia Journal* 21:1-2 (1995): 1-27.

8. George Marcus, "Ethnography in/of the World System: The Emergence of Multi-Sited Ethnography," *Annual Review of Anthropology* 24 (1995): 95-117.

9. Kathryne Cho, "Korean Brazilians: A People in Transition," M.A. thesis, University of California, Los Angeles, 1999; Kyeyoung Park, "'I'm Floating in the Air': Creation of a Korean Transnational Space among Korean-Latino-American Re-Migrants," *Positions: East Asia Cultures Critique* 7:3 (1999): 667-695.

10. Edna Bonacich and Richard Appelbaum, *Behind the Label: Inequality in the Los Angeles Apparel Industry* (Berkeley: University of California Press, 2000); Miriam Ching Yoon Louie, *Sweatshop Warriors: Immigrant Women Workers Take on the Global Factory* (Cambridge, MA: South End Press, 2001).

Recommended Resources

Between a Rock and a Hard Place: A History of American Sweatshops, 1820 to Present, http://americanhistory.si.edu/sweatshops/.

Co-op America's Guide to Ending Sweatshops and Promoting Fair Trade, www.sweatshops.org.

United Students Against Sweatshops, www.studentsagainstsweatshops.org/.

Seoul, South Korea

Members:	Goals:
Textile Manufacturer (1-2 people)	1) Make textiles 2) Find new export markets 3) Sell product 4) Make a profit
Gov't Officials (1-2)	1) Promote exports of textiles overseas 2) Help the manufacturers sell their products overseas

Buenos Aires, Argentina

Members:	Goals:
Garment Manufacturer (1-2)	1) Buy materials in S. Korea 2) Find cheap labor 3) Make garments 4) Find markets for your products
Sub-Contractor (1-2)	1) Find subcontracts 2) Find cheap labor 3) Return complete products
Labor (2-3)	1) Earn enough money to feed your family

Sao Paolo, Brazil

Members:	Goals:
Garment Manufacturer (1-2)	1) Buy materials in S. Korea 2) Find cheap labor 3) Make garments 4) Find markets for your products
Sub-Contractor (2-3)	1) Find subcontracts 2) Find cheap labor 3) Return complete products
Labor (3-5)	1) Earn enough money to feed your family

Los Angeles (CA), United States of America

Members:	Goals:
Garment Manufacturer (1-2)	1) Buy materials in S. Korea 2) Find cheap labor 3) Make garments 4) Find markets for your products
Sub-Contractor (2-4)	1) Find subcontracts 2) Find cheap labor 3) Return complete products
Labor (4-8)	1) Earn enough money to feed your family

Handout

Globalization's "Race to the Bottom" Creates Sweatshops

Sweatshop Watch
www.sweatshopwatch.org

Globalization calls for the elimination of trade barriers such as tariffs and quotas in order to increase international trade. Yet, the promotion of global trade comes at the expense of workers' rights. Globalization enables major corporations to place production in countries with cheapest labor or weakest enforcement of labor laws, creating what is called a "race to the bottom." In efforts to attract garment contracts, factories all over the world cut wages, "sweating" profits out of workers. Major retailers benefit from the race to the bottom that creates a near endless supply of cheap sweatshop labor.

The California garment industry is a $30 billion dollar industry with Los Angeles as its capital. The industry peaked around 1996 with approximately 140,000 garment workers, but has declined to about 90,000 due to global competition. After the passage of North American Free Trade Agreement (NAFTA) in 1994, major retailers shifted much work to Mexico due to cheaper labor and less governmental enforcement of wages, environmental standards, and working conditions. For example, before NAFTA, Guess was the largest manufacturer in California, sewing 97 percent of its clothing in Los Angeles. In 1997, facing a union organizing campaign and recognizing cheaper labor across borders, Guess moved most of its production out of the United States. Levi's recently announced it would also follow suit by closing down its last factory in the United States and laying off two thousand workers. Promises of growth and local development associated with free trade policies have also been used with third world countries, but the value of wages has actually dropped in Mexico since NAFTA. Two new trade agreements, the Central American Free Trade Agreement (CAFTA) and the Free Trade Area of the Americas (FTAA), both extensions of NAFTA, are currently being negotiated and would further exacerbate the race to the bottom.

Globalization creates a system that forces workers to compete around the world for the lowest wages. Although the California minimum wage is $6.75, few garment workers in Los Angeles receive this amount due to the competitiveness of the industry. Sweatshop conditions exist where some garment workers are paid as little as $3 to $4 an hour, not to mention the long hours, unsafe working conditions, and lack of overtime pay. Yet, the conditions in California are relatively better than conditions in other countries. Thus, the global competition creates sweatshop exploitation and job flight to countries with cheap labor.

Through globalization, corporations rake in huge profits. Retailers consciously choose where to place production and how workers are treated. Consumers too benefit from the cheap price of goods. However, consumers can help stop sweatshop exploitation in several ways:

- Supporting anti-sweatshop campaigns that are worker-led by writing letters of support, attending a rally, or joining a boycott.
- Buying clothing made by unionized workers, a cooperative, a fair trade organization, or other entities that work with the interest of the worker in mind.
- Opposing economic globalization by writing letters to elected officials.

Additional Reading

Sweatshops in Our Backyard!

Sweatshop Watch

Most people know by looking at the tags on their clothes that apparel is made all around the world, and many have heard horror stories about companies like Nike profiting from sweatshop labor in overseas factories. But people may not know that similar sweatshop conditions exist right here in the United States.

Garment Workers in Los Angeles

- Most workers are paid $2 to $5 per hour in many factories.
- Piece-rates average between five and forty cents. Most workers are paid only for what they sew. For example, a Los Angeles garment worker was paid just three cents for each elastic that she sewed into a halter-top; she earned just $9 or $10 for a full day's work because she could only sew 300 each day. Although employers are supposed to guarantee workers the minimum wage regardless of how many pieces they sew, many employees do not get it.
- Workers labor ten to twelve hours a day, six to seven days a week with no over-time pay. Many factory owners keep false time records for their employees. So, if a worker begins each day at 6:30 a.m. and ends at 8 p.m., they are not allowed to punch in or out at those times. Instead, the factory manager will punch timecards for each employee at hours that reflect an eight-hour workday. Sometimes work-ers are forced to sign fake time cards to receive their checks. False records make it extremely difficult for a worker to prove a complaint for back wages.
- Cash pay is common. Some employers will even deduct taxes but not report it to the government. Some employers deduct a "cash" fee as well.
- Workers endure frequent verbal abuse and sometimes also physical abuse.
- Hazardous conditions in the factories are common—poor ventilation; very dim light; dirty, crowded factories; blocked fire exits; dirty bathrooms; locked bath-rooms; no drinking water; rats and roaches.
- Workers sustain workplace injuries such as repetitive motion injuries, respira-tory problems, muscle aches, vision problems, back injuries, and constant fatigue.

Who Are the Hardworking People Who Endure This Abuse?

- They are women—roughly 75 percent of the garment workforce is female.
- They are also immigrants—70 percent are Latino immigrants mostly from Mexico and Central America, and approximately 15 percent are Asian immigrants from China, Thailand, and other countries.
- The majority are undocumented and have limited English language skills, making them even more vulnerable to abuse and exploitation in the workplace.

A Los Angeles Garment Worker's Experience

Maria P.
Sweatshop Watch

In one factory, I worked ten, eleven, sometimes more than twelve hours a day, and then I would bring work home. They didn't let us take lunch or take bathroom breaks. In fact, they locked the bathroom door and we had to ask for the key to go to the bathroom. The owner gave it to us when she wanted to. If there was an order that had to be finished fast, we couldn't take lunch. There were rats and roaches in the factory, and we would get all bitten by the fleas from the rats. They would yell at us when they wanted an order done faster or if something didn't come out right. If they needed an order finished, I would have to work sometimes until one or two at night. I would be falling asleep at my machine. The owner would pay me between $130 and $180 a week according to the amount I sewed until I told her I was supposed to be earning the minimum wage. I was owed $270 in minimum wage plus two to three hours overtime pay. When I complained, the owner said she needed to make money too, so she would only pay me by the piece. But she lowered the piece rates from thirty cents to fourteen cents. That was when I left.

Chapter 7

Expressive Therapies for Asian American Clients:

The Value of Nonverbal Sand Tray Therapy

Michi Fu

Traditional modes of psychotherapy which heavily rely on the comfort and ability of the client to articulate their concerns may not be helpful to clients from an Asian American and Pacific Islander background. Therapies that incorporate nonverbal methods may be more effective in counseling Asian Americans and Pacific Islanders, who have difficulty verbalizing their problems. This chapter focuses on techniques involved in Sand Tray Therapy as a starting point for a larger discussion on alternative therapies that may be suitable for Asian Americans and Pacific Islanders. This activity can be used in classes on cross-cultural psychology, Asian Americans' mental health, and Asian American contemporary issues as a way of facilitating a discussion about the cultural assumptions in traditional counseling theories. This activity could also be used in workshops for training therapists and clinicians to expand their strategies for working with Asian American and Pacific Islander clients.

Objectives

- To raise awareness about the cultural assumptions embedded in traditional counseling theories.
- To sensitize people to the barriers Asian Americans and Pacific Islanders may face in seeking help.
- To introduce Sand Tray Therapy and other alternative therapies which incorporate nonverbal techniques.

Time

- Thirty to forty-five minutes

Number of Participants

- No more than twelve people

  - Two people are needed to facilitate this activity.
  - One person is needed to administer the session.
  - One participant constructs the actual sand tray. It is preferable that one participant be allowed to construct the sand tray at a time, although it is also possible for clients to participate as one unit (e.g., a couple, a family, etc.).
  - Up to ten people may observe as long as they are not intrusive during the construction and intervention stages of the session.

Materials Needed

Minimum Materials Needed

- Rectangular container: The container should be sturdy and able to hold large amounts of sand. The majority of Sand Tray Therapists generally agree on measurements (approximating 20" x 30" x 3.5"). Though it is possible to have a container of an unusual shape (e.g., octagon), the idea is to have a "blank slate" for your client to work in. An optional item for your container would be a cover to keep the sand clean and sand tray from being a distraction when not being used. Authentic wooden or glass sand trays certified by play therapists can cost as much as $300 through catalogs and the Internet, however, comparable plastic underbed storage units can be purchased for as little as $10 at retail stores.
- Sand: Ideally, the tray should have at least three pounds of fine grain sand (play sand quality). This allows for enough sand for the participant to manipulate hills and valleys. Some argue that fine grain sand is crucial to minimize distractions (e.g., gritty or inferior sand may serve as a distraction, thus compromising the "blank slate" for your clients to work on). To further minimize distractions, it is often helpful to comb over the sand with a flat surface (e.g., ruler) to create an even surface. Many play therapists debate on the color of sand preferred in this type of therapy. White or natural colored sand is perhaps most common in starter kits. Other colored sand is available and often used. Sand can cost up to $100 (not including shipping and handling) or less than $5 at hardware stores.
- Figurines: A good thing to keep in mind collecting figures is that you want a wide range of objects. It is ideal to have objects that are scaled similarly (up to two inches tall) of various shapes, sizes, and forms. The basic collection will contain objects found in everyday life (e.g., people, animals, furniture, vehicles/transportation, furnishings, foliage, architectural structures, etc.). Remember that your participant's imagination will be limited to the number and types of objects you offer in your sand tray collection. The ideal (and impossible) collection contains objects that could represent the world.
- Basket: A basket is essential for allowing the participant to gather the objects they'd like to include in their final product. This is handed to your client when introducing the sand tray and giving instructions on how to go about collecting the items and constructing the sand tray. Your basket can be of any size and shape

as long as it allows for your participant to gather the objects comfortably. Baskets can range anywhere from $1 at discount stores to $50 at higher-end stores.

- Stand: You should consider investing in a stand to hold your container so that the sand tray is readily accessible to people of all ages and physical conditions. Therefore, an adjustable stand is preferable. Be sure that your stand is sturdy enough to hold heavy items, yet easy to manipulate. A TV stand from a retail store could be used and costs as little as $15. Otherwise, sand tray display stands are also available through play therapy catalogs and websites for up to $250.

Optional Materials

- Multiple trays
- Wet versus dry sand (water)
- Different colored sand

Background

Traditional counseling theories have developed from Western cultures. Such theories often depict the counseling experience as a series of verbal exchanges between the therapist and patient.[1] Clients are often expected to divulge intimate details with their therapists in order to work toward a therapeutic goal. Counselors in training are often grounded in such theories, with little regard given to the compatibility of applying such methods to clients of various backgrounds.

Asian American cultural values often conflict with help-seeking behaviors of the mental health profession. One common issue is the "loss of face" associated with revealing personal or family problems to an outsider; consequently, Asian Americans often only seek psychotherapy as a last resort.[2] This is also a reason why the severity of presenting problems among Asian Americans tends to be higher than those of other groups, such as clients of European descent. For example, twenty-four-year-old "Jesse" is a single female of mixed racial descent. She is a "local" Chinese and Japanese American, whose family has been in Hawai'i for four generations. She was self-referred for personal counseling due to symptoms of depression. Although her depression was severe to the point that she often spoke of suicidal ideation, she was resistant towards seeking the help she needed. When I referred her for a psychiatric consultation, she declined the psychiatrist's recommendation of antidepressant medications citing her primary concern as fear of having her parents discover her mental illness when receiving the statements from the family's health insurance company.

In addition, Asians and Asian Americans commonly conceptualize many of the problems Westerners would define as mental health related issues as medical illnesses.[3] This has been cited as one of the reasons why Asian Americans are often referred to mental health professionals by medical professionals. Hence, concerns are typically presented as somatic, even if related to mental health issues. For example, anger management issues could be described by recurring migraine headaches, and anxiety symptoms could be presented as stomach-aches. An example would be twenty-two-year-old Taiwanese client "Farah," who often complained of headaches when the stress of her studies overwhelmed her.

Language barriers also serve as another obstacle to traditional Western based therapies, which may rely on the verbalizations of clients to guide the therapy process.[4] This is true for immigrants with limited English language abilities as well as second and third Asian Americans who do not feel comfortable articulating their problems. Asian American and Pacific Islander clients often have difficulty verbally expressing their emotions to others.[5] In addition, the language structure of many Asian values does not adequately provide emotionally descriptive words to convey various feelings. For example, there are varying degrees of conveying anger in the English language (annoyed, frustrated, outraged, etc.), while there are only a limited number of ways to express anger in the Chinese language. Therefore, many of the Asian languages do not provide the optimal forum to express one's emotions.

Many of the cultural barriers to Asian Americans seeking treatment are also found among Pacific Islanders. This has been found true in the author's clinical work with clients of Asian and Hawaiian descent. There are many similarities in the cultural values of other Pacific Islanders (e.g., collectivistic culture in which elders recommend solutions for family problems). It should also be noted that the intergenerational transmission of cultural values among various Asian American families indicates the relevance of this chapter beyond the recent immigrant family. Therefore, depending on the level of ethnic identification, a third or fourth-generation Asian American with resilient cultural values may adopt similar attitudes toward professional help seeking behaviors.

Recently, therapists have recognized the need to utilize alternative methods of conducting therapy with Asian clients that rely less on verbalization.[6] Potential advantages of allowing clients of Asian descent to process their issues nonverbally would be to break down language barriers, allow for face-saving, and encourage clients to be creative in expressing themselves. In addition, nonverbal techniques could be perceived as less invasive and therefore less threatening to clients and their worldviews.

Sand Tray Therapy is often used to facilitate therapy with clients of various presenting issues. This mode of therapy may be used as an assessment or intervention technique. When used as an assessment technique, the sand tray constructed is a reflection of the participant's inner world. As an intervention technique, the therapist works with the client to reconstruct the inner world. It should be noted that there is a discrepancy in the field of mental health regarding the level of training required to consider one a Sand Tray therapist; however, the intention of this chapter is to encourage therapists to consider other forms of working with Asian American and Pacific Islander clients.

Sand Tray Therapy often takes less time than the traditional mode of verbal therapy if clients' first language is not English, if clients are from a cultural background that does not encourage openly expressing emotions, or if clients are more comfortable using non-threatening modes of communication. Sand Tray allows for the clients to reveal themselves to their therapists without having to speak. This mode of therapy can be used cross-culturally and creates less tension for those who are unaccustomed to utilizing face-to-face, verbal therapy.

I have used Sand Tray Therapy for over five years and find it an effective device for many Asian American and Native Hawaiian clients who do not feel comfortable with more traditional methods. The case study of "Linda," a second-generation twenty-seven-year-old Korean American female, helps illustrate the effectiveness of this technique. Linda was initially referred by her physician for hearing voices. She relayed being reluctant to disclose her symptoms to a therapist due to concerns that she would be breaking her family's trust. After three sessions, she finally disclosed high family conflict, which would usually result in audio hallucinations insulting her or commanding her to leave the house. She had difficulty conveying the family conflict without feeling guilty, yet her symptoms were clearly tied to a recent family discord. Sand Tray Therapy seemed to be a less intrusive method of having Linda describe her inner turmoil. She created scenes in which a large spider (her father) would oppress the happier characters (herself and her brother). I would help her to role play what the happier characters could say or do when the spider was expected again. Eventually, she was able to transfer these skills to her home-life environment and finally experience tension relief. We would use the sand tray often when she could not verbalize how she felt but was clearly distressed. We used scenes and images to symbolize her outer world with skills she could eventually transfer successfully.

Suggested Procedures

This activity is divided into four sections: 1) introducing the concept of sand tray, 2) allowing the clients to survey and select items they would like to include in their sand tray, 3) construction of the sand tray scene, and 4) sharing of the sand tray scene to the therapist.

1. Introduce the activity to your client. Clients are oftentimes curious about the objects they see in the therapy room. It is helpful to let them know the objects are utilized in alternative ways to conduct therapy, which have been proven to be effective. I direct their attention to the objects and the sand tray, allowing them to make an informed decision about the nonverbal activity we will be engaging in. *Suggested Introduction*: "Today, we can use the sand tray during our therapy session."

2. Give ample time to the client to sift through the objects and select those which they would like to include in their finished product. This phase could take from a few minutes to fifteen minutes, depending on how thorough your client is. Some may prefer to be more meticulous with selection and placement of their figurines. Others may spend the majority of their time reshaping the sand. *Suggested Discussion Prompt*: "Here is a basket for you to fill with as many objects from the shelves as you would like. When you're through, you may create a scene in the sand tray. Take as long as you'd like. I'll be out of your way so you can move about freely. I won't be talking to you or interrupting you during this time so you can let me know when you're finished creating your scene."

3. Review the sand tray together. This is the only opportunity for the administrator to interact in the client's sand tray. You should construct questions and possible follow-up prompts that encourage the client to share how he/she constructs her/his inner world. This usually lasts from five to fifteen minutes. *Prompts to encourage sharing of the world*: "Great job. Let's take a look at what you created. Let's pretend that this is a scene from a movie. Tell me what's going on in this scene." *Follow-up Prompts*: "Now please tell me who the main character is. What happened before this scene? If this is a story with a beginning, middle, and end, what happens to end this scene?"

4. Wrap up the sand tray exercise: The client has spent valuable time expressing their inner thoughts and sharing this with their therapist. It is often helpful to let them know you respected their work and appreciate the energy they used to create the sand tray. I sometimes emphasize that the sand tray will remain undis-

turbed for the remainder of the session, but may not be intact upon their next session so as not to raise expectations that their scene will be available for their next visit. At times, it is also helpful to let the client know that they may engage in the activity again in later sessions. *Possible Closing Statements*: "Thank you for sharing your sand tray with me. You did a great job. I'm going to set this aside. We don't have to take it apart right now, but it may not be here the next time you come in."

5. Allow some time for the breakdown of the sand tray, which should be done after the participant leaves the room and prior to your next client. Before breaking down the scene, you may choose to take a Polaroid, digital image, or videotape the scene to document for future reference.

Possible Challenges

1. Participants may ask you to create the sand tray with them. *Suggested Response*: "This is your time to create whatever you want. I will watch you as you build, but be out of your way until you finish your scene."

2. Clients may try and engage you with conversation as they are selecting objects from your shelves or constructing the sand tray. *Suggested Response*: "I want to be sure that you get your own time to select objects and create your scene. I don't want to interrupt or distract you, so I'm going to stay out of your way until you tell me that you're done."

3. Participants may take an excessive amount of time selecting objects or creating the scene. *Suggested Response*: "If we run out of time during today's session, I can try and keep your objects or sand tray intact so that we can continue this exercise during our next session."

4. Clients may not want to engage in Sand Tray Therapy. *Suggested Response*: "If you don't feel comfortable trying this activity, you don't have to. I want you to feel at ease in your sessions."

Variations

Besides Sand Tray Therapy, other projective therapies may also be useful in helping clients in sharing their concerns. I briefly discuss how to incorporate Wire Sculptures into therapy.

The Wire Sculpture is an exercise typically used to demonstrate one's Emotional Intelligence Quotient, also known as EQ. This is a method used to help understand and express our emotions.[7] Mayer and Salovey incorporate similar creative methods to assist in regulating emotions in the self and in others.[8] Materials necessary are: wire cuttings of at least one millimeter in diameter and ranging from four-to-twelve inches. Have clients quietly reflect on how they're currently feeling or have been feeling for the past week. When they are ready, have them choose a wire cutting and instruct them to bend the wire into a shape representing their feelings. This should take anywhere from one to five minutes. After they are through shaping their wire, have them display their sculpture. Ask them to imagine their sculpture is on display in a museum. Have the artist give a title and description for their sculpture. Oftentimes, the inspiration behind the wire sculpture gives a telling insight as to what they were feeling. This is a simple and effective way to access the client's feelings in a creative manner.

Notes

1. I. Yalom, *Love's Executioner & Other Tales of Psychotherapy* (New York: Perennial, 2000).

2. G. K. Hong and M. D. Ham, *Psychotherapy and Counseling with Asian American Clients: A Practical Guide* (Thousand Oaks, CA: Sage Publications, 2001).

3. M. P. P. Root, "Guidelines for Facilitating Therapy with Asian American Clients," *Psychotherapy* 22 (1985): 349-356.

4. M. K. Ho, "Differential Application of Treatment Modalities with Asian American Youth," in *Working with Culture: Psychotherapeutic Interventions with Ethnic Minority Children and Adolescents*, eds. L. A. Vergas and J. D. Koss-Chioino (San Francisco: Jossey-Bass, 1992), 192-203.

5. D. W. Sue and S. Sue, *Counseling the Culturally Different* (New York: Wiley, 1999).

6. J. A. Kottler, *On Being a Therapist*, 3rd ed. (San Francisco: Jossey-Bass, 2003).

7. D. Goleman, *Emotional Intelligence* (New York: Bantam, 1995).

8. J. D. Mayer and P. Salovey, "What is Emotional Intelligence?" in *Emotional Development and Emotional Intelligence: Implications for Educators*, eds. P. Salovey and D. Sluyter (New York: Basic Books, 1997).

Recommended Resources

C. Baker, "Healing in the Sand: Navajo Sand Painting and Sandplay," *Journal of Sandplay Therapy* 2 (1993): 89-103.

D. H. Hendrix, "Metaphors as Nudges toward Understanding in Mental Health Counseling," *Journal of Mental Health Counseling* 14 (1992): 234-242.

Transpersonal Sandplay Therapy Center, www.sandplay.net.

Chapter 8

Are High Achieving Asians Individualists?

Dharm P. S. Bhawuk and Vijayan P. Munusamy

Often people confuse achievement with individualism. However, a close observation of high-achievers from Asia shows that though they may be very competitive in work and studies, they are not as rational as Caucasian Americans when it comes to managing relationships. Critical incidents are presented to demonstrate this important difference between individualists and collectivists in general and how it applies to Asians and the Pacific Islanders.

Objectives

- To sensitize students to differences in social exchange across cultures.
- To help students understand how Asian Americans can be competitive in some domains and cooperative in other domains.
- To help students understand the theory of individualism and collectivism, particularly the difference in social exchanges in these types of cultures.

Time

- A one-and-one-half-hour session (or two forty-five minute sessions)

Number of Participants

- Five to fifty people

Materials Needed

- Overheads
- Critical incidents and explanations (included at the end of this lesson plan)

Background

Schwartz defined achievement as personal success, which is demonstrated through one's competence in accordance with social standards. In individualistic culture, social standards include individual achievement.[1] Like many other individualistic standards, individual achievement has also influenced the social standards of Asians. For example, personal wealth and education are often considered a part of social standards in Asia where collectivism is valued.

Does collectivism facilitate individual achievement? According to McClelland, individualistic achievement does not belong to collectivists.[2] He asserted that collectivist norms are not the norms for high achievers and that collectivism constrained the motivation to achieve.

Does this then mean that high achieving Asians are individualists? Bhawuk and Udas found that successful Nepalese entrepreneurs considered independence, individual merit, internal control, competition, and hedonism to be important.[3] At the same time, Nepalese entrepreneurs also showed strong collectivist tendencies. The vast majority lived in extended families, lived near close friends, and believed that aging parents should live with their children and that individuals should help their relatives. Additional factor analytic results supported the notion that this sample was high on both competition and responsibility, a combination of individualism and collectivism.

In the United States, Asian Indians excel in many managerial and professional fields such as medicine, law, engineering, and accounting. In the academic field alone, there are more than five thousand Asian Indians serving as faculty members.[4] In Silicon Valley, 300,000 Asian Indians are employed in technology firms and they account for more than 15 percent of the high-tech startups.[5] In hotel and motel industry, Asian Indians, especially Gujaratis, control more than 60 percent of mid-sized hotels and motels.[6] It is not uncommon to hear phrases such as "Patels own more motels than Hilton and Sheraton combined."[7] Some argue that Asian children's success are contributed by their family's solidarity.[8] This conclusion was reached by Professor Emmy Werner, a professor of human development at the University of California at Davis, after her thirty years of longitudinal study on Asian Americans on the Hawaiian island of Kauai. She explains that in the western world, it has always been "I do well to show that I am No. 1," whereas in many of the Asian American families, the idea is to do well to give the family a sense of pride and accomplishment.

Family plays an important role for Asians to excel. A student of Fijian ancestry describes the involvement of his family in these words: "I believe my parents were very strict with my upbringing. In grade school as well as high school, I was always under pressure to perform well. The fear of being frowned on or even just reprimanded drove me to strive for academic achievement. Eventually, through grades and the respect of my peers, I have grown to not fear the repercussions of performing poorly, but to take pride in the quality of my own work." This experience is something that many Asian Americans can relate to.

Such a socialization process also makes them high achievers, but what is often overlooked is that these people are also relational in other social exchanges, much like the Nepalese entrepreneurs. The critical incidents presented in this module will help students understand the rational and relational aspects of social exchange, and how Asian Americans may use them both in different domains.

Suggested Procedures

1. Hand out critical incidents as homework. Ask students to come to class prepared with their response to the issues and questions raised in the incidents.
2. Ask students to discuss critical incidents one to three in small groups, one incident at a time, and ask them to present one or two important ideas to the class. State the key ideas at the end of the discussion of each of the incidents, and then ask students to discuss the next incident. Continue this process until all the critical incidents are discussed in the class.
3. Make a brief presentation on the theory of individualism and collectivism to synthesize the discussion at the end of the discussion of all the critical incidents.

Critical Incident 1: A Scholarship Dilemma

Lee was an undergraduate student from Korea at a small mid-western college in the United States. He was very happy with life in general; he had a wonderful academic adviser, a full scholarship from the college and friends who were warm and hospitable. At the end of the first year, his college's Scholarship Coordinator, Nancy Smith, asked him to apply for an international scholarship that was offered specifically to Korean students. Nancy told Lee that getting an international scholarship would be good for the college and its outreach program. It would also look good on Lee's résumé. Lee being the only Korean in the program and a high achiever was definitely a fit for the scholarship. Lee had known about this scholarship much earlier but he was not keen on applying, as this scholarship did not pay for summer tuitions and book allowance. Lee's plan was to take courses in summer and try to graduate as early as possible. When he explained this to Nancy, she advised him that he could apply for a summer scholarship a month before the summer program started. Lee was still not keen on applying for this scholarship, as he would be losing around $300 in book allowance, which the international scholarship did not offer.

His academic adviser, George Moss, however, encouraged him to apply, as it would help the college in its outreach program bringing more Korean students. Besides, Moss reminded him that his current scholarship was subject to an annual review, and it would not do any harm if he applied for the international scholarship. Lee finally agreed to apply although he knew that he would be losing the book allowance.

As expected, Lee won the international scholarship. His college scholarship was immediately withdrawn and was given to another student. A month before the summer program started, he submitted an application for a summer scholarship. Two weeks before the summer semester, he received a letter from Nancy informing him that due to insufficient funds and a highly competitive pool of applicants, his application wasn't considered for the summer scholarship. She advised Lee to request the international scholarship fund to assist him for summer school fees.

Lee was flabbergasted since he was aware that he was one of the top students and the College could easily find a way to support his summer tuition, considering the sacrifices that he had made for boosting the outreach program of the college.

Lee spoke to his adviser who suggested that he petition to Nancy, considering that he had made sacrifices by accepting the international scholarship, and he had helped the college in its outreach effort. Lee wrote the petition and also spoke to Nancy personally. His adviser also wrote a letter of recommendation supporting his case. In a few weeks Lee received a letter from Nancy stating that his request had been turned down due to shortage of funding. The letter made a special note of the fact that Lee's scholarship was not his right but a privilege.

How can you explain Nancy's decision? How would you advise Lee to help him deal with this situation? Discuss the issues from the perspectives of Nancy and Lee.

Explanation for Critical Incident 1: A Scholarship Dilemma

Lee comes from a collectivist culture. Collectivists are relational, and relationships are characterized by long-term duration, unequal exchange and non-rationality.[9] In this case, Lee thinks that by agreeing to apply for the scholarship when the college needed him, he would develop a communal relationship even though it came with a price of reduced financial support. He did not point out that he would be losing $300 in book allowances and would be taking a risk in applying for a summer scholarship as he felt that being direct and forthright regarding financial matters might be perceived as rude. He expected Nancy to understand his predicament implicitly.

Collectivist cultures have a holistic view of the world, and the self is thought to be of the same substance as other things in nature, and cannot be separated from the rest of nature.[10] Therefore, the relationship between the self and other people or elements in nature is much closer, and people feel much interdependence. On the other hand, individualist cultures usually hold a Cartesian worldview, in which the self is independent of other elements of nature, people, and situations.[11] An individualistic person, therefore, takes more control over elements of nature or situations around him- or herself, and feels more responsible for his or her behaviors. Moreover, as a collectivist, Lee felt he was also obligated to what the superior (adviser) advised him to do.

Nancy, who is likely to be an individualist, thought that it was an exchange relationship. She thought that Lee's agreement to apply for the international scholarship is rational and in his best interest. Thus, Nancy does not feel any obligation toward Lee. Furthermore, she might have felt that Lee should have taken charge of his affairs and should have rejected the request if it did not benefit him. This conflict in understanding relationship between individualist and collectivist arose mainly because exchange relations are viewed as superficial by collectivists.

Clark and Mills discuss the difference between exchange and communal relationships.[12] In an exchange relationship, people give something (a gift or a service) to another person with the expectation that the other person will return a gift or service of equal value in the near future. The characteristics of this type of relationship are "equal value" and "short time frame." People keep a mental record of exchange of benefits and try to maintain a balanced account, in an accounting sense.

In a communal relationship, people do not keep an account of the exchanges taking place between them; one person may give a gift of much higher value than the other person, and the two people may still maintain their relationship. In other words, it is the relationship that is valued and not the exchanges that go on between people when they are in communal relationships. For example, Foster finds that in a Mexican peasant village, which is likely to be collectivist, usually there was a series of exchanges between two people in which what is given never quite matched what is received.[13] Thus, the exchange goes on for a long time unless the series is broken by some unavoidable situation. Lee accepted the international scholarship since he sensed a common fate with his college and its officials. Nancy, on the other hand, was simply maximizing the benefits to the college because that was her job. Mills and Clark suggest that in this type of relationship people feel an "equality of affect" (i.e., when one feels up the other also feels up, and when one feels down the other also feels down).[14] It is similar to the sense of common fate found among collectivists that Triandis describes, or to what appears as collectivists having a feeling of involvement in others' lives.[15]

Critical Incident 2: Monitoring the Lab

Jing, a Chinese undergraduate student at a mid-western university, was working in the computer lab around noon on a bright, sunny, beautiful Saturday. She was alone in the lab. The lab monitor, Rebecca, who was a student in her department, approached her and asked her if she would take care of the lab on her behalf. Rebecca told her that some of her good friends were at the racecourse and she would like to join them. Rebecca also indicated to her that she was very fond of betting at the racecourse. Rebecca's duty was until 5 p.m., and she was paid $7 an hour as a lab monitor.

As a student majoring in information technology, Jing had worked as a lab monitor before. In fact, she did so once every two weeks and in lieu of her services was given a key to the lab like other communication and information system students. Jing also knew Rebecca as a fellow student and had taken a course with her, but she was not really a friend of Rebecca.

As Jing had planned to work in the lab all afternoon, she volunteered to take care of the lab on Rebecca's behalf. Rebecca was happy to hear this and wanted to compensate Jing for five hours. Jing, however, refused to accept the $35 compensation and said that it was her pleasure to help Rebecca.

Should Jing have taken the money? Should Rebecca have insisted on paying the money? Discuss the issues from the perspectives of both Jing and Rebecca.

Explanation for Critical Incident 2: Monitoring the Lab

Jing is likely to be a collectivist and generally collectivists like to deal with people they know or trust.[16] When the person is unknown to them, collectivists try to establish common root, or try to connect through some similarity in their background. In the Asia Pacific region, it is common for people to develop relationships by inquiring about the hometown of the person, the school he or she went to, the person's native language, etc. And collectivists attempt to integrate the new person into their primary network of family, relations, and friends.[17] This, however, doesn't mean that individualists do not ask these questions. They do, but the objective is to simply build the rapport. Relationships are based on functional and rational exchanges rather than shared common root or similarity in backgrounds. Therefore, in individualistic culture, people are more task-oriented than relationship-oriented. In this incident, Rebecca, who is likely to be an individualist, went directly to the task by asking Jing to work on her behalf. Jing most likely agreed, not because of Rebecca's predicament but mainly because of their previous relationship.

Collectivists are relational, and their relationships are characterized by long-term duration. If students take the same course together and have some interaction with each other, collectivists are likely to view each other as a friend, whereas an individualist is likely to acknowledge the person as an acquaintance. Collectivists often are involved in unequal exchange (e.g., "I help you in monitoring the lab, you will help me in proofreading my term paper"), and non-rationality (e.g., "Even if I have to bear extra responsibilities in monitoring the lab, I will do it without any compensation"). Though Jing had to bear extra responsibilities as a lab monitor, she happily accepted, hoping that this would lead to a long-term relationship. Jing sees this as an opportunity and as an investment to develop a communal relationship.

Jing probably would have considered accepting the compensation if Rebecca had demonstrated that the value of her help was much more than the compensation she offered. It would have further helped if she tried to convince her that the $35 compensation was just a friendly gesture. For example, Rebecca could have said that if Jing did not accept the small compensation, it would be difficult for Rebecca to ask for her help in the future. A relationship is usually taken into account before a collectivist makes "Yes" or "No" statements, unlike an individualist who would often decide based solely on rational exchange.

Rebecca offered Jing $35 as that was a fair compensation for her hours (equal exchange). Rebecca looks at it as a market-exchange type of relationship—"If you work for me, I will pay you." For Rebecca, it is Jing's problem if she does not want to accept the compensation. As an individualist, it is difficult for Rebecca to relate to the idea that Jing is not accepting the compensation because she would like to have a long-term relationship beyond the transaction.

As a collectivist, Jing would expect Rebecca to help her in the future when the need arose. Jing's expectation would not be based on equal exchange but rather on the principle of helping each other, and her request might even sound as an exploitation to Rebecca (e.g., "I just asked her to help me monitor the lab, but now she wants to borrow my car!"). If Rebecca doesn't fulfill Jing's request, Jing might withdraw from the relationship and might not even consider "market-exchange" types of relationship with Rebecca in the future. Axing communal relationship might not bother Rebecca, but losing the "market-exchange" type of relationship might be a concern for her.

Critical Incident 3: A Nomination Letter

Ravi, a student from South Asia, was one of the recipients of the Distinguished Service Award at a prestigious educational institution in the United States. Among other factors in determining recipients for this award is the valuation of nomination letters that are submitted by other college students. In the letter, nominators need to explain the outstanding contributions that the nominee has made to the college and how those differ from what are usual and expected from other college students. The selection committee did not accept self-nomination.

Nguyen, an ambitious student from Vietnam, approached Ravi to write him a nomination letter for the award. Nguyen knew Ravi through community activities organized by their student association in which Ravi presided in the previous year. Ravi was shocked by the request as he understood that nominations for this award were normally done voluntarily and often without the knowledge of the nominee. That was the case for him when he was nominated to receive the award the previous year. Though the reason for his nomination was announced during the award ceremony, the person who nominated him was not identified.

A day later, he received another nomination request from another Asian student, Akbar. Ravi went to clarify with the award's coordinator whether it was a normal practice for nominees to request for such nomination letters. The coordinator (though he was not assertive) clarified that it was acceptable for a nominee to make such a request.

Ravi was reluctant to write the nomination letter as he still felt that nominations should be done voluntarily, and it would be unfair for other qualified candidates who did not request such nomination. In the end, however, he conceded to the request from both Nguyen and Akbar.

Why do you think Nguyen and Akbar came to Ravi for nomination? Why did Ravi write the nomination letter in the end? Discuss various issues from the perspectives of Nguyen, Akbar, and Ravi.

Explanation for Critical Incident 3: A Nomination Letter

In Asia, people value awards and achievements highly. It is not unusual to see pictures of a family member receiving an award (e.g., during a graduation ceremony) in the living room of an Asian home. It is also a common practice to list one's academic qualifications (e.g., MS, Ph.D., etc.) on business cards. Clearly, social recognition is one of the reasons why Asians are so competitive in their work and studies.

In this critical incident, we see how two students are competing for an award. Both Nguyen and Akbar felt that they were qualified for the award but were afraid that they might not get nominated if they did not toot their horns. In individualistic culture, people say, "I did this, this and this," whereas in collectivist culture, it is always, "we did this, this and this." As such, they might have felt that their individual contributions might not receive a fair recognition leading to a nomination for the award, as they never promoted their work. They would have probably nominated themselves had the procedure allowed for that.

As previously mentioned, Asians value award, and in this instance we see how Nguyen and Akbar wanted the distinction beyond the value of equality espoused by collectivist cultures. Clearly, achievement and distinction are seen as much more valuable in this context.

They might have approached Ravi because he was senior to them and a past winner of the award. In collectivist culture, seniority is important, and it is the role of the seniors to take care of the subordinates' needs, whereas in individualistic culture everyone takes care of his or her own needs. Also, in collectivist cultures, smooth interpersonal relations are valued and people make an effort to be agreeable, even in demanding situations. This explains why Ravi nominated Nguyen and Akbar even though he felt that this would be unfair to other deserving students with whom he had worked when he was the president of the student association.

Notes

1. S. H. Schwartz, "Universals in the Content and Structure of Values: Theoretical Advances and Empirical Tests in 20 Countries," in *Advances in Experimental Social Psychology*, ed. M. Zanna (New York: Academic Press, 1992), 1-66.

2. D. McClelland, *The Achieving Society* (New York: Van Nostrand, 1961).

3. D. P. S. Bhawuk and A. Udas, "Entrepreneurship and Collectivism: A Study of Nepalese Entrepreneurs," in *Asian Contributions to Cross-cultural Psychology*, eds. J. Pandey, D. Sinha, and D. P. S. Bhawuk (New Delhi: Sage Publications, 1996), 307-317.

4. Embassy of India, "Indian Americans: A Story of Achievement," www.indianembassy.org/indusrel/clinton_india/india_americans.html.

5. *Ibid.*

6. Chhavi Dublish, "America's Patel Motels," *BBC News UK Edition*, October 10, 2003, http://news.bbc.co.uk/1/hi/world/south_asia/3177054.stm.

7. W. H. Arthur and M. H. Usha, *An Immigrant Success Story: East Indians in America* (Philadelphia: University of Pennsylvania Press, 1990).

8. A. Quindlen, "The Drive to Excel," *The New York Times*, late city final edition, February 22, 1987, sec. 6, 32.

9. H. C. Triandis, *Individualism and Collectivism* (Boulder, CO: Westview Press, 1995).

10. J. Galtung, "Structure, Culture, and Intellectual Style: An Essay Comparing Saxonic, Teutonic, Gallic, and Nipponic Approaches," *Social Science Information* 20 (1981): 817-856.

11. H. R. Markus and S. Kitayama, "Culture and the Self: Implications for Cognition, Emotion, and Motivation," *Psychological Review* 98 (1991): 224-253.

12. M. S. Clark and J. Mills, "Interpersonal Attraction in Exchange and Communal Relationships," *Journal of Personality and Social Psychology* 37 (1979): 12-24.

13. G. M. Foster, "The Dyadic Contract: A Model for the Social Structure of a Mexican Peasant Village," in *Peasant Society*, eds. J. M. Potter, M N. Diaz, and G. M. Foster (Boston: Little, Brown & Co., 1967): 213-229.

14. J. Mills and M. S. Clark, "Exchange and Communal Relationships," in *Review of Personality and Social Psychology*, ed. L. Wheeler (Beverly Hills, CA: Sage Publications, 1982), 121-144.

15. Triandis, *Individualism and Collectivism*; C. H. Hui and H. C. Triandis, "Individualism-Collectivism: A Study of Cross-cultural Researchers," *Journal of Cross-Cultural Psychology* 17 (1986): 225-248.

16. D. P. S. Bhawuk, "Leadership through Relationship Management: Using the Theory of Individualism and Collectivism," in *Improving Intercultural Interactions: Modules for Cross-cultural Training Programs*, vol. 2, eds. R. W. Brislin and K. Cushner (Thousand Oaks, CA: SAGE Publishers, 1997).

17. *Ibid.*

Chapter 9

Representations of Asian Americans in Advertising:

Constructing Images of Asian Americans

Maria Mami Turnmeyer

American consumers have been warned about *false* advertisements—flashy presentations designed to seduce them into buying on impulse. Along with the false flash, advertisers use tempting images that suggest *the good life.* As the global marketplace expands, competition increases and advertisers shift gears and follow ever-changing trends of the buying public. Presentation has become a primary concern of advertisers, while striving for realistic and non-stereotypical representations continues to be the least of all concerns.

Print advertisements can serve as a text, much like an essay or short story, designed to send consumers a specific message. The subtext, implicit and explicit messages concerning race and gender, is the focus of the following activities. The lesson plan can be utilized in courses that focus on race and critical thinking, introductory classes in Asian American Studies and classes on Asian American women and men, and media classes that focus on representations of Asian Americans in the mainstream and popular culture.

Objectives

- To assist students in realizing the ways in which print advertisements have both the ability to construct and deconstruct stereotypes about Asian Americans.
- To promote and organize classroom discussions.
- To promote critical thinking skills by using observation and composition skills.

Time

- This activity is primarily a homework assignment, which will lead into a classroom discussion, ending in critical reflection of individual and group work.

Number of Participants

- Five to forty students

Materials Needed

Magazines are selected by instructors and/or students; students may select magazine advertisements based on the following criteria:

- Favorite magazines (usually mainstream magazines)
- Specific-interest magazines
- Magazines students may not be familiar with

Background

Advertisers often compose print ads that either consciously or unconsciously maintain stereotypes about Asian Americans. Often, stereotyping in ads is overlooked simply because the viewing audience understands that ads are designed to sell products. When treated as a text, advertisements become a narrative to be unraveled.

In 1994 Charles Taylor and Ju Yung Lee found that Asian American models appear predominantly in "business, science, women's, and general interest magazines" and that in print advertising, stereotyping of Asian Americans is frequent and problematic.[1] The first problematic is their sheer invisibility in magazine ads. After a close study of 1,616 ads in various magazines, they discovered that only 4 percent of the ads utilized one Asian American model. Taylor and Lee point out four specific ways in which Asian Americans are stereotyped in magazine ads. While rarely seen in mainstream magazine ads, Asian Americans are predominantly in ads for technology and science-based companies where they appear in work-related settings as background models and not the primary images.

Asian American magazines, such as *A*, feature Asian American models (both male and female) in realistic representations. However, Taylor and Lee's focus is on the ways that Asian Americans are represented in mainstream magazine advertising. Their research shows the underrepresentation (if not entire lack) of Asian Americans in mainstream magazines. Taylor and Lee conclude that when Asian American models are used in print ads, they are usually portrayed in ways that "distort" the reality of Asian Americans and perpetuate stereotypes.

The following is a very brief analysis of more recent magazine ads and extends the insights of Taylor and Lee.

- The 225-page May 2002 issue of *Rosie* (a mainstream publication) features a single female Asian American model and echoes the findings of Taylor and Lee that Asian Americans are nearly absent in mainstream publications. The print model is wearing a print suit designed and sold by Fashion Bug Plus Sizes. Though the use of a full-figured Asian American female model breaks the stereotype of the petite, fragile Asian American woman, the print of the clothing modeled is problematic. The full-figured woman models a matching casual suit that displays large, colorful palm trees and fronds. The exoticization of a palm-laden paradise is evident, and the result is a stereotypical construction of the Asian American as exotic.

- The March 2002 issue of *Small Business Opportunities* (an interest-specific magazine that is also mainstream) also features only one Asian American model—and once again, the model is female. The single ad (in a total of 162 pages) is for North American Vending Machines. The advertisement features eleven "real life" models of success. The success stories are related to the audience through captions under the photographs. However, the Asian American woman, professionally dressed and photographed, does not have a caption to illustrate her experience with North American Vending Machines. The lack of a captioned narrative is an effective silencer of the Asian American woman's voice. As Taylor and Lee found in their research, Asian Americans are portrayed in stereotypical ways—in this case—the silent, yet successful, Asian American.
- The 168-page September 2002 issue of *Atlantic Monthly* (a mainstream magazine with a large audience) also has only one Asian American model. In an ad for Sidemen's Healthcare Technologies, a female Asian American model portrays a physician. Though the ad features an Asian American as successful and intelligent (leading the viewer to believe the ad is a fair and empowering representation), it is also maintaining the model minority stereotype: that *all* Asian Americans succeed in the sciences. Upholding the model minority stereotypes can be detrimental in that it suggests that Asian Americans who do not fit the mold are somehow deficient.

Although Asian Americans are nearly invisible in mainstream magazines, when they are present in ads they are represented in the following ways.

- Asian American men are seldom pictured in print advertisement.
- Asian American women are exoticized.
- Asian American men, when present in ads, are feminized (or desexualized).
- Asian Americans are not depicted in fundamental roles, such as family settings and other settings in everyday American life.
- In some cases (especially in location/city/state-specific magazines), Asian American women are used primarily to advertise strip clubs, massage parlors, and escort services.

A student in my writing course shared an advertisement for Camel cigarettes. The ad featured an olive-skinned woman with black hair in a short, red Chinese dress. The advertisement did not utilize a photo of a model, but instead opted to use a cartoon. Aside from the words "Camel Cigarettes," the ad featured no other print language. The student concluded:

- The use of a cartoon woman to replace an actual Asian American woman causes concern because "art" can create images instead of using photo images.
- The woman in the ad appears to be Asian because she is wearing Chinese-style dress—but the dress enhances the cartoon woman's legs (because the dress is very short). This type of drawing promotes the exoticization of Asian women.
- The cartoon Asian woman in the ad is tempting the audience with a silver tray of cigarettes, and this, in a way, promotes the idea of an Asian woman as a temptress or a Dragon Lady.

The student concluded that the Camel advertisement upheld stereotypes of Asian American women. The advertisement did so by portraying Asian American women as "bad, silent, exotic, and mysterious."

Another student in the same class clipped an ad for computers that featured a new high-speed computer. The photographed advertisement depicted an office setting in which several Caucasian males stood surrounding a seated Asian American woman. The print ad reads "Faster is Better." The student pointed out that though it seemed to be a complimentary ad (since the Asian American woman was seated at the center), the ad was problematic because it upheld the model minority stereotype that Asian Americans work hard, and the message, "Faster is Better," seemed to connote the woman's sexuality. The student also noted that the computer company was a small, unknown company and remarked that a larger company (such as IBM) might not make such a blatantly stereotypical and sexually charged ad.

Suggested Procedures

The following activity is designed primarily to allow students to discover and analyze the many ways that stereotypes of Asian Americans in magazine ads perpetuate the stereotyping of all Asian Americans. The activity also allows students to design alternative ways that advertisers can both present their products and represent Asian Americans with truth and realism.

This activity works best when assigned as a homework assignment. Completed work should be shared in a group environment in which all students can participate.

1. After carefully reviewing the entire magazine, students should compose a written observation paper (approximately three pages in length) in the following format:

Name of Magazine: _____

Type (or genre) of Magazine: _____

Date of Issue: _____

Number of advertisements that
feature Asian American models: _____

Total number of advertisements
in magazine: _____

Selected Advertisement: _____

Company: _____

Product: _____

2. Treating the advertisement as a text, address the following:
   - If the model were a character, what might he/she say?
   - Is there an apparent conflict in the advertisement? If so, please describe it.
   - What is the overall tone of the advertisement?
   - Does the advertisement maintain or break pervasive/common stereotypes about Asian Americans? (Describe your response in detail.)
   - Does the advertisement contain language that is potentially derogatory or participates in the maintenance of stereotypes?
   - Does the ad contain images that reinforce stereotypes? Does the ad exoticize and/or orientalize Asian Americans? (Describe your response in detail.)

- If you could rewrite the narrative (or re-create the advertisement), how might you do so and why?
3. Group discussion: After completing the above assignment, each student should be allowed to give a brief (three-to-five minute) summary of findings. Instructors may wish to "go around" or "round robin" the entire class before opening up the discussion for the entire class. All students should view all ads. (Instructors may tailor this activity over two or three class meetings, depending on available.)
4. Concluding activity (additional component): Students should compose a two-to-three page essay that incorporates all findings from the homework assignment and class discussion.

Notes

1. Charles Taylor and Ju Yung Lee, "Not in *Vogue*: Portrayals of Asian Americans in Magazine Advertising," *Journal of Public Policy and Marketing* 13:2 (1994): 239-246.

Recommended Resources

Sonia Maasik and Jack Solomon, eds., *Signs of Life in the USA: Readings on Popular Culture for Writers*, 4th ed. (Boston: Bedford, 2003).

Signs of Life is an excellent text that instructs students on how to utilize semiotics, or the reading and interpretation of signs (language and imagery). Chapter 2, "Brought to You B(u)y: The Signs of Advertisements," is particularly useful to instructors and students because it contains readings that demonstrate careful analysis of print advertisements. Chapter 2 also contains a portfolio of advertisements that serve as examples of the implicit and explicit motivations of advertisers and the ramifications on gender, social structure, and race relations.

Chapter 10

Ripping Up Culture:
Helping Students Reconnect with Their Cultural Values

Masaru Torito

Many Asian Pacific American students have a strong hold on their cultural values, but they just don't know that they do. However, in geographical areas where there is only a small Asian Pacific American population, such as Colorado, there is a lot of pressure on youth to adapt to the norms of the dominant white culture and to lose their cultural heritage. As Asian Pacific American youth start to enter college, the pressure to conform while away from their families can consciously and subconsciously affect their lives. This activity will help students reconnect with their cultural values. This activity is especially useful for student organizations as part of leadership training.

Objectives

- To help Asian Pacific American students realize the impact of losing their cultural values and to help them regain these values.
- To provide students the tools to combat their feelings of cultural loss and enable them to fight for their right to keep their cultural values.
- To help students articulate oppression and privilege.
- To enable students to build a sense of community with other minorities, whether they are other Asian Pacific Americans, LGBT (lesbian-gay-bisexual-transexual) students, and other people of color.

Time

- Preparation time: thirty minutes for the facilitators to understand the activity and to make sure that they have the skills to handle the discussion afterward.
- Preliminary discussion: ten minutes for the facilitators to establish ground rules for the activity.
- Activity: fifteen to thirty minutes for the facilitators to have the students think about and write down the values most important to them.
- Discussion: thirty minutes to two hours for the facilitators to conduct a discussion

to deconstruct the activity. Emotions are going to be high, and it is important to help the students process these emotions. At the very least, this will take thirty minutes, but it is essential that facilitators conduct this activity when they can be flexible with time in order to allow the students to handle their emotions.

Number of Participants

- Ten to twenty students and preferably at least two facilitators

Prerequisites

For facilitators: to understand privilege and oppression and to know about grassroots movements and resources that can help direct the energy of students following this activity. Most important, there must be *trust* among facilitators as well as the students. If people have not established trust, they should not attempt this activity.

For students: to establish ground rules for interaction. An example is helping students become familiar and comfortable with speaking in "I" statements. Confidentiality is also needed; students need to know that what they share with other students will stay with the people in the room. Facilitators should remember that *trust* must also exist among the students involved.

These prerequisites, especially the ground rule of confidentiality, should be established early in the discussion, and the students should be reminded of them just before the activity. If students are prepared for this very emotional and personal activity, they will be open to share their feelings with others and gain the full benefits from it.

Materials Needed

- Note cards (standard 3" x 5" size); six cards per student
- Large writing board for conducting discussion of the activity

Background

In many areas of the United States, such as Colorado, there aren't any large Asian Pacific American communities. In these areas there is often a large rift between the younger generation—such as high school and college-age students—and their elders. The tensions between the generations come to a high point when the younger generation has to decide on the direction for their lives; whether it's college or the business world, Asian Pacific youth face dilemmas and challenges leaving family members in order to follow their personal dreams.

Once away from family members and community epicenters, these youth confront strong social pressures. Many times they will find themselves as the only Asian Pacific American in their classes and dorms. In isolated college towns they will not be able to find a traditional meal, much less a home-cooked meal. To find comfort, often students will drive for an hour to hang out with friends and family. Moreover, when it comes to finding communities on their campuses that share similar cultural values, many students become lost in the dominant white world of the educational system. There may be only a few activities to participate in, and for the most part they are forced to adapt as much as they can to the white culture that surrounds them.

This situation described our campus life in Colorado, especially when Asian Pacific student leaders tried to mobilize fellow students against several racist incidents. When we talked to fellow students around these issues, they would shrug them off as if racism did not exist. In other words, the problem was not that these students did not have enough time to get involved in fighting racism, but rather that they had difficulty seeing that the situation existed. We would call meetings and we would stress the importance of fighting racism against members of our community, but we found that fellow students mostly came for the social interaction with other Asian Pacific Americans. However, as we looked deeply at the reasons why students came to our meetings, we found hope. We realized that students were directing their energy first at trying to build a sense of community before they could begin to deal with the racism they face in society. Thus, as student leaders, we needed to find ways for people to build a sense of community by reconnecting with their cultural values in order to tackle racism plaguing our communities.

Our campus has a small Asian Pacific community, but the resources that we have are immense. We have a student government that has a $27 million budget that is controlled entirely by the students. We have scholarship programs that offer not only financial help but also tutoring and counseling. We have full-time faculty who are there to help students put together different events and activities. We have an Ethnic Studies program that offers a degree in Asian American Studies. We also have access to local and national organizations with resources to help students. In other words, we had all the necessary resources, but we lacked the participation of students.

As student leaders, we also had energy and commitment, but we needed to find a way to solve the problem of mobilizing fellow students. To find direction, we decided to focus on building leadership skills and with the help of national organizations we put together a leadership retreat. We had Asian Pacific students from nearby states get together for three days to participate in activities that would help mobilize other students into action.

The activity described below had the biggest impact on all of us. People were crying, and some were so angry that they wanted to hit the wall. We were all shocked and surprised by what happened. From our perspective, the activity worked to mobilize students. We immediately connected with all the reasons why we were in a small room for three days. We were fighting for ourselves—our identity—but we were also fighting for our families and our communities. It humbled us when we realized the sacrifices our parents made to get us to where we are, and we wanted to reconnect with our cultural values to make them proud.

The discussion deconstructing the activity was also very helpful. It gave us an outlet for the powerful emotions that we were feeling. It gave us a way to channel that energy in a very productive manner. We realized that we had a common bond with one another. Our cultural values were different, but the emotions were the same. The activity was like a slap in our faces, and we wanted to work together to stop the loss of our cultural values.

We did this activity a year-and-a-half ago, but we still stay in touch with one another working on issues and building coalitions.

Suggested Procedure

1. The activity begins with a discussion led by the facilitators of ground rules, such as confidentiality.
2. Facilitators then pass out five note cards to each student and tell students to think

about five important values in their lives. Facilitators instruct students to write down each value on a separate note card and to not show their cards to others. Examples of values that students identify usually relate to religion and family.

3. Next, the facilitators tell each student to choose one value that they could give up. Facilitators should allow students lots of time to think about which value they are willing to give up. After students have made their decisions, the facilitators ask the students to hold up their cards containing that value. The facilitators politely take away those cards from students.

4. The facilitators repeat this step two more times, having students decide two more important values in their lives that they can give up. However, the facilitators provide a decreasing amount of time for students to make their decisions. Also, when facilitators take away students' cards, they become more impatient and ruder.

5. The facilitators then ask each student to hold up their remaining two cards. The facilitators instruct students to hold these cards up high. The facilitators quickly go around the room and snatch the remaining two cards from each student, acting like thieves taking away valuables.

6. When all the cards have been collected, the facilitators destroy the cards. They tear them apart, stomp on them, spit on them, or do whatever they feel is necessary to destroy the cards.

7. The reactions of the students will be mixed. Most will sit there with shocked expressions. Some may cry, others will get angry, but most will sit silent and shocked. Facilitators should use this time to first allow students to react to the activity and then conduct a discussion to help synthesize feelings.

8. In the discussion, facilitators should relate this activity to the ways that the dominant white culture forcibly takes away the important cultural values of Asian Pacific students. Facilitators should also emphasize the need for students to build a sense of community in order to reconnect with their cultural values.

If the students and facilitators are able to stay in touch with one another over a period of time, they can discuss how this activity has continued to affect their lives and their involvement in community issues.

Part II

War, Colonialism, and Imperialism

Chapter 11

Paradise and the Politics of Tourist Hawai'i

Wayne Au

I mages of the island state of Hawai'i have been marketed to mainstream Americans since World War II. This tourist image has been used to gloss over real cultural, social, and historical realities of the peoples there, with a particular emphasis on misrepresenting Native Hawaiians. This activity uses an unlikely but appropriate text, the tourist brochure, to enter into a dialogue and critical analysis of our preconceived notions about Hawai'i.[1] This activity can be used in an introduction to Pacific Islander American Studies, media and pop-culture critique, and/or beginning analysis of U.S. imperialism of the late nineteenth century. This activity has been used in high school and college classrooms as well as among educators at conference workshops, and would also work well for diversity training and teacher education.

Objectives

- To encourage self-examination of preconceived notions about Native Hawaiian history and culture.
- To help participants understand the real ecological, economic, political, and cultural effects of the tourism industry on Native Hawaiians.
- To deconstruct tourist advertising media using historical and social data.
- To develop critical/comparative reading skills.

Time

- One-and-a-half to two hours or two forty-five-minute sessions

Number of Participants

- Five to fifty people (twenty-five ideally)

Materials Needed

- Tourist Brochures—abundantly available for free from your local travel agency; get enough for individuals or groups to share, with as much variety as possible.
- Handout: Tour Guides vs. Trask: comparative chart (included with this activity).
- Excerpts from *From a Native Daughter: Colonialism & Sovereignty in Hawai'i.*

Background

Ever since World War II, Hawai'i has been one of the mainstays of the mainstream, U.S. imagination. The sovereign kingdom *cum* U.S. military installation has been the destination *du jour* for fantasy seeking Americans. Perhaps Native Hawaiian sovereignty activist and scholar Haunani-Kay Trask said it best:

> Just five hours away by plane from California, Hawai'i is a thousand light
> years away in fantasy. Mostly a state of mind, Hawai'i is the image of
> escape from the rawness and violence of daily American life.[2]

Indeed, the annual piligrimage to Hawai'i could be seen as one of the birthrights of the American dream where middle-class Americans, having finally amassed enough capital through their individual hard work, can now exercise their economic muscle by taking the kids to the beach.[3]

The problem is that it was someone else's beach. As is pointed out in the excerpt of Trask's article included as part of this activity, the sovereign kingdom of Hawai'i was illegally overthrown by outside forces with U.S. military and economic interests at the fore. Sue Wheat writes that as of 1994 "95 percent of Hawaiian land [was] owned or controlled by 74 major landowners, mainly foreign or from mainland America. Over half is held by the federal and state governments. And 405,000 hectares—a quarter of the total area of Hawai'i—is used by the U.S. military."[4]

All this is to say that Native Hawaiians have borne the social and economic brunt of Hawai'i's transformation into a playground for tourists and a military outpost. Almost one-third of those receiving Temporary Aid for Needy Families in Hawai'i have Native Hawaiian blood. Native Hawaiians or part-Native Hawaiians make up 23 percent of the AIDS and 16 percent of the domestic violence cases in Hawai'i. Native Hawaiians also make up 40 percent of the homeless families in the state. These are particularly stark numbers considering that Native Hawaiians make up less than 9 percent of the total population.[5]

Former director of the Center for Hawaiian Studies at the University of Hawai'i, Manoa, Lilekala Hameieleihiwa, remarks that Native Hawaiians "have the worst health of any ethnic group in Hawai'i, including the lowest life expectancy and the highest rates of infant mortality. Hawaiians comprise a majority of the homeless and high school dropouts, few of the university students and many of the prison inmates. And every Hawaiian family has relatives fleeing to mainland America in search of better economic opportunities in a less racist and anti-Hawaiian setting."[6]

And outside of a formal apology granted by President Clinton in 1994, Native Hawaiians have not received much of anything from the U.S. government in return for their land. Further, the fluctuating tides of tourism continue to gouge the state's natural and financial resources, all the while marketing and selling Native Hawaiian culture as part of the appropriation and packaging of "paradise."

Historical, cultural, economic, and ecological details are overlooked and manipulated by the tourism industry, leaving out or distorting the truth of the very real impacts of this industry. Recognition of the Native Hawaiian right to sovereignty and their subsequent rights to self-determination is a central part of this issue, because Native Hawaiians, with extremely high rates of infant mortality and poverty accompanied by equally low levels of education, have paid the highest price for America's "right" to vacation in the islands.

Suggested Procedure and Discussion

1. Write the word "Hawai'i" on the board and ask the participants to brainstorm what images, sights, sounds, smells, etc. come to mind. Compile a group list on the board. In the event that one of the participants is from Hawai'i, ask them to actively observe their peers' responses and see what is said about their former home.

2. Direct the participants to get into groups of four or five. Pass out the handout, "Tour Guides vs. Trask" (see handout) and go over it with the whole group. Give each group a few tourist brochures—enough for each individual to have one if possible. The best brochures are those with lots of pictures of people and places.

3. Have the participants "read" their brochures and analyze them in terms of the history of Hawai'i, the culture of Native Hawaiians and other issues related to tourism. They should fill out the squares in column one of the handout based on what messages they learn or infer from the brochures.

4. Individually—on the back of the handout is fine—participants should write a profile of "Tourist Hawai'i" that includes climate, geography, architecture, plants, animals, and people. Make sure they describe the actual physical characteristics of the people in terms of race, class, gender, and perceived temperament. Have the participants write about the Hawai'i that the brochures have defined for them.

5. After they have finished the first column of their handouts and their profiles of "Tourist Hawai'i," reconvene as a large group for a discussion about what they learned and a sharing of what they wrote. Use this as a jumping off point for asking some of the following questions:
   - How is Hawai'i depicted?
   - What does the land look like?
   - Who are these brochures supposed to sell Hawai'i to?
   - Whose point of view is represented in the brochures?
   - Who and what is being sold as an attraction?
   - How are Pacific Islanders depicted in your brochures?
   - What kind of definition of Hawai'i does the brochure provide us with?

6. Distribute copies of the excerpt of *From a Native Daughter* by Haunani-Kay Trask. Have them read the article either individually, as a group, or perhaps as homework if used in a class, filling out column two of their handout comparing what Trask has to say with the tourist brochures. If necessary go over the following vocabulary words:
   - Colonization: when one country or nation forcibly takes over another for political or economic gain.
   - De-colonization: the effort of the colonized to undo colonization and its effects.

- Propaganda: publicity intended to spread information in order to persuade or convince.
- Complicitous: contributing to or allowing wrongdoing.
- Collaborationist: someone who works together with someone else for a common goal.
- Cosmogonic: theory of the creation of the universe.
- Ideological: having to do with the ideas that form the basis of a political, religious, social, or economic theory.
- Commercialization: taking something and making it into a packaged, marketable product with disregard to the truth or history of the product.
- Indigenous: native to a region.
- Dispossess: to deprive of possession, to take away.

7. Proceed with a full group discussion about how the columns compare, including reactions to Trask's article. Participants could look at how the depictions were similar or different, who benefits from particular depictions and why, and why the depictions are so different.

8. As a closing activity, participants could write a letter to a local travel agency, airline, or travel section of a local newspaper that compares what they found in the brochures with what they learned in the article by Trask. They could even write a letter to Trask herself. Their letters should include how they think Hawai'i should be portrayed in promotional literature, if at all.

A note on discussions. In the past this discussion has aroused a range of reactions from participants. Some have been saddened by the reality of the conditions facing Native Hawaiians, remorseful of vacation time spent there in the past, and even reluctant to visit in the future. Some participants have responded with a "who cares" attitude, saying things like "Trask is just whining. I'm going to go there and have fun no matter what anyone says." This particular response has almost always been the knee jerk reaction of someone who does not want their privilege of going where they please challenged, regardless of the real consequences. Still others are infuriated at the injustice as demonstrated through the history of Hawai'i and have chalked Native Hawaiians up as yet another group who has suffered and is still suffering under the yoke of U.S. racism and colonialism.

What's key in any discussion about a potentially inflammatory issue is that all voices be brought to the fore. Although risky, most groups of thirty or so individuals will contain varied opinions on any given subject, and it is this diversity which the facilitator must count on to carry the lesson through. Participants can agree or disagree with Trask, on tourism, or anything. Regardless of their personal perspectives, participants can at least understand that no matter where they step, their footprints carry the weight of history with them—that their actions, as tourists in this case, have consequences and may even hurt someone else as an immediate byproduct. As a facilitator, it is this perspective I have brought to the discussions and used to handle dissenting voices, but by and large participants have been sympathetic to the plight of Native Hawaiians if for no other reason than the statistics presented in the readings.

Notes

1. Previous versions of this activity have appeared in *Beyond Heroes and Holidays*, eds. Enid Lee

et al. (Washington, D.C.: Teaching for Change, 1998); and *Resistance in Paradise*, eds. Debbie Wei et al. (Philadelphia: American Friends Service Committee, 1998).

2. Haunani-Kay Trask, *From a Native Daughter: Colonialism & Sovereignty in Hawai'i*, 1st ed. (Monroe, ME: Common Courage Press, 1993).

3. D. Brown, *Hawai'i Recalls: Selling Romance to America: Nostalgic Images of the Hawaiian Islands, 1910-1950* (Honolulu: Editions Limited, 1982).

4. S. Wheat, "Paradise Lost," *Geographical Magazine* 66:14 (August 1994).

5. L. J. Foo, *Asian American Women: Issues, Concerns, and Responsive Human and Civil Rights Advocacy* (New York: Ford Foundation, 2002), www.fordfound.org/publications/recent_articles/asian_american_women.cfm.

6. Wheat, "Paradise Lost."

Recommended Resources

Candace Fujikane and Jonathan Y. Okamura, eds. "Whose Vision? Asian Settler Colonialism in Hawai'i," *Amerasia Journal* 26:2 (2000).

"Hawai'i—Independent & Sovereign," www.hawaii-nation.org/.

"Perspectives on Hawaiian Sovereignty," www.opihi.com/sovereignty/.

The Tour Guide vs. Trask
Comparative Text Chart

Using the following chart as a guide, compare the Hawai'i described by the tourist brochures with the Hawai'i described in Trask's article.

Category	Column 1: Tour Guides	Column 2: Trask
History of Hawai'i		
Native Hawai'ian Culture		
Hawai'i's Environment		
Tourist Lifestyle		
Tourist Economics		
Effects of Tourism		

"From a Native Daughter: Colonialism and Sovereignty in Hawai'i"

Haunani-Kay Trask

Excerpted and reprinted from *From a Native Daughter: Colonialism and Sovereignty in Hawai'i* by Haunani-Kay Trask (Monroe, ME: Common Courage Press, 1993); rev. ed. (Honolulu: University of Hawai'i Press, 1999).

I am certain that most, if not all, Americans have heard of Hawai'i and have wished, at some time in their lives, to visit my Native land. But I doubt that their history of how Hawai'i came to be territorially incorporated, and economically, politically, and culturally subordinated to the United States is known to most Americans. Nor is it common knowledge that Hawaiians have been struggling for over twenty years to achieve a land base and some form of political sovereignty on the same level as American Indians. . . . But despite all of this, . . . five million Americans will vacation in my homeland this year and the next, and so on into the foreseeable capitalist future.

Just five hours away by plane from California, Hawai'i is a thousand light years away in fantasy. Mostly a state of mind, Hawai'i is the image of escape from the rawness and violence of daily American life. Hawai'i—the word, the vision, the sound in the mind—is the fragrance and feel of soft kindness. Above all, Hawai'i is "she," the Western image of the Native "female" in her magical allure. . . . Tourists flock to my native land for escape, but they are escaping into a state of mind while participating in the destruction of a host people in a Native place.

History

Before there existed an England, an English language, or an Anglo-Saxon people, our Native culture was forming. And it was as antithetical to the European developments of Christianity, capitalism, and predatory individualism as any society could have been.

The economy of pre-*haole* Hawai'i depended primarily on a balanced use of the products of the land and sea[1]. . . . The *'ohana* (family) was the core economic unit in Hawaiian society.

As in most indigenous societies, there was no money, no idea of financial profit from exchange. . . . In other words, there was no basis for economic exploitation in pre-*haole* Hawai'i . . .

The genius of mutually beneficial political system of pre-*haole* Hawai'i was simply that an interdependence was created whereby the *maka' ainana* [people of the land] were free to move their *'ohana* to live under *ali'i* [chiefs] of their choosing, while the *ali'i* increased their status and material prosperity by having more people living within their *moku* or domain. The result was an incentive for the society's leaders to provide for all their constituent's well-being and contentment. To fail to do so meant the loss of status for the *ali'i*.

. . . My people believed that all living things had spirit and, indeed, consciousness, and that gods were many and not singular. Since the land was an ancestor, no living thing could be foreign. The cosmos, like the natural world, was a universe of familial relations. And human beings were but one constituent link in the larger family. . . . Nature was not objectified but personified, resulting in an extraordinary respect for the life of the sea, the heavens, and the earth. Our poetry and dance reveal this great depth of sensual feeling—of love—for the beautiful world we inhabited.

When Captain James Cook stumbled upon this interdependent and wise society in 1778, he brought an entirely foreign system into the lives of my ancestors. . . . He brought capitalism, Western political ideals, and Christianity. Most destructive of all, he brought diseases that ravaged my people until we were but a remnant of what we had been on contact with his crew.

In less than a hundred years after Cook's arrival, my people had been dispossessed of our religion, our moral order, our form of chiefly government, many of our cultural practices, and our lands and waters. Diseases, from syphilis and gonorrhea to tuberculosis, small pox, measles, leprosy, and typhoid fever killed Hawaiians by the hundreds of thousands, reducing our Native population (from an estimated one million at contact) to less than 40,000 by 1890.[2]

In [1893], the "missionary gang" of white planters and businessmen plotted with the American Minister to Hawai'i, John L. Stevens, to overthrow the lawful Native government of our last ruling *ali'i*, [Queen] Lili'uokalani. . . . As they had rehearsed so many times before, the *haole* businessmen and their foreign supporters immediately organized themselves as a "Committee of Safety" to create a new, all-white regime and to seek immediate military help from Minister Stevens. Agreeing to land the Marines and to recognize the *haole* "Provisional Government," Stevens played out his imperialist role.

Confronted by the American-recognized provisional government, and facing an occupying U.S. military force across from her palace, Lili'uokalani ceded her authority—not to the provisional government but to the United States—on January 17, 1893.

As a result of these actions, Hawaiians became a conquered people, our lands and culture subordinated to another nation. Made to feel and survive as inferiors when our sovereignty as a nation was forcibly ended, we were rendered politically and economically powerless by the turn of the century . . .

Hawaiians continue to suffer the effects of *haole* colonization. Under foreign control, we have been overrun by settlers: missionaries and capitalists (often the same people), adventurers and, of course, hordes of tourists.

In Hawai'i, the destruction of our land and the prostitution of our culture is planned and executed by multinational corporations (both foreign-based and Hawai'i-based), by huge landowners (like the missionary-descended Castle and Cook—of Dole pineapple fame—and others) and by collaborationist state and county governments. The ideological gloss that claims tourism to be our economic savior and the "natural" result of Hawaiian culture is manufactured by ad agencies (like the state-supported Hawai'i Visitor's Bureau) and tour companies (many of which are owned by airlines), and spewed out to the public through complicitous cultural engines like film, television, and radio, and the daily newspapers. As for local labor unions, both rank and file and management clamor for more tourists, while the construction industry lobbies incessantly for larger resorts.

Despite our similarities with other major tourist destinations, the statistical picture of the effects of corporate tourism in Hawai'i is shocking:

Fact: Over thirty years ago, at statehood, Hawai'i residents outnumbered tourists by more than two-to-one. Today, tourists outnumber residents by six-to-one; they outnumber Native Hawaiians by thirty-to-one.

Fact: According to independent economists and criminologists, "tourism has been the single most powerful factor in O'ahu's crime rate," including crimes against people and property.

Fact: The Bank of Hawai'i has reported that the average real incomes of Hawai'i's residents grew only 1 percent during the period from the early seventies through the early eighties, when tourism was booming. The Census Bureau reports that personal income growth in Hawai'i during the same time was the lowest by far of any of the fifty American states.

Fact: More plants and animals from Hawai'i are now extinct or on the endangered species list than in the rest of the United States.

Fact: More than 20,500 families are on the Hawaiian trust lands' list, waiting for housing or pastoral lots.

Fact: Hawai'i has by far the worst ratio of average family income to average housing costs in the country. This explains why families spend nearly 52 percent of their gross income for housing costs.

Fact: Nearly one-fifth of Hawai'i's resident population is classified as near-homeless, that is, those for whom any mishap results in immediate on-the-street homelessness.

These kinds of random statistics render a very bleak picture, not at all what the posters and jingoistic tourist promoters would have you believe about Hawai'i.

. . . [T]he commercialization of Hawaiian culture proceeds with calls for more sensitive marketing of Native values and practices. After all, a prostitute is only as good as her income producing talents. The talents, in Hawaiian terms, are the *hula*; the generosity, or *aloha*, or our people; the *u'i* or youthful beauty of our women and men; and the continuing allure of our lands and waters, that is, or our place, Hawai'i.

The point, of course, is that everything in Hawai'i can be yours, that is, you the tourist, non-Native, the visitor. The place, the people, the culture, even our identity as a "Native" people is for sale. Thus, the magazine, like the airline that prints it, is called Aloha. The use of this word in a capitalist context is so far removed from any Hawaiian cultural sense that it is, literally, meaningless.

Thus, Hawai'i, like a lovely woman, is there for the taking. Hawaiians, meanwhile, have little choice in all this. We can fill up the unemployment lines, enter the military, work in the tourist industry, or leave Hawai'i. Increasingly, Hawaiians are leaving, not by choice but out of economic necessity.

. . . Now that you have heard a Native view, let me just leave this thought behind. If you are thinking of visiting my homeland, please don't. We don't want or need any more tourists, and we certainly don't like them. If you want to help our cause, pass this message on to your friends.

Notes

1. The word *haole* means white foreigner in Hawaiian. "Pre-*haole*" refers to the period before contact with the white foreign world in 1778.

2. David Stannard, "Disease and Infertility: A New Look at the Demographic Collapse of Native Populations in the Wake of Western Contact," *Journal of American Studies* 24:3 (1990): 325-50.

Chapter 12

Racializing the "Enemy":

Japanese Americans after 12/7/41 and American Muslims and Arabs after 9/11/01

Vivian Tseng

Through analysis of cartoon images (including those by Dr. Seuss), students analyze the racial construction of Japanese and Japanese Americans after the attack on Pearl Harbor on December 7, 1941 and of Muslims, South Asians, and Arab Americans after the attacks on the World Trade Center and Pentagon on September 11, 2001. Students view cartoons of Japanese and Arab Muslims and are challenged to analyze the use of particular imagery (i.e., exaggerated physical characteristics, animal images, etc.) to portray the "enemy." Portions of this exercise were adapted from a lesson plan entitled "Historical Lessons on Wartime and Race Relations" by the Ask Asia Society.[1] High school and college educators, community activists, and trainers can use this exercise to facilitate critical analysis of the images people encounter in their everyday lives. This exercise is particularly suitable for Asian American Studies courses at the introductory level and in specific areas such as history, war, and media.

Objectives

- To develop skills for analyzing racialized images in students' daily lives (i.e., in cartoons, billboards, magazines, movies, TV, etc).
- To understand *how* Japanese, Muslims, and Arabs were constructed racially— What images were used to represent them? How were facial and other physical features exaggerated? Which animals were used to represent the "enemy"?
- To understand *why* Japanese, Muslims, and Arabs were constructed racially— How did racialized images affect public opinion? Why were animal images used to represent the "enemy"? How did racialized images affect government policies?

Time

- Thirty to sixty minutes

Number of Participants

- From small seminar to large lecture classes

Materials Needed

- Cartoon images on PowerPoint, overheads, or slides; or educators can use paper handouts of cartoon images.

Background

Within hours after the September 11, 2001 (9/11) terrorist attacks on the World Trade Center and Pentagon, television news compared the attacks by Muslim fundamentalists to Japan's bombing of Pearl Harbor on December 7, 1941 (12/7). For Americans used to thinking of war as an event in distant lands, these two attacks shook their sense of safety and security here in the "homeland." During the months following both attacks, the public's conception of the "enemy" took on an increasingly racialized form. Japanese Americans, Arab Americans, Muslims, and South Asians were viewed as having particular racial characteristics, including physical and personality characteristics. This racial construction of the enemy fueled support of a war abroad and the erosion of civil liberties within the United States. After the bombing of Pearl Harbor, the United States declared war on Japan and 120,000 Japanese Americans were confined to internment camps.[2] After the 9/11 attacks, the United States declared a "War on Terror" and bombed two Arab and predominantly Muslim countries, Afghanistan and Iraq, and American Muslims, Arab Americans, and South Asians became the targets of increased hate crimes and racial profiling.[3]

Legal scholar Jerry Kang has argued that there were important lessons to be learned from Japanese American experiences after Pearl Harbor. He writes that "the more important lesson (from 12/7) . . . is not that wartime creates mistakes; instead it is that wartime coupled with racism and intolerance creates particular types of mistakes. Specifically, we overestimate the threat posed by racial 'others' (in WWII, Japanese Americans; today, Arab Americans, Muslims, Middle Easterners, immigrants, and anyone who looks like 'them')."[4] Scholars were not the only ones to respond to the similarities being drawn: Japanese American activists, such as Nikkei for Civil Rights and Redress in Los Angeles, perceived similar threats to civil liberties and quickly built alliances with the American Muslim community.

Racializing the Enemy

I embed this exercise within a section of the course on the social construction of race and the sociohistorical significance of particular stereotypes and caricatures (see also racial formation theory by Omi and Winant).[5] This exercise focuses on how the "enemy" is racially constructed during times of war and conflict, and how these constructions are used to bolster public support for war and to erode civil liberties. Both 12/7 and 9/11 attacks renewed questions as to "Who is an American?" and allowed White Americans to distinguish themselves from the racialized other.

After the bombing of Pearl Harbor, racialized images of Japanese as a treacherous, sly, and warlike enemy were evoked in propaganda posters and cartoons to bolster public support for war.[6] *Time*, for example, published an article entitled, "How to Tell Your Friends from the Japs" (December 22, 1941). The article depicted two Chinese and two Japanese men, with text contrasting the difference between Japanese enemies and Chinese "friends." Chinese and Japanese men were described using stereotyped physical features (i.e., shape of noses, height differences, gaits, etc.) and personality traits. Two months after the bombing of Pearl Harbor, President Franklin Roosevelt issued Executive Order 9066, which authorized the confinement of 120,000 Japanese Americans on the West Coast to internment camps. Japanese Americans were evacuated from their homes en masse without individual determinations of guilt. Although the United States was also at war with Germany and Italy, German and Italian Americans were never interned en masse. The war against Japan ended with the dropping of two atomic bombs on Hiroshima and Nagasaki, the only time in world history when nuclear weapons have been used against a foreign country.

After the terrorist attacks on 9/11, President George W. Bush declared a "War on Terror" that resulted in U.S. attacks on Afghanistan and Iraq. Political cartoons in U.S. newspapers depicted Muslims and Arabs as fanatical and uncivilized, again eliciting anger, scorn, and ridicule among Americans. There were sharp increases in hate crimes and racial profiling against Middle Easterners, Muslims, and South Asians in the United States.[7] Attorney General John Ashcroft detained over 1,000 "suspected" terrorists, most of them South Asian and Middle Eastern, and refused to reveal the names of those held and the specific charges against them. These actions were followed by broader-reaching and more systematic policies by the Immigration and Naturalization Service, which required boys and young men from the Middle East, Korea, and Africa to be part of a "special registration" process. In a similar vein, Congressman Howard Coble publicly justified the internment of Japanese Americans during World War II and made direct linkages to Arab Americans following 9/11. Representative Coble, who also served as Chairman of the Subcommittee on Crime, Terrorism, and Homeland Security, stated on a radio talk show that "Some [Japanese Americans] probably were intent on doing harm to us . . . just as some of these Arab Americans are probably intent on doing harm to us."[8]

Content-wise, this exercise teaches students about the racialized construction of Japanese and by extension Japanese Americans after 12/7 and of Arabs and Muslims and by extension American Arabs, Muslims, and South Asians after 9/11. Skill-wise, this exercise teaches students how to deconstruct and decode racialized images. In line with critical pedagogy, this exercise does not lecture students on race theory and the construction of race. Rather, it provides students with a set of stimuli (cartoon images) and asks *them* to analyze how and why the "enemy" is racialized during times of war and conflict.

Suggested Procedures

This exercise consists of three parts. First, it begins with the political cartoon depicting firefighters raising the U.S. flag at "Ground Zero," the site of the World Trade Center. This cartoon reproduces the historic photograph, by Joe Rosenthal, of U.S. soldiers raising the American flag in Iwo Jima. Second, students are shown cartoon images of Japanese during World War II and of Middle Easterners and Muslims following 9/11, and asked to critically examine how and why the two groups are racially constructed in the images. Students note that depicting Japanese, Arabs, and Muslims as animalistic dehumanizes them, creating feelings of anger, scorn, and superiority in the audience. Then, students are challenged to consider the impact of these images on public support for World War II, Japanese American internment, U.S. attacks on Afghanistan and Iraq, racial profiling, and hate crimes. Third, students are presented with Gallup Poll findings on public opinion of Japanese following 12/7 and of other public opinion polls of Arabs and Muslims after 9/11.

I recommended that instructors spend considerable time on *each* image, allowing students ample time to thoroughly digest each image and deconstruct it. For each image, I often repeat the same questions until an array of students have thoroughly deconstructed the images. After each discussion question below, I list responses students typically provide.

Historical Context: How Are 12/7/41 and 9/11/01 Connected?

Show: *Flag-raising at Ground Zero* (Figure 12.1)—Political cartoon of firefighters and police officers raising the U.S. flag after 9/11. This cartoon mimics the famous historical photo, "Flag-raising at Iwo Jima," which represents the U.S. victory in "the Pacific Theatre." The battle was very bloody; about one-third of all Marines who died in combat during World War II were killed in Iwo Jima. Even if students do not know the exact historical context for this photo, they often recognize the image. You can access this photo at www.iwojima.com.

Ask: What do these images represent? How do they make you feel about the United States? (i.e., pride in America, America won't be defeated, valor, courage, strength, etc.).

Show: *Jerry Kang (2001) quote* (Figure 12.2)—"The more important lesson (from 12/7/41) . . . is not that wartime creates mistakes; instead it is that wartime coupled with racism and intolerance creates particular types of mistakes." This is a useful segue into the next section, in which race is examined more explicitly.

Analysis of Cartoon Images: How and Why Is the "Enemy" Racialized?

Show: *WWII poster ("Warning! Our Homes Are in Danger Now") and quote* (Figure 12.3)—According to the National Archives, "public relations specialists advised the U.S. Government that the most effective war posters were the ones that appealed to the emotions." This poster seeks to evoke fear of the enemy with Germany and Hitler leering over the United States.[9]

The quotation (on the left side) is from the *Government Information Manual for the Motion Picture Industry* (produced by the Office of War Information). Read aloud, or have a student read aloud the quote.

Ask: What is depicted in this poster? Ask this repeatedly until the poster is thoroughly analyzed (i.e., Hitler and Japanese man hovering over the United States, animal imagery such as claw-like hands, apelike faces, bulging eyes, big teeth, etc.) Why would the Office of War Information suggest that "civilians must have the war brought home to them"? Why would that be important? (i.e., to elicit fear of the enemy, to get Americans to support the war effort, etc.) Why would the Office of War Information provide these instructions to the motion picture industry? Why target Hollywood? (i.e., to use Hollywood for propaganda purposes, movies can manipulate emotions, etc.) What tactics are used in the poster to bring the war home to Americans? What images does the artist use to make Americans feel the war is at their doorstep? (i.e., show Japan and Germany as menacing, hovering over the United States with knife and gun; this contrasts with the representation of the United States using a quaint row of homes at the bottom of the poster).

Show: *Political cartoons of Japanese following 12/7/41* (Figures 12.4 and 12.5).

Ask: What images are used to portray Japanese in these images? (i.e., monkeys and apes, vermin, demented psychopaths, slanty eyes, silly grins, buck teeth, pig nose) Why were these images chosen to represent Japanese? (i.e., to make less human, to dehumanize, to seem like they are laughing at us) What feelings are they meant to incite in you? What purpose does it serve to incite these feelings in the U.S. public? (i.e., humor, anger, scorn, feelings of superiority, etc.) How would feelings of anger, scorn, humor, and superiority in the public affect their support of the war? How would these images impact the public's perception of Japanese Americans? of the internment? (i.e., increases support for war, make people not care about them, etc.)

Discussion Points

Recap how racial images are chosen to represent Japanese and the impact these images have on the public.

- Animal images are used to dehumanize the enemy, to make Americans seem superior
- Dehumanization helps build public support for the war, public is less likely to question war and violence against "others"
- Racialization and dehumanization has an emotional impact on its audience; it creates feelings of anger, scorn, fear, superiority which can then be used to manipulate support for war and other government policies

Show: *Political cartoons of Arabs and Muslims following 9/11/01* (Figures 12.6 and 12.7)

Ask: What images are used to portray Arabs and Muslims in these images (i.e., monkeys and apes, bulging eyes, skinny and scrawny, turbans, unruly facial hair, camels, swords, demented psychopaths, frightened faces, dumb comments)? Why do you think these images were used (i.e., to make less human, to dehumanize, to make them seem less civilized than Americans, to make them seem dumb, crazy, vicious, to make Americans feel that they are superior)? What feelings are they meant to incite in you? What purpose does it serve to incite these feelings in the U.S. public (i.e., anger, humor, scorn, feelings of superiority, etc.)? How would feelings of anger, scorn, humor, and superiority in the public affect their support of the war? How would these images impact the public's perception of Arabs and Muslims? (Educators can also discuss INS Special Registration process for Middle Eastern immigrants, FBI, and other law enforcement surveillance of Middle Easterners, screening at airports, hate crimes, etc.) (i.e., increases support for war, make people not care about them, justifies differential/racist treatment of Muslims and Arabs because they are seen as less than Americans, etc.)

Implications: What Impact Do These Images Have on the U.S. Public?

Show: Public opinion polls pertaining to Japanese Americans after 12/7 and American Arabs and Muslims after 9/11 (Figure 12.8).

Discussion Points

How is history being repeated? What can be done to break the cycle of racialization and dehumanization? Discuss Congressman Howard Coble's (Republican—NC; chairman of House subcommittee on homeland security) statements defending Japanese American internment during a call-in radio show in which a listener suggested that Arabs in America should be interned.

Student Reactions

I generally find that students enjoy this exercise and that it provides some relief from difficult interpersonal discussions of racism, inequality, oppression, and power; but at times, there is some student resistance and defensiveness. A few students react with comments such as "People should lighten up," "It's just for fun," or "Don't take it so seriously." At these points, I find it beneficial to redirect and challenge students by asking them, "Why would it be important to take these images seriously? What impact do these images have collectively and over time? How might they contribute to hate crimes and racial profiling?" Better yet, it is helpful to redirect these questions to the class so that students with varying viewpoints are engaged in dialogue with one another, rather than solely between students and instructor.

At other times, students comment that "Everyone gets stereotyped. White people get stereotyped, too." This poses an opportunity for the entire class to discuss the implications of stereotyping and racism. For example, why didn't law enforcement racially profile young, white men after Timothy McVeigh was implicated in the Oklahoma City bombings? Why did initial reports jump to the suspicion that Middle Eastern terrorists were to blame? When white men are found to be guilty of domestic terrorism or other acts of violence, why aren't they profiled as a racial group? What societal forces allow it to happen to young men of color?

Variations

Community Panel: I have conducted this activity in conjunction with a panel created for a large, lecture class. The panel consisted of a Japanese American former internee, a Japanese American activist working to protect civil liberties after 9/11, a Filipino American activist, and Muslim student activists. This panel format with presentations, followed by questions and answers works well for a large lecture class. Possible topics for the panel include:

- Erosion of civil liberties during war: Japanese American internment, U.S.A. Patriot Acts I and II, INS special registration of Middle Eastern, Asian, African immigrants
- Hate crimes
- Racial profiling
- Student and community activism, coalition-building

Images of Asian Americans: Throughout my courses, I show different images of Asian Americans and ask students to deconstruct the images and their implications. Below are suggested images.

- *Time* article, "How to Tell Your Friends from the Japs" (December 22, 1941): racializes Japanese and Chinese as having particular facial and bodily features and personality characteristics
- *Time* cover, "Those Asian-American Whiz Kids" (August 31, 1987): racializes Asian Americans as nerds and geeks, posing with glasses, books, and computer
- Abercrombie and Fitch t-shirts of "Buddha Bash—Get your Buddha on the floor," "Wong Brothers—Two Wongs can make it White," "Pizza Dojo—Eat in or Wok out," "Wok-n-Bowl—Let the good times roll, Chinese food and bowling": use of humor in racializing Asian Americans (http://www.boycottaf.com)

Notes

1. Ask Asia Society, "Historical Lessons on Wartime and Race Relations," <http://www.askasia.org/teachers/Instructional_Resources/FEATURES/AmericasCrisis/Aftermath/RaceRelations.htm>.

2. Geoffrey S. Smith, "Racial Nativism and Origins of Japanese American Relocation," in *Japanese Americans from Relocation to Redress*, eds. Roger Daniels, Sandra C. Taylor, and Harry H. L. Kitano (Seattle: University of Washington Press, 1991).

3. Stephen Lee, "U.S. Intervention in the Middle East, the 'War on Terror,' and Domestic Hate Crimes: An Amerasia Journal Chronology," *Amerasia Journal* 27:3/28:1 (2002).

4. Jerry Kang, "Thinking through Internment: 12/7 and 9/11." *Amerasia Journal* 27:3/28:1 (2002): 45.

5. Michael Omi and Howard Winant, *Racial Formation in the United States from the 1960's to the 1980's* (New York: Routledge Press, 1986).

6. Smith, "Racial Nativism."

7. Lee, "U.S. Intervention in the Middle East."

8. Associated Press, February 5, 2003. "Coble Says Internment of Japanese-Americans Was Appropriate."

9. The National Archives, "Powers of Persuasion," <http://www.archives.gov/exhibit_hall/powers_of_persuasion/powers_of_persuasion_home.html>.

Recommended Resources

Cagle's E-mail and E-toons, <http://cagle.slate.msn.com/politicalcartoons/>.

Russell C. Leong and Don T. Nakanishi, "After Words: Who Speaks on War, Justice, and Peace?," *Amerasia Journal* 27:3/28:1 (2002).

Sut Jhally, *bell hooks: Cultural Criticism and Transformation* (Northampton, MA: Media Education Foundation, 1996), videorecording.

Figure 12.1 Flag-raising at Ground Zero, Marshall Ramsey, Jackson Mississippi, The Clarion Ledger

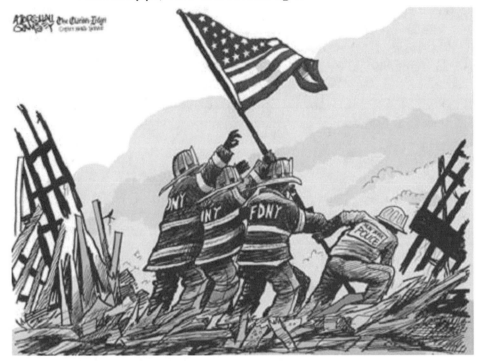

Reprinted with permission from Copley News

Figure 12.2 Jerry Kang quote *(Amerasia Journal, 2002)*

Racism and War:

Thinking through internment: 12/7 and 9/11
by Jerry Kang (2002)

> **"The more important lesson . . . is not that wartime creates mistakes; instead it is that wartime coupled with racism and intolerance create particular types of mistakes."**

Overheads/Handouts

Figure 12.3 WWII poster and quote

"Civilians must have the war brought home to them. Every individual must be made to see the immediacy of the danger to him. . . . He must be made to understand that he is an integral part of the war front, and that if he loses the war, he loses everything."

Government Information Manual for the Motion Picture Industry

Produced by the General Motors Corporation, 1942. NARA Still Picture Branch (NWDNS-44-PA-2314) Courtesy National Archives and Records Administration.

Figure 12.4 Political cartoons of Japanese following 12/7/41

Dr. Seuss Collection, University of California, San Diego.

Figure 12.5 Political cartoon of Japanese following 12/7/41

Dr. Seuss Collection, University of California, San Diego.

Figure 12.6 Political cartoons of Arabs and Muslims following 9/11/01

Daryl Cagle, Slate.com.

Overheads/Handouts

Figure 12.7 Political cartoons of Arabs and Muslims following 9/11/01

Courtesy Bruce Plante, *Chattanooga Times Free Press.*

Figure 12.8 Racializing the "Enemy": Public Opinion following 12/7 and 9/11

Gallup Polls following 12/7/41:

Percentage of Americans that think each adjective describes Japanese

- Sly   63%
- Treacherous 73%
- Warlike   46%

Various Polls following 9/11/02:

Percentage of Americans that support the following:

- Would be more suspicious of people they *think* are of Arab descent   46%
- Favor requiring people of Arab descent to undergo special, more intensive security checks when flying on American planes   60%
- Believe that Arabs living in this country should be put under special surveillance as the Japanese Americans were following Pearl Harbor   32%

After September 11, 2001:
An Asian Pacific American Perspective

Sin Yen Ling
Asian American Legal Defense and Education Fund

Reprinted with permission from the *Backlash: Final Report, 2001 Audit of Violence Against Asian Pacific Americans by the National Asian Pacific American Legal Consortium.*

The September 11, 2001 attacks transformed New York City into a war zone and a hotbed of hate violence, racial profiling, and police scrutiny of foreigners perceived to be terrorists. In the disorder following the collapse of the World Trade Center, emergency workers dug through the rubble for survivors, and relatives searched for loved ones at makeshift medical triage sites. Lower Manhattan was quarantined, and access to major bridges and tunnels was prevented or limited. Against this backdrop, South Asians, Arabs, and Muslims were pulled out of their cabs, beaten, and shot at.

In the months that followed, the impact of September 11 on South Asian American working-class and immigrant communities was tremendous, as many stayed home in fear. Some who ventured outside the relative safety of their homes were chased down by drivers shouting,"I am doing this for my country!" In one incident, subway riders stood by and watched as a Bangladeshi American rider was beaten senseless.

School attendance fell among South Asian, Muslim, and Arab students in the New York City public school system. Students going to school were pelted with rocks, but the New York City Board of Education did not initially acknowledge the violence. South Asian American storeowners in Richmond Hill, Jackson Heights, Flushing, and Floral Park received death threats, and their stores were vandalized with Molotov cocktails. Mosques and temples were also targeted with hate crimes. Members of the Sikh American community, perceived to be Arab because of their dress, were singled out in attacks in New York and elsewhere. Some seeking assistance were met with non-responsive police officers or were told, "It's petty, and they have men busy digging down at the World Trade Center." As law enforcement failed miserably to address the needs and fears of the victims, the community protected itself by draping the American flag in store windows, affixing stickers saying "Proud to be an American and a Sikh" to their cars, and even using fabric with flag prints for their turbans. Some in the South Asian community displayed the flag to deflect hate, while others displayed it proudly as a patriotic gesture.

As President Bush denounced racial violence, his administration mounted a snowball campaign that eroded the civil rights of Arab Americans, South Asian Americans, Muslims, and Sikhs. Local, state, and federal laws passed in response to the attacks validated aggressive racial and immigrant profiling, by which South Asian men were subjected to illegal interrogations and arrests without depositions.

The National Guard and the New York Police Department stopped and questioned Arab Americans, South Asian Americans, Muslims, and Sikhs inquiring as to immigration status and personal background and demanding papers proving citizenship. In one incident, NYPD officers asked all passengers on a train in Queens to evacuate, except two South Asian men carrying black bags. The two were searched and asked to raise their pant legs so that their socks could be patted down.

In Brooklyn and Queens, the FBI and INS raided communities largely populated by

Additional Reading

South Asian Americans, Arab Americans, Muslims, and Sikhs. Without search warrants, homes were searched and personal property confiscated. Undocumented men were brought to county jails and correctional facilities in the New York metropolitan area, where some sat for weeks without being charged for any crime. The detainees were questioned thoroughly by INS officials and asked to disclose information about relatives in the United States. In some cases, the detainees were transferred to another state in the remote Midwest. INS refused to notify attorneys of the transfers, and the detainees were not informed until the early morning of their long drive and plane ride.

In November, Attorney General John Ashcroft ordered local police departments to assist in the questioning of 5,000 immigrants of South Asian and Arab descent. The government rounded up Arab American, South Asian American, Muslim, and Sikh men between eighteen and thirty-three who had recently entered the United States on visas and who had no connection to terrorist or criminal activities. In the New York City area, eighty-six interviews were conducted. Although the interviews were "voluntary," the local police were ordered to go to the homes of interviewees who could not be reached by phone. Some of those interviewed spoke to federal agents without legal representation. Along with the detention of thousands of Arab Americans, South Asian Americans, Muslim Americans, and Sikh men, the government's action amounted to an unjust roundup and racial profiling.

Some secondary issues flowing from September 11 also affected the city's Asian Pacific American community. In the initial months, the media coverage focused on disaster assistance to Battery Park City (which bordered the World Trade Center) but ignored Chinatown and the Lower East Side, with its large Chinese and Latino populations. Chinatown, a major tourist attraction located two miles from the WTC and home to 100,000 residents, was paralyzed as police denied access to visitors and cars. Caregivers without proper identification could not attend to the elderly living on certain streets. Parts of Chinatown lacked phone lines for months. Small-business revenue declined between 30 and 70 percent, and there were layoffs, capacity reductions, and shutdowns, especially in the important garment industry that employs more than 10,000 workers. Drawing the eligibility zone for most relief at Canal Street left half of Chinatown unaccounted for. In addition, Chinatown residents breathed noxious fumes drifting north from the World Trade Center, and the government revealed little to the public about the toxicity levels.

Located just north of "Ground Zero," the Asian American Legal Defense and Education Fund relocated to a temporary midtown office and immediately fielded complaints of hate violence against Asian Americans across the nation. On September 15 and 22, AALDEF convened emergency community meetings of over 300 concerned groups to address the anti-Asian backlash and the need for a broad-based response. We spun off working groups to develop a unified response to the backlash and to plan community outreach, education/youth organizing, media outreach, and legal support.

Additional Reading

Teaching about Hindus and Muslims in the United States of America:
"And all they will call you will be deportee"

Amir Hussain

This activity is designed to facilitate discussions of both Hinduism and Islam. For courses on world religions that include a section on Hinduism, this activity serves as a background to the discussion of the caste system. For courses on world religions that include a section on Islam, this activity serves as a background to the discussion of Muslim minority communities. In both instances, the activity also helps in any discussion of class and societal hierarchies in North America. The activity could be used in a senior level high school class or in lower or upper-division college courses that deal with Hindus or Muslims.

Objectives

- To help students understand about societal divisions in North America.
- To understand divisions in Hindu societies and compare those divisions to North American societies.
- To study about Muslim experiences as members of minority religious communities.
- To help students think both empathetically and critically about Hindus and Muslims as well as themselves.
- To learn about the struggles of Latinos in North America and to connect those struggles to other communities.
- To learn about the work of Woody Guthrie, one of the most important American songwriters of the past century.

Time

- Thirty-five minutes
  - Seven minutes to read the handout

- Five minutes to listen to the song
- Three minutes to write a short response to the handout and song
- Twenty minutes for class discussion.

Number of Participants

- Six to sixty students

Materials Needed

- Handout of AP news story and lyrics to Woody Guthrie's song
- Music only or video and music recording of Woody Guthrie song (I use a videotape entitled *A Vision Shared: A Tribute to Woody Guthrie and Leadbelly*, from CBS Music Video Enterprises, 1988)
- Equipment to play music CD, tape, or video

Background

Most Americans know little of two of the largest religions in the world: Hinduism and Islam. I teach undergraduate courses on Islam and world religions at a large public university in Southern California. Many of my students come to my classes with negative stereotypes associated with Hindus and Muslims. Since September 11, 2001, they have come with even more negative assumptions about Muslims.

Hinduism is an almost exclusively Asian religion. It is sometimes surprising to people that Islam is also largely an Asian religion. The countries with the largest populations of Muslims are Indonesia, Pakistan, India, and Bangladesh. Hinduism and Islam are also American religions, with substantial communities in North America. In fact, according to the 2001 Census of Canada, Islam is the second largest religion in Canada (behind Christianity). Islam may well also be the second largest religious tradition in the United States.

In North America, there are major Hindu temples in Penn Hills, Malibu, Kauai, Aurora, and Atlanta, and smaller temples in various cities and towns. Since Hinduism is not a unitary tradition, there are many Hindu identities in North America and elsewhere. Some temples are dedicated to Vishnu, others to Shiva, and others to various Hindu gods and goddesses. Some Hindus consider themselves to be monotheists (seeing the various gods and goddesses as manifestations or incarnations of one divine reality), while others view themselves as polytheists. There is no one way to be Hindu. The major caste divisions in Hinduism are *brahmins* (seers), *kshatriyas* (administrators), *vaishyas* (craftspeople), and *shudras* (unskilled laborers), as well as those who fall outside the system (untouchables).

North American Muslims are split into three main ethnic divisions. The majority (about 35 percent) of North American Muslims are South Asian. Approximately 33 percent are Middle Eastern, and some 25 percent are African American. About 70 percent of North American Muslims are Sunni, while 30 percent are Shi'i. There are also various Sufi (mystical) communities throughout North America. Muslim immigration to North America increased with the changes in immigration laws of the late 1960s and early 1970s in Canada and the United States. Muslims in America run the gamut from educated professionals to working class laborers.

South Asians in general (and Hindus and Muslims in particular) have often been marginalized in the United States and Canada. They are members of ethnic, linguistic, and religious minority communities. The differences among South Asian communities were historically ignored in North American society, and groups as diverse as Sikhs from the Punjab, Tamils from South India, and tribal peoples from Northern Pakistan were lumped together under the racial epithet "Paki." As a boy growing up in Toronto in the 1970s, I still vividly remember the racist bumper stickers that I saw on some cars, "Keep Canada Green. Paint a Paki." South Asians, being brown, were constructed as "nonwhite" and discriminated against.

I use the assignment outlined below to teach about both Hindus and Muslims. In the section of my world religions class on Hinduism, we discuss the caste system. Officially, caste has been outlawed by the Indian government. Unofficially, it is still a very powerful force in Indian society. Before we discuss caste in Hinduism, I ask my students to think about caste and other divisions within American society. To facilitate this discussion, I give them the attached handout. The first part tells the story of the deaths of immigrants trying to illegally cross the Mexico-U.S. border. The second part gives the lyrics to a song by Woody Guthrie, "Deportee (Plane Wreck at Los Gatos)." I will then play a recording or a videotape of the song. The song and article encourage students to examine the divisions in American societies. After we have done this, we can then talk about the divisions in Hindu societies.

In my introduction to Islam class, I use this assignment to talk about the vision of Islam as an "alien" religion and of Muslims as an "alien other." This occurs, for example, in countries as diverse as India and the United States, where Muslims are stereotyped as foreign invaders. We use this assignment to talk about who "belongs" in society and who doesn't, who is regarded as a person and who isn't. Since I teach at a university where a large number of students are Latino, this assignment has great relevance to them. It is this connection of experiences, among several different cultures, that I find to be a very powerful learning experience.

Hindus and Muslims often have had common experiences with Latinos in the United States. All three groups (as well as others, of course) are stigmatized as immigrants who are brown and do not speak English. They are seen as "foreigners who take away jobs from (White) Americans." What is conveniently forgotten is that their labor is needed. Agriculture in California, for example, depends on a continuing supply of migrant labor. And often it is South Asian doctors who work in rural areas where "American" doctors are in short supply. Perhaps it is because our labor is needed that it is devalued by those in positions of power and authority.

With the terrorist attacks on September 11, 2001 came a sharp rise in hate crimes against Muslims, Arabs, and those who "looked the part." These hate crimes were documented by the Council on American-Islamic Relations (CAIR). In fact, the first person killed in a hate crime following September 11 was a Sikh. In the fall of 2003, Sikh taxi drivers became the targets of hate crimes and killings. Following the attacks, a national registration program was created in the United States for men who were visitors from several Muslim countries. As a result of this program, many men were imprisoned on visa technicalities, while others left the United States to seek asylum in Canada. That registration program was replaced with a new system at the end of 2003. Many Americans have protested the U.S. Patriot Act, which was rushed through Congress following the attacks, as an instrument to threaten the status of civil rights for all Americans.

Fortunately, many Muslims in the United States (who were innocent of any terrorist activity and were themselves threatened by the terrorist attacks) received support and sympathy from other Americans. The first group to stand alongside Muslim Americans was Japanese Americans. During World War II, Japanese Americans were placed in internment camps, even though the vast majority of them were loyal Americans. This support was heartening to American Muslims. Another venue of support was Cornerstone Theater, which produced a play about the Muslim communities in Los Angeles (*You Can't Take It With You: An American Muslim Re-mix*) in October 2003.

Following the attacks, many Muslims took the opportunity to speak to other people about Islam and Muslim life. They spoke in private homes and workplaces, as well as in public settings such as schools, community centres, mosques, synagogues, churches, etc. However, due to the backlash and hate crimes, many other Muslims did not want to be identified as Muslims. There was a decrease in attendance at some mosques, and a marked decline in contributions to Muslim charities, three of whom had their assets frozen amid allegations that they gave funds to terrorist organizations.

It is important to remember that a great many South Asians (both Hindu and Muslim) immigrated to America precisely because they wanted to live in a pluralistic and democratic society where they could succeed on their own merits. Abraham Verghese describes with his characteristic brilliance the situation of a young Indian intern seeking a visa to come to America. When asked by the visa officer the real reason why he wants to come to America, the intern speaks the following words, which could easily come from the mouths of countless American Muslims and Hindus:

Vadivel, who had held on to his American dream for so long that he could speak with the passion of a visionary, said, "Sir, craving your indulgence, I want to train in a decent, ten-story hospital where the lifts are actually working. I want to pass board-certification exams by my own merit and not through pull or bribes. I want to become a wonderful doctor, practice real medicine, pay taxes, make a good living, drive a big car on decent roads, and eventually live in the Ansel Adams section of New Mexico and never come back to this wretched town, where doctors are as numerous as fleas and practice is cutthroat, and where the air outside is not even fit to breathe." The consul gave him a visa.[1]

It is important to remember that the vast majority of South Asians in North America are immigrants or the children of immigrants. They—we—came to North America because of the opportunities that were available here and not, for whatever reason, in the country of origin.

Suggested Procedures

I give my students a packet of readings at the beginning of the semester. Included is the handout at the end of this lesson plan. When we get to the section on Hinduism in my world religions class, we discuss the caste system. This is done after introducing the students to India and after a discussion of the beginnings of Hinduism. I find it important for students to discuss societal hierarchies and divisions in American society, before discussing divisions within Hindu societies. In the class period before we do this activity, I ask the students to read the handout. Some of them will have done so when we begin this exercise, others will not.

1. I give the students about five to seven minutes to read the attached handout.
2. I play them a video recording of Arlo Guthrie and Emmylou Harris singing the

Woody Guthrie song, "Deportee." The video is introduced by Bruce Springsteen, who talks about how Woody worked towards a world where there was less hatred and oppression. Arlo Guthrie (Woody's son) then introduces the song and explains how his father came to write it after hearing on the radio about the deaths of Mexican migrants, who were referred to only as "deportees." This takes about five minutes.

3. I ask the students to begin writing their reactions to the story and video. In this class, my students keep learning journals, and I tell them that they might discuss this issue further in their journals. But the point of this exercise is to get them to write their thoughts and reactions for only one or two minutes. I find that this increases the amount of discussion that will follow. I also ask students to think about divisions in American society, and if there are any people who fit outside of those societal divisions, who are marginalized or outsiders. This takes about three minutes. Some possible framing questions are: a) Is there a caste system in America? b) Are there people that we don't consider as "people"? If so, who are they? c) Are there societal divisions in American society? If so, what are they? d) Do some people have more rights than others in American society?

4. For twenty minutes, we discuss the story and video. Many students identify class distinctions in America. They often identify the homeless, the disabled, the mentally ill, migrant workers, prisoners, and others as people that fall outside the lines, and are often not considered as people. Most students see hierarchies in American society, whether they are based on class, gender, race, sexuality, etc. Sometimes, there is disagreement about divisions in American society. Very few claim that there are no divisions and that anyone can succeed in America. Other students will often challenge these claims. This makes for a very interesting discussion among students, and my job is usually to moderate that discussion. I make it clear that the caste system in Hinduism is not the same as the class system in America, but that before we look at one society, we need to properly understand our own. Since many of my students are Latino, this assignment has great personal relevance to many of them.

Variations

I use this same exercise in my introduction to Islam in class. In that class, the last third of the course is spent on the modern phenomenon of Islam. In that section, we discuss the experiences of Muslims as members of minority religious communities in countries such as India, England, Canada, and the United States. In many of those countries, Muslims have been stereotyped as a species of alien outsider. I do the exercise in the same way, except that we use our discussion of American society as a bridge to understanding the experiences of Muslims.

Notes

1. Abraham Verghese, "The Cowpath to America," *The New Yorker*, June 23 and 30, 1997, 74-7.

Recommended Resources

The syllabi for all of my courses and other resources are given on my web page, www.csun.edu/~ah34999/.

The Woody Guthrie Foundation and Archives is on the web at http://www.woodyguthrie.org.

The best web page for the academic study of Islam is www.uga.edu/~islam/.

A good page for Hinduism is www.clas.ufl.edu/users/gthursby/rel/hinduism.htm.

The reading on Hinduism for my world religions course is Vasudha Narayanan, "The Hindu Tradition," in *World Religions: Eastern Traditions*, 2nd edition, edited by Willard G. Oxtoby (Toronto: Oxford University Press, 2002). The reading on modern Islam for my introduction to Islam course is Omid Safi, ed., *Progressive Muslims: On Justice, Gender, and Pluralism* (Oxford: Oneworld Publications, 2003). Other helpful books are:

Michael M. J. Fischer and Mehdi Abedi, *Debating Muslims: Cultural Dialogues in Post Modernity and Tradition* (Madison: University of Wisconsin Press, 1990).

Christopher John Fuller, *The Camphor Flame: Popular Hinduism and Society in India* (Princeton: Princeton University Press, 1992).

Yvonne Yazbeck Haddad and Jane I. Smith, eds., *Muslim Minorities in the West: Visible and Invisible* (Walnut Creek, CA: AltaMira Press, 2002).

Violence Raises Tensions, Stakes Along U.S.-Mexico Border

Pauline Arrillaga, Associated Press Writer
August 19, 2000

Brackettville, Texas: The first shot struck near his right foot, kicking up a spray of dirt as Javier Sanchez ran for his life through a thicket of cedar and sage. When the second shot rang out, he looked back to see his companion fall.

Sanchez took cover in the brush. The old man with the gun lit a pipe and sat down for a smoke. A few hundred feet from where Sanchez hid, Eusebio de Haro lay bleeding in a clump of cactus—shrieking in pain, pleading for water.

Water was all they had wanted in the first place.

According to investigators and the story Sanchez recounted for lawyers, he and de Haro had hiked nearly two days to this isolated homestead 45 miles north of the border. The day before had been 105 degrees. While the temperature had dipped, the men were tired and thirsty, their water jugs almost empty.

"Excuse me, please," Sanchez had called out to the house trailer, an oasis in this arid patch of South Texas range. A woman came to the door. And in his best English, Sanchez implored: "Could we get some water?"

But the woman refused. Instead, she cried out to her husband: "Call the Border Patrol!" Sanchez and de Haro took off down the road; the couple followed in their truck. When they spotted the two men, they got out and ordered them to sit tight; the Border Patrol was on its way.

That's when Sanchez spotted the gun and fled.

Hiding now in the brush, Sanchez saw the woman approach de Haro, who begged for help. She suggested he stick his finger in the bullet hole to stop the bleeding.

Five minutes passed. Ten. Twenty. Finally, de Haro fell silent.

Sanchez crept away. The next day, when he turned himself in, authorities confirmed what he'd known in his heart: In that clump of Texas cactus, Eusebio de Haro had bled to death.

The shooter claimed self-defense, but authorities dismiss that. De Haro, they note, was shot in the back of the leg as he ran.

Investigators call the slaying of de Haro on May 13 an isolated incident in a region where landowners are so used to illegal immigrants they sometimes leave water out so their livestock tanks aren't drained.

Isolated, even though de Haro was the third immigrant shot by South Texas residents since November. One of them, a 16-year-old boy, also died, and the shooter was charged with murder.

Isolated, even though seven white youths are accused of beating and using a pellet gun to wound five elderly migrant workers last month in San Diego.

Handout

Isolated, even though armed Arizona ranchers have detained trespassing immigrants.

To immigrant rights advocates, de Haro's death was yet another example of how treacherous the journey north has become. On top of the usual risks of extreme temperatures, drowning, and unscrupulous smugglers, migrants face a growing threat of vigilantism.

"There's a climate of violence that's being created by the presence of armed agents, infrared sensors, helicopters with night-vision scopes and guns—a real sense from the U.S. government that there's actually a war being waged," says Sasha Khokha of the National Network for Immigrant and Refugee Rights. "It's very easy, then, to imagine immigrants as the enemy."

Some 8,270 Border Patrol agents stand guard over the 2,000-mile boundary between the United States and Mexico. That's a 122 percent increase from six years ago, when the government announced a plan to block traditional crossing routes.

Droves of agents and equipment were shipped to the most popular immigration corridors: El Paso; San Diego; Nogales, Ariz.; and Brownsville, Texas. While traffic dropped in those areas, it increased in more remote places such as El Centro, Calif.; Douglas, Ariz.; and Del Rio, Texas—places not only more dangerous because of their rugged landscapes but also not used to the onslaught of illegal crossers.

In Douglas, the Border Patrol apprehended an average of 147 immigrants daily in 1995. That's risen to 729 people daily, and Douglas is now the nation's busiest illegal crossing route. Empty water jugs litter ranches, fences have been cut, cattle slaughtered for food.

Since October, the Border Patrol has documented 32 cases of Arizona residents detaining illegal crossers, sometimes at gunpoint.

"When I see 'em on my place, you betcha I round 'em up and call the Border Patrol," says Roger Barnett, who patrols his 22,000-acre cattle ranch in Douglas with a sidearm. Barnett alone has detained more than 1,000 immigrants in the past year.

In Arizona, citizens can detain trespassers but may not point guns or use force unless they fear for their lives. No Arizona ranchers have faced charges for holding immigrants, local law officers say. Even when a rancher allegedly pointed his gun, the migrants declined to press charges.

The law varies from state to state, however. In Texas, such detentions could be considered false imprisonment, says Jim Harrington of the Texas Civil Rights Project. Citizens "can call the Border Patrol if they want, but to take the law into their own hands is just part of this old cowboy mentality."

David Aguilar, a 22-year Border Patrol veteran who supervises most of the Arizona border, bristles at claims that the government's strategy has contributed to confrontations. He says sporadic violence between residents and migrants is inherent on the border.

Border residents aren't the only ones turning to arms. People-smugglers and some migrants have begun carrying weapons, too, says John Keeley of the Center for Immigration Studies in Washington, D.C.

More migrants died crossing the border in the first nine months of this fiscal year than in all of last year: 239 compared with 230, according to Border Patrol statistics. Most were heat-related deaths or drownings, but 14 are suspected homicides. The agency recorded no homicides the previous year.

Cases under investigation include two in which immigration officers shot migrants who allegedly assaulted them, as well as the killing of de Haro.

"I'm going to take a swing up north," de Haro told his father a year ago in April.

He was 22, the eldest of 14 kids in a family that worked hard to get by. As a boy, when drought didn't ravage the crop, he helped harvest corn on his family's ranch in the central Mexican town of San Felipe. He pitched in, too, at his dad's fireworks shop.

But de Haro dreamed of a better life across the border.

"When he told me he wanted to go, I didn't even argue," says his father, Paciano de Haro Bueno. "You earn as much up there in an hour as you do here in a week."

Near Dallas, de Haro found a job making cabinets, earning $8 an hour. He sent money home and to the mother of his infant daughter in Kerrville, Texas, where he had worked in construction. Whenever he called home, his siblings would stand in line—oldest to youngest—for the news from up north.

In January, de Haro's family spoke with him for the last time. Sometime after, he was deported from the United States and made the fateful decision to return.

By the time the sheriff and paramedics arrived at the shooting scene in Brackettville, de Haro was dead. Blood soaked the dirt beneath him. Cactus thorns protruded from his right cheek and shoulder. Cans of tuna fish, green beans, and cola, which he'd clutched when he fled, were scattered on the ground. In his pockets were two disposable razors, some papers, 53 American cents, and a couple of Mexican coins.

The autopsy confirmed de Haro was shot from behind. The bullet went through his left thigh, severing an artery.

Samuel Blackwood, a 75-year-old retiree from Arkansas, was initially charged with murder but later indicted on a downgraded charge of deadly conduct. He is free on bail while awaiting trial. His wife, Brenda, was not charged.

Neither Blackwood nor his attorney returned messages, but Kinney County Sheriff L. K. "Buddy" Burgess says the Blackwoods claimed the shooting was self-defense.

A $15 million wrongful-death lawsuit has been filed against the Blackwoods by de Haro's parents. George Shaffer, a lawyer investigating the case on the de Haro family's behalf, hopes to make an example of the Blackwoods.

"The fact that someone is here illegally," he says, "does not give you license to shoot them."

On July 31, the Border Patrol held a town hall meeting in Brackettville—part of a program that was in the works before de Haro died and became more relevant afterward. The Del Rio Border Patrol sector, which includes Brackettville, anticipates it will become the next immigration hot spot.

"Once Arizona's under control, you're still going to have 1 million people trying to go through, and they've got to go somewhere," says Carlton Jones, sector spokesman. The town hall meetings, he says, are meant to get agents and ranchers talking before any onslaught begins.

In Arizona, the Border Patrol has beefed up a special ranch response unit, and Aguilar says there have been no reports of ranchers detaining immigrants since May.

However, a Texas group is calling for armed volunteers to head to Arizona this fall. There, they'll help ranchers repair damage caused by trespassing immigrants.

And, if necessary, detain them.

Deportee (Plane Wreck at Los Gatos)

Words by Woody Guthrie; music by Martin Hoffman
TRO (c) Copyright 1961 (renewed) 1963 (renewed)
Ludlow Music, Inc., New York, NY

The crops are all in and the peaches are rotting,
The oranges are packed in their creosote dumps.
They're flying 'em back to the Mexico border
To take all their money to wade back again.

Goodbye to my Juan, goodbye Rosalita,
Adios mis amigos, Jesus y Maria.
You won't have a name when you ride the big airplane,
All they will call you will be "deportee."

My father's own father, he waded that river.
They took all the money he made in his life.
My brothers and sisters came workin' the fruit trees,
They rode the big trucks 'till they laid down and died.

Some of us are illegal, and others not wanted (*Somos ilegales, Y mal recibidos*)
Our work contracts up and we have to move on. (*Se a caba el contrato, Y de alli a caminar*)
Six hundred miles to that Mexican border,
They chase us like outlaws, like rustlers, like thieves.

Goodbye to my Juan, goodbye Rosalita,
Adios mis amigos, Jesus y Maria.
You won't have a name when you ride the big airplane,
All they will call you will be "deportee."

The skyplane caught fire over Los Gatos Canyon,
A fireball of lightnin' and it shook all the hills.
Who are these dear friends, all scattered like dry leaves?
The radio tells me, "They're just deportees."

Goodbye to my Juan, goodbye Rosalita,
Adios mis amigos, Jesus y Maria.
You won't have a name when you ride the big airplane,
All they will call you will be "deportee."

We died in your hills and we died in your deserts,
We died in your valleys, we died in your plains.
We died 'neath your trees and we died 'neath your bushes,
Both sides of the river we died just the same.

Goodbye to my Juan, goodbye Rosalita,
Adios mis amigos, Jesus y Maria.
You won't have a name when you ride the big airplane,
All they will call you will be "deportee."

Is this the best way we can grow our big orchards?
Is this the best way we can grow our good fruit?
To fall like the dry leaves and rot on my topsoil,
And be known by no name except "deportee."

Goodbye to my Juan, goodbye Rosalita,
Adios mis amigos, Jesus y Maria.
You won't have a name when you ride the big airplane,
All they will call you will be "deportee."

The Woody Guthrie Foundation and Archives is on the web at www.woodyguthrie.org.

Hate Crimes Immediately after September 11, 2001

National Asian Pacific American Legal Consortium

Excerpted from *Backlash: Final Report, 2001 Audit of Violence Against Asian Pacific Americans* by the National Asian Pacific American Legal Consortium.

NAPALC and its affiliates documented 507 bias-motivated hate crimes against Asian Pacific Americans in 2001, which represented almost a 23 percent increase from those documented in 2000. The increase in anti-Asian violence is attributable in part to the backlash after the tragic terrorist attacks on September 11, 2001. In the following three-month period, NAPALC and its affiliates documented nearly 250 bias-motivated incidents and two murders targeting Asian Pacific Americans. Below are selected incidents from the report.

September

Fullerton, California: A Sikh American couple was selling ice cream from their truck when they were chased and threatened by a man wielding a baseball bat. The assailant, who believed the couple to be of Afghan descent, was convicted of two felony counts during his trial but served only a brief jail sentence.

Anaheim, California: A Pakistani American man's home was burned to the ground. Earlier in the day, the victim had received threatening phone calls telling him to "Get the hell out of here and go back to your own country!" to which he had responded, "This is my country! Why don't you go somewhere else?" The Pakistani victim left for work, thinking he had only been the target of prank callers. When he later returned home, he found his house on fire.

Augusta, Georgia: A Pakistani American woman reported that two teenagers in a jeep tailed and blocked her car. The drivers gestured with their hands as if they were aiming imaginary pistols at the woman and said, "Go back to your country, wherever you came from." The woman, who had her eight-month-old son in the car, said she feared for her life and the life of her child.

Woodbridge, New Jersey: The two-year-old daughter of a South Asian American man was playing outside her apartment complex when a number of teenagers started to pelt her with stones while yelling racial slurs.

Cleveland, Ohio: A Sikh house of worship was the target of arson as bottles filled with gasoline were hurled into the temple's windows.

Tulsa, Oklahoma: A twenty-eight-year-old Pakistani American man was hospitalized after he was beaten and kicked by three men as he attempted to enter a gas station to visit a friend who worked in the station's convenience store.

Union Grove, Wisconsin: A male forty-seven-year-old Indian American convenience store operator was threatened by a man who came into the store and yelled at him, "You must go back to your country!" The perpetrator also asked the victim whether he knew people involved in the terrorist attacks on the East Coast and whether they conspired so he could raise gasoline prices. A man was arrested in relation to the case and charged with disorderly conduct as a hate crime.

Troy, Illinois: A female Indian American gas station owner was threatened by two men who claimed that they would firebomb her property. According to the men, she was "one of those fucking Arabs," and her property needed to be destroyed to "send a message to all the Arabs."

Somerset, Massachusetts: An Indian American-owned convenience store was set on fire when three teenagers threw a Molotov cocktail through the window. The teens were apprehended and charged with assault with the intent to murder, malicious and willful burning, and committing a hate crime. The local police chief vowed not to take the incident lightly, especially because there were people working in a pizza parlor attached to the store when the fire started.

Lower Merion, Pennsylvania: A male Pakistani American worker at a convenience store was threatened at gunpoint by an off-duty police officer. The officer pointed a gun at the victim in the parking lot of the store, threatened his life, and referred to him as "Arabic." The suspect was arrested after turning himself in to the local police. He was charged with aggravated assault, terrorist threats, ethnic intimidation, harassment, and reckless endangerment.

Tulsa, Arizona: An Indian American man was attacked by three men as he was leaving his apartment. A police spokesperson said that "three people jumped on him. They knocked him down and covered his eyes, then beat on him." After addressing him with an expletive, the men further threatened him, saying, "We are going to cut you like you cut our people."

Eagen, Minnesota: A South Asian American woman was walking to her car in the parking lot of a store when three male assailants came from behind and pushed her into a car. They then punched her in the stomach and elbowed her in the back. The assailants stated, "That's what you people deserve," before running away.

Frederick, Maryland: A Sikh American man was driving on a highway when he was targeted by a white male in a truck who pointed his finger towards the victim, pretending to shoot. The assailant then rolled down the window of his truck, pointed a rifle at the victim, and fired one shot before driving away.

October

Artesia, California: At their restaurant, which served primarily Islamic food, an Indian Muslim family received phone threats and accusations about being terrorists. Because of the hate calls, the owners hired a security guard to watch over the restaurant as a safety precaution. However, one Friday evening, the family returned home from their restaurant to find that their house was burned down. The victims were too scared to report the incident to the police.

San Diego, California: A thirty-nine-year-old South Asian man was walking on a street when he was hit on the head with a baseball bat by two white male assailants shouting ethnic slurs.

Detroit, Michigan: A Pakistani American man was threatened with death by an assailant over the phone. The assailant, who randomly selected the victim's name from a phone book because it appeared to be an "Arab-sounding" name, faced federal charges by the U.S. Attorney's Office.

Seattle, Washington: A forty-seven-year-old Sikh American man was attacked by a man with a cane in the lobby of his motel. The attacker shouted, "You still here? Go to Allah!" and knocked the victim unconscious with two blows from the cane. The victim required nine stitches as a result of his injuries, and the assailant was arrested and charged with second-degree assault.

November

Los Angeles, California: A white male attacked a Bangladeshi security guard while he was on duty outside of a mosque's entrance. When two African American Muslim women tried to enter the mosque, the suspect began to yell, "Terrorists! Go home to your own country!" When the security guard attempted to stop him from harassing the women, the suspect attacked the security guard and attempted to choke him. The assailant was placed under house arrest with an electric monitoring device and given three years on probation. In addition, he was fined $5,000, which was to be given to the mosque, and was required to compensate the victim for any expenses incurred from the attack.

Palermo, New York: An interfaith religious center, where many of the area's Sikhs meet to worship, suffered extensive damage in a fire set by unknown arsonists. State and federal authorities are investigating the incident as a possible hate crime. Temple officials have publicly stated their belief that the fire was a deliberate attempt to target Sikhs after the terrorist attacks.

Stone County, Mississippi: A twenty-year-old male Pakistani international student was detained on a visa violation following an INS raid on a Greyhound bus. While in custody at a correctional facility, the victim was stripped naked and brutally beaten by inmates who referred to him as "Bin Laden." The assault resulted in a ruptured eardrum, a broken tooth, and fractured ribs. The victim claimed that the officers at the correctional facility made no attempt to assist him despite his cries for help.

December

Northridge, California: A Sikh American man was beaten by two men with metal poles at his liquor store. The victim attempted to explain that he was Sikh and had no association with the accused terrorist, but the assailants continued with the assault.

Additional Reading

Chapter 14

On the Curses and Blessings of War:

Discussions for a Filipino American Experience Class

Allan Aquino

This classroom activity is framed around a student-moderated discussion of the Philippine-American War (1899-1902), a key event in the experiences of Filipino Americans. Once erroneously referred to as a mere "insurrection," the American military's invasion and settlement of the Philippines was a horribly genocidal campaign that nonetheless led to (what many consider) the archipelago's modernization. Thus, attitudes toward the war have often been polarized in terms of "curses" or "blessings," to borrow ideas from past classes. Awareness of the war is not common, and some believe it is due to historical repression or amnesia. While, arguably, the average American may have never heard of the war, it is all the more troubling that many Filipino Americans are unaware of the war and its potential influence upon their own lives.

Objectives

- To induce dialogue and debate on the adverse and beneficial effects—the perceived curses and blessings—of war.
- To nurture understanding of the roots and complexity of the Filipino American experience.
- To encourage practical critical thinking by having students, in addition to discussing the war, consider the current state of Philippine-American relations and contemporary Filipino American life, especially amidst the modern "War on Terrorism."
- To encourage students to organize their own methods of interactive learning.

Time

- Forty-five minutes to one hour

Number of Participants

- Twelve to sixty people (adaptable—see section on "Variations")

Prerequisites

- Pre-assigned readings for students (see Recommended Resources). In addition, student moderators, who will prepare discussion statements, should be pre-selected by the instructor and the students themselves. A viewing of the video *Memories of a Forgotten War* is highly recommended.[1]

Materials Needed

- A list of discussion statements prepared by the student moderators; examples will be outlined later.
- A chalk or dry-erase board.

Background

By the beginning of the twentieth century, the U.S. government, roused by the ideals of Manifest Destiny, annexed Spanish colonies during the aftermath of the Spanish-American War—namely Puerto Rico, Cuba, and the Philippines. The acquisition of the Philippines was secured after the "Mock Battle of Manila," a more or less staged conflict orchestrated to preserve Spanish dignity. Spain preferred to lose (on record, that is) its sole Asian territory to an emerging global power like the United States, rather than to what was deemed a primitive Filipino peasantry that had, by and large, succeeded in its struggle for independence.

It is believed that the United States was primarily interested in annexing the Philippines in order to secure a strategic military stronghold, a stepping stone to Asia. Contrary to many popular accounts, the Philippines was not merely purchased from Spain for twenty million dollars after the 1898 Treaty of Paris; this money was given to Spain as war reparations.[2] Most notably, America's acquisition of the Philippines was not without extreme consequences.

Philippine independence was verbally recognized by an intervening U.S. government during the Philippine Revolution (1896-1898). Soon afterward, however, U.S. officials declared the Philippines unfit for self-government. President William McKinley claimed divine inspiration behind his decision to "civilize" the Philippines through military intervention.[3] Thousands of American troops, many of whom were veterans of the so-called Indian Wars, began landing in the Philippines in June of 1898, the same month that Filipino leaders declared independence and elected the country's first president.[4] Violent conflicts between Filipinos and Americans began with the mindless shooting of Filipino *insurrectos* in June of 1899.[5]

Thus, the Philippine-American War began, ultimately resulting in the death of approximately a million Filipinos. The United States succeeded in pacifying Filipinos with a technologically advanced army; indeed, many military innovations like rapid-fire ammunition, long-range cannons, and high-caliber handguns were first put to use in the Philippines. And though the war was declared over in 1902, it is estimated that full-scale battles ensued through 1912, particularly the so-called "Moro Wars" against Filipino Muslims, who persisted in resisting the American occupation.[6]

Several accounts of American brutality against Filipinos during the "civilization" campaign are well documented. In order to make a clear statement against the futility of resistance, American General Jacob H. Smith (better known as "Howlin' Jake") was assigned by President Theodore Roosevelt to retaliate against a bloody rebellion on the island of Samar. "I want no prisoners," Smith declared to his troops. "I wish you to kill and burn; the more you kill and burn, the better it will please me."[7] Generals like Smith, thus, green-lighted widespread arson and public executions of any Filipino over the age of ten, as people of that age were feasibly "capable of carrying arms." As a message to Filipinos around Manila, the Philippines' capitol and political center, U.S. gunboats casually sailed down the Pasig River and engaged in target practice on suspected Filipino guerrilla camps.[8] American atrocities so shocked even the American public that an Anti-Imperialist League was established, and the most visible and vocal member was Mark Twain.[9] Likewise, African Americans stationed in the Philippines, sympathizing with Filipino oppression (described as an "affinity of complexion" by one black infantryman), often deserted, sometimes serving in the Philippine armed forces.[10] Nonetheless, through sheer attrition, the United States subdued an otherwise fledgling Philippine republic. For Filipinos, any public advocacy of independence was outlawed under the American regime.

After the Philippine-American war, however, the American government immediately established modern hospitals, industries, roadways, energy, sewage, and public transportation systems. Most notably, public schools were widely established.[11] Education in English was made accessible for Filipino men *and* women, unlike the earlier Spanish-era educational system that was reserved for the elite and strictly patriarchal *ilustrado* class.

Students in Filipino schools during the early twentieth century were taught by transplanted WASP teachers, known collectively as "Thomasites," and studied topics like the American constitution and the life and times of icons like George Washington and Abraham Lincoln.[12] In the eyes of many, the United States held true to its promise to "benevolently assimilate" the Philippines. Not surprisingly, the modern Philippine constitution, first drafted after World War II, closely follows the American model.

In 1903 the Pensionado Act was passed in a concurrence with the American postwar agenda, thereby creating an official exchange program for Filipino students to enroll in American universities. The intention of the *pensionado* program was to instill "American ways," which would later be reapplied and passed on in the Philippines. Thousands of Filipinos came to America, sponsored by the U.S. government, while some came as self-supported *paisanos*. From 1922 to 1939, the total number of Filipino students fluctuated from as low as twenty to as high as two thousand.[13] Other Filipinos came as laborers who were recruited by American businesses to replace excluded laborers from China, Japan, and Korea. Many of these laborers came to the United States to make ends meet (some of them being *paisanos*) and support their struggling families in the postwar Philippines. Inevitably, many Filipinos, then as now, chose to form communities in America, thereby establishing foundations for the Filipino American experience.

All in all, through the decades following the Philippine-American War, many Filipinos in the Philippines and the United States alike adopted a new language: American English. They easily adopted American etiquette, wardrobe, mannerisms, and many other cultural "isms." Filipinos learned to speak and write prolifically in English, an ability that, no doubt, aided their settlement in America. Notably, the urban landscapes of the Philippines today are teeming with facets of American pop culture, many of which are found in everyday lingo, music, fashion, and local businesses. (Coca-Cola and Starbucks Coffee are staple elixirs for modern Philippine youth.) *Taglish*, a blending of Tagalog and English, has been a common language among Filipinos of different ethnic backgrounds in the Philippines and in Filipino America.

Unlike other Asian immigrants, Filipino acculturation to American life is, by some, deemed a relatively smooth process. Notably, Filipino Americans, despite their large and quickly-growing populations (numbering second only to Chinese Americans) are relatively invisible in American life, seldom forming discernible "Filipinotowns" in major cities. It is said that the need for an ethnic "town" is not so much a necessity for Filipinos, as their American heritage has greatly aided their assimilation processes. In considering the perceived "curses" or "blessings" of this dynamic for Filipino Americans, one thing is certain: it is rooted in a century-old legacy of American military violence.

As mentioned before, in referring to America's wars in Asia during the twentieth century, many Americans only know about the wars in Japan, Korea, and Viet Nam. Sadly, the Philippine-American War is largely repressed or ignored in both the Filipino and American memory. In many U.S. history texts and courses, it is footnoted as a mere "Philippine Insurrection," thereby suggesting that the conflict was akin to a "sour grapes" tantrum against a dominant parent-figure.

Since the Philippine-American War, the Philippines has served as an ideal epicenter for the American military in Asia. Some argue that this dynamic has been most advantageous in providing protection for the Philippines against potentially oppressive forces in Asia, while providing the United States a strategic base of operations for its wars in Asia.

Currently, the U.S.-Philippine Visiting Forces Agreement (VFA), drafted in 1999, is hotly debated. Although the U.S. military cleared away its Philippine bases in 1992, the VFA reinstates American "intervention" rights in the Philippines under "justified" conditions. Hence, the VFA is all the more relevant to the post-9/11 world; the Philippines, after all, has been unceremoniously included in President Bush's blacklist of terrorist-harboring nations connected with the Al Qaeda network. The recent installment of U.S. troops in the southern Philippines to help combat the Abu Sayyaf terror cell bespeaks parallels with the "Moro Wars" of yesteryear.

Needless to say, post-9/11 policies have impacted contemporary Filipino American life. In 2002 alone, the Aviation and Transportation Security Act (ATSA), which federalized airport security jobs, forced many Filipino airport screeners, not yet eligible for naturalization, to lose their jobs. The Absconder Apprehension Initiative, designed to crack down on immigrants who had overstayed their visas, has led to mass deportations. Most recently, ten airport workers in Texas, supposedly linked with Abu Sayyaf, were arrested and detained.[14]

Amidst these concerns, the need to discuss the Philippine-American War today is all the more urgent, particularly for Filipino Americans.

Suggested Procedures

1. During the first or second week of a course, students should sign up for facilitation groups to moderate a discussion activity on one course topic. Sign-up sheets, photocopied for the instructor and each student, should include relevant contact information (i.e., e-mail addresses). Student moderators (as they will be referred to

hereon) should meet prior to their discussion date and consult with the instructor. Ideally, for a dialogue and debate on the Philippine-American War, about four moderators are needed: two to co-facilitate separate student teams (the dynamics of which will be explained in step 2), one to read and clarify discussion statements (to be explained in step 3), and one to record ideas raised by students (as explained in step 5).

2. At the beginning of the activity, the moderators instruct students to physically stand and assemble at one end (front or back) of the classroom as a single group. From then on, a series of provocative and open-ended statements—each prepared by the moderators—will be read one by one. After each statement, the students will react and reassemble as two separate teams as described in step 3. Every statement should be deceptively simple, sometimes bold or absurd by nature (depending on one's biases), and thematically linked to the Philippine-American War, the "Americanization" of the Philippines, and the Filipino American experience from past to present, particularly in the post-9/11 world. Examples of past discussion include the following:

   We need war in order to establish peace.

   The Philippine-American War was ultimately a great blessing for the Filipino people.

   If not for the Philippine-American War, the Philippines would have remained unstable and unfit for government.

   If the Philippine-American War never happened, the Philippines would not have modernized.

   Americanization has made Filipinos more socially acceptable than other Asians in American life.

   The U.S. military is a vital presence in the Philippines; how else can the country be saved from the threat of terrorism?

   The arrest, interrogation, and prosecution of Filipino Muslims are justified; anyone could be a terrorist?

   If not for the Philippine-American War, I wouldn't enjoy the life I have in America today.

   Since Filipino American students are typically legal residents or citizens of the United States, such statements have tended to be "pro-American" in tone, compelling them to consider all statements in the context of their own lives.

3. Each statement should be repeated or explained by the moderators, if necessary. After a single statement is read, each student must choose one of two sides of the classroom—respectively marked (on a chalk or dry-erase board) as "I agree" and "I disagree"—and move and stand on their chosen side. (As a guideline, past moderators have told students: "Ask yourself, 'Why do I agree or disagree?'") By now, the students are literally divided along ideological lines; while, at first, it may appear that the exercise could encourage antagonism or opposition, the ultimate purpose (which must be made crystal-clear even before the activity begins) is the sharing of ideas. Free expression, with appropriate consideration, should be highly encouraged.

4. For each statement there is no middle-ground or a "maybe" response; each student must choose a side and be willing to articulate the reasoning behind her or his choice. For time purposes, two or three students from both sides should be allowed to speak; it is best that a variety of students speak. In order to promote

participation, moderators are empowered to call upon any student (especially those who are quiet). Naturally, moderators, with the aid of the instructor, must make sure that all dialogues remain respectful, fair, and free of unnecessary conflict. Typically, by the time the activity is scheduled, the students will have some degree of rapport with each other. In order to maintain the freshness of the activity, moderators, on a given impulse, may personally support or play devil's advocate with any of their classmates' ideas. Whenever necessary, instructors should provide relevant insights or background information. In the unlikely instance that heated conflicts arise, the moderators and the instructor should tactfully intervene and remind the students that no class activity should ever be taken personally.

5. When time is called for the end of the activity (i.e., during the "wrap-up" minutes of a class session), the recording moderator should list on the board the general ideas gleaned from the discussion. During this time (or during a follow-up session, if necessary) the class should collectively examine these ideas and determine if they agree on any common themes, thereby illustrating that, despite differences in personal viewpoints, the students share an ideological common ground.

In past discussions, students have generally agreed that U.S. military intervention, in the Philippines or elsewhere, may not always be "justified," that war must only be a "last minute" necessity, and that events in the Philippines may have some degree of influence on the contemporary transnational-by-nature Filipino American community.

Variations

In a large class, the moderators may subdivide the class into smaller groups. For a past class containing more than sixty students, for instance, moderators divided the class into four separate groups, each with their own individual set of discussion topics and subfacilitators. In addition, moderators may exhibit visual aids (pertinent photographs, charts, etc.) and encourage students to share their reactions to the images. In a past discussion on the Philippine-American War, such a dynamic was framed around an old newspaper illustration depicting "Howlin' Jake" Smith executing young Filipino boys.

Notes

1. Camilla Benolirao Griggers and Sari Lluch Dalena, *Memories of a Forgotten War* (New York: Kawayan Films/Third World Newsreel, 2001), videorecording.

2. Teodoro Agoncillo, *History of the Filipino People*, 8th ed. (Quezon City, Philippines: Garotech Publishing, 1990).

3. William McKinley, "Remarks to a Methodist Delegation," in *The Philippines Reader: A History of Colonialism, Neocolonialism, Dictatorship, and Resistance*, eds. Daniel B. Schirmer and Stephen Rosskamm Shalom (Boston: South End Press, 1987).

4. Walter L. Williams, "United States Indian Policy and the Debate over Philippine Annexation: Implications for the Origins of American Imperialism," *Journal of American History* 66:4 (1980); Renato Constantino, *The Philippines: A Past Revisited (Pre-Spanish—1941)* (Quezon City, Philippines: Renato Constantino, 1987).

5. Eric Gamalinda, "Myth, Memory, Myopia," in *Flippin': Filipinos on America*, eds. Luis Francia and Eric Gamalinda (New York: The Asian American Writers' Workshop, 1996).

6. Luzviminda Francisco, "The First Vietnam: The Philippine-American War, 1899-1902," *Letters in Exile: An Introductory Reader on the History of Pilipinos in America* (Los Angeles: UCLA Asian American Studies Center, 1976).

7. Agoncillo, *History of the Filipino People.*

8. Francisco, "The First Vietnam."

9. Howard Zinn, *A People's History of the United States* (New York: HarperPerennial, 1995).

10. Willard B. Gatewood, *"Smoked Yankees" and the Struggle for Empire: Letters from Negro Soldiers, 1898-1902* (Fayetteville, AK: University of Arkansas Press, 1987).

11. Fred Cordova, *Filipinos: Forgotten Asian Americans* (Dubuque, IA: Kendall/Hunt Publishing, 1983).

12. Carlos Bulosan, *America Is in the Heart* (New York: Harcourt, Brace, and Company, 1946).

13. Emily Porcincula Lawsin, "A History of the *Filipino Student Bulletin*," *Filipino American National Historical Society Journal* (Seattle: FANHS Publications, 1996).

14. Filipino American National Historical Society (FANHS) and *Filipinas* Magazine, "Chronicle of a Continuing Journey," *Filipinas* (October 2003).

Recommended Resources

Stanley Karnow, *In Our Image: America's Empire in the Philippines* (New York: Ballantine Books, 1989).

Thomas Carter, *Land of the Morning: A Pictorial History of the American Regime* (Quezon City, Philippines: Historical Conservation Society of the Philippines, R.P. Garcia Publishing, 1990).

Filipinos and the "Negritos Americanos":
Empire and Racial Bonds

Allan Aquino

The U.S. government's demand for African American soldiers during the Spanish-American War led to the formation of all-black units in Cuba and the Philippines. From the outbreak of the Philippine-American War, however, black soldiers displayed considerable sympathy for the Filipino independence movement, identifying Filipinos as "kinsmen." Such tones of anti-imperialism compelled the U.S. War Department, in 1899, to question whether blacks should be sent to the Philippines at all. Thus, Filipinos admirably referred to African Americans as "Negritos Americanos," embracing them as "very much like ourselves, only larger."[1] ("Negritos" is a Hispanic-Filipino term referring to dark-skinned indigenous peoples like the Aetas of Luzon.)

Filipinos were generally called "niggers" by white soldiers, thereby distinguishing them from the "darkey troops." African American soldiers, quick to identify such racism, foresaw a grim, destructive future for Filipinos under the American regime. Excerpts from a letter sent by Sgt. Patrick Mason of the Twenty-fourth Infantry to the *Cleveland Gazette* (November 1899) revealed the moral dilemma of blacks in the Philippines:

> Dear Sir:
>
> I have not had any fighting to do since I have been here and don't care to do any. I feel sorry for [the Filipinos] and all that have come under the control of the United States. I don't believe they will be justly dealt by. The first thing in the morning is the "Nigger" and the last thing at night is the "Nigger." You have no idea the way these people are treated by the Americans here. . . . The natives are a patient, burden-bearing people.

As chronicled in Gatewood's collection of letters from black soldiers, John W. Galloway, another member of Patrick Mason's unit, recorded his conversations with natives, illustrating the "affinity of complexion" between blacks and Filipinos. An excerpt from his letter to the *Richmond Planet* (December 1899) has the following dialogue:

Ques. Do the Filipinos hold a different feeling toward the colored American from that of the white?

Ans. Before American occupation of the islands and before the colored troops came to the Philippines, Filipinos knew little if anything of the colored people of America. We had read American history in the general but knew nothing of the different races there. All were simply American to us. . . . Of course, at first we were a little shy of you [black soldiers], after being told of the difference between you and them [white soldiers]; but we studied you, as results have shown. Between you and him, we look upon you as the angel and him as the devil.[2]

Thus, many African American soldiers deserted.[3] Their desertions were "invariably of a different character" than those from white regiments; whites "deserted because [they were] lazy and idle," while blacks deserted "for the purpose of joining the insurgents," thereby raging against the principles of American oppression against nonwhite peoples.[4] In some cases, African Americans defected to the Philippine forces, training Filipinos to more effectively combat the white regiments. Of all such soldiers, the most famous was

David Fagan of the Twenty-fourth Infantry. He became a high-ranking Philippine officer, wreaking havoc on the American forces for two years.[5]

By 1903, after the "official" end of the Philippine-American War, about five hundred African Americans remained in the Philippines, often marrying Filipino women and establishing professional livelihoods.[6] A letter from Twenty-fourth Infantry member T. Clay Smith to the *Savannah Tribune* (October 1902) posited a belief that, in the midst of American racism, African Americans would do well to emigrate to the Philippines:

> Dear Sir:
>
> Several of our young men are now in business in the Philippines and are doing nicely . . .
>
> However, color prejudice has kept close in the wake of the flag and is keenly felt in that far-off land of eternal sunshine and roses. I think, everything considered, that the Philippines offer our people the best opportunities of the century and would advise emigration.[7]

Notes

1. Willard B. Gatewood, *"Smoked Yankees" and the Struggle for Empire: Letters from Negro Soldiers, 1898-1902* (Fayetteville, AK: University of Arkansas Press, 1987).

2. *Ibid.*

3. *Ibid.*

4. Stephen Bonsal, "The Negro Soldier in War and Peace," *North American Review* 186 (June, 1907).

5. Frederick Funston, *Memories of Two Wars* (New York: Scribners, 1914).

6. Gatewood, *"Smoked Yankees" and the Struggle for Empire.*

7. *Ibid.*

Chapter 15

Addressing Redress:
Japanese Americans' Reparations for Their Incarceration during World War II

Wayne Au

In the fall of 1990, Japanese Americans received reparations/redress, or repayment, from the U.S. government for losses suffered during their mass incarceration during World War II. Reparations is a highly inflammatory topic that raises complex historical and emotional issues of American injustice. Japanese American reparations presents profound implications regarding the "repayment" of African Americans for profits from enslavement or possibly the return of illegally acquired lands to Native Hawaiians and Native American tribes. This chapter, developed as a role-play, explores issues surrounding reparations. Further, this role play can be used to raise issues of "national defense" and "homeland security" as, similar to Japanese Americans after the bombing of Pearl Harbor, many Arab Americans were targeted following the Sept. 11, 2001 World Trade Center bombing. This activity is best suited for high school and college-age students and is ideal for courses in U.S. history, Asian American Studies, Ethnic Studies, civics/government, and African American Studies. Before using this role play, instructors should cover the incarceration of Japanese Americans, with particular emphasis on the wartime experiences leading up to, and hardships during, the incarceration and the constitutional rights and principles of democracy that were violated in the process.

Editors' Note: This role-play focuses on the role of the Japanese American Citizens League (JACL) in the redress movement. Two other community groups—National Coalition for Redress and Reparations and National Council for Japanese American Redress—also played leadership roles but are not included in this role play.

Objectives

- To familiarize participants with differing perspectives and issues surrounding the movement for Japanese American redress.
- To give participants an opportunity to come to their own conclusions regarding Japanese American redress and its potential implications for other U.S. communities.

Time

- Two forty-five minute sessions

Number of Participants

- Fifteen to fifty people (around thirty is recommended)

Materials Needed

- Role sheets for six groups (see handouts)
- A sign with the name of each role—large enough for other groups to read
- A set of "Getting into Your Role" sheets for all groups but the CWRIC group
- A specific "Getting into Your Role" sheet for the CWRIC
- Handout of "Japanese American Redress: What Really Happened" and questions

Background

redress—*n* 1. the setting right of what is wrong: *redress of abuses*. 2. relief from wrong or injury. 3. compensation or satisfaction for a wrong or injury. - *vt*. 4. to set right; remedy or repair (wrongs, injuries, etc.). 5. to correct or reform (abuses, evils, etc.). 6. to remedy or relieve (suffering, want, etc.). 7. to adjust evenly again, as a balance.[1]

Language is powerful. It is used to define how issues are framed, it sets the terms of debate and discussion, and it has an immense impact on how events are interpreted and understood. The language and terms used to describe, reflect upon, and analyze Japanese American incarceration have been struggled with and clarified greatly over the last fifty-plus years. In light of this, it is necessary to discuss some of the issues surrounding the terminology associated with the incarceration of Japanese Americans during World War II.

Japanese American: For this activity, I use the term "Japanese American" to describe persons of Japanese ancestry, both citizen and non-citizen, living in the United States.

U.S. Military Euphemisms: During the forced removal and incarceration of Japanese Americans during WWII, the U.S. military referred to it as an "evacuation" where "Japanese" were sent to "assembly centers" and later placed in "relocation centers." More correctly, Japanese Americans were "excluded" from the West Coast and imprisoned in "incarceration camps" surrounded by barbed wire fences and armed guards.[2] David Takami adds:

"Evacuation" was a government euphemism for the West Coast deracination of Japanese Americans, a word usually applied to removal of citizens for their own safety in time of flood, landslide, or other imminent danger. "Internment" technically applies to prison camps run by the U.S. Justice Department. . . . The distinction is critical: the internment of enemy aliens during a war has a basis in law—specifically the Alien and Sedition Acts of 1798—and it is governed by international accord in the form of the Geneva Conventions. The roundup and incarceration of American citizens had no legal precedent and singled out a race of people.[3]

Internment vs. Incarceration: Although "internment" is popularly used to describe the forced removal and imprisonment of all Japanese Americans, technically only non-citizen "enemy aliens" can be interned during times of war. It is more inclusive and technically correct to use the term "incarceration" or "mass incarceration" to describe the treatment of all Japanese Americans, citizen and non-citizen alike, who were imprisoned in camps.[4] Many articles still refer to the internment, and the official government Commission on Wartime Relocation and Internment of Civilians (CWRIC in this role-play) used the term "internment" to refer to everyone who was moved and imprisoned regardless of citizenship.

Before any discussion of redress can happen, it is necessary to understand the events surrounding and conditions of Japanese American incarceration during World War II. What follows is a brief summation of key events.

On December, 6, 1941, Japanese planes bombed Pearl Harbor, and on December 7, the Federal Bureau of Investigation began arresting Japanese Americans under the pretense of being a threat to national security. Within three months, on February 19, 1942, Executive Order 9066 was signed by President Roosevelt giving the U.S. government the power to exclude civilians from any area it chose. In March General DeWitt issued Public Proclamation #1 and began removing people from their homes. More than 110,000 Japanese Americans were forcibly moved and incarcerated in concentration camps. It must be noted that no Japanese American was convicted of committing espionage, treason, or terrorism during the war.

To understand the lasting impact of these events, one has to imagine being forced to close your business or be forced to resign from your job, put all of your things into no more than a few suitcases, leave your house—either selling everything or being lucky enough to have a trustworthy friend who could watch your property—be portrayed as a traitor, feel ashamed of your culture and yourself for not being considered "American" enough, and generally have your community physically and emotionally shattered.

It wasn't until January of 1945 that the war department announced that all exclusion orders be rescinded based on a Supreme Court ruling that "loyal" citizens could not be forcefully detained, and in 1948 President Truman signed the Japanese American Evacuation Claims Act providing $38 million to repay Japanese Americans for their losses. This amount covered only a small fraction of losses. Upon returning home, many were met with signs in shops that read "No Dogs and Japs Allowed" and often found it impossible to comfortably re-settle.

Japanese Americans were not the only people incarcerated by the U.S. government during World War II. Eight hundred and eighty-one Aleuts, who were U.S. citizens, were forcibly removed from their fishing villages by the U.S. military, only to return home later and find their villages virtually destroyed.[5] Additionally over 2,000 Latin Americans of Japanese ancestry from eleven countries, 84 percent from Peru, were forcibly incarcerated by the U.S. government in camps in Texas.[6] About 800 Latin Americans of Japanese ancestry were sent back to Japan for prisoner-of-war exchanges, and 900 were deported back to Japan.[7] At least 10,000 German Americans and 1,600 Italian Americans were incarcerated, moved or detained in some form.[8] There are key differences between the treatment of Japanese Americans and German and Italian immigrants. Unlike the Japanese Americans, people of German and Italian ancestry were detained and incarcerated on an individual, case-by-case basis. Aleuts and people of Japanese ancestry, however, were subjected to mass incarceration.[9]

The Redress Movement

The issue of redress for incarceration had simmered in different parts of the Japanese American community for a long time. Even as early as 1942, some individuals had written letters to the president protesting the incarceration and demanding something be done. These letters are sometimes seen as being the first attempts to obtain redress.[10]

There are competing stories about how the redress movement started, and by and large it seems that there were at least two main groups. Talk of redress had been tossed around the National Japanese American Citizens League (JACL) at least since 1970, but JACL seemed reluctant to proceed, passing the responsibility on to individual chapters for development. Meanwhile, in Seattle, Henry Miyatake with the help of Mike Nakata and Shosuke Sasaki developed what became known as the "Seattle Plan"—the first concrete plan for financial reparations to individuals, and one that focused on the psychological and emotional effects of incarceration in addition to the financial losses. This plan received resistance from National JACL.[11] Key leaders within National JACL were concerned with the political and social risks involved with seeking redress. It seems that these leaders always followed the Nikkei delegation in Congress (a delegation composed of Japanese American Congressmen), some of whom were opposed to redress.[12] The Seattle JACL chapter, with its Seattle Evacuation and Redress Committee, was seen by the national organization as an instigator that continually pushed them to act on the issue of redress. Tensions mounted between the two groups, and at one point the Seattle chapter considered seceding from JACL.[13]

Politically speaking, the Japanese American community did not educate and organize around the issue of redress specifically, but several actions took place that focused on the injustice of the mass incarceration which helped build support for obtaining redress. The Manzanar Committee in California regularly organized pilgrimages to the Manzanar incarceration site, helping raise awareness of the history of incarceration.[14] In Seattle in 1970, the Museum of History and Industry displayed the "Pride and Shame" exhibit, which was created with the support and input of local Japanese Americans. This exhibit presented a history of Japanese Americans in the Northwest, and it included incarceration as part of its subject matter. This was significant because in the Japanese American community issues considered shameful—such as being incarcerated by one's own government—were rarely discussed publicly. In 1975 a "Day of Remembrance" was organized, during which thousands of Japanese Americans gathered and followed the same route taken when they were incarcerated over thirty years prior. This was a large commemoration that received media attention, and it added to the growing community and political support for reparations.[15]

Executive Order 9066, the 1942 order granting the U.S. government the power to forcibly remove the Japanese Americans from specified regions, was finally rescinded in 1976 by President Ford. This symbolic act created the political space for National JACL to stand behind the redress movement, and in 1978 it announced its own proposal of $25,000 and a trust fund for educational purposes. Soon after, in 1980, Congress passed a bill supporting the creation of the Commission of Wartime Internment and Relocation of Civilians (CWRIC) to study the incarceration. Even U.S. Senator Hayakawa of California, who opposed redress itself, could support the idea of studying the issue of incarceration. After all, a commission and study are not the same as redress.[16]

After conducting research and hearing hours upon hours of public testimony, in February of 1983, the CWRIC issued its report, *Personal Justice Denied*, outlining the gross injustices experienced by the Japanese American community at the hands of the U.S. government. J. Edgar Hoover is quoted as saying, ". . . The decision to evacuate was . . . based primarily on public and political pressures rather than on factual data."[17] The CWRIC recommended a formal presidential apology and $20,000 given to each person incarcerated. On August 8, 1988, after a nationwide organizing and lobbying effort, President Reagan, following the CWRIC's recommendations, signed HR442 into law. On October 10, 1988, the first letters of apology and $20,000 checks were given.[18]

Some Japanese Americans were opposed to the idea of redress. For example, some veterans viewed redress as being unpatriotic. They resisted supporting it until the "Day of Remembrance" took place, where Shimabukuro notes that many veterans began to change their views.[19] Additionally some Japanese American farmers of California's central valley and of Idaho were opposed to reparations. These farmers had done well economically after returning to their land after incarceration, and some didn't want to risk backlash against themselves and other Japanese Americans if they made noise about redress. Interestingly enough, the internal community resistance proved to be the biggest opposition to redress. As redress advocates talked to White and African American individuals and community groups, they generally were greeted with support. And outside of a few vehemently racist groups like the Americans for Historical Accuracy, there seemed to be little organized resistance.[20]

Unfortunately the other incarcerated groups—German Americans, Italian Americans, and Japanese Latin Americans—were squeezed out of receiving redress during the political process. In the case of the Japanese Latin Americans, since none were U.S. citizens or "legal" residents at the time of their internment, their chances of receiving redress were effectively argued out of Congress.[21] It wasn't until more recently, in 1999 after a series of court battles, that some Japanese Peruvians were given $5,000 in redress for their incarceration.[22] Fortunately the Aleuts did receive redress, but didn't get it until 1988—the same year as Japanese Americans. Aleuts received $12,000 and a government trust fund.[23] It should be noted that all of these groups were included in Miyatake's original version of the Seattle Plan for redress.[24]

Implications and Extensions

The discussion of Japanese American redress could be extended to contemporary issues surrounding repayment of African Americans, Native Americans, and Native Hawaiians. In 2001 there was a groundswell examining the amount of money U.S. insurance companies gained from the enslavement and trading of Africans, and more recently there have been analyses of the amount of lost wages due to African Americans. One researcher used the prices of enslaved Africans from the 1860s as labor value, compounded the interest, and estimated the lost wages to equal $2 to $4 trillion.[25] If, assuming that it is agreed that the trading and exploitation of Africans was wrong from a legal, moral, or humane perspective, then shouldn't African Americans be entitled to some form or repayment for the injustices they suffered—especially if many large U.S. corporations made their profits from that very same slave trade? And what of Native Americans who, other than receiving land for reservations, have essentially paid for the creation of the United States through their near genocide? This question is particularly important considering that the U.S. government broke treaties, spread disease or actively refused to stop European American encroachment on Native American lands.

Finally, in the case of Native Hawaiians, the U.S. government has openly acknowl-edged that Hawai'i was taken illegally when in 1893 a military junta made up mostly of Americans forcefully removed Queen Lili'uokalani from her position as sovereign of the Hawaiian Nation. Technically this amounted to an act of war since no treaty was ever drawn up with the Hawaiian Nation, and U.S. warships supported the overthrow. The implication is that from a strictly legal perspective annexation and statehood should not exist. The Native Hawaiian population has been decimated since first European contact, and as a people they have been dispossessed of their land. Currently Native Hawaiians, like Native Americans, suffer extreme poverty and have the highest infant mortality rates and the lowest education levels in the state.

Suggested Procedures

1. Write or post the definition of "redress" at the front of the room. Explain to partici-pants that they will be taking part in a role play about Japanese American Redress for their incarceration during World War II.

2. Rather than letting participants form their own groups, hand out the six role sheets—S.I. Hayakawa, the Americans for Historical Accuracy, the National JACL, the Seattle JACL Chapter, Congressman Mike Lowry, and the Commission on War-time Relocation and Incarceration of Civilians (CWRIC)—semi-randomly and have students form their groups according to their roles. (I recommend making sure those who have stronger leadership skills are spread out evenly among the groups).

3. Hand out signs to the six groups to be posted nearby or placed on each group's table, and ask them to read their role sheets and follow the directions. Hand out the "Getting into Your Role" sheets and ask students to complete these sheets. Remem-ber: the CWRIC gets its own "Getting into Your Role" sheet. Each group, except for the CWRIC, should make a decision about Japanese American redress in the space provided on their sheets. Once everyone has completed their "Getting into Your Role" sheets, each group should prepare a presentation for the CWRIC, which will be making a decision on whether or not redress should be given.

4. While the groups are preparing their presentations, have the CWRIC go on a "fact-finding" mission. Individually each member of the CWRIC, using the space on their sheets, should ask questions to each of the other groups. Then the CWRIC should reconvene and prepare to hear the presentations of each group. This allows the CWRIC to learn about each group's position individually in a more "scientific" manner, without the information being based on presentation skills, and it rein-forces the individual group's responsibility to support their positions within the role-play.

5. Have each group make its presentation to the CWRIC. Allow questions from the floor and the CWRIC after each presentation. The instructor can mediate the pre-sentations or assign a member of the CWRIC to preside over the whole process (they are representing the U.S. government after all). Expect this part to get ener-getic and possibly loud as students launch into their respective positions and arguments.

6. After the discussion has reached a standstill and/or participants have exhausted their arguments, allow the CWRIC to meet, come to a decision and explain their reasoning.

7. Breaking up from their groups, participants will read the "What Really Happened" and answer the questions. Reconvene for a full class discussion about the issues and implications for redress for other U.S. communities.

Discussion Guide

Discussion after a role play can be fun, but the facilitator has to allow room for participants to let the emotions generated be released. I remind everyone that the role-play is over, and that all of the participants are now back to being themselves and not their roles. This helps re-center everyone on their own perspectives rather than the perspectives of their roles.

One of the central questions of this role play is whether or not participants see the incarceration of Japanese Americans as just or unjust. Historical evidence does show that even the U.S. government admitted to wrongdoing, despite groups like the Americans for Historical Accuracy holding on to racist views.[26] Given the evidence put forth in the role-play, participants should discuss the concept of justice thoroughly.

Because of the particular contexts in which I have done this role-play, I have not experienced a tremendous amount of resistance to the ideas embedded in it. In general, because of the U.S. government's admitted culpability and apology, most participants have agreed that incarceration was wrong for moral, legal, or political reasons. However, disagreement has arisen around two specific questions: 1) Can we hold the people of the past to our current standards of right and wrong today? (In other words, can we blame the U.S. government for making its decision within the context of WW II?) This question is obviously a broader and more philosophical one than the role-play specifically invites, but it is a common argument for many people. I always follow this up with still more questions: How do we make judgments about anything or anyone in the past? Can we condone Hitler as being a man of his times, for instance? Or can we justify the enslavement of Africans because it was "legal" much of the time it was practiced or that their enslavers didn't know they were being racist? 2) Based on the assumption that incarceration was unjust, the next question is which type of reparations is best? This is a specific disagreement within the role-play, and although we know what type of reparations Japanese Americans did get, there is no clear answer as to which would have been "best."

The discussion should be extended to current issues, specifically the events following the September 11, 2001 destruction of the World Trade Center in New York. Given that the U.S. government rounded up many American Islamic and Middle Eastern people, often forcefully and secretly with no trial or legal representation for those detained, what is an appropriate response to the U.S. government's actions? Can we justify these actions, particularly in the face of similar actions taken against Japanese Americans during WWII? What is the relationship between individual/group rights and national security? Is it necessary to sacrifice one for the other?

Notes

1. *Random House Compact Unabridged Dictionary* (New York: Random House, 1996).

2. Densho Project, "Terminology and Glossary," www.densho.org/assets/sharedpages/glossary.asp?section=home.

3. D. A. Takakmi, *Divided Destiny: A History of Japanese Americans in Seattle*, 1st ed. (Seattle: University of Washington Press and Wing Luke Asian Museum, 1998), 7.

4. Densho Project, "Terminology and Glossary."

5. "Aleut Internment and Restitution," National Parks Service, U.S. Department of the Interior.

6. E. Kusher, "Japanese-Peruvians: Reviled and Respected," *NACLA Report on the Americas* 35 (2001): 29.

7. "Internment of Japanese Americans in Concentration Camps," http://academic.udayton .edu/race/02rights/intern01.htm.

8. J. Brooke, "After Silence, Italians Recall the Internment," *New York Times* (August 8, 1997), 10.

9. W. Au, interview with Alice Ito, Seattle, 2004.

10. W. Au, interview with Robert Sadamu Shimabukuro, Madison, WI, 2003.

11. R. S. Shimabukuro, *Born in Seattle: The Campaign for Japanese American Redress*, 1ˢᵗ ed. (Seattle: University of Washington Press, 2001).

12. Au, interview with Robert Sadamu Shimabukuro.

13. Shimabukuro, *Born in Seattle*.

14. Au, interview with Robert Sadamu Shimabukuro.

15. Shimabukuro, *Born in Seattle*.

16. Au, interview with Robert Sadamu Shimabukuro.

17. Quoted in Shimabukuro, *Born in Seattle*.

18. Densho Project.

19. Au, interview with Robert Sadamu Shimabukuro.

20. *Ibid.*

21. *Ibid.*

22. J. Ma, "Redress-Fund Suit Thrown Out: Restoring Lost Interest Is Up to Lawmakers, Not Courts, Judge Rules," *Asian Week* (November 25, 1999), 21.

23. Aleut Internment and Restitution.

24. Shimabukuro, *Born in Seattle*.

25. D. Conley, "The Cost of Slavery," *New York Times* (February 15, 2003), 25.

26. R. Walker-Willis, "Americans for Historical Accuracy," www.hemet411.com/afha/.

Getting into Your Role

AHA, S. I. Hayakawa, JACL (both), M. Lowry

Here you will be presented with five possibilities for Japanese American redress. For each one write your perspective from the point of view of your role-play. Ask yourself what the person or group in your role-play would think? Why?

1. No redress or reparations for Japanese Americans at all.
2. Government Apology Only—The U.S. government would offer a formal public apology to the Japanese American community. No redress or reparations would be offered.
3. Public Education Campaign—The federal government would set aside funds to pay for education programs about the incarceration of Japanese Americans.
4. The Seattle Plan—Japanese Americans can "check off" a box in support of reparations on their federal tax forms. This plan would grant $10,000 for each person affected by the U.S. government's decisions during World War II, starting with the eldest first.
5. Straight-up Reparations—The U.S. government would pay interned Japanese Americans a sum of $20,000 and apologize for any wrongdoing.

Final Decision

What position/s (it may be a mix) does your group want to advocate for? Why?

Getting into Your Role

Commission on Wartime Relocation and Internment of Civilians (CWRIC)

As the CWRIC you must make a decision about redress for Japanese Americans. Before you do anything though, you need to do some "fact-finding" to help you make an informed decision. Use the following space to take notes on the position of each person or organization. Here are the five possibilities you will have to choose from:

1. No redress or reparations for Japanese Americans at all.
2. Government Apology Only—The U.S. government would offer a formal public apology to the Japanese American community. No redress or reparations would be offered.
3. Public Education Campaign—The federal government would set aside funds to pay for education programs about the incarceration of Japanese Americans.
4. The Seattle Plan—Japanese Americans can "check off" a box in support of reparations on their federal tax forms. This plan would grant $10,000 for each person affected by the U.S. government's decisions during World War II, starting with the eldest first.
5. Straight-up Reparations—The U.S. government would pay incarcerated Japanese Americans a sum of $20,000 and apologize for any wrongdoing.

S. I. Hayakawa—Position on Redress? Justification?

Americans for Historical Accuracy—Position on Redress? Justification?

National Japanese American Citizens League—Position on Redress? Justification?

Seattle Chapter Japanese American Citizens League—Position on Redress? Justification?

Congressman Mike Lowry—Position on Redress? Justification?

Once you've done your fact-finding, prepare to hear everyone's presentations and write your decision here. What recommendation will you make to the U.S. government regarding redress for Japanese Americans? (It may be a mix of the options.)

S.I. Hayakawa

Read this role sheet out loud as a group or quietly to yourself. This role is who you are (temporarily, of course). As a group review the five options for reparations in the "Getting into Your Role" sheet, and make a decision about which option you support. As a group prepare a presentation to the CWRIC, which will make the decision on redress. Be prepared to ask critical questions of other groups since they do not necessarily share your perspective on the issue.

You are S.I. Hayakawa, former president of San Francisco State University, and now U.S. Senator from California. You were born in Canada and lived in Chicago during World War II, and you and your family were never placed in camps since you lived outside the geographical area covered by Executive Order 9066. Even though you are Japanese American, you can't stand all the whining on the part of other Japanese Americans about so-called incarceration and the even more ridiculous redress demand when, in your eyes, no harm was done!

In fact, as you see it, Japanese Americans were lucky that they were treated so nicely during World War II. You wrote, "The fact that Americans did not panic at the presence of Japanese immigrants in their midst, the fact that angry mobs did not descend on Japanese communities, shooting, looting, and burning homes . . . shows that by 1941 American racial attitudes, even with the war going on, had matured profoundly."

Besides, in your opinion, the camps weren't all that bad—really, you prefer to call them "relocation centers" and think of them as "safe refuges" that were the "best thing that could have happened" to Japanese Americans. These relocation centers provided protection. The U.S. government couldn't have made a better decision. It was wartime, and the safety of the U.S. government was at stake. What else could it have done?

Besides, what's with all the focus on the past? As far as you're concerned, Japanese Americans need to recognize they got a good deal and should just stop crying. Life isn't so bad, is it? They need to stop worrying about what happened and start looking to the problems ahead.

There are five options about redress on the table, which will you choose?

Americans for Historical Accuracy (AHA)

Read this role sheet out loud as a group or quietly to yourself. This role is who you are (temporarily, of course). As a group review the five options for reparations in the "Getting into Your Role" sheet, and make a decision about which option you support. As a group prepare a presentation to the CWRIC, which will make the decision on redress. Be prepared to ask critical questions of other groups since they do not necessarily share your perspective on the issue.

You are the Americans for Historical Accuracy. You are patriotic Americans who completely oppose reparations for Japanese Americans. In fact, not only do you think that incarceration wasn't that bad, but because there are no remaining signs of incarceration, you are not even sure if the "camps" were even real. As far as you can see, the movement for redress is really a political ploy by misinformed liberals to slander such great leaders as President Franklin Roosevelt who signed Executive Order 9066 incarcerating the Japanese Americans. The Japanese Americans would have you think that Roosevelt was a racist! What a load of junk! He was great because he made the wartime decisions that had to be made, including the correct one to remove the Japanese threat from the West Coast through incarceration.

Why should the Japanese get redress payments anyway? Redress assumes that the U.S. government did something wrong in the first place, something "unconstitutional." Well, the only body in the U.S. capable of judging constitutionality is our Supreme Court, and in 1944, the U.S. Supreme Court upheld the evacuation and incarceration of Japanese as constitutional. Forget redress! Real Americans would understand that relocation was necessary to our security.

National Japanese American Citizens League (JACL)

Read this role sheet out loud as a group or quietly to yourself. This role is who you are (temporarily, of course). As a group review the five options for reparations in the "Getting into Your Role" sheet, and make a decision about which option you support. As a group prepare a presentation to the CWRIC, which will make the decision on redress. Be prepared to ask critical questions of other groups since they do not necessarily share your perspective on the issue.

You represent the National Japanese American Citizens League (JACL). According to your own literature, the JACL was established to "secure and maintain the human and civil rights of Americans of Japanese ancestry and others victimized by injustice." And you know that the internment was an injustice. Over two-thirds of those interned were U.S. citizens—whose constitutional rights were taken away in the blink of an eye. And you've seen and experienced the trauma that internment brought. Families were sometimes split up. The whole Japanese American community was left in disarray. People lost their homes and their businesses, all with absolutely no proof of guilt or any wrongdoing by a single Japanese American.

You're not sure what to do about reparations, however. On the one hand, you represent the Japanese American community, so you know you have to act in their best interests. But what are those best interests? Should you struggle with the U.S. government and try to gain some form of reparations? Or is it best to just keep cool and not make waves? There is an old Japanese saying, "The nail that sticks out gets pounded back in." If you stand up for Japanese American rights, will you face anti-Japanese attacks from the American public? It's risky, especially considering how hard National JACL worked to prove your loyalty to the U.S. government during WWII—you told the Japanese American community to cooperate with the government and even helped the FBI as they rounded up community leaders. Can you risk your political clout with America by appearing to be un-American?

As an organization you are in favor of the idea of reparations but not so sure about the reality. Over the course of three national conventions you have discussed the issue of reparations and even set it as an organizational priority. But you just haven't been able to make the commitment to actually take steps to making reparations happen. Maybe you can work for a form of reparations that wouldn't cause too much trouble.

Japanese American Citizens League (JACL)—Seattle Chapter

Read this role sheet out loud as a group or quietly to yourself. This role is who you are (temporarily, of course). As a group review the five options for reparations in the "Getting into Your Role" sheet, and make a decision about which option you support. As a group prepare a presentation to the CWRIC, which will make the decision on redress. Be prepared to ask critical questions of other groups since they do not necessarily share your perspective on the issue.

You represent the Seattle Chapter of the Japanese American Citizens League (JACL). You are frustrated and maybe even fed up with what's been happening in regards to redress/reparations. You know Japanese Americans deserve to be repaid for the supreme injustice their community has been handed by the U.S. government. Your communities were uprooted, splintered, and destroyed. Families were broken up, businesses had to be sold in last second desperation or were even looted and taken over by white Americans—never to be returned. You lost your homes, your history.

Also you're frustrated with the National JACL. They're wimps who are scared to push for reparations, scared to make waves. You even considered pulling the Seattle Chapter out of National JACL because it keeps saying it would support redress but keeps just saying it and not taking much action. After all redress was first brought up in the 1970 JACL convention, made a priority at the 1972 and 1974 conventions, and here it is the 1980s but nothing has hardly happened. Also, every time you try to push your plans for reparations, National JACL keeps giving you the run around.

You know that some say that the camps were "not so bad," that it was "for your own protection," and even that camps didn't exist. Please? Some of you were there. Your parents were there. Some of your grandparents were there. You witnessed all the pain and heartbreak, the suffering, the shame. You felt it yourself. There were barbed wire fences, there were gun towers, and the guns were pointed into the camps at you and your families—not pointed outside "for your protection."

Worse than that, you were disrespected, treated with contempt, spit upon, called racist names, and considered guilty of espionage and treason against the U.S. government—with absolutely no proof! You need the government to acknowledge its wrongdoing. Most of the Japanese Americans incarcerated were U.S. citizens! Your constitutional rights were taken from you and stomped on like yesterday's garbage. You know you deserve reparations; the question is, in what form?

Congressman Mike Lowry

Read this role sheet out loud as a group or quietly to yourself. This role is who you are (temporarily, of course). As a group review the five options for reparations in the "Getting into Your Role" sheet, and make a decision about which option you support. As a group prepare a presentation to the CWRIC, which will make the decision on redress. Be prepared to ask critical questions of other groups since they do not necessarily share your perspective on the issue.

You are U.S. Congressman Mike Lowry, representative of the 7th Congressional District of the State of Washington. You became involved when at a campaign fundraiser you were asked if you would support a bill for Japanese American Redress. You answered, "Yes, of course."

Later you stated that you have had "strong feelings about this and related types of invasion of civil liberties all [your] life," and that you were "most familiar with the internment."

It turns out that in 1943, after the Japanese Americans had been incarcerated, you lived by Minidoka, one of the concentration camps in Idaho, and your parents had always talked about "what a terribly unfair thing it was!" You've always felt that incarceration was wrong, and now you have the chance to do something about it.

You're a long-time politician, so you're familiar with the political system and know many ways that you could help the Japanese American community get redress for the wrongs committed against them in the past. There are five possibilities for redress on the table; which will you support? Which do you think will get through?

Commission on Wartime Internment
and Relocation of Civilians (CWIRC)

You are the Commission on Wartime Internment and Relocation of Civilians (CWIRC). You are representatives of the U.S. government. Your group was created by an act of Congress in order to determine the reasons why Japanese Americans were interned during World War II. You are important. You are all powerful. You are the official eyes and ears of the government. What you find or don't find will make or break this idea of redress for Japanese Americans.

As a group you are supposed to be neutral, but you are also politicians appointed to this commission. You have to weigh what you think is right with public opinion of what is right at all times—that's the nature of politics. What you report to Congress, and the world for that matter, will become the official record of what happened to Japanese Americans during their incarceration. If you decide there was "just cause" for incarceration, then that is what will go on the record. If you find there was an injustice committed, then that is the story history will tell.

More importantly, you and you alone will make the recommendation to the government whether or not to grant any form of redress to Japanese Americans, and if you do decide in favor of redress you must state exactly what form.

Your job: Once you have read your role and considered the questions at hand, each person on the commission must go into the community on a "fact-finding mission" and ask questions of the other groups. Figure out who's who? Which side are they on? What type or types of redress do they want? What is their point of view? Take notes on their answers on the sheet provided.

Japanese American Redress: What Really Happened?

The Players

S. I. Hayakawa was a politician and semanticist. He was well known for his stance against Ethnic Studies and student strikes when he was president of San Francisco State College in the late 1960s. He opposed redress for Japanese Americans as a U.S. Senator. Many thought that his stance on internment—that it might have been necessary and not so bad—and redress were influenced by the fact that his family was not interned since they lived in the Midwest during World War II. To be fair, he supported the creation of the CWRIC because it was not in fact redress, just a commission.

The Americans for Historical Accuracy is an organization started by Lillian Baker, who spent a lot of time trying to prove, among other claims, that the incarceration camps either didn't exist or weren't that bad at all. Even though Baker has passed away, the group's website is up and running, where they attempt to provide evidence to support their perspectives. To quote their website, "Realize the truth of the west coast evacuation/ relocation of the Japs."

Congressman Mike Lowry was a Washington State representative who went on to become governor. He played a key role in the drive for redress. Specifically, Lowry's continued political support within the machinations of Congress was instrumental in making redress happen.

CWRIC was a Congressional commission that heard hours and hours of community testimony in different cities. The CWRIC issued a report *Personal Justice Denied*, which catalogued the experiences of the Japanese American community and included their recommendations in favor of redress to the tune of $20,000 for each survivor of internment.

Seattle JACL Chapter, which almost severed ties with the national group, created the "Seattle Plan" that included redress for Italians, Germans, Aleuts, and Japanese Peruvians who were also interned or incarcerated. When the National JACL was dragging its feet on the issue of redress, the Seattle Chapter kept pushing the matter. Some would argue the Seattle Chapter was the real force in initially putting redress in motion.

National JACL is a politically savvy organization. Although it rarely admits it, the JACL helped the U.S. government during internment. After Japan bombed Pearl Harbor, the U.S. military asked for names and locations of important community leaders, and the JACL gave up the information in hopes of proving Japanese American loyalty to the government. It was a move consistent with the JACL's compliant approach to dealing with U.S. politics and power, which also was reflected in their slow move towards redress. Always cautious and politically conservative, eventually the National JACL got on board with redress and did end up backing a plan, but it wasn't without a lot of internal political struggle within the organization and political headway made in the government. To be clear, the JACL takes its role as an advocate for the rights of Japanese Americans very seriously and has done substantial work to those ends.

Redress: After many years traveling through Congress, eventually all the necessary bills were signed, and in the fall of 1990 the oldest Japanese Americans who were still living—starting with those 100 years or older—received letters of apology and their redress checks for a flat sum of $20,000. This same sum was paid to all U.S.-born Japanese Americans who were incarcerated. All leftover money from this program was rolled over into funds to support educational programs about the incarceration. Note: In 1988 Aleuts were also given redress ($12,000) for their incarceration, and in 1999 some Japanese Latin Americans who were taken out of countries like Peru and interned by the U.S. Government received $5,000.

Implications

1. Based on the labor values of the 1860s, compounded with interest, some scholars have estimated that $2 to $4 trillion dollars of "back pay" is owed to African Americans for the work done and profits made from during slavery.
2. Some German companies are paying up to $5 billion in reparations to Jewish "slave laborers" interned by Nazis during WW II.
3. The U.S. Government has openly admitted to illegally taking Hawai'i from Native Hawaiians in 1898, and even apologized for its actions (but has given no redress).
4. After the September 11, 2001 attacks on the World Trade Center in New York, several thousand Muslims and Arab Americans were rounded up by the FBI and detained without legal representation, evidence of any wrongdoing, due process or having their whereabouts be told to anyone—even family members. Several Arab Americans, and some who just "looked" Arab, were killed by other angry Americans.

Questions

1. What is your personal opinion on the issue of redress for Japanese Americans?
2. Considering that the U.S. government has openly apologized to Native Hawaiians for the illegal overthrow of their government and African Americans for slavery, could or should these communities receive some form of redress too? What form could it take? Explain your answer.
3. In relation to the issue of internment and incarceration, what is the relationship between freedom and safety? Was it necessary to incarcerate Japanese Americans in 1942 as a potential threat to national security? To protect them from the other American people? Was it necessary to forcefully detain Muslims and Arab Americans as potential threats to national security after September 11, 2001?

Handout

Part III

Community Building, Learning, and Organizing

Chapter 16

Making Student Leadership Development an Integral Part of Our Classrooms

Glenn Omatsu

Generally, professors and students in Asian American Studies recognize the importance of student leadership development as a crucial part of college life. However, most today see leadership training as mainly occurring outside the classroom through student organizations and extracurricular activities. In other words, consciously or unconsciously, they have adopted the traditional framework of the university—i.e., separating academic work from students' activities outside the classroom—and have forgotten that an early goal of Asian American Studies was the elimination of this firewall. This lesson plan shows how leadership training can be incorporated into the classroom, especially by redefining it around the concept of "Shared Leadership." This activity also can be used by advisers working with student organizations, by teachers in high schools, and by activists in community groups.

Objectives

- To respond to the needs of community groups and society as a whole by making leadership training an integral part of our courses.
- To overcome students' prevailing stereotype of leadership (i.e., defining a leader in terms of decision making, commanding others, and possessing charisma) by helping students understand the deep roots of this traditional concept in Western colonialism.
- To introduce the concept of "Shared Leadership" as a new paradigm that is crucial for our communities and our world today.
- To integrate student leadership training into ongoing coursework, such as class projects, so as to provide actual arenas for students to practice new leadership skills.

Time

- This lesson plan takes only fifty to seventy-five minutes to carry out; however, it's important to embed this activity in the overall course. I've never done this lesson plan as a "stand-alone" exercise. I've always integrated it into a term-long class project. In other words, it's essential to provide students with actual arenas to carry out the new leadership skills they are developing. For example, I've used this lesson plan to help students conduct community-based research projects, organize educational programs both on and off campus, and plan large-scale activities such as fairs, conferences, rallies, and picketlines.

Number of Participants

- Five to forty people

Background

Ask staff from community groups about what they feel students need to learn in college, and you will hear a common answer: Students need to learn leadership skills. They need to learn these skills in college, so that they can help their communities. Surprisingly, this same answer comes from personnel managers in both big and small companies. When asked to identify qualities they look for in hiring recent college graduates, they rank leadership skills as the main factor. As I will explain later, today's community groups and companies have a definition of leadership that is different from the traditional definition. Community groups and companies equate leadership with the ability to work well with others. This expanded understanding—what I call the paradigm of "Shared Leadership"—is significant for our world today.

Sadly, in college classrooms today, few students learn the leadership skills they need for their future jobs or to serve our communities. In most universities, the development of leadership skills is not part of the academic curriculum but relegated to "extra-curricular" activities—i.e., it is regarded as part of students' non-academic activities in clubs and organizations.

Of course, at various times in U.S. history, student movements have challenged this narrow definition of college curriculum by demanding an education relevant to their lives and promoting the mission of universities to uphold democracy, social justice, educational equity, and diversity. In the late 1960s, for example, students fought for the creation of Asian American Studies and Ethnic Studies and emphasized service to communities, student participation in their own learning, and student leadership development at the very center of new curriculum. During the past three decades, students have had to defend this new framework against constant efforts to impose more traditional academic practices into curriculum.

Today, for most students, learning leadership skills in college is not easy because they need to do this in addition to their academic work. This challenge is especially difficult for students who need to work in order to pay for their education. Unlike students from more well-off families, working-class students may not have the time to participate in student groups in order to learn leadership skills. Moreover, not all student groups in college understand their critical mission for providing students opportunities for leadership development. By their nature, some student groups are simply social clubs, while others are narrowly defined around a particular function.

Given these realities, faculty have a responsibility to incorporate leadership training into their classrooms. However, carrying out this responsibility requires seeing leadership and leadership training in a new way. It requires overcoming traditional concepts about leadership and embracing a new approach. What is the traditional concept that needs to be rejected, and what is the new concept that must be embraced?

Like other Americans, faculty and students today have a stereotyped image of what constitutes a leader, and this stereotype is anchored in a concept of leadership that emerged over the past few centuries mainly in the Western world. According to this definition, a leader is a strong and powerful individual—someone who makes decisions, commands many others, and speaks with charisma. A leader is the rare human being embodying special qualities not often found in one person; in fact, from this very definition, most human beings are followers and not leaders. Almost always, this image of a leader is that of an older male, and usually it is associated with CEOs in corporations, the U.S. president, and generals in the U.S. military. Not surprisingly, leaders in all these institutions are older men and overwhelmingly White. Could this concept of leadership be related to patriarchy, racism, and colonialism that have been among the defining (and often hidden) features of the Western world?

Of course, in reality, even in today's corporations, the U.S. presidency, and the military, leadership does not revolve around a single executive. In even these highly patriarchal institutions, leadership is based on teamwork. A general, a CEO, and even a president become effective leaders only if they are able to work well with others. Crises in leadership in these institutions usually reflect breakdowns in the capacity to work together, and leadership is defined as the ability of people to coordinate their work and meld disparate skills. Thus, within even the most patriarchal institutions in the modern world, the best leaders are those who have the ability to assemble a team consisting of people with different talents; the days are long past when a leader is seen as one individual embodying multiple qualities associated with leadership.

Why has this shift in thinking about leadership occurred in the most powerful institutions symbolizing Western society? The short answer is that today's world is much more complex than the world of earlier centuries. Corporations and businesses are no longer led by "captains of industry" who manage assembly lines; and wars are no longer always fought on battlefields requiring standing armies.

There is also a longer answer to this question. For the past several centuries, grassroots movements in every part of the globe have advanced democracy, expanded human rights, and challenged Western ideologies based on patriarchy, racism, and colonialism. In other words, grassroots movements for social justice have also reshaped our thinking about leadership by developing a new model that stands in opposition to the traditional model. We can call this new grassroots model "Shared Leadership." In many ways, it is not new since it draws from the ideas of leadership that have long existed among indigenous peoples around the world, from cultures that have not been dominated by patriarchy, from immigrant communities in Western nations, from national liberation movements, from the women's movements, and from the work of community groups and NGOs (non-governmental organizations). What is new about Shared Leadership is the way that innovative thinkers have adapted these legacies to respond to the special challenges in the twenty-first century, a world of complexity and interconnectedness, where the very survival of the human species depends or our capacity to work together.

At the grassroots level of community groups—and increasingly even in corporations—the approach that is most treasured is Shared Leadership. Shared Leadership is the ability of a person to work well with others—as part of a team. Shared Leadership requires strengths and abilities not normally associated with the patriarchal version of leadership: the capacity for nurturing others and bringing out their best talents, the ability to mediate conflict, the quality to both express empathy and compassion for others and educate others about the importance of these feelings, and the talent for encouraging different viewpoints while upholding one's core values and principles. Shared Leadership is based on a commitment to dignity, equality, democracy, and transformation in human beings. Thus, Shared Leadership is closely associated with grassroots movements for social justice around the world.

Some have defined Shared Leadership as the vision of leadership needed for the twenty-first century. In fact, as mentioned earlier, both staff at community organizations and personnel managers of both big and small companies now identify Shared Leadership as the number one quality that they look for in college graduates that they hire. They have come to redefine leadership in terms of the capacity of an individual to work well with others. In other words, even in corporations—the bastion of capitalism in the Western world—leadership is now conceptualized as an individual's ability to work well with others to get things done.

Yet, even though thinking about leadership has begun to shift in even the most patriarchal institutions of Western society, the traditional notion of leadership continues to influence popular thinking. Thus, most students today do not consider themselves leaders—even when they possess skills to work well with others. Why is this happening?

It's not unusual for old ideas to continue to influence society even when they have outlived usefulness. But with the concept of leadership, something else is happening that makes acceptance of new ideas difficult. In Western societies, thinking tends to be dualistic—as "either-or" thinking—and people are taught to think dualistically from an early age. A person is either a leader or a follower, and certainly not both. Similarly, it's hard for people raised in Western cultures to conceptualize Shared Leadership since there has been so much emphasis on seeing only certain qualities (e.g., decision-making, charisma, etc.) associated with leadership, while other important qualities (e.g., nurturing, mediation of conflict, etc.) are not. Thus, to embrace Shared Leadership, it is not enough to reject old ideas. It is also essential to constantly recognize the ways that many different leadership styles exist within a group and that all members contribute to the leadership of the group. So how can teachers embrace Shared Leadership and use this new paradigm to carry out student leadership training in our classrooms?

First, it's important to recognize that most leadership training programs in the U.S. are based on the Western concept of leadership. Thus, young people are trained in command and direction functions: to run meetings, give orders to others, speak in public, etc. These programs are based on the assumption that there is a leadership crisis in most communities—that there are not enough leaders. In reality, the training programs that our communities need are not those built around the Western model. The crisis facing our communities today is not the absence of leaders but the presence of too many self-proclaimed leaders who have difficulty working with others. In short, we need new leadership training programs that teach people how to work together, that uncover the leadership skills within each individual, and that help people learn how to fuse the different leadership styles together to work effectively. In other words, we need leadership training programs based on the concept of Shared Leadership.

All of us commonly hear that leaders are not born but are made. But how are leaders "made"—i.e., how is leadership developed? Is it necessary for people to go to special leadership training institutes and spend large sums of money? Can they learn leadership skills by listening to inspiring and charismatic people?

The most effective leadership training programs occur in everyday settings—i.e., in the course of a community group planning an event, a student group holding a meeting, or a class of students carrying out a group project. These everyday venues potentially can serve as opportunities for leadership development for all members. However, for these everyday venues to be transformed into leadership training sites, a shift in consciousness of the members of the group is essential. This shift requires rejecting not only the old ideas of Western leadership but also the prevalent thinking that leadership development can only happen on "special" occasions—e.g., at leadership institutes. Instead, members of the group must transform their consciousness to see the work of the group itself as a leadership institute. This also requires moving beyond the dead-weight of Western thinking that counterposes "getting things done" to "training people to get things done." In Western societies—where people are educated from their early years to see the development of things in stages—it's difficult to conceptualize two different things, in this case, "training" and "getting things done," as able to happen at the same time.

In an organization based on Western thinking, when tasks are divided up people who can do things well receive assignments based on their skills. Those individuals striving to develop new leadership skills are encouraged to practice on these skills and to observe existing leaders but not necessarily to take up new tasks requiring these skills. Within these organizations—whether they are corporations, the military, clubs, or even gangs— a powerful leader will usually choose one younger individual and serve as a mentor to teach that youth leadership skills. Often, this younger person is defined as the next leader, the "heir apparent."

In contrast, organizations infused with the ethos of Shared Leadership see task division and leadership training much differently. Rather than counterposing the two things, members see task assignments as an opportunity for leadership development. Usually, this happens by assigning an experienced person to work with a less experienced person and having the two work together to complete the task. Similar to the traditional organization, mentoring occurs at every step. But unlike the traditional organization, *each member* of the group is a mentor for other members since all members have leadership skills that they can help others develop. Thus, organizations where shared leadership prevails are organizations infused with a culture of mentoring. They are tight-knit organizations characterized as a community of mentors.

This "culture of mentoring" helps to explain the process of leadership development in groups and also classrooms promoting Shared Leadership. A mentor is a trusted advocate, ally, and guide. A mentor nurtures growth, helping the mentee to realize the potential within them. The mentor does this through a combination of methods: by modeling new behavior, by having the mentee assist in a new task (such as through an apprenticeship), or by allowing the mentee to work individually with guidance.

Let's take a simple example of how this approach to leadership development would work for a college student in a classroom working on a project organized around the model of Shared Leadership. Among Asian American students, one commonly identified new leadership skill that many want to develop is public speaking. Since most students only gain experience speaking in public in college classrooms where they are graded, many associate public speaking with fear and a heightened sense of self-consciousness. There are some students who are experienced public speakers; usually they have developed their abilities outside the classroom as teachers in youth clubs and churches and possibly even through family gatherings. In a class project characterized by Shared Leadership, the teacher would pair the more experienced speakers with the less experienced. However, the teacher would also train the more experienced speakers to serve as mentors; they would be trained not to push the less experienced students into situations where they would speak before a crowd of fifty or a hundred people. Instead, the more experienced student would watch for opportunities in everyday life to gradually introduce the mentee to public speaking: for example, to help with a short announcement or to take responsibility for a small part of a presentation while the experienced speaker does the main part. (For those interested in learning theory, the ideas presented here are similar to concepts developed by Vygotsky, especially his "zone of proximal development.")

Class projects contain many such opportunities for leadership development. In fact, think of what would happen if teachers consciously adopted the Shared Leadership model and conducted leadership development for students as part of ongoing work on class projects. If each semester students did a leadership training exercise in a class, think how many new leaders would emerge from that classroom. If that same exercise were conducted each succeeding semester, think how many new leaders would graduate from that college. And think even more expansively: what would happen if thousands of classrooms across the U.S. did the same? What impact would this have on responding to the needs of our communities and changing society?

Suggested Procedures

My lesson plan for student leadership development is an integral part of my overall courses. I'm not sure if it's possible to carry out this lesson plan as a "stand-alone" assignment. Thus, in the descriptions below I work from the assumption that this lesson plan is embedded in ongoing coursework and connected to a class project. For example, I've used this lesson plan in past classes to help students mobilize for peace and justice and against the U.S. invasion of Iraq, to help third-grade immigrant students in an inner-city school, and to take the initiative in redefining the future of Asian American Studies (see class websites below).

- "Mobilizing for Peace and Justice"
  www.sscnet.ucla.edu/aasc/classweb/winter03/aas116/index.html
- "Community Education: Youth Empowerment"
  www.sscnet.ucla.edu/aasc/classweb/fall01/aas197j/
- "Asian American Social Movements: The Role of Students in Defining the Future of Asian American Studies"
  www.sscnet.ucla.edu/99F/asian197j-1/webmag99.htm

1. Generally, I carry out this lesson plan in the second or third class session of the term. Thus, this exercise also helps students learn about each other by interacting together.
2. In the class sessions preceding this lesson plan, I've focused on building good group

dynamics in my class by encouraging students to recognize the "full humanity" of fellow students. The concept of "full humanity" is adapted from the ideas of Korean immigrant journalist K.W. Lee who teaches the importance of rejecting simplistic and stereotypical descriptions of people, especially racial groups, and to embrace a full understanding of their ideas and aspirations. In college classrooms students are quick to classify others, such as "political" or "non-political," from what they hear in early discussions. Thus, I've found it helpful in initial class sessions to emphasize the need for students to understand classmates in terms of their "full humanity" through careful listening and sustained interactions. During initial class sessions, I also devote time to discussions about the class term-long project and the responsibilities of students—individually and collectively—to complete this project. These earlier discussions set the stage for introducing this activity on leadership development. I want students to know that leadership development is an important component of the class project, not only for their own self-development but for future service to our communities.

3. I begin the lesson plan by asking the roomful of students a question: "How many consider yourselves to be leaders?" Typically, in a group of thirty or forty Asian American students only a handful will raise their hands. I ask two or three who have raised their hands why they consider themselves leaders. I then focus on those who did not raise their hands and ask them why they don't consider themselves leaders. Usually, the points they raise highlight the contradiction between qualities that they possess, such as being able to work well with others, and the fact that these qualities are not defined as leadership qualities. This discussion begins to highlight assumptions and the need to expand our thinking about what constitutes leadership.

4. I hand out the assignment (see handout) and talk briefly about the difference between "traditional leadership" and "Shared Leadership." If I've done a good job facilitating the earlier discussion about different ideas about leadership in our classroom, this presentation is simply a summary of ideas that students have already expressed.

5. Next, I state that one key goal of our class project is student leadership development. Thus, it's important to learn about existing leadership strengths of each student and also for each student to identify one new quality that will be developed through work on the project. I explain that in most settings it's easy for individuals to only focus on what they can do well. However, if everyone in our communities did this, there would be no leadership development. Instead, we need to create our classroom as a training ground where each student can use existing leadership skills while at the same time developing one new skill. In other words, within our class we shouldn't counterpose leadership development to "getting things done efficiently" (a common dilemma in Western society). We can do both simultaneously by having those who are strong in a particular skill work with others wanting to develop that skill.

6. I pair up students, being careful to have students work with someone they don't know well. Students then ask each other three questions and take notes on what their partner says: 1) Do you consider yourself a leader? 2) What is one leadership quality that you feel you have? 3) What is one new leadership quality that you want to develop this semester through work on our class project? For the last two questions, I ask students to be specific rather than general. I then have each pair report back to the class.

7. During the report-back, I take notes, identifying each student's existing leadership skill and the one new skill for a chart I will hand back at the next class. If during the report-back, the skill mentioned is too general, I ask the student to make it more specific. For example, if a student states that the partner wants to "become more organized," I find out what that student wants to focus on during the semester to develop better organizational skills. If another student mentions that the partner wants to "work better with others," I help the student identify what this means in the context of our class project. Generally, in an Asian American Studies class, many students will identify public speaking as the new skill they want to develop. However, through discussion some will clarify their answer by stating that they want to feel more comfortable speaking before large groups, while others want to focus on their role in small groups, such as committees.

8. At the conclusion of this workshop, I mention again that a key goal for our class project is leadership development. Thus, by the end of our project, each student will have had an opportunity to develop a new leadership skill. I encourage students to think about their remaining time in college from this same framework. In other words, if each semester, each student works on developing one new leadership skill, think about how many skills that student will be able to contribute to their community upon graduation. Similarly, if a student establishes the habit of continuing to develop new leadership skills each year, think about how many leadership skills that individual will have twenty years from now.

9. I also emphasize that another reason we do this exercise is to allow each member of the class to hear about the existing leadership skills of all other class members and the new skills each wants to develop. In this way, our class can function as a community helping each person develop new skills. Also, by doing this exercise, we as a class can avoid common conflicts relating to different styles of leadership that crop up in groups. In student groups (and also most community groups), there is usually not a discussion about each person's concept of leadership until there is a leadership crisis. Crises are not the best times to carry out this type of discussion since ideas about leadership get caught up in personality conflicts and other issues. Usually, group conflicts are rooted in different styles of leadership. For example, one person may criticize another for "not being a strong leader" due to the belief that a leader needs to be a charismatic speaker. The leader being criticized may lack this quality but may be very effective in nurturing others and mediating group conflict. In an argument between two people holding different concepts about leadership, there can be no resolution until there is understanding about their different ideas about leadership. Obviously, it's better for groups to have this type of discussion before problems arise. In fact, envision what would happen if in student and community groups, people regularly held discussions about the importance of melding together different styles of leadership and recognizing the importance of each member's leadership skills. Making these practices a regular part of group practices could have a revolutionary impact on our communities. These are also points that I ask students to ponder.

10. For the following class, I hand out a chart of each student's existing leadership skills and the new skill they would like to develop. I then lead a discussion to correct any mistakes and to further clarify points.

11. In future class sessions, when students are assigned to work committees for the

class project, I ask students to review the leadership chart and consider assignment of tasks from the perspective of existing leadership skills and new skills to be developed.

12. Among students who are strongly influenced by the Western concept of leadership, it's fairly common to turn over a particular task to a new student, not offer much help, and rationalize their actions as implementing Shared Leadership. For example, Student A is an experienced public speaker, while Student B wants to develop this skill. The class project requires one student to make a speech at an educational event; therefore, Student A tells Student B to give the speech "in order to develop your new leadership skill." This is not Shared Leadership! Shared Leadership requires Student A to help Student B. For public speaking, I often pair an experienced student with a new student and have the experienced student present the main part of the speech and the new student a smaller part.

13. Throughout work on the class project, I monitor students' interactions to watch if they are practicing Shared Leadership. Far too often, Western colonialism distorts people's perception about what they are doing and what they think they are doing. In other words, people may say they are doing something in one way, when in reality they are doing it in the opposite way. Often in a classroom, students heavily influenced by the Western concept of leadership will embrace Shared Leadership in words, but not in actions. It's the role of teachers as mentors to help these students overcome their colonized minds.

Assignment Variations

Originally, I created this lesson plan as a workshop for a student group I advised in the early 1990s at UCLA, the Asian Pacific Languages and Cultures Committee (APLCC). The group was created by an energetic group of students who demanded that UCLA provide classes in South and Southeast Asian languages and cultures. The students came from outside the ranks of existing student groups but quickly developed the political savvy to wage a successful campaign that eventually led to the creation of language classes in Tagalog, Hindi, Thai, and Vietnamese. The students' victories are all the more remarkable given the context of severe budget cuts occurring at UCLA, which led to the elimination of a number of classes. How, then, did the students achieve their remarkable victories? One of their strengths was their commitment to student leadership development. The original founders of APLCC recognized that their campaign would require at least five years—beyond the time that they would be on campus. Thus, from the beginning, they emphasized leadership training for new students who would continue this campaign. The original founders also recognized that UCLA administrators were adept at the game of "divide and conquer." Administrators always wanted to identify student leaders and only negotiate with these individuals, often causing bitter divisions between those few who knew what was going on and the many others who were not due to "the sensitive nature of discussions." From the beginning, APLCC founders rejected the game of administrators. When asked by administrators to identify the group's leaders, APLCC members stated that they were all leaders and practiced a system of rotating representatives to meet with administrators. In all student groups, however, individuals emerge with special skills. APLCC was no exception. At a critical point in their campaign, one student emerged as crucial for dealing with administrators, critically analyzing trends in the university, and boldly speaking at campus rallies. The emergence of this leader, however, created internal tensions as APLCC members grappled with how to best utilize this member's skills while not becoming dependent on her. The Leadership Training Workshop served as a way to deal with this situation and to better conceptualize APLCC's concept of Shared Leadership.

I mention this story because it's important to see that my lesson plan emerged from a real-life situation and responded to practical questions facing student activists. Understanding the lesson plan in this way means that others using it should do so flexibly, feeling comfortable to adapt it to particular needs facing students on their campuses.

Recommended Resources

Bruce Kokopeli and George Lakey, *Leadership for Change: Toward a Feminist Model* (Gabriola Island, British Columbia: New Society Publishers, 1983).

Lev Vygotsky, *Mind in Society: The Development of Higher Psychological Processes* (Cambridge, MA: Harvard University Press, 1978).

Margaret Wheatley, *Leadership and the New Science: Discovering Order in a Chaotic World* (San Francisco: Berrett-Koehler Publishers, 1999).

Leadership Training Workshop

Leadership Styles: Two Different Approaches

The top-down style of leadership—otherwise known as the "command style"

A) A group is defined by a single, supreme leader who "rules" over all.
B) The leader's main responsibility is to direct and command members of a group.
C) To carry out these command functions, the supreme leader must possess multiple skills:
   1) Serving as spokesperson for the group (through speaking and writing)
   2) Functioning as the group's chief negotiator with other forces
   3) Serving as military field commander in struggles with the "enemy"
   4) Serving as the group's political strategist
   5) Promoting internal group cohesion and motivating the membership (interpersonal skills)
   6) Training one "heir apparent"

Alternative concept of leadership: the grassroots approach of Shared Leadership

A) A group functions collectively—with a large number of leaders, each able to contribute specific skills, such as:
   1) Serving as spokesperson (through speaking and writing)
   2) Representing the group in negotiations with other forces
   3) Serving as military field commander in struggles with the "enemy"
   4) Developing political strategy for the group
   5) Fostering intra-group harmony and the concept of teamwork
   6) Recruiting new members
   7) Managing tasks and overseeing group responsibilities
   8) Fostering a "culture"—or atmosphere within the group—that promotes learning, membership development, and fun
B) The group is comfortable with having many styles of leadership; no one style is defined as the most important style.
C) The group provides a nurturing atmosphere, enabling all members to grow in their leadership skills and to learn new skills.

Common Misconceptions about Leadership

A) "There is one—and only one—style of leadership for a group."
B) "For any group, there is one—and only one—leader. A few members of the group are 'developing leaders,' while the rest are 'followers.' "
C) "Leaders are born, and not trained; a person either has leadership ability or does not."
D) Even when people recognize the existence of different leadership styles, they tend to believe that "one style (usually the 'command style') is more important than other styles."

Handout

Exercise for Class Members

A) Self-evaluation
1) Do you consider yourself a leader? Why or why not?
2) What is (are) your main strength(s) as a leader? What is your "leadership style"?
B) Self-development
1) Identify one new facet of leadership that you would like to develop this semester through our class project
C) Group activities (for discussion)
1) Based on class tasks for the coming period, how can we assign people to effectively utilize their existing leadership skills and styles, and to help them to develop new leadership skills and styles?

And remember:

- Leadership training is an important part of an organization's development. Groups that want to grow and succeed will always invest time in leadership training for their members.

- Develop your leadership skills as a youth; it will be much harder to learn about different leadership styles as you get older.

- Leadership training—and organizational activities overall—should always be fun and educational.

Chapter 17

Beyond the Egg Rolls, Fortune Cookies, and Paper Fans:

Seeing the Residential Side of Chinatown

Andrew Leong

As the title of this assignment implies, most outsiders with no understanding of Chinatown have the notion that it is really not a community at all. It is an invention for the tourist. No real people live here since all they see are restaurants and curio shops. When the tourist leaves, Chinatown shuts down only to reopen the next morning with the arrival of the next tour group. This conception is also the predominant notion for policymakers. If no one lives in Chinatown, then they do not need to protect this space. Furthermore, if this is a prefabricated place, there is no need for it when a more profitable use is demanded.

This exercise is designed to dispel these notions in order for students to see that Chinatowns are occupied by real people who have to cope with the detriment of the tourist-trap mentality on a daily basis. I have used this exercise in introductory Asian American Studies classes, for year-long projects focused on assessing the impacts of commercial developments in Boston Chinatown, in classes on social differences, and in a graduate policy practicum. High school students also can participate in this activity (although security may become an issue if the students conduct the tour by themselves; I suggest that a parent to accompany the students but not influence their perspectives and thus the outcome of the assignment).

Objectives

- To help students see Chinatown as more than a repository for the restaurant and tourist industries and as a living residential community.
- To assess students' stereotypes about Chinatown and begin a discussion.
- To have students compare conditions in Chinatown with other communities.
- To have students explore how race and class impact a community.

Time

- One-and-a-half to two hours for a student to conduct a self-guided tour
- One-and-a-half hours for debriefing with the class
- Optional: two-hours instructor-guided tour with the class after the debriefing. This tour would be dramatically different from their self-guided tours since students would have the benefit of hindsight developed from their earlier tours plus additional information that the instructor offers on the community.

Number of Participants

- Five to fifty persons

Materials Needed

- Walking tour map with highlighted route
- Notepads and pencils for students. Optional: camera and tape recorder for more detailed records

Background

Most students (Asian Americans or not) have visited Chinatowns to eat and to shop, but their perspective of the community is from that of an outsider. Most students have had only limited interaction with this multi-faceted community, notably lacking contact with the residential and non-English-speaking population.

Similarly, public policymakers deal only with the business class of Chinatown (more often than not the English-speaking sector). Previously they consulted only with particular spokesmen, such as the Chinese Consolidated Benevolent Association, or "Chinese Six Companies," which acted as the voice for the community. However, since the 1960s, due to a growth in both nonprofit service organizations as well as progressive advocacy organizations, the power of these traditional organizations has waned.

Although Chinese restaurants originally catered to the needs of the Chinese immigrants, after World War II and military servicemen's exposure to "Oriental" and "Polynesian" food, the restaurant industry in Chinatowns began to target outsiders. Thus, it is the traditional business organizations that have created and maintained the tourist images in order to entice outsiders to Chinatown. These businessmen assert that they are simply giving people what they want. Tourists come to Chinatown to see ducks and chickens hanging in windows with their heads still on; go to restaurants and eat seemingly foreign foods with chopsticks (even though they may be ordering American inventions like "chop suey" or crunchy chow mein noodles) and end the meal with the obligatory American invention, the fortune cookie; view supposedly Chinese pagoda-like architecture or buildings; traverse in Oriental grocery stores where live animals like fish and chicken are sold; and hear people who are Chinese speaking with an accent.

Meanwhile, the visitors fail to see the residential component of Chinatown. When I have done political or environmental tours of Boston Chinatown, invariably people are shocked to find a residential area. Some are amazed that parts of Chinatown do not look very "Chinese"—that they look like other parts of the city.

On issues that relate to Chinatown, the traditional organizations continue to have a voice in the public policy arena. For example, with the recent decline in business activities due to the SARS outbreak, most spokesmen voiced concerns for Chinatown businesses. Yet, one questions whether that voice truly represents the range of perspectives within Chinatowns. Furthermore, while most of the organizational representatives have their offices in Chinatown, they do not reside there. If they do not live in the community that they purport to represent, their views are limited. They may not be aware of the nuances that residents are knowledgeable about—such as seeing or hearing the traffic that spews out with the closing of nightclubs at 2 a.m. Nor would they see the constant onslaught of triple parking on weekends and the piling up of garbage by the end of the day—generated by weekend visitors.[1]

Since the business sector has the goal of increasing the profits of restaurants and shop owners, this sector promotes measures that focus on these interests. The result is usually negative for residents who have to deal with the consequences of decisions made by the businesses. One infamous example is the relocation of the adult entertainment district in 1974 next to Boston Chinatown. At city council hearings residents spoke against the relocation, but restaurant owners supported this measure since it meant more business for Chinatown. Such short-sighted views meant that Chinatown had to deal with the effects of having the only adult entertainment district to be legally zoned in Boston. Residents had to deal with the associated crime that came with such a zoning: drug dealing, prostitution, "johns" driving around, and petty crime.

On a different front, the development of new office or luxury residential complexes—thus gentrification—also impacts Chinatown.[2] The business sector usually supports new developments with the hope for more foot traffic, while residents are opposed to developments that could potentially eliminate and price-out current residents. With "empty nesters" coming back to chic urban living and with many Chinatowns located in downtown areas, residential real estate is becoming a premium in most Chinatowns.

The composition of Chinatowns is also changing. Chinatowns have evolved into a center or hub of Asian American activities. In most Chinatowns one is beginning to see other businesses aside from those owned by Chinese. This change was accentuated in the early 1980s as a result of the Vietnamese refugee resettlement. Some ethnic Chinese from Vietnam began opening businesses Chinatowns, usually in areas that other Chinese would not occupy. These small businesses had the effect of enlarging as well as stabilizing the base of Chinatowns. Not only are there *pho* restaurants but there are also grocery stores owned and operated by Vietnamese, catering to the needs of that community. After that came the expansion by other Asian ethnic groups. By the 1990s we began to see the emergence of other non-Chinese businesses—with Japanese, Thai, Malaysian, Korean, Filipino restaurants opening up in Chinatowns across the country. Although their numbers remain relatively small in comparison to Chinese businesses, they are indicative of a change that is ongoing.

Suggested Procedures and Discussion

Pre-Tour Discussion

Prior to the tour, ask students to write down brief statements about what their perceptions are of Chinatown. This list will then be compared with their views after the tour. No formal readings are necessary for the exercise. In fact, it is better to have students do assigned readings after the exercise. This would enable them to analyze their stereotypes of Chinatown. Questions to have students consider before they embark on the tour include:

- Have you been there before? How often and for what purposes? Older students usually relate that they have a favorite restaurant, while younger students may talk about a "Sanrio" shop for Hello Kitty or other toy items. Instructors should inform students that the above activities are not the purpose of this tour.
- What images or thoughts come to mind when we mention "Chinatown"?
- Where do these images come from? How much comes from TV or film?
- Who comes to Chinatown?
- Is Chinatown only for the Chinese?
- Do all occupants of Chinatown speak Chinese? Are there U.S. citizens in Chinatown?
- Does anyone live there?
- Who works there?
- What kind of economic activities go on there (commercial, industrial, service, etc.)?
- What's the economic status of the people (residents, workers, passers-by)?
- What's the racial/ethnic mix of the population?

Tour Directions and Suggested Guidelines

1. Provide a highlighted walking map to students with an emphasis on the residential components and other elements that make up an ethnic enclave. For instance, if there are any murals that are important symbols for the community, then the tour route should cover these sites. The attempt is to highlight the negative and positive elements composing this community.

2. Tell students they are to conduct this tour by themselves and take notes. Some students may have traveled to Chinatown before or may live there, and for these students, the goal of the tour is to look at Chinatown from a different perspective. For instance, I always instruct students to look above eye-level. Even for students that have lived in Chinatown, this act of looking up and seeing things that have always been there becomes a revelation. Especially in the business section of Chinatown, one can notice that buildings have multiple functions aside from being restaurants and shops. Since there is mixed-zoning, people usually live above the businesses. There are also upper floors that are occupied by family associations and other groups. In Boston one notices that the structures themselves tell a story since there are quite a few buildings built on top of existing older buildings; as such, the original pitched rooflines can still be seen. Moreover, are there any historical markings? How old are these buildings? Have the functions of these buildings changed over time?

3. Instruct students to observe specific things during their tour in order to later examine the socioeconomic-political context of Chinatown (see handout for more detailed instructions). For instance: who lives there (class and race)? Who works there? How safe is it? How crowded or dirty is it? How large is the area, and what do the "boundaries" consist of? List details as to the time and day of the visit.

4. Encourage students to use all their senses. For instance, does it sound or smell differently in various sections of the community? How does Chinatown feel de-

pending on where one is? Is there more or less sunlight in certain areas? Is there more or less wind in certain areas? Is it louder or quieter in different areas? In lieu of having students conduct a speedy tour, encourage them to stop at certain sections just to be able to note observations.

5. Ask students to recount what images they had of Chinatown prior to the tour. Does Chinatown look like their perception of how Chinatown "should look like"? What classes of people live and work there? What types of people visit Chinatown and for what reasons? What were the differences in a "before" and "after" comparison?

Post Tour Discussion

1. Encourage students to share the thoughts and feelings they had about the self-guided tour. For instance, for most first-timers engaging in this effort, some may have felt reticent about traversing through Chinatown alone. Would there be gangs waiting around the corner? These feelings are natural to the extent that stereotypes of Chinatown dominate the perceptions that the students have about this community. This is where the pre-tour discussion would be crucial.

2. Ask students to share what their notions are of Chinatown and how those views may have been changed by the tour. Most students during the discussion become extremely quiet because they feel they do not have anything to offer since they may not know Chinatown, nor do they know how conditions "ought" to be. They should be encouraged to engage in the discussion based on their knowledge of other communities in comparison to what they observed in Chinatown.[3] It is important to continually ask students "why" they think a particular condition exists in Chinatown. Some of the above questions in the pre-tour discussion can be revisited based upon new information acquired from the tour. Other questions below can also direct the way towards a valuable debriefing exercise:

   - What schools, parks, libraries, social services, recreation exists for the benefit of the community (compare it to your own community)? How big are the parks and what kind of play structures exists for children? How many basketball or volleyball courts are there for younger adults? What open space is there for elderly residents? How many trees are there versus how many parking lots or garages?
   - On the other end of the spectrum, what undesirable elements exist in the community?
   - Is there an overabundance of factories, industries, and institutions?
   - What is the traffic pattern like compared to other neighborhoods?
   - What are differences in services and facilities? For instance, why is trash pick-up only once a week in Chinatown but three times a week in nearby upscale Beacon Hill? Why are there greater traffic calming features in other communities (e.g., speed bumps and pedestrian walking right-of-way signs)?
   - What signs of change do you notice? Are there buildings that were recently fixed up? Recently built? Are there abandoned buildings and vacant lots?
   - Can you see signs of different periods of development? Are the buildings old or new? Do they show signs of having been used for a different purpose in the past (e.g., factory buildings that are now housing or offices)?

- What are the "important" (or important-looking) buildings? Think about the meaning of why some buildings are built or decorated to look important— what do they say about the society that built them? Who defines "importance"?
- How do your impressions change as you walk through different areas? Are changes abrupt or gradual? Do these changes mark a boundary between neighborhoods?
- What issues seem to dominate the attention of this community?
- What do you think are the strengths and challenges of this area for the people who live and/or work there?
- Do residents have a choice of whether to live in or outside of Chinatown? Why?
- Why do we need Chinatown?

Variations

Similar tours can be conducted for other communities such as Vietnamese, Cambodian, Korean, Japanese, Filipino, and Asian Indian communities in town. For a more challenging exercise, instructors can have students tour Chinatown and adjacent areas. The main point is to get students to begin asking:

- Where is and who defines Chinatown?
- How does the demarcation of "Chinatown" impact this community?
- What are the differences between neighboring areas and Chinatown (e.g., allotted residential and guest parking, open space, cleanliness, noise differences, etc.).

Comments from students have yielded these statements:

- "Cars in the nearby community were nicer; same with houses and cleaner streets."
- "The nearby community seemed dead, even on weekends, when Chinatown is bustling with activities and people."
- "The highway divided Chinatown from other communities."
- "Historic designations were in adjacent neighborhoods but not in Chinatown."
- "Other areas were listed as a "neighborhood" on city maps, but not Chinatown."

Future Activities

Students should be encouraged to read local neighborhood publications, where there are articles relating to issues of concern for the community. Whereas mainstream newspapers and books cover certain issues, they usually do not have in-depth coverage of local issues that neighborhood publications have. Lastly, have students read about urban renewal policies and their impacts on communities.[4] Although the literature might be scant on Chinatowns, the instructor can encourage students to do further research around the following questions:

- Did this Chinatown use to be bigger?
- Why is it located next to a major highway (and why are most Chinatowns next to highways)?

- Why is it zoned or near adult entertainment activities?
- What are the threats (real or potential) that this community faces?

Locate local literature that provides background history on the formation and development of Chinatown. Have students delve into oral histories on the impact of urban renewal in the community.[5] They can conduct interviews with residents, social service providers, and others engaged with the community. After the above debriefing in class, students can be encouraged to conduct small-scale research projects,[6] such as an environmental audit where they can go out and count the number of trees or measure the amount of green space in Chinatown. Similarly, I have conducted audits of how many parking garages or lots there are in Chinatown. This provides a reference guide to visualize the priority of land-use policies for a community. Students can do the same audit for the community they reside in to provide a comparative study of possible disparities between neighborhoods.

Through these engagements with the community, students will be better able to understand the plight of the community and what roles they can play in order to keep this historic, vibrant, and necessary community alive for future generations.

Sample Notes and Reflections from Students after the Tour

Karen Wong (Chinese American student): "I don't particularly enjoy living behind a major highway. The air pollution is like poison that the families who live in the community are breathing all of the time. It is also very noisy regardless of the time and day. The highway is like an eye sore. . . . One could see the significant changes in this neighborhood, which has been designated 'Parcel C' by city officials. It is land that is being developed for luxury condominiums. These sites once had a mural painted on the back of a building, a drawing that represented the Chinatown neighborhood. But, that is history now. The painting is gone, and I feel that part of my childhood is gone. I remember growing up with this drawing and people of all races would come and view and get a better insight of the community. . . . I grew up on this side of the street. Between the planes landing at Logan Airport and the noise pollution from the highway, I don't know how I survived all these years. I guess this brings me back to my original question. Why our community? To have a major highway built around a community is not an ideal place for any community. I noticed that Tyler Street is mostly made up of families of recent immigrants who lived here because of cheap rent, and the condition of the homes is not good. I noticed that the new bio-medical is under construction and this particular building is pretty high and does not fit in with the neighborhood. New England Medical Center is buying a lot of properties surrounding the neighborhood and turning the old YMCA into a parking lot."

Rita Labad (African American student): "It appeared quiet and not 'very Asian.' I realized later that this impression was based primarily on stereotypical thoughts of what Chinatown should look like. I think that the expectation was that the buildings around me should portray designs of the China revealed in movies and books. . . . I knew then that I had to put all of my perceptions in check and continue the journey through Chinatown with an open mind. . . . It was obvious to me that I was walking through the residential section of Chinatown. The neighborhood streets were narrow, the one children's playground appeared to have been constructed with only two children in mind. . . . there was a noticeable difference here from my neighborhood. . . . there are other issues which need addressing. For example, adequate and decent housing, and much needed recreational facilities. There is the distinct evidence that in fact the development of the neighborhood never for one moment included the well-being of its established neighborhood residents; hence, it was placed in the shadows of the many institutions erected to date. Today, I view my neighborhood with different eyes, and more attention is paid to the residents there. I live in a predominantly white neighborhood with beautiful hedges, well-manicured lawns, streets lined with the perfect trees and kept clean by town workers, beautiful parks, and large playgrounds. . . . My question remains, why do the people in my neighborhood deserve all this and the people in Chinatown do not?"

Notes

1. Doug Brugge, Andrew Leong, and Amy Law, "Environmental Health in Boston Chinatown," in *Asian Americans: Vulnerable Populations, Model Interventions, and Clarifying Agendas*, ed. Lin Zhan (Sudbury, MA: Jones and Bartlett, 2003), 43-67.

2. Andrew Leong, "A Case Against Liberty," *Pacific Citizen* (December 2002), 28.

3. Andrew Leong, "We Protect Southie, Fenway—Why not Chinatown?" *The Boston Sunday Globe* (November 23, 1997), sec. D, 7.

4. Zenobia Lai, Andrew Leong, and Chi Chi Wu, "The Lessons of Parcel C: Reflections on Community Lawyering," *UCLA Asian Pacific American Law Journal* 6 (Spring 2000).

5. Philadelphia Folklore Project and Asian Americans United, *Look Forward and Carry on the Past: Stories from Philadelphia's Chinatown*, videorecording, 2002.

6. Andrew Leong, "The Struggle Over Parcel C: How Boston's Chinatown Won a Victory in the Fight Against Institutional Expansion and Environmental Racism," *Amerasia Journal* 21:3 (Winter 1995/1996): 99-119.

Recommended Readings

Although there are several works on Chinatowns, most are about bigger cities such as New York City—see Jan Lin, *Reconstructing Chinatown: Ethnic Enclave, Global Change* (Minneapolis: University of Minnesota Press, 1998), or San Francisco—see Chalsa M. Loo, *Chinatown: Most Time, Hard Time* (New York: Praeger, 1991). For studies of local communities, it is often worthwhile to look at masters theses and doctoral dissertations at universities within the area. Also, websites contain valuable information about local Chinatowns (e.g., Seattle: www.seattlechinatown.org/history.asp.

Boston Chinatown Walking Tour

Andrew Leong

For your walking tour of Chinatown, you are encouraged to take this walk alone, but if you don't feel comfortable doing that, go with only one other person. What we want is your impressions of the neighborhood(s) through which you're walking, not as modified by others. Even if you're familiar with this area, pretend you've never been there before and give it a fresh look.

Much of the time, when we're walking in the city, our minds are on something else and we aren't very aware of our surroundings. But, if you really pay attention to where you're walking, you can learn a great deal from the environment. In this exercise, you're not being asked to do formal research on the area through which you're walking; you are being asked to be as observant and aware as possible and to think about the meaning of what you're seeing, hearing, smelling, touching, etc. You should jot down some notes during your walk and afterwards write down some of your thoughts for discussion to hand in next week at our class—where we'll compare impressions. Please note the day and time you took your walk. As you walk, try to figure out some of the things we spoke about in class, taking notes as you go along. Some of the questions below will serve as a reminder of the things that you should look for during your tour:

- **Current socioeconomic factors**: Who lives here? Who works here? What kind of economic activity goes on (commercial, industrial, service)? What's the economic status of the people (residents, workers, passers-by)? What's the racial/ethnic mix of the people?
- **Neighborhood change**: What signs of change do you notice? Are some buildings recently fixed up? Recently built? Are there abandoned buildings, vacant lots? Are there buildings in bad shape, mixed in with rehabilitated ones?
- **Neighborhood history**: Can you see signs of different periods of development? Are the buildings old or new? Do they show signs of having been used for a different purpose in the past (e.g., factory buildings that are now housing or offices)?
- **"Important" Buildings**: What are the "important" (or important-looking) buildings? Think about the meaning of which buildings are built or decorated to look important—what do they say about the society that built them? Who defines "importance"?
- **Boundaries, borders**: How do your impressions change as you walk through different areas? Are changes abrupt or gradual? Do some of these changes seem to mark a boundary between neighborhoods?
- **What do you like or dislike about** the areas you're walking through?
- What do you think are the **strengths and challenges of this area** for the people who live and/or work there?

Chapter 18

Mobilizing Students to Respond to Community Needs:

Organizing a Class around a Community Project

Glenn Omatsu

Thirty years ago, teaching a class in Asian American Studies meant participating in grassroots movements for social change. At one time, students took classes to join campaigns against evictions, to support struggles for worker rights, and to help low-income residents mobilize against corporate greed. Faculty created classes to fulfill their responsibility to the communities that nurtured them. Unfortunately, today, it is rare to find these classes in universities. This chapter describes ways that faculty and students can reintegrate these classes into the Asian American Studies curriculum.

Objectives

- To emphasize the responsibility of faculty to create classes in Asian American Studies to serve communities, especially the needs of low-income immigrants.
- To highlight the historic mission of students—armed with knowledge from Asian American Studies—in our communities.
- To engage faculty and students in grassroots movements where they can learn from the experiences of low-income immigrants.
- To promote humility as an important quality that faculty and students can gain from interactions with immigrant workers.

Time

- Forty-five minutes for each assignment, followed by a reflection paper and discussion

Number of Participants

- Ten to thirty people

Background

"Knowledge is too important to remain in the classroom."

For the past several years in my service-learning classes involving community projects, I've used this slogan to help students understand their historic role as community educators. Far too often in conventional classrooms, students learn to conceptualize knowledge as capital—i.e., as something to accumulate for individual advancement. They also learn to perceive knowledge as coming from individual endeavors such as reading or doing library research or from a dyadic relationship with a professor. Based on this perspective, they regard knowledge as only coming from scholars. Worse yet, some see knowledge as something to flaunt, usually at the expense of others who do not have it. Of course, powerful institutions in Western society, such as universities, perpetuate these myths. In this sense, many of us are still affected by primitive and savage approaches to knowledge—those promoted by kings, emperors, high priests, corporate CEOs, etc. who, recognizing that "knowledge is power," define its quest as outside the realm of common people. I mention these ideas because they serve as a starting point for any community project in Asian American Studies. Students—as well as professors—are constantly influenced by conventional thinking about the nature of knowledge, and we need to remind ourselves that embedded within Asian American Studies is a very different approach.

Asian American Studies arose from grassroots movements of students and community people who were also simultaneously involved in other political movements such as support of national liberation struggles abroad and defense of worker rights. Participation in these movements fashioned an approach to knowledge that clashed with the ideas promoted in traditional classrooms. The new approach was not unique to Asian American Studies; it also serves as the foundation for Black Studies and Chicano Studies and is integral to the philosophies of indigenous peoples worldwide. Specifically, knowledge is not individually constructed and certainly not an individual possession; knowledge emerges from interactions with others. Thus, by its very nature, knowledge is social and needs to be shared with others. Otherwise, any understanding is incomplete. Moreover, knowledge does not come only from those "above us"—e.g., professors. To make our knowledge whole, we must also educate ourselves with the wisdom of the communities that nurtured us—i.e., we must seek out wisdom from our families, from low-income community residents, and from immigrant workers. In short, knowledge is a complex process involving social interactions, personal reflections, critical awareness, and social action. To emphasize only one aspect of this process produces a distorted understanding of our world and ourselves as human beings.

Thus, based on this perspective of knowledge, the founding mission of Asian American Studies emphasized the responsibility of teachers and students to serve communities. The founding mission highlighted the power of students to serve as agents of social change. Students could promote change by joining in solidarity with the struggles for social justice of residents and by bringing back Asian American Studies to their communities. The founding mission also highlighted the responsibility of faculty to create classes to help students fulfill their historic role.

For the past several years, I have used the above ideas as the foundation for building my service-learning classes around community projects. Some of the classes have been complex. One class in 1995 mobilized students to support the unionization efforts of Latino immigrant workers at the New Otani Hotel in Los Angeles Little Tokyo; the students organized educational forums both on campus and in Little Tokyo focusing on the solidarity between Asian Americans and Latino Americans. I've created other classes to train students as community educators to defend affirmative action, to protect immigrant rights against anti-immigrant campaigns, and to build a campus movement against the invasion of Iraq and for global peace and justice.

How did I create these courses? In this chapter I describe one project and the steps involved. Before I identify these steps, though, I want to re-emphasize the need to build the course around the founding mission of Asian American Studies. I have seen other classes that did not do this; instead, they were built on a traditional viewpoint of knowledge. Unfortunately, community groups have had many bad experiences with academics working from the traditional framework. I have heard horror stories of students refusing to share research findings with community groups on the grounds that the groups were not entitled to their findings—only their professors were, since the professors were giving them the grades. I have seen examples of communities exploited by researchers, such as cases where professors have received large follow-up grants for research but community groups nothing. I have also heard professors argue with community groups over "their right" to do research on issues they deem important even when the groups have urged the researchers to focus on critical needs. On perhaps a different level, I have heard community groups complain about devoting valuable time to supervising students who were gone after a few weeks. Obviously, creating a positive interaction in a project between professors-students on the one hand and community groups on the other is difficult. However, here, I want to emphasize the importance of building this relationship—from the university end—on the mission of Asian American Studies and not traditional academia.

In late 2001, Leslie Ito of Visual Communications (VC) contacted me about a new project. Leslie, a community activist and a graduate of the UCLA Asian American masters' degree program, identified the need for a video documentary on grassroots Asian American labor struggles in Los Angeles. Such a documentary, Leslie believed, could be used in classrooms and also by community groups. This documentary could highlight the voices of immigrant workers and their leadership in defining solutions to issues such as racism, sexism, and corporate exploitation. She asked filmmaker Robert Winn and performance artist Alison Delacruz to help with the documentary. Due to her work with VC—the nation's oldest Asian Pacific film and video organization—Leslie recognized the importance of involving workers in this project. She contacted four groups—Korean Immigrant Worker Advocates (KIWA), Garment Worker Center, Pilipino Workers Center, and Asian Pacific American Labor Alliance (APALA)—and asked them to serve on the project committee. Leslie wrote proposals for funding and asked me to serve as "lead scholar." The VC documentary was completed in late 2004 and titled "Grassroots Rising!"

At about the same time that Leslie contacted me, Rena Wong, then a UCLA undergraduate majoring in Asian American Studies, talked to me about sponsoring a new class on Asian Pacific American labor. Rena felt that issues relating to workers were not sufficiently addressed in existing classes. At UCLA, students in Asian American Studies have a tradition of not only suggesting classes but also initiating them. Rena wrote a proposal to the University of California Institute of Labor Education (ILE) for research support to create the course and for funding of a teaching assistant. After successfully getting ILE funds, she met with administrators from Asian American Studies to negotiate my hiring for the class for 2002. In short, all the hard work in creating this course was done by Rena.

She planned to serve as the course Teaching Assistant during her first year of graduate work at UCLA but decided instead to forego graduate work to work as a union organizer.

When the UCLA course was approved, I talked to Leslie about ways we could have students help with the VC project. According to Leslie, the immediate need was preliminary research. VC did not have the capacity to research historical and current-day Asian Pacific labor struggles in Los Angeles. We identified several struggles: the campaign by the Immigrant Workers Union and KIWA to unionize Korean and Latino workers at Assi Market in Koreatown, the ongoing work of KIWA to fight for rights of Latino and Korean restaurant workers in Koreatown, the campaign of the Garment Worker Center to gain justice for immigrant workers at Forever 21, the campaign by Thai and Latino workers for garment retailer accountability arising from the infamous El Monte slave shop, the efforts of the Pilipino Workers Center to help low-income immigrants, the activities by Asian Pacific American Labor Alliance (APALA) supporting unions, and past labor struggles in Southern California such as the 1903 Oxnard sugar beet strike uniting Japanese and Mexican workers and historic struggles of Filipino farmworkers. I had been involved in most of the current struggles and could help guide the students for their research.

In consultation with Leslie and Rena, I decided to focus my UCLA class on research for the documentary. I required students to do participatory research and not traditional research due to the needs of community groups. Participatory research—similar to community-based research—involves the students in the struggles they are studying. Research topics are defined by community representatives working with the researchers. Students are not "objective" researchers but become participants in these movements. Questions of objectivity, thus, are redefined as students grapple with understanding relationships between powerful oppressors and relatively powerless people struggling for justice. In addition, due to their participation in the struggle on a short-term basis, students reflect on their privileged status as college students and think about the ways they can use their talents to help communities both now and in the future.

To train students in participatory research, I needed to overcome their preconceptions about both the nature of research (i.e., the way they saw knowledge) and about communities. Most UCLA students come from relatively privileged backgrounds, and it is not unusual for students in my class to have never visited ethnic enclaves in Los Angeles. Moreover, UCLA students have been conditioned to do research by going to the library or else by interviewing experts such as professors or community leaders. In contrast, for this project, I required students to attend community meetings, interact with staff from community groups, interview immigrant workers, and participate in picket lines and other actions. With this chapter, I include two lesson plans that I created to shift student thinking away from a traditional approach to research and toward the participatory model needed by community groups. These assignments also focus on ways that students can learn from immigrant workers, especially in terms of their own leadership development.

Also to promote student accountability to the communities they were researching, I defined the final exam as a presentation by students to Visual Communications staff. Grading was done jointly by VC staff and me. For their presentations, most of the student research teams created video projects. All of the projects were very good, and two—one on garment workers' struggles and the other on the Koreatown Assi market workers' campaign—were outstanding. I have since used these two student-created videos in other classes as examples of participatory research projects that have value for community groups. All of the student research teams also produced written reports that were given to

VC staff. These reports—along with the course syllabus and other homework assignments—are posted on our class web magazine.

Asian Pacific American Labor Studies, UCLA, Winter Quarter 2002

www.sscnet.ucla.edu/aasc/classweb/winter02/aas197a/index.html

Let me now summarize the steps involved in creating a community project in a class:

- It's best to create projects around issues that professors are already involved in. In that way, professors will have some initial ideas about the particular needs of the campaign and the ways that students can help. In the spirit of the founding mission of Asian American Studies, professors should focus on community projects that help the relatively powerless confront the powerful.
- Ideas for the project should be discussed with the community group. If the professor is involved in the campaign, this is not a problem. However, if the professor is not involved, he should become involved. This would help to build accountability throughout the course of the project and beyond.
- It is challenging to create a project that serves the needs of both students and the community. Sometimes these needs do not correspond. For example, college classes run according to a rigid schedule. At UCLA, the term is ten weeks long. In contrast, community movements follow no such timetable. Thus, it's important for professors to discuss with the community group what realistically students can accomplish. The project should be something that tangibly contributes to the campaign. Otherwise, both the group and students will end up feeling frustrated, and community staff especially will feel that the time they invested in students was wasted.
- Community projects often have needs that students cannot fill, despite the best of student and faculty intentions. Sometimes groups need research that students cannot do. For example, the VC documentary needed students fluent in different Asian languages, far beyond the capabilities of students in my class. Thus, it is largely up to the professor to identify the skills (and limitations) of students and to discuss with community groups how to best utilize these skills. Faculty can also identify university resources that can be used for community projects. For example, at resource-rich institutions such as UCLA, students have access funding that can be very helpful for community groups. Professors and students should creatively think about ways of redirecting these resources to help community projects.
- Community groups want student support for their projects. However, groups are not organized to either supervise students or systematically teach about the campaigns. These are the responsibilities of faculty unless the group has explicitly asked for these roles. It is also important for faculty to train students in humility in their interactions with residents, especially immigrant workers (see sample assignments). It's also important to remember that through projects students (and faculty) are in the community to help groups, not the other way around.
- Because staff from groups do not have the time to meet student needs relating to leadership training, professors should focus on it in the classroom (see chapter 16).
- Finally, professors should take responsibility for completion of the class project

and finish any uncompleted student portions themselves. For example, in my labor class, one project was the creation of a bibliography on Asian Pacific labor struggles, both historical and current. This bibliography has obvious value for community groups and researchers. However, since no student from my class volunteered for this project, I completed it myself. It is available online on the class website.

- Should professors organize students around a single project or multiple projects? I prefer a single project—with many components—so that students can have a shared experience rather than dispersing students to several groups, but my answer may reflect my own limitations as an organizer. I am not adept at overseeing work in different campaigns, but I know that there are other professors who are comfortable supervising several projects. For multiple projects, though, I believe that professors have all the responsibilities outlined above.

Two Sample Assignments to Learn from Immigrant Workers

To help students carry out participatory research, I create assignments that combine reflection with social interactions, critical awareness, and social action. The two sample assignments described here are reflection papers that help students at elite institutions like UCLA understand their connection to immigrant workers and their responsibility to use their privileges to serve communities.

Both assignments focus on the peculiar nature of class dynamics in our communities at the beginning of this century and the key role of students in responding to this situation. Today's dynamics sharply contrast to thirty years ago when most Asian Pacific Americans were working-class, and there was only a very small segment of professionals (i.e., doctors, lawyers, etc.), almost all practicing within their ethnic community. Today, class stratification in our communities is vastly different. Due to new immigration policies and the economic advances made by some sectors, our communities consist of different strata that may or may not interact with each other. There is still a large working-class of mainly new immigrants and a large small business sector. However, we now have a large professional sector. Unlike their counterparts of three decades ago, these professionals are relatively young and generally work outside the ethnic economy, in corporations and government agencies. Large in number and still increasing, these professionals have created their "own community" through various Asian Pacific groups in fields ranging from law and business to the arts and literature. Today's Asian Pacific college students, especially those at elite institutions, will join the ranks of this professional sector. Thus, in a relatively short time span of thirty years, we now have an interesting phenomenon: at elite universities where there are large numbers of Asian Americans, it is not unusual to find relatively privileged students who have grown up in the suburbs among families of other professionals and who are comfortable with the concept of being part of the Asian community but who have never interacted with immigrant workers. For these students, their only sense of solidarity with these sectors is an abstract bond of race or ethnicity. The two assignments require students to move beyond this abstraction.

Having students carry out participatory research rather than regular research also enables students to learn from immigrant workers. However, in order to learn from workers, students need to overcome the deeply ingrained attitude that there is nothing to learn. This attitude, of course, is reinforced by universities where students associate teaching only with professors. How, then, can we subvert this viewpoint? While obviously requiring a protracted approach addressing class stratification, I share these assignments as ways of expanding student thinking.

Suggested Procedures

Assignment 1: Connecting Students to the Experiences of Immigrant Workers

1. This is the first assignment for the course, and I explain how it will help students with their participatory research project.
2. I lead a discussion on changing class dynamics in today's Asian Pacific American communities and the new opportunities and dangers these changes bring.
3. We discuss the resources and talents students in the class possess and ways that students can use these to help the campaigns of immigrant workers.

Assignment 2: Learning from the Legacy of Immigrant Workers

1. I give this assignment a week or so after students have participated in the leadership training exercise (see chapter 16) and have completed some research. I hand out the assignment and ask students what they know about Filipino immigrant labor leader Philip Vera Cruz. If there are students with little understanding, I have other students talk about his impact on history. I ask one student to read the quotation from Vera Cruz about leadership and have students interpret the quotation and assess its relevance for their own lives, such as their work in the class project. I then review our leadership workshop and explain that I developed it from the Vera Cruz's ideas. In this sense, Shared Leadership is a legacy passed along to this generation of students by immigrant workers.
2. I ask students to reflect on what they have learned from their encounters with immigrant workers and community organizers through their participatory research projects. Do students see the ways that today's immigrant workers use the approach of Shared Leadership to wage their campaigns?
3. Finally, I ask students to reflect on their own work in class committees from the framework of Shared Leadership. Are students applying this approach for our class project? If so, how? If not, why not? I include these questions because often students from elite institutions interpret Shared Leadership as the absence of leadership. In reality, Shared Leadership requires shared responsibility.

Recommended Readings

Grace Lee Boggs, 1969. *Education to Govern: A Philosophy and Program for Learning Now!*, James and Grace Lee Boggs Center to Nurture Community Leadership, Detroit, 1969, www.boggscenter.org/edgovern.htm.

David Werner and Bill Bower, *Helping Health Workers Learn: A Book of Methods, Aids, and Ideas for Instructors at the Village Level* (Palo Alto, CA: Hesperian Foundation, 1982).

Joan Wink, *Critical Pedagogy: Notes from the Real World*, 2nd ed. (New York: Addison-Wesley-Longman, 2000).

Assignment 1: Connecting Students to the Experiences of Immigrant Workers

This assignment provides students an opportunity to think about the relationship between their lives as UCLA students and the lives of Asian Pacific immigrant workers and to think about ways that students can use their talents and resources to support labor movements for justice.

Thirty years ago when the field of Asian American Studies began, class dynamics in our communities were very different from now. Thirty years ago, almost all students taking Asian American Studies classes at elite institutions like UCLA came from backgrounds closely connected to the lives of low-income workers in their communities. Many had parents who worked in low-income jobs. Others had parents who operated small businesses in ethnic enclaves. A small number came from families in professions, but most of these professionals (i.e., doctors, lawyers, etc.) worked in ethnic enclaves and interacted with low-income workers daily. Today, class dynamics in our communities are different, and the differences affect the consciousness of students at universities like UCLA. For example, today, while there are still large numbers of Asian Pacific workers and small business people in ethnic enclaves, there are now unprecedented numbers of professionals living in suburbs. Professionals today—unlike those of a generation ago—are no longer restricted to careers in ethnic enclaves. Today, Asian Pacific professionals are more likely to be found "outside" the enclave economy in the corporate and public sectors and may have very little contact with immigrants in ethnic enclaves.

Thus far, few in Asian American Studies have examined how today's changing class dynamics affect the consciousness of students, especially at elite institutions. Today, at top-ranked universities across the nation there are growing numbers of Asian American students, most coming from suburban families with professional backgrounds. This growth has created an unprecedented situation—for the first time in history, our communities potentially have access to power and resources previously denied to them. However, it's also important to remember that this new development is occurring at the same time that many other people are losing access to higher education due to the end of affirmative action and the rising cost of college education. Moreover, worldwide we see a growing gap between rich and poor, the haves and have-nots.

1. Today, some have characterized the overall situation described above positively as a period of great opportunities for Asian American students at elite institutions like UCLA. Others have identified this period as one of danger. Still others have identified this period as containing both great opportunities and great dangers. What is your viewpoint? Would your viewpoint be similar to or different from that of low-income immigrant workers?
2. As a student taking an Asian American Studies class, how do you think that today's community class dynamics have shaped your own consciousness? In this period, does your status as a student taking a class in Asian American Studies at UCLA present new responsibilities and new possibilities?
3. In this period, what are specific ways that you as a UCLA student can use your skills and talents and access to resources to support the struggles of low-income immigrant workers?

Sample Assignment

Assignment 2: Learning from the Legacy of Immigrant Workers

This assignment helps students reflect on what they are learning from their research and their conversations with immigrant workers and community-based labor organizers.

The late Filipino immigrant labor leader Philip Vera Cruz once wrote: "Leadership, I feel, is only incidental to the movement. The movement should be the most important thing. If the leader becomes the most important part of the movement, then you won't have a movement after the leader is gone. The movement must go beyond its leaders. It must be something that is continuous, with goals and ideals that the leadership can build upon."

Philip Vera Cruz's vision of leadership is rooted in the concept of Shared Leadership that has long characterized the movements of Asian immigrant workers. Historically and today, one of the greatest contributions of immigrant workers to our community is to expand thinking about leadership. Vera Cruz's vision of leadership stands in contrast to the prevailing concept of leadership in society that emphasizes command and management functions, charisma, and personality qualities relating to individual advancement such as assertiveness. Thus, in the minds of most Americans, a leader is like a general in the military, a CEO in a corporation, or the U.S. president. From the prevailing framework, Asian immigrant workers are not leaders.

For this Journal, write an essay responding to the following two questions:

1. Based so far on your research and your conversations with immigrant workers and community-based organizers, what have you learned about their conception of leadership of the campaigns they are involved in? Mention specifically those you have talked to so far. How does their approach compare to the thinking about leadership of most UCLA students you encounter? How does their approach compare to your own approach, such as in student groups, church groups, on the job, etc.? Are there things that you and other UCLA students can learn from the approach to leadership of immigrant workers and community-based organizers? If so, what specifically? If not, why not?

2. For your committee work for our class project and for your work in our class as a whole, evaluate how well you are contributing based on a Shared Leadership approach. Note: remember that Shared Leadership does not mean the absence of leadership but rather a willingness to follow in the tradition of immigrant workers by contributing one's talents and energies to advance the work of all. In other words, Shared Leadership means shared responsibility.

Sample Assignment

Chapter 19

Bridging Generations:
Bringing the Experiences of Illness, Health, and Aging into the Classroom

Grace J. Yoo

The nursing home is a potential site for instruction, discussion, and learning. This classroom project helps students not only learn about Asian American history but also understand the continuum of the Asian American experience in terms of aging, health, and disability. This exercise can be used in classes in introductory Asian American Studies, Asian American women, contemporary Asian American issues and health and aging courses. This chapter highlights the positive learning outcomes achieved through such an exercise.

Objectives

- To facilitate intergenerational and intercultural dialogue between older immigrant Asians and younger college students.
- To sensitize students to the needs and issues of older, monolingual Asian immigrants.
- To encourage students to think of the Asian American experience from a life course perspective.
- To understand the implications of language, age, and disability and Asian Americans in a health care setting.
- To understand the physical, psychological, and sociological aspects of aging for older Asian immigrants.
- To create opportunities for networking with classmates and identifying resources available for older Asian Americans.

Time

- The first-time visit to a nursing home will take sixty to ninety minutes, usually after lunch.
- The classroom project will continue for sixty to ninety minutes each week.

Number of Participants

- Two to forty students; participants should work in pairs.

Background

In 1993, my Korean immigrant grandfather, Yong Chang Park, was hit by two devastating strokes. Unable to move and requiring twenty-four-hour care, my aunts and uncles decided he needed the care of professionals. He was eventually moved to a skilled nursing facility where he spent the last two years of his life. My grandfather, who had been a minister in the ghettos of Korea and who later migrated in the 1970s to minister to new Korean immigrants in Los Angeles Koreatown, was now unable to speak or move. He could no longer use words to inspire and encourage others. He was under the care of others for everything—from bathing, eating, standing. The highlights of his day were the Korean-speaking visitors who visited and prayed for his recovery.

Being the oldest grandchild, but having relocated to the San Francisco Bay Area, I drove or flew to Southern California and visited him often. Even my wedding took place within blocks of his nursing home. Unable to speak or move, he would often point to my wedding program. This was an accomplishment for him. Even though he was confined to a wheelchair, he had made it to his first grandchild's wedding. For two years, I witnessed my grandfather's ups and downs and his eventual decline while residing in a nursing home. His experience in a nursing home fueled my desire to incorporate this into my research and teaching.

Age, Illness, and Health: Void in Asian American Studies

In 1999, I started teaching full-time at San Francisco State University in the Asian American Studies department and realized it lacked community service projects directed towards the aged. Through a community service grant from SFSU, I embarked on developing a project that would make the experiences of older Asian Americans come alive to students. The reality of these life experiences was often not within Asian American Studies texts. Rather, what took center stage were topics such as race relations, second-generation identity issues and recovering our history. These topics were the experiences of young to middle-aged Asian Americans. The voices and experiences of the old, monolingual, and disabled were non-existent in these texts. Rather, what preoccupied classroom discussion and the minds of students in my courses were the experiences of those able-bodied, working adults between eighteen to sixty-five years of age. A major missing aspect was and still continues to be the voices of limited-English speakers, the ill, old, and disabled. The invisibility of this experience has led many within and outside the Asian American community to believe that we are the "healthy" minority.

Emerging trends shatter this model minority stereotype. The trends illustrate that

Asian Americans are not the healthy minority; rather they experience health problems but also barriers to care. For example, Asian American women are more likely to die of cancer that any other racial and ethnic group in the country.[1] Among Asian American men, cardiovascular disease, diseases of the heart and stroke, is the number one cause of death, followed by cancer.[2] Moreover, older Asian Americans constitute the fastest growing ethnic group sixty-five years and older in the United States today. Between 1990 and 2000 the Asian American population over sixty-five increased by more than 75 percent, becoming one of the fastest growing parts of the American population.[3] The majority of Asian Americans over the age of sixty-five, are foreign-born and non-English speaking. For older Asian immigrants, everyday stressors such as cultural conflicts, social isolation, role change, financial problems, and racial discrimination, can impact stress and lead to higher levels of depression.[4] Chinese American women over the age of sixty-five have three times the suicide rate of white women in the United States. Among women over seventy-five, the rate is seven times that of white women.[5] The projection for 2050 is that the elderly population will represent almost one-fifth of the Asian American population.[6]

Do Asians Care for Their Own?

There is a widespread assumption within and outside the Asian American community that Asian American families take care of their own—more specifically that they take care of their aging and sick family members. The literature on Asian ethnic families furthermore promotes this common assumption that there is a willingness of adult children to care for their aging parent and an expectation of the old to be cared by them. Not only has the limited research on Asian immigrants and their aging parents promoted this, but also federal policies have encouraged and promoted this assumption. The 1996 Federal Welfare Reform Law that barred federal assistance to older legal immigrants was in part passed with the message that Asian immigrant households would take care of their aging parents.[7] However, at these hearings, there were reports of Chinese immigrant elders being abandoned by their adult children.[8]

Although the traditional Asian family is seen as strong with filial ties, there is lack of critical discussion of how adult children in a new country who are overworked, lack resources, and lack time and money can provide the emotional, social, and financial needs of their aging parents.[9] Moreover, there are changes in how older Asian immigrants view support provided by their adult children. In several focus groups conducted with older Korean immigrants in the San Francisco Bay Area, elders voiced that they did not want to rely on their adult children because of their hurried and busy lives.[10] "My children call to see if I am all right, or see if I have died. Sometimes I say to them, 'Why do you call me? Are you calling to see if I am dead? Even if I were dead, what could they really do for me?' I just try to handle things on my own and try to solve on my own any difficulties that I face," states an elderly Korean female.

Moreover, even among American-born Asians, there are changes in the amount of support that they can provide to their aging parents. Acculturated adult children may find that they do not live in close proximity to their aging parent because of job placement. Among Japanese Americans, structural and cultural changes across generations have resulted in an increased need for utilization of long-term care facilities, like skilled nursing facilities.[11] Even though older Asian immigrants would like to be taken care of by their adult children, they also realize that they could easily be a burden to their busy adult children.[12] The reality is that as the Asian American population grows, as immigrant adult children feel the pressures of surviving in a new country, and as more acculturated adult children move for job mobility, more Asian American families are utilizing formal care, such as nursing homes, for their aging family members.[13]

Life in a Nursing Home

Seventy-five percent of nursing home residents are over the age of seventy-five and suffer from multiple chronic diseases and functional impairment.[14] For most Americans, the nursing home is associated with an unpleasant, depressing environment. As a result many who enter a nursing home enter reluctantly. Previous research has shown that racial and ethnic minorities have avoided use of long-term care facilities, like skilled nursing facilities, because of costs, stigma of family abandonment, fear of social isolation and low quality of care.[15] For Asian immigrant elderly, three significant losses occur for those entering into a nursing home: loss of family, loss of culture, and loss of community.[16]

As a doctoral student, I spent a year conducting interviews and observations in nursing homes throughout the San Francisco Bay Area. I particularly focused on the experiences of older Chinese and Korean immigrants. For many of these elders, entering a nursing home brought major changes. Due to language barriers, they faced constant social isolation. Oftentimes, Chinese and Korean immigrants residing in a nursing home were unfamiliar with the food served, the activities and the language of the nursing home environment. Moreover, these elders experienced multiple challenges in receiving assistance for their daily needs. All whom I studied faced limitations in mobility due to strokes, arthritis, or pulmonary diseases. A few elderly had cognitive impairments due to dementia or Alzheimer's disease. These elders needed assistance twenty-four hours a day, but due to their limited English or lack of English, language was a barrier to receiving care. Moreover, this also increased their isolation and loneliness. These residents were frustrated, but oftentimes their health care providers were also frustrated because of their inability to understand these residents. Because of language barriers, family members often provided tangible and emotional support to their aging family members. Family provided met needs that were often neglected, ignored, or dismissed by nursing home staff. However, a major barrier many families faced was the lack of time they could spend with their elderly family member.

Bridging Generations

Research has shown that a nursing home resident's sense of isolation decreases with companionship. Moreover, visits by friends and family enhance a resident's self-esteem. As a result, the visits by students can be a learning experience, but also visits can improve the quality of life for many monolingual Asian elderly residents. Simply talking to a resident in his or her language can benefit the elder's well-being. Talking with elders has shown to provide stimulation. Moreover, activities that students can organize such as ethnic food, music, or videos can also provide stimulation for the elderly.

Suggested Procedures

Because of varying schedules of students, this assignment should be an option in lieu of writing a research paper. Many of my students who take this option often volunteer to opt out of writing a research paper and grow and learn tremendously. This assignment is not limited to bilingual Asian students. In my previous courses, both bilingual and non-bilingual Asian and non-Asian students have been part of this weekly assignment.

The site of the intergenerational service-learning experience can be any nursing home or long-term care facility that has monolingual Asian elderly immigrant residents.[16] Paired up with a bilingual student, students will interact with elders in pairs or teams. It is initially challenging having students feel comfortable stepping inside a nursing home. Oftentimes, this is the first time a student has been in a nursing home and the first time they have witnessed frailty, disability, and dying. The suggested activities in building rapport with the nursing home residents should help ease some of the students' initial fears. Moreover, the instructor should encourage students to talk and write about their concerns in class discussions and in the weekly written assignments.

There are several things that these paired students can do each week, including conducting oral histories, simply visiting or letting elders reminisce. If residents are unable to speak, they could still provide companionship by showing ethnic videos or reading newspapers to residents. The following are some questions they could ask the residents.

Early Life

- Where you were born?
- How many brothers and sisters do you have?
- What did you do for a living?

Family Life

- Did you marry?
- How many children do you have?
- Where do they live?
- How many grandchildren do you have?

Coming to America

- Why did you come to the United States?
- What was it like your first couple of years?
- What did you do for a living?

Present Life

- Who are your friends?
- Are your satisfied with the nursing home?
- What is your relationship like with your adult children?
- What is it like communicating with the staff here?
- What have been the best years of your life so far?

Students must keep a reflective journal. They must also present a final paper on their experiences and present their experience in an oral presentation. Meetings with the elderly take place outside the classroom and can be sixty to ninety minutes each week. The reflective weekly journals should critically assess the experience and answer some of the following questions.

1. What happened while you were there?
2. Did you experience any difficulties?
3. Describe your feelings about this experience.
4. What changes did you observe? About yourself? About the residents? About the staff?
5. Does the experience stimulate thoughts about older Asian immigrants residing in nursing homes?
6. Does the experience suggest changes in your feelings or behaviors about older Asian immigrants?

In their weekly journals, my students evaluate this learning experience as positive and one that has challenged their assumptions and perceptions of older Asian immigrants, disability, health, and family. Students revealed a deeper understanding of what it means to be old, non-English speaking, low-income, and disabled. For example, one student writes about his observations of the resident that he visits:

"Mr. Park's life in the nursing home is very simple. He basically stays in his room and watches TV, reads his newspaper, or takes a nap. Every Tuesday morning, a Korean minister visits the hospital to share the gospel with Korean elders. I can only imagine how valuable it was for Mr. Park to have us pay him a visit every week."

Through their weekly journals and a final paper on the experience, students write what they have learned. Often many write about their thoughts about how their older resident has changed because of their visit, but they also write about deeper philosophical, existential questions like the meaning of life that also surface during this classroom project. One male student writes about the time spent with his elder:

"One hour visits every week for seven weeks are only seven hours. Within those seven hours, we may not have heard enough of Mr. Park's life stories, but we did have the chance to share our friendship and value the moments of sharing. We may not have had the chances to ask all the questions that we wanted to ask Mr. Park, but we had the chance to ask ourselves the questions about life in general and what life means for Mr. Park as a Korean elder."

Another undergraduate female reflectively asks herself how she will grow old and who will take care of her:

"If I can I make it to be that old, I wonder what I will be like at that age. If I can't take care of myself, who would help me? What would I do? I don't know, but I had these kinds of thoughts during my visits at the nursing home."

The assignments bring out the depth of student thinking. Students are not afraid to talk about aging and disability and the sights that they observe in the nursing home. Moreover, they are quite aware of the valuable service they provide by visiting these elders. Staff members at the local nursing homes are also quite aware of the profound difference a visit by students can make to the lives of monolingual Asian elders. One staff person writes:

"Efforts on behalf of her students have had positive consequences for both residents and students. The benefit to elders of repeated, respectful one-on-one attention is immeasurable. Bilingual students helped the monolingual Asian elders overcome isolation and communicate their life stories. The regular visits became the highlight of the week for residents. The benefit to student participants in this project can be measured by the eagerness both to expand and to continue their service to the hospital."

Despite the difficulties with such an intergenerational program, the students who have been part of this project seem to be drawn to these residents in a very powerful way. The students utilize their minds, time, and most of all their hearts in understanding the living conditions of older Asian immigrants in nursing homes.

Variations

What can teachers and students do if they are far away from a skilled nursing facility that has Asian immigrant elders?

First, faculty should conduct their own research by talking with directors at nearby long-term care facilities. If there is a growing Asian American population on campus, nearby long-term care facilities will reflect this. Faculty can also talk with local aging organizations and Asian immigrant churches to see if there are specific needs that elderly face. Some elderly may not live in a nursing home, but there could be specific needs that community-dwelling or homebound elderly may need that students can help fill through a community service project in an Asian American Studies course.

How should teachers prepare for this assignment with limited bilingual Asian American students?

When there are limited bilingual Asian American students enrolled in courses, faculty can use creative ways in recruiting bilingual students to help with this project. By offering independent study units, faculty may be able to entice bilingual students. They receive units and also learn and help peers in meeting with monolingual Asian elderly nursing home residents.

If bilingual students are unavailable to help with the project, faculty and students can still facilitate a meaningful interaction between residents and students. By identifying the language that the elderly resident speaks, students can identify audio-visual material they could present to the resident, such as CDs or videotapes. In fact, a weekly video showing in a particular language can be something that residents look forward to each week.

Notes

1. P. A. Wingo, L. A. Ries, H. M. Rosenberg, D. S. Miller, D. S. and B. K. Edwards, "Cancer Incidence and Mortality, 1973-1995: A Report Card for the U.S.," *Cancer* 82:6 (1998): 1197-207.

2. D. L. Hoyert, H. C. Kung, "Asian and Pacific Islander Mortality, 1992," *Monthly Vital Statistics Report*, supplement 46:1 (1997).

3. National Asian Pacific Center on Aging, www.napca.org.

4. T. Kaugh, "Changing Status and Roles of Older Korean Immigrants in the United States," *International Journal of Aging and Human Development* 49 (1999): 213-29; A. C. Mui, "Depression among Elderly Chinese Immigrants: An Exploratory Study," *Social Work* 41 (1996): 633-45; and A. C. Mui, "Living Alone and Depression among Older Chinese Immigrants," *Journal of Gerontological Social*

Work 30:3/4 (1998): 147-66.

5. U.S. Public Health Service, *The Surgeon General's Call to Action to Prevent Suicide* (Washington, D.C.: Department of Health and Human Services, 1999).

6. National Asian Pacific Center on Aging.

7. G. J. Yoo, "Constructing Deservingness: Federal Welfare Reform, Supplemental Security Income and Elderly Immigrants," Ph.D. dissertation, University of California, San Francisco, 1999.

8. *Ibid.*

9. Y. Song, "Life Satisfaction of the Korean American Elderly from a Socio-psychological Analysis," *Korean Journal of Population and Development* 21 (1992): 225-41.

10. G. J. Yoo, S. T. Wong, and A. Stewart, "The Changing Meaning of Family Support among Chinese and Korean Immigrant Elderly," unpublished paper.

11. *Ibid.*

12. Hikoyeda and Wallace, "Do Ethnic-Specific Long Term Care Facilities Improve Resident Quality of Life? Findings from the Japanese American Community," in *Social Work Practice with the Asian American Elderly*, ed. Namkee Choi (New York: Haworth Press, 2002).

13. G. J. Yoo, "Asian Immigrant Elderly in Nursing Homes," paper presented at the Annual American Sociological Association Meeting, New York, 1996.

14. Jeanie Kayser-Jones, "Decision Making in the Treatment of Acute Illness in Nursing Homes," *Medical Anthropology Quarterly* 9 (1995): 236-56.

15. Michael Maclean and Rita Bonar, "Ethnic Elderly People in Long Term Care Facilities of the Dominant Culture: Implications for Social Work Practice and Education," *International Social Work* 2 (1986): 227-36.

16. Types of long-term care facilities are Residential-Care Facilities (RCFs), which provide meals, sheltered living, and some medical monitoring-supervision of medications and surveillance of symptoms and signs of problems; Intermediate-Care Facilities (ICFs), which provide room and board and regular (not round-the-clock) nursing care for those unable to live independently; and Skilled Nursing Facilities (SNFs), which provide twenty-four hour nursing care by registered nurses, licensed practical nurses, and nurses' aides. SNFs are for those who need intensive nursing care and rehabilitation.

Recommended Resources

Tim Diamond, *Making Grey Gold: Narratives of Nursing Home Care* (Chicago: University of Chicago Press, 1992).

D. Shenk and J. Sokolovsky, *Teaching about Aging: Interdisciplinary and Cross-Cultural Perspectives* (Washington D.C.: Association for Gerontology in Higher Education, 1999).

Chapter 20

Oral History and Multiculturalism

Mariam Beevi Lam, James Lam,
Michael Matsuda, and Diep Tran
Orange County Asian and
Pacific Islander Community Alliance

This lesson plan gives students an opportunity to conduct oral histories of individuals in their families, schools, neighborhoods, or communities. Students will learn that history is not simply a listing of dates, wars, and leaders but the stories of real people whose lives were impacted by the events of their time. Oral history captures the voices of "unsung heroes": individuals who have made positive impacts in their community but are unrecognized in traditional U.S. textbooks. The collecting of oral histories can be a powerful learning tool for students at the college and high school level for a range of classes, such as U.S. history, Asian American history, Asian American women, Asian American contemporary issues, research methods, and other race and Ethnic Studies and Women Studies courses. The procedures outlined here can be also be used for community-based organizations that are interested in collecting the histories and perspectives of people in their communities.

Objectives

- To observe the human or personal side of history by learning about the people in the community who are essentially "living" histories.
- To compare the histories of different ethnic groups and to locate patterns of commonality.
- To identify the cultural diversity and history of the local community, and to appreciate the contributions that diverse groups have made to the economic, political, and social development of the community.
- To understand the social, political, and economic conditions that force individuals and families to take drastic measures, such as moving to a new area or another country.

- To open a new avenue for communication with an older generation.
- To appreciate the interrelationship of literature and history.
- To realize that history is constructed, and that students can participate in writing history.
- To follow the process of preparing a manuscript for publication, including gathering information, organizing, writing, editing, rewriting, and formatting.

Time

- One week.

Materials Needed

- A sample interview outline is included with this lesson plan. This particular outline was previously used in an interview of a former South Vietnamese military officer who spent close to a decade in a Vietnamese Communist re-education camp.
- Examples of oral histories conducted by students are in the "Primary Sources" section of the OCAPICA curriculum guide, *Vietnamese Americans: Lessons in American History*. These are interviews of a Vietnamese prisoner of war and of a refugee.
- A sample agreement form for interviewees is included with this lesson plan.
- Tape recorders and, at most, two blank recording tapes are needed for each team of students.

Background

Oral history allows us to collect and hold on to invaluable information that can otherwise slip away with each passing generation. But beyond preventing the loss of historical events and facts, oral history helps expand what is perceived and valued as history. Because oral history depends on the spoken word and not on written sources, it expands history beyond that which has been defined by the powerful, famous, and wealthy. Oral history allows us access to the voices, experiences, and perspectives of individuals and people who have been ignored or even oppressed. As such, oral history is also an act of cultural and sociopolitical resistance. For example, underrepresented women and marginalized communities have used methods of oral history to record and document their own histories, in the absence of traditional historical documentation. These groups have utilized oral history to document their stories and added to the fabric of American history. In academia, disciplines such as Women's Studies and Ethnic Studies have particularly valued oral histories because the stories of such groups have often been undervalued and documented. Oral history, therefore, fills the gaps within traditional curricula, creating a redefined and transformed history—a history that provides us with a much more inclusive and accurate picture of the past.

Teachers will see the value of oral history as a flexible teaching tool that can be used to explore many different topics or subjects. This lesson allows students to understand and appreciate the ethnic and cultural diversity of their local community. This activity is adapted from several lesson plans created by Elaine Seavey and Richard Oakes Peters; *An Oral History Primer* by Sherna Berger Gluck; and the instructional video, *Adventures in Oral History: Using Oral History in K-12*, a collaborative project of California State University,

Long Beach and Long Beach Unified School District and directed by Sherna Berger Gluck and Karen Harper.

Suggested Procedures

Teachers may want to do additional research in the area of oral history. An Internet search on "oral history" or "oral history guide" will give an abundance of resources. Also, local colleges may house an oral history program that could provide additional resources. For example, teachers in Southern California can utilize the oral history programs at California State University, Fullerton and California State University, Long Beach. Both programs offer courses in oral history, instructional materials and videos, and archival materials. The website of the CSULB program (www.csulb.edu/depts/history/relprm/oral01.html) is a valuable resource that contains an excellent oral history primer, from which this lesson is adapted.

Introducing the Project

Introduce the oral history project to the students and tell them that they will be working in teams. Explain to the students that many history books tend to focus on famous people and big events and ignore ordinary people and everyday events. But everyone has a story to tell about his or her life; we all have interesting life experiences to share. Oral history preserves the stories and conversations of people who have participated in or lived through important political, cultural, and/or economic developments. Oral history captures these personal experiences and eyewitness testimonies. An oral history project involves students in the pursuit of history, where they can learn new, unexpected facts and stories that strengthen and personalize their understanding of history. Oral history projects also provide students with an opportunity to participate in the actual writing of history.

Defining the Topic

The first step is to define the main topic to explore. Explain to students the purpose and objectives (listed above) of the project, and that the general themes are "multiculturalism," "diversity," and/or "immigrants and immigration." Ask the students to identify all the racial and ethnic groups in the local community. To further define the main topic, ask the students to brainstorm historical events or experiences shared by members of each ethnic/racial group. Along with ideas that you may have, suggest the following ideas:

- Experience of a Vietnamese refugee who escaped Vietnam in the late 1970s and 1980s.
- Experience of a Vietnamese prisoner in a Communist re-education camp.
- Adjustment and acculturation experiences of newly-arrived immigrants and refugees from Eastern Europe or Africa.
- Native American childhood memories of separation from families and tribal affiliations.
- Experiences of African Americans in schools prior to and after the *Brown* v. *Board of Education* case (desegregation).
- Experiences of Japanese Americans in U.S. internment camps during World War II.

- Experiences of Native Hawaiians in Hawai'i and other Pacific Islanders during and after the Pearl Harbor attack.
- Experiences of European immigrants during the Depression.
- Experiences of Latino migrant workers in the early 20th century.
- Factors that influenced people's decisions to immigrate to the United States or to move to Orange County.

Researching for Background Information

Divide the class into teams of two students each. Teams should decide on topics of interest to them—topics they would like to further explore. To prepare the students for the interview, ask them to conduct some background research on their topic. Information could be gathered on specific topics derived from the brainstorming session or on general characteristics and experiences of ethnic/racial groups. Suggest they look at newspapers, magazines, textbooks, novels, maps, photographs of an era or place, Internet census data, and other websites. Remind students to formulate and record their thoughts and questions that they may want to ask in the interview as they are collecting and analyzing background information.

Identifying the Narrator

After further defining the purpose and focus of each project, each team will identify an individual who could help shed light on the chosen subject or information they have gained from the background research. To foster understanding of different groups, each team must choose an interviewee who belongs to a different racial or ethnic group than those of the team members. Ask the students where they would likely find people who are willing to volunteer for the project. How could they widen the pool of potential interviewees? Who are some of the people they know in the community? Neighbors? Other teachers and administrators in their school? Members of their church or temple? Immediate family members or relatives? Grandparents? Members of civic groups, senior citizens center, or community organizations? Parents of friends?

Stress the importance of safety for the students. Are they personally familiar with the potential interviewees? Or do the interviewees come from a trusted source? The teacher can also have his or her own list of trusted individuals who would be willing to participate in the project. Interviews could also be conducted at the school site.

Make sure that the people chosen by the teams somewhat represent the actual diversity of the local community.

Preparing the Interview Outline

The next step is an extremely important one. With the information obtained from the background research, each team should construct an interview outline (see sample interview outline). The outline is a general list of topics and questions; students should use it to help them in their interviews and should not strictly adhere to it. The interviewers should remember to maintain the oral history as an open-ended process that allows the interviewee to shape the narrative in his or her own style. An oral history may not necessarily be sequential or chronological. The interviewer is there to simply guide the narrator.

Contacting the Narrator

Now, each team should be ready to contact the person it plans on interviewing to ensure their cooperation. Explain to the potential interviewee the purpose of the class oral history project, ensuring that they know its plans and intentions. Give the interviewee a general outline of what will be covered. Also discuss the taping of the interview, if this is the means of recording the interview, and the length of the interview. This initial contact may be in writing, orally, or both. Then arrange an interview appointment at a convenient time for the narrator. It is recommended that teams reconfirm with the narrator before setting off for the interview.

Conducting the Interview

Remind the teams to practice using any equipment, such as a tape recorder, before the interview. Use good quality, sixty-minute tapes. Remember that tapes have a few seconds of "lead time," so warn students to not begin recording the moment they turn on the tape recorder. Students should label tapes by writing the narrator's name, date, and purpose on each side of the tape. If one side is blank, write "blank" on it.

Upon arrival, students should politely greet their narrator, introduce themselves, and thank the narrator for volunteering. Once having sat down with the narrator and set up the equipment, the students should record on the tape the date, location, and the names of participants of the interview. To help smooth the interviewing process, students should not turn the tape recorder on and off; they should do so only when the tape needs to be turned over or when the narrator asks for it to be turned off.

Students should begin the interview with the most general question to see where this leads them, before asking more detailed questions. Such basic questions include: "Can you tell me about. . . ?" or "Can you describe. . . ?" Students should ask open-ended questions and avoid questions that result in "yes" or "no" answers. Ask follow-up questions that would yield the most detail. Remember to formulate questions that answer "who-what-when-where-and-why."

Students should not strictly adhere to the interview outline. They should listen attentively and pursue the direction of the interviewee's narrative with additional questions that could capture more detail, rather than simply moving to the next question on the outline. Remind students to be flexible. They should not let periods of silence fluster them. Ask only one question at a time. Keep questions short and clear. Do not interrupt. Give the narrator a chance to think about the question. Allow plenty of time for the narrator to answer. Respond positively with nods and smiles. Students should be polite and respectful of the narrator's wishes. If the narrator asks for a break or that the tape recorder be turned off, the team should comply. Since this oral history project is a team effort, suggest to the students that they take turns asking questions. Remind them to respect and to consider each other's feelings, opinions, and input.

Remind students to take notes during the entire interview, as a reminder for later questions, clarification of details, or additional research. Also, students should take note of non-verbal cues, which may improve the students' analysis of the interview and the narrative. Some behaviors could be captured on tape, such as long pauses, laughter, or sighs. But there are equally important non-verbal behaviors; for example, the narrator may become particularly nervous, distracted at specific points in the interview, or may tear up as they narrate.

Students should end the interview at a reasonable time. One and one-half hours is usually enough time for the scope of this lesson. Once the interview is completed, thank the narrator for volunteering and sharing. Remind the interviewee that the narrative will be used for the class project and ask the interviewee to sign the agreement form (see sample agreement form). Take the time to thank the narrator and answer any questions the narrator may have about the project. Before the students depart, they should leave contact information (classroom teacher's information) for the narrator in case he or she would like to contact someone about the project. Remind students to send a thank-you card or letter to the narrator shortly after the interview.

Processing the Interview

The teams should get together as soon after the interview as possible. This could be for a short period of time, but it is important for the team to process the interviewing experience and to take additional notes of each member's observations and thoughts.

The next step is for students to transcribe their interviews. First, students should attempt to record the narrative verbatim and ignore grammatical structure. After completing the transcript, students should help each other with the editing process, with final approval from the teacher. The final stories could be completed in a variety of formats, from question-answer to story narrative. All final stories should give credit to those who contributed information for the project. Photographs, newspaper clippings, and other documents could be incorporated into the story.

At this point, teachers have discretion on how the students should present their stories in a final product. Teams can simply turn in their stories and make presentations to the rest of the class. Or, to make this class project more exciting and worthwhile, they should consider the possibility of publishing the oral histories as the final product of the project—a compilation book of oral histories of real people from their local community. Students would be involved in the production and publication of a book that could incorporate collected photographs, newspaper clippings and other pertinent materials. This process would further engage the students in the oral history project and could help develop computer literacy skills. Each team's narrative would be a chapter in the book, and it would be the responsibility of each team to design the layout of their chapter. Teachers who have used this method have reported that students feel a high sense of excitement and accomplishment after the book copies come back from the printer. The book could also be shared with the entire school.

Each team can make a presentation on their individual chapter to the rest of the class and share their experiences in conducting the oral history project.

Assessment/Closure

After the class sharing of oral histories, an important closure activity is necessary to help students evaluate their experience with the oral history project. A group discussion and/or writing assignment could address the following questions:

1. What did you learn from an oral history interview that you would not have learned from reading a book?
2. What did you learn that you did not know before about this particular person, historical event or time period, or ethnic/racial group?

3. Is there additional historical or other information that you would like to know or pursue about your interviewee, a particular event/time period, or an ethnic/racial community?

4. In hindsight, what could you have done to improve your oral history project (i.e., your interviewing skills or the questions asked)? What additional questions would you ask?

5. If any, what skills did you gain from completing this oral history project? Any improvements in your speaking or communications skills? Your ability to communicate with an older generation? Your ability to develop the questions that can get the information you need? Your listening skills? Your writing skills?

Sample Topical Outline

Topic: The Story of a Vietnamese Prisoner of War

Personal and Family Background

1. Tell us about growing up in Vietnam.
   Where were you born/raised?
   How many were in your family?
   What did your family do for a living?
   What do you remember about growing up there?
   What was your schooling there?
   What were your plans for the future when you were going to school?
   What made you join the military?

Life in Vietnam

2. Tell us about your life in Vietnam after 1975.
   Why were you unable to escape Vietnam shortly before or after the fall of Saigon?
   When were you imprisoned by the new Vietnamese government?
   Where was the prison located?
   How were you treated in the prison?
   What was a typical day in prison? Please describe.
   Were your family members able to visit you in the prison?
   When did the Vietnamese government release you from prison?
   What was life like for you after your release?

Leaving Vietnam

3. Tell us when and how you left Vietnam.
   How old were you at the time?
   Why did you and/or your family leave?
   What were your plans?
   By what means did you leave Vietnam?
   Did you leave any immediate family members behind?
   Did you have any reservations about leaving your homeland?

4. Tell us what you expected life to be like in the United States.
   What was your definition of the American dream?
   What is your definition of the American dream now?
   Do you think you or your family can attain it?

Settling in the United States

5. Tell us your first impressions of the United States.
   Did you know anyone here?
   Where did you first settle? Why there?
   Did you know or meet other Vietnamese people here?

Handout

Life in the United States

6. Tell me about your life in the United States.
   How did you go about finding a job?
   Housing?
   Making friends?
   What was the most challenging adjustment for you?
   Have you experienced any acts of prejudice or racism?
   How did your life here compare to your life in Vietnam?

7. Were you able to maintain Vietnamese customs? Language?
   What difficulties did you face maintaining your culture?
   To become an American, do you think you can retain your culture?
   Did you maintain ties with Vietnam? Visit?

Reflections

8. Looking back on your experience, what would you have done differently?
   Would you have stayed in Vietnam?
   What would you do differently in the United States?

AGREEMENT FORM

Your story (oral history) is valuable for our Oral History Class Project on the topic of
_____. We are students at _____
School. If you are in agreement, please complete and sign the form below.

I hereby give to the ORAL HISTORY CLASS PROJECT and/or the _____
SCHOOL for educational uses and purposes outlined in the class, the following tapes of the
interviews recorded on (dates):_____.

Unless otherwise specified below, I place no restrictions on non-commercial access to and
use of the interviews.

Name: _____   _____
                  (Please print)   Phone/e-mail

Address:_____City:_____Zip: _____

_____   _____
      Signature of interviewee   Date

_____
Name of interviewer (Please Print)   Phone/e-mail

_____
Name of interviewer (Please Print)   Phone/e-mail

_____
Name of interviewer (Please Print)   Phone/e-mail

School Address:_____ City: _____Zip: _____

Signature of Teacher: _____

Date:_____

===

I wish to place the following restrictions on the use of the recorded interviews: Please check
and initial those restrictions you wish to place on the use of your interview(s):
_____ I wish to be identified by a different name: _____
_____ I wish to restrict access to the materials until (date): _____
_____ Other (specify): _____

I/we agree to abide by these restrictions:

Signed by: _____ Date:_____

Position _____ Phone/email:_____

If you should wish to make inquiries at any future date about your interview, feel free to contact _____, Teacher and project supervisor at _____.

Chapter 21

Bridging Asian American and African American Communities

Ajay T. Nair

Many institutions of higher education embedded in urban settings strive to forge and strengthen links with surrounding communities.[1] According to Ramaley, partnerships between institutions and communities can be appropriate ways to address large-scale reforms.[2] These lesson plans were developed in response to 1) a movement for Philadelphia school reform, 2) a growing tension between racial/ethnic groups in Philadelphia public schools, and 3) the aforementioned movement to strengthen links between local communities and institutions. The lessons move beyond volunteerism and community service by helping elementary school, high school, and college students develop a better understanding of multicultural societies and the larger meaning of community through service learning.[3] In addition, through this service-learning project, we help students develop a strong sense of civic and social responsibility.[4]

Objectives

- To enable students to better understand how to develop friendships across racial/ethnic, language, geographic, socioeconomic, and intergenerational boundaries.
- To help students recognize qualities of friendship and transfer that knowledge to their own behavior.
- To develop a respect for difference.

Time

- Session one: one hour (autobiography)
- Session two: one hour (icebreaker/book background)
- Session three: one hour (friendship bracelet)
- Session four: one hour (jump roping activity)
- Session five: two hours (local ethnic community tour)

Number of Participants

- Five to thirty student teachers

Materials Needed

- Session 1: journal, paper, pencil, chart paper, markers
- Sessions 2, 3, and 4: chart paper, markers
- Sessions 3 and 4: string, tape, and Sook Nyul Choi's book, *Halmoni and the Picnic*
- Session 4: jump ropes
- Session 5: permission slips, tour guide, bus rental, chaperones

Background

Asian American Studies emerged from student and community activism that was part of a larger social movement seeking to transform society.[5] Today, despite the "changed terrain," Asian American Studies can and must serve as a vehicle for community service without "neglecting curriculum and pedagogy."[6] The strategic academically based community service course that inspired these lessons strives to foster structural community improvement by creating a space where students can develop friendships across racial/ethnic, language, socioeconomic, geographic, and intergenerational boundaries.[7]

In a 1997 film produced by Asian Americans United of Philadelphia, a student from University City High School in West Philadelphia declared that the school is not safe for Asian people. "When we walk down the hallway, we hear, "Oh! We smell fish." They push us a lot. Me and my friends, we get into fights every single day."[8] The racial composition of University City High School is 97 percent African American.[9] Despite the similar forms of oppression and discrimination faced by people of color, racial conflict such as this is not uncommon today.[10]

According to the American Friends Service Committee, several factors contribute to the sources of tension between people of color. The mainstream media promotes negative stereotypes of people of color. These damaging images can result in hate violence. In addition, people of color are encouraged to work against each other in a system where individuals and communities compete for scarce resources. The mainstream promotes the idea that anyone in the United States can succeed if they try hard enough. Asian Americans have often been held up as models by the mainstream, promoting the "pull yourself up by your own bootstraps" mentality despite the significant barriers that exist within the diverse Asian American community.[11] Vijay Prashad writes, "we (Asian Americans) are not simply a solution for black American but, most pointedly, a *weapon* deployed against it."[12]

In school settings, racial stereotypes against Asian Americans such as the model minority myth can create racial conflict. Asian American students in such a situation may withdraw from the school community or fight back, physically or verbally.[13] "The portrayal of Asian Americans as a hardworking, successful group is usually accompanied by invidious comparisons to Blacks," further exacerbating racial tensions between the two groups.[14]

As a reform mechanism, the service-learning model here can help communities of color find common ground by promoting the larger meaning of community. The model can also help urban K-12 public schools offer students the validation and personalized attention needed, without overextending the budget or teaching staff. Based on preliminary analyses, the use of this model has managed to do just this. The students report having left the class feeling more self-assured and motivated. The reflection papers especially reveal feelings of optimism about the future, improved notions of self-worth, and belief in academic ability.[15]

For this project, Penn's Asian American Studies Program and the Pan-Asian American Community House partnered with two local community schools: Philadelphia's Franklin Learning Center High School (or Franklin for short) and the Alexander Wilson Elementary School (Wilson). The strategic, academically-based Asian American Studies service-learning course enrolled both high school and college students. The course strove to cultivate a heightened sense of civic awareness and responsibility for college and high school students, while concurrently providing a supportive, safe space of intellectual and emotional encouragement for the high school and elementary school participants.[16]

Together, the high school and college students facilitated Asian American Studies lessons in Wilson Elementary School using cooperative learning teams to promote cross-race friendships and to provide character education for the elementary school participants.[17] The lessons were developed in accordance with the core curriculum of the School District of Philadelphia, which emphasizes key character education concepts. The course culminated with high school and college students creating change projects designed to address issues impacting Asian Americans in urban schools.

The lessons discussed in this chapter were piloted in a second grade class at the Wilson Elementary School in West Philadelphia. During the pilot year of the program, 94.5 percent of the students enrolled in the school were African American, and 86.5 percent were from low-income backgrounds.[18] The second-grade class was comprised of twenty-eight students with a variety of academic abilities. The ten college students were pursuing a variety of majors (i.e., business, English, nursing, engineering, and urban studies). The students were traditional college age, and the majority had attended elite private schools all over the country. Most were from middle-class or upper-middle-class backgrounds. All of the students identified as Asian American. Seven Asian American high school students from Franklin High were selected to participate in the course through the Future Leaders Program (FLP), sponsored by Penn's Asian American Studies program, Pan-Asian American Community House and Young Scholars Program. FLP is open to high school juniors and seniors in the Philadelphia School District. Tuition was paid by the Young Scholars Program. Costs for textbooks and travel were covered by the Asian American Studies program. Potential first-generation college students were especially encouraged to apply.

The objectives of the course for the high school and college students were to 1) challenge assumptions and prejudices on social, political, and racial issues, 2) strengthen and assess self-awareness and personal skills related to service and leadership, and 3) develop an appreciation of social and civic responsibility. The academic component provided an opportunity for training and reflection. Thus, all participants in the project were learners. This model helped to avoid the traditional paternalism associated with service-learning projects.[19]

A study by Nair and Nakiboglu indicates that the service-learning model employed here can help urban K-12 students.[20] Students attending Franklin High School and Wilson Elementary School, both urban institutions affected by recent Pennsylvania school reform mandates, gained from their extended interaction with the Penn undergraduates. Specifically, these elementary and high school students have shown signs of considerable intellectual and emotional development through their participation in the course. The Penn students involved have enhanced their sense of civic responsibility and citizenship through their participation in the course.[21]

Suggested Procedures

The Asian American children's book selected for activities with elementary school children was titled *Halmoni and the Picnic*.[22] It was chosen because the storyline is able to facilitate students' critical thinking of concepts such as friendship, respect for difference, and teamwork. In *Halmoni and the Picnic*, a Korean American girl named Yunmi and her grandmother, Halmoni, explore friendship through everyday interactions in the community. Halmoni has come to the United States to visit Yunmi and her family. Yunmi enlists the help of her friends in an effort to help her grandmother overcome the difficulties she is facing in adjusting to American culture. Halmoni establishes meaningful cross-race friendships throughout the book. With the help of Yunmi and her friends, Halmoni is able to see beyond cultural differences and find commonalities with people she normally would not have interacted with.

Other factors that contributed to the selection of the book included the realism of the characters, the lively illustration, and the rich description of an ethnic culture. Although the concepts were rooted in the experience of an Asian American child while the lessons were being taught to African American children, we found that the story-line and subtleties of this book transcended racial boundaries.

Two activities offered by the California State Polytechnic University, Pomona Teachers' Asian Studies Summer Institute website were adapted for use in these lessons.[23] The activities explore friendship through a jump rope activity and the creation of a friendship bracelet. The jump rope activity served as a natural bridge between the literature and the experiences of the African American children. Jump roping and associated rhymes like "Miss Mary Mack" have been part of most African Americans' childhood. In the lesson, students are instructed to develop chants that incorporate the theme of friendship to accompany jump roping. In addition, the curriculum of the elementary school required experiential learning activities focusing on the theme of friendship. Most important, the activities were selected because they relate directly to the story-line in the book and provided students with an opportunity to apply prior knowledge in a real world setting.

However, prior to exploring concepts such as teamwork and friendship, it was critical that students build a strong classroom community. The lessons preceding the friendship bracelet and jump rope activity sought to develop a sense of community that transcends racial and socioeconomic barriers. The lesson plans were constructed using a five-phase developmental design but can be adapted (see variations) according to particular needs. Instructions for the lesson plans focus primarily on the elementary school students, but procedures for college and high school student teachers are included.

Preparation for Session One

Begin this session with a discussion of human similarities and human diversity.

1. Before our new friends (college and high school students) come to our classroom, it

is important for us to create an autobiography about our lives so that we can share it with them and discuss how our lives are similar and different.

2. Can you tell me what kinds of things families do everyday? *Typical student responses:* "we eat dinner together," or "my mommy takes me to the doctor when I am sick." You can see that there are many similarities between each of us and our families.

3. Can you all share with me something that is special and different about you and your family? Students may describe religious affiliations, family structures (i.e., single-parent household), country of origin, or the kind of neighborhood they live in. *Prompt:* Although all of us have some things in common, we should be proud of the things that make us different. Our new college and high school friends will have both similarities and differences with all of you. Aren't you excited to meet them?

The elementary school students will create a journal in which they will record their autobiographies and reflections on prior learning. As a class, the teacher will brainstorm at least five life events for inclusion in their autobiographies. In order to brainstorm effectively, the teacher should provide guiding questions such as:

- Where were you born?
- Describe your family.
- Describe your neighborhood.
- Describe some of your favorite things to do.
- Tell me about your friends.
- What do you hope to be when you grow up?

Elementary students will be asked to create a rough draft of their responses for their autobiographies. The teacher and students will edit their rough draft together and create a final draft. The students will record their final draft into their journals. Elementary students will decorate the front cover of their journals to reflect a special moment in their lives. They will share their autobiographies with the college students.

College and high school students will share their autobiographies (in the form of a children's book) with the elementary students. College and high school students were asked to reflect on their experiences prior to coming to college and consider factors such as family background, relationship with their parents, community in which they lived, their childhood friends, and how all of these factors have influenced their worldview. They are encouraged to include as many pictures as possible in their books and to pay special attention to writing the book to meet the reading level of the elementary school students.

Session One

- Elementary school students will be pre-assigned to college student partners. Once elementary students and their college student partners break into small groups, they will share their autobiographies with each other. After sharing autobiographies, the teacher will process the lesson with the high school, college, and elementary participants. The following questions can be used as a guide:

    1. What did you learn about your group members? *Prompt:* Describe for me the

different neighborhoods, religions, and racial/ethnic backgrounds represented in the classroom.

2. What similarities did you discover between you and your group members?
3. What differences did you discover between you and your group members?
4. Can you form friendships with people that are different than you?

Preparation for Session Two

1. Tape will be placed in the shape of a rectangle on the floor.
2. The participants will be asked to secure a position on the tape.

Session Two

Instructions for "ABC" Name Game

Purpose: To encourage open communication, acceptance, and teamwork between participants.

1. Participants will identify a corner where the alphabet will begin and end.
2. Participants will place themselves in alphabetical order by first name without stepping off the tape.
3. Once participants have completed the task, have each participant say their first name to see if the task was completed correctly. *Prompt:* Did you hear any names that you have never heard before? Does anyone know the meaning of their name?

Discussion Questions

- Was it difficult to complete this task?
- What was difficult about the task?
- What did you learn from this game?
- What helped you complete the task successfully?
- How are these skills helpful in building friendships?
- Do you need to do different things to make friends with people who are from different backgrounds? *Typical student responses:* Some students will say, "no, you just need to be yourself," while others will say, "you need to be open-minded and willing to accept difference." Regardless of the response, the teacher can role-play and demonstrate that both similarities and differences are important to make friends from different backgrounds.

The teacher will inform the participants that the high school and college students will share a story during their next session. The teacher will describe the book, *Halmoni and the Picnic*, making reference to the concept of friendship. The participants will break up into their pre-assigned small groups. Have them discuss the following questions:

1. How do you decide who your friends are?
2. What do you think friendship means?
3. Do you have friends that are different than you? Do you have friends from different racial/ethnic backgrounds, religions, or neighborhoods?

4. How can you make friends from different backgrounds?

Closure

Have students hold hands while standing in a circle. Ask each person to share why friendship is important to them.

Session Three

- Activate student's prior knowledge about friendship and friends that they have. Teacher will review student responses from the previous session.
- College students will read the story aloud to their assigned group members.
- Encourage students to ask questions and review the main points of the story.
- *Prompt:* "What made Halmoni's friends her true friends?" *Typical student responses:* 1) they like each other, 2) they play games, 3) they have fun together, 4) they like the same things.
- On the chart paper, write down the students' ideas.
- Ask them what makes a good friend? *Typical student responses:* 1) they trust each other, 2) they play nicely with each other, 3) they don't fight, 4) they like the same games.
- Elicit ideas about how good friendships can develop between very different people. *Typical student responses:* 1) you can play games with anyone, 2) sometimes friends who are different can teach you new things, 3) you can teach them things about your culture, 4) if you feel lonely, you have someone to count on.
- Tell them that they are going to make friendship bracelets for a new friend (college or high school student).
- Pass out the string and tape.
- Make the bracelets.

Closure

Bring the students back together to discuss what the students learned about friendship. Share the bracelets that they made and have them introduce their new friend by sharing something new they learned about their friend.

Session Four

- Activate prior knowledge by asking students to tell you what they remember from the story. Discuss the ways that children in the story worked together. Ask them what it means to cooperate. Help them to understand that cooperation is an important part of friendship.
- Tell them that today they are going to work together in a group and create a jump rope chant. Remind them that it is important to listen to everyone's ideas.
- Ask a volunteer from each group to write down the chant.
- Practice the chant while jumping rope.
- Share the chant with the class while jumping rope.
- Encourage students to show respect for the different chants and to listen for the different qualities of friendship.

Safety Tips: Be sure to remind them not to push and shove when jumping.

Closure

Teamwork: Have them discuss what they learned about working together. Talk about the advantages of working together.

Maintaining Friendship: Students can be encouraged to write thank you notes to the college students as a way to maintain friendship. Students can use a semantic web to brainstorm qualities they liked about their college student partners.

Discussion Suggestions

- Identify strategies to help maintain friendships.
- What did you give to your new friend, and what did you receive?
- Is it difficult to make friends who are different from you (i.e., age, race, ethnicity, primary language, religion, etc.)?
- What are the benefits of making friends who are different from you?

The teacher will remind participants that they will be taking a fieldtrip to a local ethnic community. The teacher will emphasize that friends can be made from any community and that the community they will be visiting is a community with people who might have different cultures, but they can still be great friends.

Preparation for Session Five

- Collect permission slips for fieldtrip
- Reserve bus and organize tour
- All participants will write thank-you notes for their partners. Students will be encouraged to reflect on the major themes (making friends across race/ethnicity, socioeconomic status, intergenerational boundaries, etc.) of the lessons while writing thank you notes.

Session Five

Purpose: To connect concepts of the lesson outside the classroom. Students will understand that friendships can transcend race and socioeconomic background.

Instructions

- College students will serve as chaperones on a historical tour of a local ethnic community.
- The tour guide will be told in advance about the concepts emphasized in the lessons and will be asked to incorporate the idea of friendship throughout the tour.
- The tour will end with participants eating lunch together and sharing their thank you notes.

Discussion Suggestions (during tour)

- Where do you think most of the people in this neighborhood came from?
- *Prompt:* When people come from different countries they like to be around things that are familiar. For instance, tell me how Halmoni felt when she first came to America in the book we read? What things made her feel more comfortable in America?
- *Prompt:* We are currently in a neighborhood that is both different and similar to your neighborhood. Do any of you know anyone who lives in this neighborhood? How many of you have friends from different neighborhoods?
- How is the neighborhood that you live in similar to this neighborhood?
- Are there things you noticed about this neighborhood that are different from your neighborhood?
- Can you describe the neighborhoods your college and high school partners are from?
- See how easy it is to make friends from different neighborhoods. Isn't it fun?

Variations

Although the intended targets are Asian American and African American students, the lessons are applicable to any group. The lessons are designed to be conducted successively, but teachers who are constricted by time or other factors may choose not to use all the lessons or adapt lessons to meet the needs of their students. For example, teachers interested in integrating technology can instruct elementary students to write thank you letters using the computer and have them delivered through e-mail.

Notes

1. A. Nair and H. Nakiboglu, "Back to the Basics: Service Learning and the Asian American Community," unpublished manuscript.

2. J. A. Ramaley, "The Perspective of a Comprehensive University," in *Building Partnerships for Service Learning*, ed. B. Jacoby (San Francisco: Jossey-Bass, 2003).

3. K. P. Moore and J. H. Sandholtz, "Designing Successful Service Learning Projects for Urban Schools," *Urban Education* 34:4 (1999): 480-98.

4. N. M. Haynes and J. P. Comer, "Service Learning in the Comer School Development Program," *Service Learning* (1997): 79-89.

5. G. Omatsu, "Defying a Thousand Pointing Fingers and Serving the Children: Re-envisioning the Mission of Asian American Studies in Our Communities" (Los Angeles: UCLA Asian American Studies Center, 1999), www.sscnet.ucla.edu/99F/asian197j-1/Omatsu.htm.

6. Kenyon S. Chan, "Rethinking the Asian American Studies Project: Bridging the Divide Between 'Campus' and 'Community,'" *Journal of Asian American Studies* 3:1 (2000): 17-36.

7. L. Benson and I. Harkavy, "Communal Participatory Action Research as a Strategy for Improving Universities and the Social Sciences: Penn's Work with the West Philadelphia Improvement Corps as a Case Study," *Educational Policy* 10 (1996): 202-03.

8. Asian Americans United, *Face to Face: It's Not What You Think* (Philadelphia: Asian Americans United, 1996), videorecording.

9. Welcome to Info Resources, *West Philly Data Info* (Philadelphia: University of Pennsylvania, 2003), http://westphillydata.library.upenn.edu/.

10. American Friends Service Committee, "Immigrants and Racial/Ethnic Tension," www.afsc.org/immigrants-rights/learn/racial-ethnic.htm#sources.

11. *Ibid.*

12. V. Prashad, *The Karma of Brown Folk* (Minneapolis: University of Minnesota Press, 2000).

13. D. T. Nakanishi and T. Y. Nishida, eds., *The Asian American Educational Experience: A Source Book for Teachers and Students* (New York: Routledge, 1995), 176.

14. *Ibid.*

15. Nair and Nakiboglu, "Back to Basics."

16. *Ibid.*

17. M. L. Clark, "Gender, Race, and Friendship Research," paper presented at the Annual Meeting of the American Educational Research Association, Chicago, Illinois, April 1985.

18. Welcome to Info Resources, *West Philly Data Info.*

19. B. Jacoby, *Building Partnerships for Service-Learning* (San Francisco: Jossey-Bass, 2003).

20. Nair and Nakiboglu, "Back to Basics."

21. *Ibid.*

22. Sook Nyul Choi, *Halmoni and the Picnic* (Boston: Houghton Mifflin, 1993).

23. Teachers' Asian Studies Summer Institute Web Page, *An Integrated Unit on Friendship Implementing Asian-American Children's Literature* (Pomona, CA: Pomona: California State Polytechnic Institute, 2003), www.intranet.csupomona.edu/%7Etassi/tassi.htm.

Part IV

Critical Thinking Teaching Strategies

Chapter 22

Understanding Privilege in American Society

W. David Wakefield

One dimension that influences our perceptions and ways we interact with people is our level of privilege. Privilege represents the failure and unwillingness to acknowledge benefits that one has received as a member in our society. Much of the literature has focused on "White male privilege"; however, privilege is a concept that cuts across racial, class, and ethnic lines and is a useful discussion in any dialogue on intercultural communication and race or ethnic relations. This exercise can be used in courses such as introductory Asian American Studies, contemporary Asian American issues, Asian American women, multicultural education, psychology, child and adolescent development, and in other courses addressing issues of race and culture in U.S. society. This exercise is also appropriate for workshops examining the complexity of race relations and intercultural communication. This activity was adapted from an activity on risk-factors and protective factors in human development used by Dr. Gale Morrison in 1999 in her graduate course titled, "Risk and Resiliency" at the University of California, Santa Barbara.

Objectives

- To enable students to explain the concept of "privilege" and how it manifests itself in the U.S. macroculture.
- To provide students the opportunity to reflect on their level of privilege and how it has affected their lives.
- To promote students' insights on different perspectives of "privilege" through peers' experiences.

Time

- Two forty-five minute sessions or one one-and-a-half hour session

Number of Participants

- Ten to fifty people

Materials Needed

- Large space outside (to allow participants to stand in a single-file line)
- Index cards (3″ x 5″ size)
- Debriefing sheets

Background

Multicultural or culturally pluralistic settings are often considered a panacea for the development of positive racial and ethnic relations. Yet, the reality of how "privilege" influences intercultural interactions is often overlooked when considering the benefits of culturally diverse communities. Privilege is often defined as the set of advantages an individual has, simply as a result of being a member of a specific group.[1] For example, a White American is privileged by the neighborhood in which she or he was raised and by being raised in a two-parent household by highly educated parents. These advantages provide these individuals more opportunities and more access to resources (e.g., private schools, exceptional public schools, "good neighborhoods," etc.) than their low-privilege counterparts.[2] Access to education is one illustration of how privilege can have an advantageous effect.

In contrast, low-privilege individuals have one or more disadvantages that are usually stigmatized in our society. For example, a first-generation Thai American lesbian raised in a single-parent household has lower relative privilege (i.e., being nonwhite, non-heterosexual, non-traditional family structure) than the White American described above. Privilege is a useful construct for discussing issues of stratification in U.S. society because it cuts across the dimensions of gender, race, ethnicity, and class. The concept of privilege often explains why some people in our society have more or less advantages than others.

Being White is often associated with high privilege since in U.S. society White is the default racial group.[3] "Whiteness" has historically been used as the standard for the dominant culture in the United States, and being nonwhite is typically connected to stereotypically negative aspects of American society. As a result, simply being White can elevate one's status and privilege.[4]

One way we can view the effects of privilege in our society is through the incidence and prevalence of racial discrimination. "Privilege" often creates societal inequalities and leads to social stratification. Naturally, one way we can see these inequalities is through the racial discrimination that results. Racial discrimination, or the active behavioral expression of racism, is defined here as denying members of certain racial groups equal access to scarce and valued resources, both material and social.[5] This definition can easily be applied to discrimination on the basis of ethnicity as well. All racial and ethnic minorities continue to be frequent targets of discrimination.[6] Moreover, young people in particular often confront racial or ethnic discrimination as a regular part of their daily lives.[7] For example, Asian American college students often report their teachers expect them to perform extraordinary well in math and science and perform poorly in verbal and written communication. Asian American students also frequently report that individuals are "surprised" if they speak without an accent.[8]

For many Asian American students, as well as other students of color, experiences with discrimination in day-to-day interactions in our society often influence how they connect and relate to their ethnic group.[9] One might expect that people who consistently see members of their ethnic group stigmatized by the dominant culture may distance themselves from their ethnic group. This may be a particular concern during adolescence when young people think about the meaning and significance of their ethnic group membership and develop their ethnic identity.[10] In contrast, White students consistently see themselves in normative roles in American society during adolescence which increases their relative advantage compared to people of color.

As our environments become increasingly diverse, it will be necessary for people to interact with people from a variety of ethnic and racial backgrounds in school, their communities, and the workplace. As a result of privilege, racial and ethnic discrimination is a thriving part of the United States, and there is no assurance that such behaviors will abate any time soon. Thus, people of color will quite likely encounter acts of discrimination during their lives, and they must develop skills to successfully cope with such behavior and maintain optimal levels of mental health and self-esteem. Conversely, White Americans must also become more cognizant of the pervasiveness of negative cultural stereotypes and discrimination.

To promote effective intercultural communication and the development of a healthy ethnic identity, many scholars in the fields of education, psychology, and Ethnic Studies have found that individuals who have clear understandings of their own biases and stereotypes—especially reflecting on their level of privilege—are better able to effectively interact with people from different ethnic, cultural and class groups.[11]

Suggested Procedure

1. Briefly discuss the concept of privilege with the entire group. The following questions may be useful in stimulating discussion with the group: Why doesn't everyone in our country have the same set of opportunities? What personal characteristics or life circumstances often influence one's access to opportunities?

2. After a brief introduction to the concept, ask participants to fold a piece of paper in half, lengthwise, so that it forms two columns. Have them title one column "Personal Benefits," and the other column "Personal Disadvantages." Ask the participants to list the advantages or personal characteristics that they *personally* have benefited from in our society as well as those that have hindered or disadvantaged them. Allow them five to seven minutes to work on this individually.

3. Have students form small groups of three to five people. Distribute two 3" x 5" cards to each participant. Ask members to share two items from each column of her/his list and describe briefly how they decided whether it was an advantage or disadvantage. After each person in the group shares four items (two from each list), each person should select two items and write them on a card (one item on each card). In the upper-right-hand corner of the card have the student write either a +1 or +2 if it is an advantage or -1 or -2 if it is a disadvantage. Use 1 for "moderate advantage or disadvantage"; use 2 for "significant advantage or disadvantage." Collect the cards. While the students are completing this task, make ten to fifteen of your own cards and mix these into the cards collected from the students.

4. Ask participants to move to the large space outside and ask them to form a single-file line. The facilitator should then stand in the middle and ask the participants to face him (note: participants should now be in a horizontal single-file line).

5. Announce that you will be reading a mixture of cards from the participants and

from a list you have previously compiled on personal advantages and disadvantages based on values of the American macroculture. Ask the participants to quickly decide whether or not the statement applies to them, and if it does to take step(s) either forward or backward as directed. Read through approximately twenty of the cards (i.e., "If you are a woman, take one step backwards." "If your parents are still happily married, take a step forward"). During this part of the activity, the participants will likely become stratified. Ask the students to stay in the same place and slowly make a 180-degree turn to see the rest of the group. Note: it is important for the instructor to scan through the cards before reading them. The instructor should eliminate advantages/disadvantages that are inconsistent with the concept of privilege. For example, some students in introductory courses might list "being a woman" as an advantage because they are not required to serve in the military. A student might also list "being gay/lesbian" as an advantage because they do not have to pay "marriage taxes." Eliminating these from the pool of cards is useful to ensure that students clearly understand the concept of privilege.

6. Have students get back into their original groups of three to five people and ask them to discuss the following questions on the debriefing sheets for ten to fifteen minutes. Have one member of the group record people's responses on the debriefing sheet.

   - How did this exercise make you feel?
   - In what ways do you think this activity reflects life in our society?
   - What do you think the differences are between people in the very front versus those in the very back? Is position (front-back) related more to opportunity or individual ability?
   - In what ways has this activity influenced your attitudes about privilege?

   Students generally respond about how uncomfortable this activity makes them feel (especially White male, high-privilege students) since this is often one of the first times that they have been confronted with their relative position and status compared to nonwhite students. Nonwhite students and women typically describe how "in-your-face" this activity is since it causes them to reflect on how certain characteristics that they have little or no control over can place them in a position of disadvantage in U.S. society. When the students discuss the nature of differences between people in the front versus the back, the conversations typically centers around the nature of opportunities in U.S. society and the "myth of rugged individualism." Most "high privilege" students explain differences based on their perception that "people work hard to achieve status," while "low privilege" students note that the lack of opportunities available and that working hard alone does not lead to high status. At the conclusion of this activity, most students gain a strong sense of the "invisibility" of privilege for members of the dominant culture and also how privilege directly limits opportunities for women and members of ethnic minority groups.

7. Bring the group back together as a whole. Facilitate a discussion asking people to share points discussed in their small groups. Typically, many participants talk about how this activity makes them feel slightly uncomfortable since many of the advantages are "unspoken" in the American macroculture and there is an explicit focus on "being disadvantaged" rather than "being advantaged" in our society. Also, participants typically raise points about how this activity raises their awareness of differing levels of opportunity that exists in American society.

Notes

1. Peggy McIntosh, "White Privilege and Male Privilege: A Personal Account of Coming to See Correspondences through Work in Women's Studies," Working Paper No. 198, Wellesley College, Center for Research on Women, 1988.

2. James A. Banks, P. Cookson, G. Gay, W. D. Hawley, J. J. Irvine, S. Nieto, J. W. Schofield, and W. G. Stephen, "Diversity within Unity: Essential Principles for Teaching and Learning in a Multicultural Society," *Phi Delta Kappan* 83 (2001): 196-8.

3. Tim Wise's ZNet Homepage, www.zmag.org/bios/homepage.cfm?authorID=96.

4. P. S. Rothenberg, *White Privilege: Essential Readings on the Other Side of Racism* (New York: Worth Publishers, 2002).

5. E. Cashmore, *Dictionary of Race and Ethnic Relations*, 4th ed. (New York: Routledge, 1996).

6. A. Hacker, *Two Nations: Black and White: Separate, Hostile, Unequal* (New York: Scribner's, 1992).

7. Willis Hawley and Anthony Jackson, *Toward a Common Destiny: Improving Race and Ethnic Relations in America* (San Francisco: Jossey-Bass, 1995); Jean Phinney and Victor Chavira, "Parental Ethnic Socialization and Adolescent Coping with Problems Related to Ethnicity," *Journal of Research on Adolescence* 5 (1995): 31-53; William D. Wakefield and Cynthia Hudley, 1997. *Responses to Racial Discrimination in Adolescents*, poster presented at the biennial meeting of the Black Caucus of the Society for Research in Child Development, Washington, D.C. (ERIC Document Reproduction No. ED408372, 1997).

8. William D. Wakefield, "Adolescents' Perceptions of Racial Discrimination," poster presented at the National Multicultural Summit of the American Psychology Association, Newport Beach, CA, 1998.

9. William D. Wakefield, "African American Male Adolescents' Thinking about Racial Discrimination," Ph.D. dissertation, University of California, Santa Barbara. 1999.

10. Jean Phinney, "The Multigroup Ethnic Identity Measure: A New Scale for Use with Adolescents and Young Adults from Diverse Groups," *Journal of Adolescent Research* 7 (1992): 156-76.

11. Rothenberg, *White Privilege*.

Recommended Resources

Center for Research on Education, Diversity, and Excellence, www.crede.org.

Lisa Delpit, *Other People's Children: Cultural Conflict in the Classroom* (New York: The New Press, 1995).

Larry Adelman and Jean Cheng, *Race: The Power of an Illusion* (San Francisco: California Newsreel, 2002), videorecordings.

Lists for 3" x 5" Cards

Write each of these sentences on 3" x 5" cards. Put the number (1 or 2) in the top right-hand corner of the cards. These numbers correspond with the number of steps to move.

Personal Advantages/Benefits

One of your parents is identified as White. (+1)

Both of your parents identify as White. (+2)

Your parents are happily married. (+1)

You are a male. (+2)

You can hold hands with your "significant other" in public without being ridiculed, laughed at, or subjected to violence. (+2)

Both of your parents have college degrees. (+2)

You have a family member who is a doctor or a lawyer. (+2)

You were able to meet your grandparents. (+1)

You grew up in a single-family home. (+1)

Your first language is English. (+2)

You worked while attending school/college. (+1)

The history of your race/gender/sexuality was taught in your high school. (+2)

You attended a private school. (+2)

You grew up in a safe neighborhood. (+2)

You are Christian. (+2)

You have used public transportation less than thirty times. (+1)

You see people of your race as heroes or heroines on TV or film on any given day. (+1)

Your parents were able to speak the same language as the majority of teachers/staff at your school. (+2)

You have NEVER been followed around a department store/mall because of your skin color. (+2)

Holidays you feel are important to you are celebrated and recognized in your school and at your workplace. (+2)

Personal Disadvantages

You see yourself as overweight. (-1)

You identify as a woman (-1)

People think that you or your parents are stupid because of an accent. (-1)

You identify as a person of color. (-2)

Your gender has never been president or vice-president of the United States. (-1)

Someone has asked you "where are you from?" (-1)

Your opinions are not taken seriously because of your gender. (-1)

Your opinions are not taken seriously because of your race. (-1)

One of your parents is a person of color. (-1)

You define yourself as gay/lesbian/bisexual. (-2)

Your first language is not English. (-2)

Your reflective listening skills have been misinterpreted as being a passive and/or submissive person. (-1)

During your childhood you lived in an apartment. (-1)

You are non-Christian. (-2)

Before the age of eighteen, you had to work to help with the household finances. (-2)

You have lived in poverty during a point in your life. (-1)

You have lived in a "dangerous" neighborhood. (-1)

One of your parents doesn't have a high school diploma. (-2)

You have relied on public transportation at some time in your life. (-1)

You were part of the Federal Lunch Program at school. (-1)

Your teacher wasn't able to communicate with your parents. (-2)

You are over fifty-five years old. (-1)

You joined the military because it was one of the few ways you were able to attend college or see the world. (-1)

You have been treated differently because of your race, ethnicity, or culture. (-2)

You've been suspected of being a "terrorist" because of your skin tone or name. (-2)

You've been told to "Go back to your own country!" (-2)

Chapter 23

An Exploration of Meaning:
Critically Thinking about History

Laura Uba

In recent years, more and more emphasis is being placed on teaching students to think critically across the curriculum. Efforts have gone beyond simply teaching students to doubt everything—an approach that has bred alienation and Manichean cynicism—or honor their opinion-filled but analysis-free journal entries. The approach described in this chapter was designed for a lower-division Asian American history class. It grew from efforts to change classic student perspectives about course work and to demonstrate different ways to look at information. It is designed to promote integrative thinking, the component of critical thinking that involves identifying meaningful patterns and connections among pieces of information. Learning to identify patterns and meanings is useful for analyzing narrative threads in influential political writings to media portrayals of gender and racial groups. Thus, this pedagogical framework is applicable to many courses, including contemporary issues, literature, and Ethnic Studies.

Objective

- To help students develop their critical thinking skills (in particular, the ability to think in integrative ways), to find meaning in events/conditions, and to connect the relevance of historical occurrences to current conditions.

Time

- First phase: about 150 minutes
- Second phase: about seventy-five minutes
- Instructors can modify time periods by varying the number of clusters students weigh, the subtlety of the underlying meanings, and the number of parallels drawn.

Number of Participants

- Fifteen to twenty-five students preferable, or up to forty students if a teaching assistant is available.

Prerequisites

- The instructor needs to create clusters of events, conditions, or behaviors (see handouts at the end of this chapter).
- Both the instructor and students should be familiar with Asian American history and have some historical and current knowledge of other minority communities.

Background

All too often, students have learned education's "three R's"—read, remember, and regurgitate information. Even when they are told to write an essay critically analyzing some topic, often they are really only required to reiterate the analysis the instructor presented in a lecture or textbook author laid out. Moreover, once information has been disgorged in a final examination, it is promptly forgotten because the students have branded it as irrelevant to other knowledge they have, problems they face, and conditions they see. When students don't know how to integrate their knowledge, don't look for meaning, and don't analyze events, history classes seem like "just a bunch of dates"—no wonder they don't want to remember the material. Years of schooling condition students. In the absence of intellectual challenges requiring thinking, students concentrate on reporting what others have thought. So when told to critically analyze events, they silently wait for the instructor to tell them what to think and repeat it.

Before students can assume the responsibility for analyzing and experience the liberation associated with independent thinking, many find it helpful to begin critically thinking within a somewhat structured domain. Consequently, the pedagogical exercise described here focuses on identifying underlying themes or meanings for a small number of events or conditions.

In this pedagogy, student groups consider clusters of events or conditions from Asian American history and identify a common, underlying thread or theme for each cluster. (Each group consists of three students; these small groups can mitigate some of the anxiety associated with facing a daunting, unfamiliar task. Social pressure usually prevents members of a small group from sitting back and waiting for others to do the thinking. Experience talking in small groups can also increase student participation in subsequent class discussions.) Students report that the activity has the secondary benefit of helping them review for examinations both because they have to recall the meaning of cluster items, such as the Gentlemen's Agreement, and because the history of Asian Americans becomes increasingly meaningful. The required body of knowledge, fodder for critical analysis, is analogous to a material cause of critical thinking.

In addition, the process of identifying meanings helps students to be more precise about what they remember. Many lower-division students are satisfied with grasping only the very general gist of what is said or written—a complacency, born of experiences in which that sufficed, that frequently causes them to overlook meanings and compounds the challenge of careful and subtle analysis.

Once all cluster themes are identified, students participate in the "Then" segment of the exercise, which is grounded in Critical Theory's view that knowledge is a way of exposing false impressions and exploitative pressures. Awareness of historical patterns and their current consequences and manifestations enables students to see commonalities among minority communities and makes them more alert to ways in which such communities continue to be perceived and exploited, which is the initial step toward pushing for social justice. This 150-minute segment is followed by a seventy-five-minute segment focusing on the commonalities and differences in the experiences of minorities. Students rely on information from lectures and reading assignments as well as knowledge they bring from other sources to assess the degree to which the historical experiences of other minorities could also be explained in terms of the same integrative themes. This segment has the additional benefit of giving students who are knowledgeable about other communities—for example, African American history—the recognition of being valued sources of knowledge, which, for minorities, is an experience absent in traditional curriculum that is irrelevant to their lives.

The second part of the exercise, the "Now" segment, highlights the relevance of what students are learning: Students look at parallels in the circumstances and treatment of Asian Americans in the past and now. They identify instances in which the event/condition/behavior patterns and cluster meanings identified earlier are manifested today. Afterward, they are again told to identify overlap between the experiences of Asian Americans and other minorities.

Suggested Procedures

The two phases of the pedagogical protocol described here, the "Then" and "Now" phases, are preceded by several weeks of discussion of Asian American history. Because this discussion triggers questions from students about why they didn't previously learn about Asian American history, we look at the way U.S. history is taught, especially in high school—we look at how it is presented from the perspective of dominant groups and carefully sliced in a way that overlooks many racial, political, and economic issues. For example, I show indexes from current high-school U.S. history textbooks and point out that "poverty" typically gets no mention or is "covered" in one page and that the only reference textbooks cite on "race" is "race riots."

Phase 1: The "Then" Phase

1. As a way of helping students find meanings behind the historical experiences and treatment of Asian Americans, I present each three-student group with the same list of events/conditions/behaviors in Asian American history (see handout).

2. The groups are told to identify what a cluster of events/conditions/behavioral responses have in common—for example, "What do the clustered items tell us about attitudes toward Asian Americans?" Insofar as meanings are not inherent in events, conditions, or behaviors, groups might identify legitimate, alternative links to the one the instructor had in mind.

3. In the face of initial uncertainty about how to approach the task and conditioned passivity in the classroom, students need a spur: They are told that all members of the first group to come up with a correct answer will receive extra credit points. (I have found that students are willing to work on the task for extra credit because,

they report, the task begins to feel like a game to them. A concomitant advantage to awarding just a few points is that failure to get them won't dishearten students or turn them off to the activity.) Soon, groups begin to raise hands because they have identified an integrative theme.

4. Often, students will come up with a theme that doesn't account for one or more of the cluster items and hope that I will tell them how those overlooked items fit. When that tactic fails, they concentrate on identifying an encompassing theme. Due to the extra-credit implications, large classes need a teaching assistant because, on occasion, groups almost simultaneously raise hands to proffer solutions.

5. As each group identifies an encompassing theme, that success is acknowledged to the class although the theme is not. Other groups must still independently identify the theme. Meanwhile, groups that have identified the theme focus on identifying other events, conditions, or behaviors that could have been included in the cluster. The results of that effort are discussed after all groups have identified the initial theme.

6. Then students are told to form completely new groups. This step is necessary because otherwise many students will try to align themselves with anyone they think is smart based on classroom performance. A new cluster is presented to the new groups with the same aforementioned instructions. The process continues until all cluster themes and potential, additional events, conditions, or behaviors are identified.

7. The "Then" phase ends with a discussion of examples of the historical experiences of other minorities that could also be explained in terms of the integrative themes. Both students and instructor provide examples. I prompt students with questions about, for example, parallels and differences in Asian Americans' and African Americans' treatment on plantations, the significance of international relations, and restrictions imposed on their right to vote.

Phase 2: The "Now" Phase

1. As in the previous phase, students form groups and identify examples of themes in Asian American communities today. At least some of their responses are based on reading assignments. Students notice that the manifestation of an old ideology often takes a more subtle form in the present.

2. The "Now" phase ends with a description of how the lives of other minorities today could be described in terms of the cluster themes or meanings. The discussion usually starts with a reference to an assigned reading or prompting questions about a current news event. In those discussions, students frequently describe experiences in their lives or cite information they have learned in other courses, which also helps students see relationships between disciplines.

Recommended Resources

Margaret Andersen and Patricia Hill Collins, *Race, Class, and Gender*, 4th ed. (Belmont, CA: Wadsworth/ Thomson Learning, 2001).

Sucheng Chan, *Asian Americans: An Interpretive History* (Boston: Twayne, 1991).

James Loewen, *Lies My Teacher Told Me* (New York: Simon and Schuster, 1995).

Finding Cluster Themes/Meanings: "Then" and "Now"

Students must identify the cluster themes/meanings in the following clusters of events/conditions.

"Then" clusters

A. What ties together these events?
 1. 1882 Exclusion Act
 2. Roosevelt's Executive Order 589 and Gentlemen's Agreement instead of exclusion
 3. Putting Japanese Americans into concentration camps
 4. Filipinos as U.S. subjects
 5. Suspicion of Chinese Americans as communists, during McCarthy era
B. What shared consequence resulted from the following?
 1. Chinese Foreign Miner's Tax
 2. Paying Asians less than white workers for same job
 3. Great Mahele
 4. Not letting Asians into unions
 5. Teachers telling Japanese Americans in Hawai'i not to become educated; one purpose of "Oriental" schools
 6. Thind ruling by U.S. Supreme Court
 7. Not fully compensating Japanese Americans for WW II internment
 8. Size of the Korean American population before 1965
C. What attitude is behind these events/behaviors?
 1. Asians couldn't become naturalized citizens
 2. 1882 Exclusion Act; Angel Island treatment
 3. 1924 Immigration Act
 4. Limiting possibility of bringing wives to the United States; anti-miscegenation laws
 5. Bad living conditions for Filipinos
 6. U.S. military rule over Guam
D. What attitude or value is behind these behaviors/events?
 1. When Filipino farm workers were no longer needed during Depression, the United States doesn't want them here
 2. Delay in granting independence to the Philippines
 3. Filipino plantation workers being closely supervised to prevent "subversive" activity
 4. Historical narratives about the United States usually start with the arrival of Europeans
 5. Payne-Aldrich Tariff Act; later, tariff against commodities from the Philippines imported to the United States
 6. Forced changes in lives of Samoans
 7. *Haole* oligarchy
E. What do the following have in common?
 1. Chinese were the first to undertake commercial sugar production in Hawai'i
 2. A Filipino American invented the fluorescent light bulb

Handout

3. Asian Americans turn California into an agricultural state by introducing irrigation to previously infertile areas.

4. Importance of Japanese Americans in MIS/442/100 and Filipinos during World War II

F. What attitude underlies these behaviors and policies?
1. Discrimination against Chinese for having queues
2. Issei accepted more than Chinese in the first modern wave of immigration
3. World War II claim that Japanese Americans were un-American
4. Government refugee resettlement plan
5. Anglo-conformity as unhidden, unchallenged goal

G. What do the following have in common?
1: Filipinos using Naval service to become citizens
2. Lawsuits
3. South Asians' farm cooperatives
4. Secondary migration of Southeast Asians
5. Korean plantation councils and sworn brotherhoods
6. Unpaid family labor

H. What do the following have in common?
1. Reason early Filipino immigrants didn't get into business as much as Chinese Americans had
2. Japanese came after the United States had outlawed contract labor
3. Ability of some Southeast Asian refugees to escape conditions in Southeast Asia

I. Repeated patterns: Put a checkmark next to all of the above that are also true for other minorities.

"Now" Phase

- Put a star next to conditions that still affect Asian Americans.
- Put a cross next to conditions that still affect other minorities.

Note: Students do not see the "answers" listed here.
A. International relations affecting treatment of Asian Americans
B. Impediments to the development of power among Asian Americans
C. Ways in which Asians were discouraged from coming to the United States or staying here
D. Colonialist attitude/exploitation
E. Unacknowledged contributions of Asian Americans
F. Pressures to acculturate
G. Coping strategies employed by Asian Americans
H. Role of luck

Handout

Chapter 24

Generative Thinking:
Using a Funding Proposal to Inspire Critical Thinking

Daniel Hiroyuki Teraguchi

One of the arduous tasks for an educator is designing an assignment that teaches students to interrogate an issue from multiple angles using a variety of methodologies that lead them to deeper understandings about the complex world they live in. When students are given writing assignments on critical thinking, they often describe and summarize rather than analyze. Part of the problem is that some have not been given techniques to help them analyze an issue, while others are simply disengaged. In response, I have created four fun and engaging activities around a process that I call Generative Thinking that exposes students to critical thinking techniques and that culminates with a funding proposal assignment to provide a practical mechanism for students to demonstrate their problem-solving skills.

Because Generative Thinking is a process of engaging students in critical thinking rather than being topic-driven, it is useful in content-specific courses such as public policy and introductory classes in Asian American Studies. Community-based organizations may also find it useful as a collaborative brainstorming exercise that produces fundable ideas and strong drafts of grant proposals. In addition, elements of Generative Thinking can be used in diversity-focused workshops to help faculty incorporate empowerment pedagogies into their courses.

Objectives

- To increase students' capacity to critically analyze issues from multiple angles using a variety of methodologies.
- To strengthen students' ability to articulate their analyses through multiple forms of expression and in public venues.
- To engage students in various forms of expression to flush out their ideas and to approach problem-solving from multiple vantage points.
- To enhance students' learning capacity by exposing them to non-traditional teaching methods, so they are better able to survive in a variety of educational settings.
- To foster a culture of innovation and inquiry where students develop their capac-

ity to formulate questions and their courage to ask them.
- To produce a product that could have practical applications to a community-based organization, the field of Asian American Studies, and/or students' personal interests.

Time

- The four activities are designed to span three weeks for a class that meets twice a week for an hour and fifteen minutes, but they can be adapted to different time periods. However, the culminating exercise, the funding proposal, is enhanced when all four steps are implemented sequentially over an extended period.

Number of Participants

- Ten to thirty people

Materials Needed

- Poster-size Post-It Notes
- Two to three color markers per student
- A room with movable chairs/desks and wall space to display the posters

Background

One of the strongest links Generative Thinking has to Asian American Studies is its empowering pedagogical style that yields a critical thinking product; this emerges from a developmental process that integrates student experiences and course content. Generative Thinking attends to a fundamental principle of Asian American Studies, which is to create a supportive learning environment through empowering pedagogies that are inclusive and learner-centered and that respect and respond to student needs and cultures.[1] Furthermore, Generative Thinking establishes a non-threatening environment that enables students of color who have been disenfranchised in other classes a space of visibility.

Another central concept to Generative Thinking is using different forms of communication to increase the capacity of students to be better critical thinkers. With different forms of expression, the students are pushed to explore new ways of viewing an issue. For example, one activity is having students communicate their thoughts through drawings but by using any language other than English. This activity enables students to understand the perspective of students whose first language is not English in U.S. society. This activity reverses the tides of power and privilege for students who only speak English, and it pushes them to express their ideas in a form that they may not be as comfortable doing. Creating this empowering and exploratory space inspires innovative thinking and empathetic knowledge. Moreover, empathetic knowledge is a key element in critical thinking because it helps students realize that their position can limit their understanding of an issue. Generative Thinking deliberately exposes students to different forms of expression, such as acting, drawing, talking, and writing. The goal is to have students explore an issue from multiple vantage points through different forms of communication, which can reveal new approaches to solving that issue.

My inspiration for these activities came from Dr. Peter Nien-chu Kiang's assignment that he uses in his "Boston's Asian American Communities" course at the University of Massachusetts, Boston. I have applied the Generative Thinking process in my Fall 2003 Asian American Studies course at the University of Maryland College Park, "Asian American Communities: The D.C. Metro Area."

Suggested Procedures

Setting the Tone

Before implementing the Generative Thinking process, the instructor needs to establish a classroom culture that encourages creative forms of expression, promotes active learning, and fosters students leadership. Students need a comfortable and exploratory space to contribute their experiences in multiple formats to enhance their learning and the learning of the class as a whole. Otherwise, students will struggle to find their voice and feel uncomfortable performing the activities embedded in the Generative Thinking process.

To establish this type of classroom culture, I start with a non-traditional method of doing class introductions. I ask students to draw their introduction on a poster by using symbols and pictures that have special meaning to them and that they want to share with their classmates. To level the playing field for students whose first language is not English, I do not allow students to use any English words on their posters, but they may use any other language. After about ten minutes, students display their posters and are given two to three minutes each to explain them to the class. To help students understand their relationship to the class as a whole, I have students address three questions in a writing assignment.[2] The questions are: How are you like no one? How are you like some? And how are you like everyone?

During the next class, I give them an opportunity to take a leadership role in the success of the class by developing a fair and just policy for students who do not turn in assignments on time. Students must decide who has voting rights as well as generate possible disciplinary policies. After much debate, I clarify the policies to be voted on and remove any aspects that I feel are inappropriate, such as asking students to financially contribute to make up for the late assignment. In my classes, the majority generally vote for a policy with three components: 1) students must make up the assignment; 2) they must do something extra; and 3) they must be disciplined. For my most recent class, students agreed that those who turned in any late assignment must write a poem to explain why their assignment was late and read it out loud in front of the class, in addition to completing the assignment. Without being prompted, all the poems contained apologies for not being good citizens in the class. Afterwards, very few students handed in late assignments; when they did, they had their poems ready.

To continue fostering a comfortable space for self-expression, I also introduce the class to improvisational skits. For these skits students divide into small groups where they must develop a short play that lifts out a particular issue from their readings or videos from class. To help students generate a storyline for the skit, I ask students to write down five emotions and pose a series of questions for them to contemplate. Questions include: What emotions were evoked after reading the article or watching the video, and how do you portray that emotion in your skit? What emotions do you want to draw on to engage your audience? What will be the morale of your story? Tying the skit to an emotion helps students communicate their feelings about a particular issue. After about ten to fifteen minutes of preparation time, each student team has two to three minutes to perform. At the end of the skit, the class must guess the moral of the skit. What is their message? How does it relate to the class?

For example, one group played off the TV show, *Blind Date*, by mismatching an Americanized Filipino (JR) with a fresh-off-the-boat Filipina (Sharon) to address generational issues within the Filipino community in the D.C. Metro Area between recent immigrants and U.S-born youth. In the skit, JR arrives at Sharon's place for dinner and is immediately scolded for not taking off his shoes. A strange odor makes JR cringe. Seeing JR react to the smell, Sharon becomes extremely nervous and embarrassed because he, obviously, finds her traditional cooking offensive. A class discussion ensues where students try to guess the moral of the skit and to probe deeper into the issue and its connection to the readings.

Although the students were resistant to performing at first, they were amazed by the power of acting out an issue. Comments from students included: "I didn't know learning could be so much fun," and "This was bizarre, but it really made me think." Once students know they are expected to use different forms of expression, they become comfortable doing so and even demand it. This sets the stage for the Generative Thinking process.

Finally, I engage students in a fun technique called the Brownie Test, designed to help them develop critical questions using a rubric to determine if a brownie is good or not. The activity starts by bringing brownies to class. Then, I ask students to write down five to ten adjectives to describe brownies. In small groups, I have students compile their adjectives into categories such as taste, appearance, texture, cost, and moistness. They must also write down five questions that they want to ask the instructor to increase the preciseness of their rating. The groups rate the brownie after eating it and asking their questions. A short discussion ensues about each group's rating. For homework, I have them apply the brownie technique to an article where they must create five questions or categories prior to reading it to determine if the article is, in fact, a good one. They are expected to hand in their questions and an explanation of whether they felt the article was good based on their questions or other factors that emerged from reading it.

Generative Thinking Process

At this point, the class expects nontraditional assignments and interactive classroom activities, and students feel fairly comfortable expressing their ideas and asking critical questions. This sets up the Generative Thinking four-step process for teaching critical thinking. Each step is described below.

Step I—Human Sculpture: The goal of this activity is to get students to visualize and then actualize different aspects of a particular idea in developmental steps. Since sculptures are immobile and have no voice, this activity is also designed to expose students to the difficulties facing groups who are unable to verbally communicate their ideas. That is, students literally have no voice in this activity because it asks them to develop a series of silent human sculptures to articulate their ideas.

It begins by dividing students into teams, either self-selected or assigned by the instructor, that must agree on a truly important issue, idea, or question and then (re)present it for the class to see, understand, and appreciate. For my most recent class, the Human Sculptures had to relate to Asian American communities in the D.C. Metro Area. To assist students, I asked them to draw several scenes on paper first to help them generate images about their bodies as expressive tools. But I do allow them to use any objects in the classroom for their sculptures. After about fifteen minutes of preparation time, the groups perform.

For example, one group of four students focused on rice rockets, the hyped-up cars that Asian American male youths show-off and drag race in parking lots of local strip malls. This topic was inspired by the loss of one of the student's friends during a recent drag race. The sequence of their sculptures began with two students mimicking driving in desk/chairs, while the others stood beside them flexing their muscles to portray how their hyped-up cars represent their Asian masculinity. The next scene had the students in their desk cars dragging down the street with the other two students in front of them trying to get out of the way while covering their ears with a frightful look on their faces. The last scene had one of the desk cars tipped over with one student and a pedestrian lying on the ground. One student is kneeling by his friend, covering his face with his hands. The other student is attending to the injured pedestrian.

After performing, the team leads a short discussion where their classmates try to guess the issue portrayed in the human sculptures, offer suggestions, and ask questions. Sometimes students are still shy in critiquing their peers' sculptures, so I have them write down questions that pop up during the performance on a piece of paper for me to ask. This empowers students to ask any question because it removes the pressure of being identified as potentially asking a silly question since no one knows who actually wrote it. After a short question and answer session, the performing students are given an opportunity to explain why they chose this topic and how it relates to an Asian American community in the D.C. metro area.

Step Two—Mural: The goal of this activity is for the groups to clarify their issue by re-displaying it through another form of communication that reflects suggestions from their peers. Each group is instructed to draft a design for a mural that illustrates their topic through a series of drawings. Students have the first fifteen to twenty minutes of the next class to draw their murals on a series of poster-size Post-It Notes, or they may bring pre-drawn panels to class. Again, no English words are allowed.

This step also provides a way for students to work individually within their student groups. Because each group will have three posters to draw their mural, I indicate that teams may draw three separate posters representing different interpretations of the issue. If groups are able to meet outside of class, I encourage them to design a single, succinct mural using the three posters. Students must decide which is best for their group because some teams have a difficult time to meet outside of class. I made this adjustment based on student feedback because team time outside of class was a major barrier for completing projects.

After the murals are completed, each team is allotted two to three minutes to explain the images in their mural to the class. To further assist groups in clarifying their topics, I have the class complete anonymous evaluation forms to provide feedback to the team. The form asks students on the mural and topic, to list areas of strengths, and to indicate areas for improvement. I collect the evaluation forms after each presentation and use them to provide written feedback to students in person or in an e-mail. I do not show the raw data to presenting teams because a few students always write inappropriate comments. The class is also encouraged to ask questions about the mural to help their classmates better articulate and clarify their topic.

Step Three—Monologues: The goal of the monologues is to have students to analyze their topic through different perspectives and engage them in empathetic understanding. That is, this activity is designed to increase students' capacity to gain empathetic knowledge of an issue by having them see the issue from another person's perspective.

To help students generate the monologues, I ask them to think about writing a screenplay, where they develop characters to represent different vantage points of their selected topic. Each member of the team is required to write at least one monologue, none of which can be from the same point of view. For example, one student group from my last class was studying the effects of HR 3244, the Victims of Trafficking and Violence Protection Act. The monologues they developed are briefly described below:

- The Victim: The students created two monologues, one showing a woman's desperate situation in Asia, and another after her arrival in the United States to highlight how she is deceived and forced into prostitution to pay off her debts.
- Yellow Fever Man: This monologue focused on a white male's fetish for Asian women and emphasized the harmful stereotypes. The students also addressed the marketability of Asian massage parlors and spas—that is, there is a demand for massage parlors and spas featuring Asian women because of Yellow Fever Man.
- Spa Owner: In this scenario, an Asian American owner of a legal spa is the victim of racial profiling and arrested by police. The students wanted to emphasize to the class that all spas are not brothels and to show the effects of a wrongful arrest. The spa owner was disgraced from being arrested, and she lost her business.
- The Ally: Although this was the least developed monologue, the students were trying to understand what might inspire an ordinary community member to help these exploited women.

Due to time constraints, all the monologues were not presented. However, I did select some for students to read to the class. For smaller classes, I encourage that all monologues be presented.

Step Four—Funding Proposal: The culminating activity is designed to offer students a way to display their critical thinking they have developed from previous steps and evoke their problem-solving skills. Each team must write a proposal to a foundation that is interested in donating one million dollars for Asian American community projects. Drawing on insights gained from the previous steps, they must determine the components of their topic that will be compelling enough for the foundation to fund it. To complicate matters for students, I limit the length of the paper to two to three single-spaced pages to encourage students to be concise. For the first time, students demanded that they be allowed to write longer papers. The sections of the funding proposal included:

- Project title and description, including goals and objectives.
- Who is involved? Is there any partnership with community organizations?
- Rationale and background/history: Why should you receive money for this project and why for this particular population?
- Description of the project—project goals and objectives: What will you accomplish?
- Strategies to accomplish your project goals/objectives.
- Evaluation: How will you know if you have succeeded? You need to document whether or not you accomplished your goals.

In class, the students were shocked that only one proposal would be funded. Another one needed minor changes in order to be funded. All others were rejected, which surprised some of the more studious students. These students indicated that if they had more space, they could have crafted a stronger proposal. I indicated to them that they needed to do a better job of determining the most compelling aspects of their topic and clearly articulating them within the proposal rather than trying to explain everything briefly. The imprecision of their strategies for accomplishing their goals and objectives was the major reason it was rejected because the funder could not figure out what they planned to do with the million dollars even though the rationale was sound.

Variations

Classes focusing on public policy issues may especially benefit from the Generative Thinking process. Examples could include the examination of the application of affirmative action to Asian Americans in higher education, Kamehameha Schools' Hawaiian-preference admission policy, the effect of the Patriot Act on different immigrant groups, and the underlying causes of Asian American youth gangs.

Notes

1. Peter Nien-chu Kiang, "Pedagogies of Life and Death: Transforming Immigrant/Refugee Students and Asian American Studies," *Positions* 5:2 (1997): 524-55.

2. S. R. Komives, "Increasing Student Involvement through Civic Leadership Education," in *Realizing the Educational Potential of College Residential Halls*, eds. P. Mable and C. Schroeder (San Francisco: Jossey-Bass, 1994), 218-40.

Recommended Resources

Mary Field Belenky, Clinchy Blythe McVicker, Nancy Rule Goldberger, and Jill Mattuck Tarule, eds., *Women's Ways of Knowing: The Development of Self, Voice, and Mind* (New York: Basic Books, 1973).

Maralee Mayberry and Ellen Cronan Rose, eds., *Meeting the Challenge: Innovative Feminist Pedagogies in Action* (New York and London: Routledge, 1999).

David Schoem and Sylvia Hurtado, eds., *Intergroup Dialogue: Deliberative Democracy in School, College, Community, and Workplace* (Ann Arbor: University of Michigan Press, 2001).

Chapter 25

Promoting Transgressions through the Automatic Reward System in the Literature Classroom

George Uba

Traditional writing assignments in the literature classroom often produce boring and repetitious critical analyses. The problem lies less with student motivation than with the conventional nature of most writing assignments and with a reward system that too often credits a safe predictability, while discouraging a riskier originality. Over the years I have experimented in my junior-level college literature course entitled "Asian American Fiction" with an automatic reward system designed to foster an environment in which students engage assigned texts originally, creatively, and transgressively. This lesson plan describes the reward system.

Objectives

- To require students to engage texts with originality, not only to enhance their interest but to help them understand how texts operate as multiple discourses whose meanings are not limited to the creator's apparent intention or to the instructor's authority.
- To help students gain consciousness of how educational practices have imposed intellectual dependency on them by systematizing and rewarding a reliance on various forms of received authority, while stifling them from critical thinking.
- To help students engage in deconstructive writing practices, while acquiring a working vocabulary of post-structural terminology.
- To increase the number of writing assignments per class, while not increasing the amount of time required of the instructor for comments and corrections.
- To encourage students to take advantage of their preexisting cultural literacies in their critical investigations of Asian American literature.

Time

- Because the automatic reward system does not involve a single activity, it cannot be reduced to a set amount of time. Going over the thesis and response paper template (see handout) usually takes more than a single one-hour class session. Also, some form of transgressive analysis takes place during virtually every class meeting. Finally, I find it very helpful to allow students to meet in small groups throughout the semester, since much individualistic thinking actually is stimulated through collective activities.

Number of Participants

- Twenty to forty students

Background

Deconstructive reading practices and post-structural principles continue to afford a valuable opportunity to wean students from their habitual reliance on received authority. I build this course on Asian American fiction on a platform of critical theory that unsettles my position and the author's position as principal authorities regarding the meanings of the text. As well, it undermines students' unexamined faith in structural unities and common-sense interpretations. I encourage students to use my own interpretations only as incentives to develop their own. I want them to understand how reading conventions and ideologies inform, shape, and customarily limit their interpretations of the literary text and how the process of approaching texts as multiple discourses facilitates the construction of alternative readings.

As in other disciplines, students in literature courses customarily tailor their critical interpretations to what they believe the instructor permits. Such displays of dependency are a function of an educational programming whose system of rewards and punishments has been internalized over the course of many years. All students have seen instances of those penalized for stepping beyond the tacit boundaries of interpretation established by the instructor—that is, punished for violating the instructor's ideological limits. Rather than try anything too risky, they opt for the safety of some form of analytical regurgitation. Notwithstanding admonishments to be original, the neophyte learns to exercise extreme intellectual caution rather than daring, to exhibit dependence rather than independence, and to seek the shallows of a safe conformity rather than risk the turbulent depths of transgression.

And yet it is the latter of these sets of terms that the majority of us in this profession surely wish to promote. While it is true that institutions, legislators, and even many educators remain married to what Freire critiques as the "banking method" of education in which the knowledgeable teacher/banker makes the intellectual deposits in the blank container of the students' minds, it is equally true that most teachers want students to be able to think for themselves, to generate original insight, to lead rather than simply to follow.[1]

The question is, how do we get them to the desired starting point, when the history of their educational experience tells them that we teachers are apt to say one thing and do another? Verbal admonishments may inspire or not (usually not), but in any case they fail to provide a method. The occasional showcase essay offers a model—but seldom a means. To promote original and transgressive textual analyses, we must start by acknowledging our students' dependence on grades. Students have been programmed to rely excessively on grades as the primary—in some cases the sole—index of their intellectual accomplishment. This reliance is profoundly reductive, of course, but decrying its existence is useless. Thus, any attempt to generate really original or, as I am calling it, transgressive readings must be placed within a *grading context* that, for our students, constitutes reality. What I rather crudely label the automatic reward system is designed to foster an educational environment that promotes intellectual daring and experimentation and that "forces" students to challenge accepted ideas (no matter how logical, convincing, well-supported, and agreed-upon they may appear to be). Most important, it is designed to habituate them to believe that they will not be penalized for taking risks and possibly not succeeding in their essays—and that they may even gain a reward, if at first only a verbal one, for making the effort in the first place.

During the semester, I give six writing assignments, of which the first four receive automatic full credit for being turned in on time. Each assignment builds in length and complexity, until students feel that they can—and indeed must—think and argue originally and embrace the principle of transgressive analysis in order to earn the higher letter grade they desire. The real objective of the reward system, however, is not grade-centered. Just as students intuit the rewards inherent in educational conformity, I want them to leave the classroom questioning this principle and better prepared to engage in other forms of free, original, and individualistic critical thinking. This system, one which I have experimented with for the last nine years, has produced consistently satisfying results. I will share two examples of original critical analyses that students developed once they were thoroughly convinced that the class really did value original, disruptive, transgressive thinking.

To begin, several years ago in a class discussion of N. V. M. Gonzalez's short story "The Bread of Salt," I lamented that while this well-told, familiar tale of youthful infatuation and disenchantment bears resemblance to and shares emotional registers with James Joyce's classic story "Araby," it does not confront the more political aspects of Spanish colonization, which instead are allowed merely to percolate beneath the story's surface. One of my students, a Filipino American math major who was unaccustomed to writing critical essays, recognized my lecture as an opportunity to develop a transgressive reading of the text. After conducting research into the folklore of the Philippines, he pursued an analysis of the text that showed how it actually operates within traditions of the *sirena*, a mermaid-type figure who lured men into captivity and destruction by offering them certain types of food. Tracing the parallels between Gonzalez's story and the *sirena* myth, the student successfully argued that the story can indeed be read as an anti-colonial text in which the young man's failure to win the heart of the wealthy niece of the "old Spaniard" constituted not failure but success—in this case the successful avoidance of the temptations of a consuming neo-colonialism. At the same time, the student's essay showed how Gonzalez's story was rooted not so much in European literary tradition as in Filipino folklore.

Another student, whose parents came to America as Vietnamese refugees, researched what previously had been an idle interest in *feng shui*, then applied her findings to Amy Tan's "Rice Husband," the well-known tale from *The Joy Luck Club* involving Lena and Harold as the mismatched interracial couple who supposedly split everything in half in the name of fairness and equality. Without denying the importance of the gender and racial assumptions that guide each character's actions, or of the different cultural legacies and family histories that further complicate the marriage, my student shifted attention to the material surroundings of house and landscape and argued compellingly that, irrespective of the characters' actions and traits, the bad *feng shui* virtually guaranteed that the marriage would fail. What is most interesting is that the student's step-by-step application of *feng shui* principles actually worked to de-exoticize an Oriental practice, an especially useful tactic when dealing with an author like Tan. Not only did the student's essay arrive at an alternative reading of the story, but it also succeeded in arguing for an alternative, non-Western science.

Such examples could easily be multiplied. Clearly, as the instructor, I too am beneficiary of an open, transgressive intellectual environment. Like others, I take no pleasure in reading boring essays that merely regurgitate ideas already discussed in class. But the rationale for this teaching practice goes beyond personal enjoyment and learning and even beyond the desire to have students think and analyze more adventurously. Rather, I want them to understand that there are ideological reasons why their analyses of situations and texts—not just literary texts either—are so often kept within accepted parameters and equally that there are ideological reasons why their analyses need not remain so confined. Beyond the reading of literary texts, I want students to apply similar deconstructive or transgressive principles to other cultural texts, whether these exist in the form of work environment, hip-hop club, place of worship, or the mainstream media. The automatic reward system, then, while respecting the students' own allegiances to achievements ratified by grades, ultimately remains committed to broader principles of critical thinking and reform. By itself, it is only an instructional method, and as Freire reminds us, educational methods and techniques are not to be confused with desired social transformations, when the larger goal "is a different relationship to knowledge and to society."[2] Nevertheless, it is in step with other pedagogical practices in pursuit of such change.

Suggested Procedures:

Pre-writing and Discussion Activities

In order to demonstrate how certain conventional "authorities of interpretation" become internalized as we proceed through our educational lives and how they serve to delimit the possibilities of interpretation, the instructor may wish to start with a sample text. Early in the semester I focus on a short story by Toshio Mori entitled "Say It With Flowers." Students readily agree that the story concerns a young florist shop worker named Teruo who faces a moral crisis when he learns that he must tell lies to the customers about the freshness of the flowers. After refusing to lie and after giving flowers away for free, Teruo is fired—but retains his integrity. After arriving at this collective and consensual interpretation, the class is encouraged to revisit the story in the context of classic Marxism. With a bit of prompting, students usually interpret Teruo's rebellion as a symbolic revolt of the proletariat, a revolt quickly crushed, as it turns out, by a managerial system that already has compromised other members of the working class. The class then examines the problematics of socialist revolt and the means by which class-centered analyses insinuate their way into texts otherwise marked by primarily humanistic concerns. At this point I direct the class's attention to something entirely different and easily overlooked: a passage in the story in which Teruo refers to the pleasure he gains through the "art" of arranging the bouquets for his customers. We contrast the passage to a couple of others in the story wherein various characters refer offhandedly to the "business" of selling flowers. Occasionally, a student knows something about *ikebana*, the Japanese art of flower arrangement. More commonly, I explain to the class some of its basic principles and how—through research—I learned about these principles. As the students examine the story from this unexpected angle, they come to see that it can be viewed both as a contribution to a pre-existing discourse on the art of flower arrangement and as an exploration of a Japanese American sensibility that has retained some vital aspect of a Japanese cultural heritage in the midst of a grasping assimilation that marks his Japanese American co-workers. As a story linking with cultural heritage, "Say It With Flowers" not only gains added dimension but pursues a different direction from what the author evidently intended and even from what a mechanical application of class analysis permits.

Response Papers

The next step is to provide students with a template (see handout) that directs them away from the rambling, unfocused, and unreflective responses they are apt to engage in and towards a more challenging and unique set of ideas. The template, which naturally can be altered or refined depending on an instructor's inclination, is a bit crude, perhaps, but nevertheless useful. I require that the two response papers each consist of two extended paragraphs whose total length should be about two typed pages. The first paragraph of the response paper begins with the line, "Most readers probably think that the text (title of work), followed by the student's thesis or interpretive statement." The template includes an example of how to develop this paragraph.

After developing and supporting this thesis idea, the student begins the second paragraph with the line, "But I contend that this story (or text) can be viewed quite differently." This sentence is followed by a second thesis or interpretive statement. After discussing the example in the template, I find it useful to work with the class on the blackboard in generating, developing, and supporting the second thesis. As the class works collectively, often—along with the instructor—struggling to develop the second paragraph successfully, the students not only gain practice in finding and using textual evidence in less obvious ways but also begin to appreciate how a successful argument is always a matter of process and of trial and error. I remind them that if they don't struggle with their second paragraph, it's likely that their second thesis statement is already too obvious to most readers. The format of the template, along with the subsequent development of each paragraph, also serves to bridge the gap between the personal or impressionistic textual engagements that response papers frequently devolve into and the more rigorous analytical demands of a critical essay.

As long as the correct format is followed, the minimum length requirement observed, and the paper submitted on the appropriate date, the student receives automatic full credit for the response papers. I read but do not comment on or return these papers. Instead, I redistribute them in small-group read-arounds, asking each group to single out for praise the most original thesis idea and the best supported paragraph.

Interpretation Papers, Group Project, Final Paper

The next three essays, labeled interpretation papers, are longer critical engagements that dispense with the two-paragraph format but continue the idea of developing the most original or transgressive thesis. The first two interpretation papers receive maximum full credit for being turned in on time. The third paper is the first assignment for which the students are not guaranteed full credit. They do know, however, that for this third paper, as well as for their group projects (research-based oral presentations) and their final papers, they will be expected to demonstrate that they have absorbed and can apply the principles underlying the entire course. They know too that if they merely summarize or repeat interpretations covered during lectures, they will receive lower rather than higher scores.

Potential Hazards

The Free Ride or Lack of Effort Myth: Surprisingly, the guarantee of full credit for the first four writing assignments seldom leads to what would seem to be the most obvious hazard: a lack of motivation or effort. Since all students are guaranteed full credit, anyone can go through the motions, write the bare minimum, be completely unreflective, and still gain the same amount of credit as another student who slaved away at the paper for days. But usually students gain a sense of immediate liberation when they understand that whatever they argue about a text—as long as it is original, as long as it transgresses or counters the more obvious or received view—will not be penalized. The verbal recognition given during the classroom read-arounds to those who have taken intellectual risks plays a definite role in providing reassurance and stimulation.

Grade Inflation: Grade inflation and the frequency of students not completing the reading assignments on time, or at any time for that matter, pose potential problems since I give no tests. Since I do not assign journals, I give brief pop quizzes at the start of many but not all classes. Even though the pop quizzes can be a form of negative reinforcement, they succeed in ensuring that students will complete at least a substantial number of reading assignments. Moreover, they provide a stimulus for class discussion. By semester's end, the variations in the pop quiz scores—along with a more stringent grading scale (see handout)—help to assure that a reasonable grade distribution operates within each class.

Lack of Written Feedback: An ongoing challenge is to ensure that there is sufficient written feedback on the three interpretation papers, so that the class feels adequately compensated for not having received written feedback on their first two response papers. Praise and recognition for a few during the read-arounds obviously cannot replace specific writing suggestions for all. Therefore, it is usually imperative to set aside a single response paper or sections from several response papers to address composition-related problems.

Difficulties of Critical Terminology: The extent to which students are able to apply actual critical concepts and terms in the course of a single semester or quarter varies substantially. Not surprisingly, students—and my students come from virtually all majors—who enter the class perplexed even by the raw, common-sense meanings of the texts are especially daunted by arcane terminology. Keeping the vocabulary reasonably simple is a good idea.

Further Activities

To make students begin to apply post-structural principles actively throughout the semester (whether or not the terminology is used), small-group activities are very useful.

- Choose (or even allow the students to select) one to two paragraphs from a story or book. Have each group identify possible concepts, motifs, or even just individual words that may possibly serve as the fulcrum for a larger discursive engagement. Have the groups explain in class how they could develop a fuller textual analysis from this starting point. For an advanced exercise and in possible preparation for the group project, have the students connect their idea to discourses existing outside of the immediate text, so that they begin to understand how literary texts too are clusters of discourses rather than self-contained organic unities.

- Ask groups of students to identify and highlight passages on consecutive facing pages that they would deem important if they were studying the text for purposes of a conventional critical analysis or a test. Then direct them to the unmarked passages and ask them to construct an interpretive strategy relying exclusively on the unmarked passages. Afterwards, have them return to one or more of the marked passages and ask them to use some portion of the previously marked passages in support of the new interpretive angle. At the end, re-emphasize how interpretations are constructs rather than mere decodings of textual or authorial clues, and how previous reading practices have shaped and in a sense pre-determined which passages tend to be identified as potential evidence bearers in the first place.

- Ask the class to identify how meanings are made in non-literary texts and to identify further the real-life consequences that result when idiosyncratic or transgressive interpretations are disallowed.

Notes

1. Paulo Freire, *Pedagogy of the Oppressed*, translated by Myra Bergman Ramos (New York: The Seabury Press, 1970), 57-74.

2. Ira Shor and Paulo Freire, *A Pedagogy for Liberation: Dialogues on Transforming Education* (South Hadley, MA: Bergin & Garvey Publishers, 1987), 35.

Recommended Resources

Henry A. Giroux, *Theory and Resistance in Education: A Pedagogy for the Opposition* (South Hadley, MA: Bergin and Garvey Publishers, 1983).

Mary Beth Hines, "Multiplicity and Difference in Literary Inquiry: Toward a Conceptual Framework for Reader-Centered Cultural Criticism," in *Reading Across Cultures: Teaching Literature in a Diverse Society*, eds. Theresa Rogers and Anna O. Soter (New York: Teachers College Press of Columbia University, 1997), 116-32.

bell hooks, *Teaching to Transgress: Education as the Practice of Freedom* (New York: Routledge, 1994).

A Template for Thesis Statements and a Discussion of Response Paper Elements

Paragraph 1 begins: Most readers probably think that . . .

Paragraph 2 begins: But I contend that this story can be viewed quite differently.

1. Sample thesis and format for paragraph 1 (based on "Immigration Blues" by Bienvenido Santos): Most readers probably think that this story shows how marriages of convenience involving Filipinos in the United States can be viewed in a positive light. Such marriages of convenience were often strategies for people facing hostile immigration policies and widespread racism. In Santos' story there are two marriages of convenience that turn out to be successful and one possible marriage of convenience that holds the prospect for success. For example, Alipio and Seniang's marriage of convenience turned out to be quite successful, even though the odds seemed to be against it. During their marriage, Alipio was clearly a devoted husband who tried to "take care of Seniang" (427), who in turn would greet him warmly at the door "wearing (his) jacket and (his) slippers" when he returned from work (427), telling him "'you keep me warm all day'" (428). Following her death, "everything had gone to pieces" for Alipio (424). He even says, "'Seniang was my good luck'" (424). Similarly, Mrs. Zafra and Carlito's marriage of convenience, though less successful than Alipio and Seniang's, still benefited each person. How might we discuss this further, using textual evidence to show how both Mrs. Zafra and Carlito benefited from the marriage of convenience? Finally, a possible marriage of convenience between Alipio and Monica could turn out to be as successful as the one between Alipio and Seniang not only because Monica is desperate to remain in the United States and Alipio is becoming aware of his need for companionship but also because their humble, likeable personalities seem to match rather well. How might we discuss this further, using textual evidence to show Monica's desperate need to remain in the country, Alipio's need for companionship, and their personality characteristics that seem to match.

2. Another sample thesis for paragraph 1: Most readers may think that the story "Immigration Blues" focuses in a humorous way on a man who lives alone and knows it but who is also lonely but doesn't know it until the possibility of companionship unexpectedly arises.

3. Sample thesis and format for paragraph 2: But I contend that the story can be viewed quite differently. I argue that the story endorses the activities of Mrs. Zafra as a rebel and a system-breaker. To support this thesis, discuss how Mrs. Zafra breaks away from the restrictive convent, where she found "the sisters and the system . . . (to be) tyrannical, inhuman" (432). Then discuss how she uses the marriage of convenience and Carlito as "an instrument for her good" (433) to help her gain self-realization as a defiant, independent person. The paragraph could also focus on how Mrs. Zafra enters Alipio's home "with the assurance of a social worker" (425), using this quote to suggest that Mrs. Zafra's form of "social work" is

not designed to preserve the social system but to "re-work" and "re-shape" it into something different.

4. Another sample thesis and format for paragraph 2: But I contend that the story shows how Mrs. Zafra exhibits the classic traits of the "liberated woman" as defined by ____ in her book ___. (Start by laying out the four to five characteristics of the "liberated woman" as defined in the book. Then, using textual evidence, show how Mrs. Zafra exhibits most or all of these traits through her attitudes, words, and/or actions.)

5. Another sample thesis and format for paragraph 2: But I contend that the story can be viewed quite differently. The story actually shows how Alipio and Monica are brought together not because of Mrs. Zafra's efforts but through the "language" of food. (Let's discuss this one in class, placing our ideas in paragraph form on the blackboard.)

AAS 321: Asian American Fiction

Course Requirements and Point Totals

Assignment	Maximum Score
Response Paper 1*	25
Response Paper 2*	25
Interpretation Paper 1*	25
Interpretation Paper 2*	25
Interpretation Paper 3	50
Group Project (collective score)	100
Group Project (individual score)	50
Final Paper	100
Class Participation	50
Pop Quizzes	50
Total Possible Points	500

Asterisked assignments (*) = automatic full credit (all essays shall be read by the instructor; however, the two response papers shall not be returned to the student or have written comments on them).

Grading Scale

To receive a grade of at least A-, the point total for the semester must reach at least 465/500 (93%). To receive a grade of at least B-, the point total must reach at least 418/500 (83.6%). To receive a grade of at least C-, the point total must reach at least 350/500 (70%). To receive a grade of at least D-, the point total must reach at least 275/500 (55%).

Chapter 26

What's Wrong with a Color-blind Perspective?
A New Model of Critical Caring for Teachers

Christina Ayala-Alcantar

Many teacher credential programs attempt to address cultural diversity through a pluralistic orientation that does not adequately address how cultural factors influence the learning process of students of color. A pluralistic orientation provides a superficial understanding of diversity such as appreciating differences, celebrating holidays, and eating ethnic foods. This approach does not allow teachers to learn how the intersection of factors such as race and social class influence both their practice and student learning. This chapter provides an opportunity for teacher candidates to explore the dilemma of making ethnicity/race "invisible" in the classroom. More specifically, this chapter will demonstrate how a "colorblind" perspective excludes the experiences of students of color and immigrant students from the classroom even though their cultural experiences permeates every aspect of their lives and shapes the ways they think, feel, and act.[1] This activity can be used in teacher training programs, teacher credential programs, and Liberal Studies courses.

Objectives

- To introduce students to the concept of a "white knight."
- To examine the problems with a "color-blind" perspective in the classroom.
- To introduce students to the concept of "uncritical caring."
- To introduce students to the idea of "silencing."
- To provide students an opportunity to reflect on their own perceptions and experiences with ethnicity/race and how this will influence their interaction with students and teaching.

Time

- Three hours.

Number of Participants

- Twenty to thirty-five students.

Materials Needed

- TV
- VCR
- Documentary *First Person Plural* by Deann Borshay Liem.[2]
- Alice McIntyre's article, "Constructing an Image of a White Teacher"[3]

Background

> "I don't see color, I only see children." What message does this statement send? That there is something wrong with black or brown, that it should not be noticed? I would like to suggest that if one does not see color, then one does not really see children. Children made "invisible" in this manner become hard-pressed to see themselves worthy of notice.[4]
> —Lisa Delpit, *Other People's Children*

Teacher education programs can play a critical role in transforming how the nation's future teachers educate K-12 students to live, work, and participate in an ever-changing, multiracial and multicultural world. To assist in this transformation university teacher education programs must provide teacher candidates with learning experiences that enable them to acquire the knowledge and skills to meet the needs of culturally diverse students. Teacher candidates must reflect on their own perceptions of and experiences with race before they fully understand the worldviews of culturally diverse students.[5] For example, teacher candidates who demonstrate sensitivity toward the lives of students of color and immigrant students often possess a positive sense of self that includes an awareness and acceptance of their own ethnic identities.[6]

The documentary *First Person Plural* provides a forum through which professors and teacher candidates can examine the role of race in their personal lives and their classrooms. The film chronicles the adoption journey of Deann Borshay Liem, a Korean national adopted by a White American family in Fremont, California. Deann begins her search for her Korean family by writing a letter to the orphanage she was adopted from and is informed that she is not Cha Jung Hee, the orphan adopted by Alveen and Arnold Borshay. Instead, she is Ok Jin Kang and is informed that her immediate family (with the exception of her father) is alive and well in Korea. It turns out that Cha Jung Hee was found and reunited with her father right before she was to be adopted by the Borshays. The orphanage decided to send Ok Jin Kang as her replacement without informing anyone that she was not Cha Jung Hee. The film explores the complex maze of her adoption, her experiences growing up with her American family, and her desired relationship with her Korean family.

While the video does not directly address teaching, the film highlights many of the ideas put forth by Alice McIntyre in her article "Constructing an Image of a White Teacher."[7] McIntyre collects qualitative research on white teacher candidates, and the article examines a portion of her findings. More specifically, she discusses the idea of "Teacher Image," which refers to how White teachers make sense of their white racial identity in relation to their practice and perception of self as a teacher.

One of the themes that emerges from her data is the notion of a "white knight." This refers to a teacher who wants to save students of color from their "deprived" lives without considering what the students really need or desire in the classroom. The emphasis is placed on being a benevolent teacher. It is similar to a missionary perspective of saving souls without regard to the convert's attitudes, beliefs, and values because the missionary knows what is best. This concept of a "white knight" alleviates White teachers from any responsibility of addressing the inequities in the educational system because the emphasis is placed on the individual level of assisting students. This allows White teachers to ignore institutional factors such as meritocracy, tracking, and intelligence testing that assist in creating an educational standard and guaranteeing that only a small number of students will excel and many others will fail. Accordingly, by only focusing on individual students in the classroom, White teachers do not have to feel responsible for the failure of the large number of students of color in our public schools.

A second issue that emerges from her data is that of "colorblindness." This theme appears when teacher candidates discussed being White teachers in relation to their students of color. In particular, teacher candidates struggled with the idea of racism and how they belonged to the larger institutional structure of education, which is racist and benefits White students. Instead they shifted the focus to their classrooms and how they were not racist in this setting because they simply saw "children not color." Thus, their "colorblind" perspective meant they were not racist but good people and good teachers. However, by minimizing the role of race in the classroom, they either silenced or marginalized the lived experiences of students of color. For example, this occurs on a consistent basis in relation to immigrant students. Many times teachers are not trained for or considerate to the experience of immigrant students. Their primary concern is teaching the child English without any regard to the emotional loss of leaving family and friends nor the culture shock students may be experiencing in a new country. Moreover, teachers may not be fully aware of the different barriers students may be experiencing in acquiring a new language and adjusting to life in the United States. Silencing occurs for these students because little time is taken to incorporate their immigrant experiences in the classroom.

Both of these ideas are addressed in relation to being adopted in *First Person Plural*. Specifically, Deann's American family provides multiple illustrations of how having good intentions (i.e., being a "white knight") and a "colorblind" perspective can create problems for people of color. The Borshay family's wish to help a poor Korean orphan illustrates the notion of a "white knight." Their desire to assist is sincere and altruistic. However, this very desire serves as a barrier in meeting the needs of their new daughter as she enters a new country and starts her life with a new family. For instance, when she arrives from Korea and they pick her up from the airport, they fail to consider the language difference. They do not have a translator with them to assist them in communicating with Deann. They are so caught up in their own excitement that they do not take a step back to reflect on Deann's wants at the time.

"Colorblindness" emerges for the family when considering the physical differences between themselves and Deann. One of the methods used by the family to address this issue was to highlight the similarities and minimize physical differences. Deann's brother discusses how their eyes are different but how they share the family smile. In an extreme example of making differences invisible, Deann complains to her parents that her ears keep sticking out when she combs her hair, and the Borshays recommend plastic surgery to remove the problem.

Michelle Fine defines silencing as processes and practices within education, which make it difficult to talk about the experiential lives of students in schools.[8] This occurs either though mechanisms in schools that do not allow certain topics to be discussed or mechanisms that discredit or minimize topics that are raised. Although the documentary does not address silencing in schools, it does reveal how Deann's American and Korean families silence certain aspects of her life. For instance, at no time does her American family provide an opportunity for her to mourn her homeland or the loss of her Korean family. Her American family is unable to deal with her sadness and loss, so they keep silent and ignore her pain. Similarly, Deann's Korean mother is unable to cope with her decision to give Deann up for adoption. She encourages Deann to accept her American mother as her real mother. Thus, her Korean mother minimizes the emotional pain Deann is experiencing in reuniting with her and her desire to rekindle a mother-daughter relationship.

The video also provides an opportunity to develop McIntyre's idea of "uncritical caring." One of the points made by McIntrye is that many teachers do not think critically about their students' lives when they talk about caring for their students. That is, they fail to consider how factors such as culture, gender, and socioeconomic status impact their students' lives and learning in the classroom. They also lack a critical exploration regarding the inequities that exist in the educational system. McIntyre argues that it is time to move away from this standard and time for teachers to support their students through "critical caring." Therefore, teachers must consider the experiential lives of their students and should challenge the structures that continue to support an inequitable public education.

Suggested Procedures

1. Before showing the video, inform students of the content of the film (i.e., the film is about a Korean woman who is adopted by a white American family in Fremont, California). Discuss the similarities between adoptive parents and teachers. Discuss how biological parents entrust their children to adoptive parents and have faith the adoptive parents will love and do everything that is best for the child. In a similar manner, parents trust teachers to properly educate and care for their children.

2. At the completion of the video, break students up into groups of three to five persons. Try to make groups as culturally diverse as possible. Have groups discuss their initial reaction to the documentary. What thoughts did they have as they watched the documentary? What feelings did they experience? What was their impression of Deann's American parents? Her American siblings? Korean family? What surprised them the most about the video? What did they dislike the most? Give students approximately five to ten minutes.

3. Ask students to share their reactions with the class as a whole. Spend approximately five to ten minutes sharing as a class.

4. Review the concept of "white knights" and "colorblindness" discussed by Alice McIntyre. Students should have read her article prior to coming to class.

5. As a group have students link these concepts to the video. Have them fill in a table with examples of family members serving as "white knights" or endorsing a "color-

blind" perspective. For each example, ask students to identify how the incident was beneficial and/or negative for Deann. Give students approximately ten to fifteen minutes in groups.

6. Ask a representative from each group to share one example from the group with the class by writing it on the board. Also, have them list the benefits and negatives. Spend approximately ten to fifteen minutes sharing and documenting examples.

7. Introduce students to the notion of silencing (educator should read Michelle Fine's article, "Silencing in Schools: What Is Said and Not Said" listed in "Notes").

8. Ask students to identify examples of silencing from the list on the board. Potential examples relate to immigration, language, culture, and ethnic identity—for example, the lack of encouragement Deann received to maintain the Korean language and her Korean name. Another example is the family's inability to learn or remember Deann's real Korean name (Ok Jin). Her sister argues that her real name is not important because she is still Cha Jung Hee to her. This example highlights how they minimize her cultural identity and worth.

9. Ask students how these examples might also occur in the classroom and at schools. What does silencing look like in schools for students of color and immigrant students?

10. Review the concept of "uncritical caring" by Alice McIntyre. As a class discuss this notion in relation to the video. Ask them how the Borshays might have acted differently with Deann if they engaged in "critical caring."

11. End the discussion with the need for teachers to participate in "critical caring" for their students. Share the importance of their moving out of their comfort level and caring for the students in a manner that is much more supportive of them as individuals and their education.

Addressing Student Concerns

1. One issue that arises while working on this exercise is the concern some students express regarding the Borshay family. They feel that it is unfair to critique the Borshay family because they had good intentions when adopting and raising Deann. I believe it is important to emphasize that is not the point. Many times teachers have good intentions when entering teaching, but they do not necessarily do what is best for the students because of their own agendas and/or beliefs. However, I do believe that is vital to explain to students that the intent is not to vilify the Borshays, but to highlight some of the issues that arise when relationships are one-sided or only one perspective is considered. I also believe the Borshays are to be admired for their courage and willingness to meet Deann's biological family. Some adoptive parents are not willing to engage in such action. While they made some mistakes, they also made some very good decisions in supporting their daughter.

2. Another issue that emerges is that many times white students are very uncomfortable with the notion of a "white knight." They want to believe that they are good people and struggle in understanding how their altruism is something negative. I believe this provides an opportunity to talk about why a person wants to become a teacher. Is it because they love children? Do they want to make a difference? Or is it because they want to educate students? What is their motivation to

teach? These are important questions to answer because if they are going into teaching for all the wrong reasons, they might want to reconsider this career.

Notes

1. The introduction of this chapter is adapted from the introduction to *Education in American Society*, an anthology edited by William De La Torre and Christina Ayala-Alcantar (Dubuque, IA: Kendall/Hunt Publishing, 2003).

2. Deann Borshay Liem, *First Person Plural* (San Francisco: National Asian American Telecommunications Association, 2000), videorecording; information about this documentary is also available on the PBS website, www.pbs.org/pov/pov2000/firstpersonplural/.

3. Alice McIntyre, "Constructing an Image of a White Teacher," *Teacher's College Record* 98:4 (1997): 653-81.

4. Lisa Delpit, *Other People's Children: Cultural Conflicts in the Classroom* (New York: The New Press, 1995).

5. G. McAllister and J. J. Irvine, "Cross Cultural Competency and Multicultural Teacher Education," *Review of Educational Research* 70:1 (2000): 3-22.

6. G. Howard, *We Can't Teach What We Don't Know: White Teachers, Multicultural Schools* (New York: Teachers College Press, 1999).

7. Alice McIntyre, *Making Meaning of Whiteness: Exploring the Racial Identity of White Teachers* (New York: State University of New York Press, 1997).

8. Michelle Fine, *Silencing in Schools: What Is Said and Not Said in Education in American Society* (Dubuque, IA: Kendall/Hunt Publishing Press, 2003).

Recommended Resource

Joan Wink, *Critical Pedagogy: Notes from the Real World* (New York: Addison Wesley Longman, 2000).

Chapter 27

Modeling Whiteness:
Minorities, Assimilation, and Resistance

Sheena Malhotra and Aimee Carrillo Rowe

The emergence of the field of "whiteness studies" offers new insights into understanding the cultural and political positioning of Asian Americans as a model minority. While we have often thought of the role of the model minority largely in terms of class, it is also productive to consider the ways in which racial differences are both accentuated and erased through this positioning. It is important to ask what a model minority is supposedly modeling. The answer is revealing in terms of understanding whiteness. As a model minority, Asian Americans are both accepted into whiteness and rejected from it. Whites use the "model" status to keep other minorities down, even as it sets Asian Americans up to strive for something that can never be fully achieved. This chapter provides an assignment that makes visible the relationship between "whiteness" and the positioning of the model minority. The exercise may be used to dialogue about the particularities of being a model minority, its relationship to whiteness and how it might function to reify whiteness and perpetuate racism in society.

Objectives

- To have students question their views about race and challenge their ethnocentrism.
- To understand that whiteness serves a universalizing function that is not limited to White bodies.
- To gain skills for self-reflexivity by learning to critically read one's own experience.
- To identify each student's own positionality in relation to whiteness in U.S. society.

Time

- Sixty to seventy-five minutes for the model minority exercise.
- An additional thirty minutes if one unpacks the racial formations that might be formed in the course of the exercise.

Number of Participants

- Twelve to forty students

Background

Asian Americans are often characterized as the model minority, a shining example to other groups of how hard work can help minorities achieve the American dream. Certain successful segments, or celebrities, from black and Latino populations may also be seen as models, but the myth is most often associated with Asian Americans. The term is highly problematic as it erases the differences between Asian ethnic groups with dissimilar socioeconomic realities, creates high pressures on this population to succeed and belies the racial difficulties most Asian Americans still experience in the United States. As any form of domination succeeds by dividing marginal groups, so the myth of the model minority is used to hold up Asian American achievements and argue that if one racialized group can make it, so can other minority groups if they just work harder.[1] This myth is created by setting up and maintaining the normativity of whiteness.

The field of whiteness studies has provided important insights into how we think about white identity. But whiteness and White identity are not the same. Whiteness is defined as a "standpoint of racial privilege" or an "unmarked" racial location.[2] We suggest that whiteness is also a process that continually produces and reifies the content matter that makes up White cultural identity. Whiteness is a process that universalizes a particular way of being in the world, privileging White cultural identity and making it seem that it is the only way or the best way to be. For example, Western logic and Cartesian binary thought often associated with white cultural identity are important ways to analyze the world. However, it is a problematic for whiteness when that logic is set up as the "only way" for everything to function and then gets used to characterize peoples and societies that use different thought systems as "uncivilized" or "primitive." White settlers were unable to see the complexity of organization in Native American societies they were colonizing because these did not fit their own linear logic and hierarchical structures. This led to Native Americans being characterized as "savages," and tribes were forced to appoint patriarchal leaders in order to "negotiate with the White man."[3]

Within the discourse of whiteness, racialized bodies are usually positioned as deficient or "the other," even as whiteness encourages them to strive to "be like White" in order to be recognized as fully human. This is seen clearly and chillingly seen in the rising popularity of eye surgeries among a small segment of the Asian American population, who are getting surgery to "correct" the shape of their eyes in order to imitate Anglicized facial construction. For Asian American students, what must be considered then are the ways that Asian-ness both conforms to and fails to meet the norms of whiteness. Sometimes, class privilege among certain Asian groups may function to disguise racial positioning temporarily and in particular contexts.

When we conceptualize whiteness as a process rather than an essentialist identity, we see it is possible for people who are not White to also engage in the performance of whiteness. White cultural identity usually falls on White bodies because those are the bodies trained since birth into that way of being. In other words, the bodies we are most accustomed to seeing performing whiteness are White bodies. But people of all colors often strive toward achieving White cultural identity in order to gain access, to be accepted or to seem "normal." There are some racial groups that may seem more able to access this whiteness than others. This exercise unpacks the dynamics and implications of this striving.

The underlying assumption of being a "model minority," after all, is that one has assimilated into the rules of the white world in an exemplary fashion. There is an internalization of whiteness that often accompanies this process, sometimes a judgment about those who have not assimilated as successfully and possibly even a self-hatred for not being quite "White" enough. Unpacking the concept of the model minority in relationship to whiteness can offer us insights into how whiteness operates and the power it yields for students who fit this stereotype and have to negotiate it on a daily basis. Also it enables us to better understand students who do not fit this stereotype and the feelings it engenders.

However, this assimilation into whiteness is always conditional. For example, Asian Indians who migrated to the United States in the 1990s as computer programmers were sometimes able to access parts of the American dream relatively quickly, although they were often paid less than white programmers for similar jobs. In the 1990s, the cap on work visas for technically trained workers was raised to bring in more of these workers in order to fuel the technology. They were seen as a desirable population because they were highly-educated, English-speaking and more important, filled a labor shortage at a particular time. However, when the technology sector crashed at the end of the 1990s, that labor shortage quickly became a labor surplus, and these same workers were suddenly seen as undesirable and characterized as "taking away American jobs." The acceptance into mainstream U.S. society, then, remains conditional, on a variety of factors, including economic trends and how well the minority group models the dominant one.

In either case, whiteness studies reveal the complexity of examining race from the side of privilege, as opposed to the side of marginality. This work can be revealing to Asian American students as they come to see the ways in which they have or have not had to negotiate whiteness and its interrelation with the myth of the model minority.

Suggested Procedures

This activity helps students to unpack the complexities of the concepts of the model minority and whiteness. The exercise is set up to appear as if it focuses on creating physical representations of race in the United States. The actual objective, however, is to unpack the dynamics of being a "model" for others—of being chosen—and its implications.

In order for this exercise to be effective, however, students should do some readings on race and whiteness. Without such readings it will be difficult to unpack the nuances of the exercise. We recommend the article by Peggy McIntosh on White privilege and male privilege because it allows students to begin understanding how white privilege functions.[4] McIntosh lists various daily and invisible privileges she enjoys, such as knowing that she can move into any neighborhood she can afford and knowing that when she speaks, she is not assumed to represent an entire race. She also compares these privileges of being White, both big and small, to the privileges of being male that often go unnoticed by men. Her article is an effective way to explore White privilege as the other side of racism. The video *The Color of Fear* is also an excellent teaching tool and can be used to help explain concepts we cover.[5] Prior to conducting this activity, instructors should also spend some time discussing whiteness as a norm and differentiating it from White cultural identity.

We find that devoting a two-week period of the semester to this assignment can greatly enhance students' understanding of whiteness and race. Studying race on its own or whiteness by itself only provides one piece of the puzzle and can sometimes lead to an oversimplified understanding of race. In many ways, the ability of model minorities to embody a desire for whiteness provides grounds for a fertile discussion of the nuances of race in the United States. Students begin to understand that while whiteness is most often associated with White bodies, it is possible for whiteness to be performed by nonwhite bodies. Just as importantly, white bodies can also resist whiteness. This exercise also helps to tease out the differentials between White cultural identity, whiteness and White privilege. Once students begin to grasp these concepts, they are able to deconstruct their own experiences with race and whiteness, no matter what their own racial positionings may be. Conducting this exercise about a third of the way into the semester can promote fruitful discussions about race and the Asian American experience in particular for the rest of the semester.

Suggested Procedures

1. Pick two student facilitators from the class. It is effective to choose students who tend to be the most outspoken and extroverted for the first pair of students. Alternatively, ask for student volunteers. Take them aside and tell them they have been chosen for their ability to grasp concepts of race and express themselves creatively. Give them a simple directive. Ask them to use students from the class in order to create a visual representation of race in America that includes a marked representation of whiteness.

2. It helps to take in visual markers that students can use in the exercise, such as bandanas. Using bandanas may be essential in more homogenous classrooms but also useful in mixed classrooms so that students can "mark" other students rather than using skin color. It allows for flexibility and can mitigate the emotional risk of the exercise. When we conducted the exercise, we gave the students different colored bandanas and explained to them that they could use the bandanas any way they wanted with the goal of creating a visual representation of race relations in the United States.

3. Give the student facilitators three minutes to discuss their concept between them and seven minutes to execute the task. Possible examples of what students might create or that you could suggest are:
   - a circle formation in which most of the class is on the outside circle and a select few (usually White students) are in the middle.
   - a start and finish-line formation where most are clustered closer to the start-line and a privileged few are close to the finish-line.
   - a more dramatically expressive formation where a heterosexual, upper-class, White male stands on a desk in the center of the room and others in the class gather around him, trying to reach his position.

4. Give the facilitators five minutes to field questions about their construction. The questions usually center on the symbolism of their formation. Sometimes other students will offer an explanation of what they saw being communicated by the facilitators in their formation. Allow the facilitators to talk about why they did what they did. They are being the "experts" on race and white privilege.

5. Repeat this exercise with one or two other pairs of facilitators (depending on time and number of students you have).

Examples from our classroom

- One pair of students used the bandanas to signify three racial groups. The "White people" were those with their bandanas tied around their arms, standing at the center of the room; the "people of color" wore their bandanas on their legs and stood in one corner of the room; the "biracial" people were represented by two people tied together at their arms.
- Another pair of students (both White women) walked around the class placing bandanas over the chests of some people and in the pockets of others and giving none to a few. The presence of the bandana signified the "racial mark" for the people who wore them; it was an unseen mark for biracial people, signified by the bandanas in their pockets; and it was absent for White people. This formation was a somewhat biologically determined representation of race, since race was conceptualized as something worn "under the skin" for some and "on the skin" for others. But other students acknowledged that race is about the social meanings assigned to those visual cues that are culturally determined.
- Another pair of students placed four chairs back to back in the middle of the room and asked four people, including the instructor (who is of mixed racial background, Angla-Chicana), to sit in the chairs and cover their eyes with a bandana. Once their eyes were covered, the rest of the class was put on their knees without bandanas, around the seated people. In this instance, the facilitators, both students of color, problematized racial relations, even as they depicted them. The blindfolded "White people" sitting in the middle of the room could not see, signifying that they were blind to who they were and unable to see how they stood on "the heads" of people of color (a reference to *The Color of Fear*). The people of color could see clearly that they were marginalized, and they knew the position of the White people better than the White people themselves. The "people of color" were also *not* racially marked (with the bandanas), which in racialized communities is possible to imagine.

Discussion

After two or three pairs of students have modeled being classroom instructors, begin the discussion to debrief the exercise. Allow at least thirty minutes for the debriefing. Begin with a discussion of the exercise. We have listed questions below that can be utilized as a starting point for the discussion. Remember that the class has already briefly discussed each of the formations that the pairs created. It is not the formations themselves that are the point of this debriefing, but the process of how the exercise was conducted.

Questions for the Pairs of Facilitators

- What did it feel like to be the "chosen ones"?
- What did it feel like to be in a position to choose which students would help form your visual representation of race and which students would not be chosen?
- When other pairs were performing the exercise, how did it make you feel? Did you feel competitive about your formation in comparison to theirs? Or did you want to help them and collaborate to build on their vision by using your experience?

Questions for the Class in General

- What did it feel like not to be chosen to lead the class?
- Who had the most power in this exercise and why?
- Did the people who never got the chance to be facilitators feel like their ideas of race relations in America got adequately represented?
- Did anyone who was not a "leader" feel like they could have done a better job for the task at hand?
- How did whiteness function in this exercise?

When we opened our classroom to questions, what was noticeable and surprising was that it was the students who were in the majority formations, not the facilitators, who had the most powerful insights about how to read the racial formations. That is, those students who were privileged in respect to being able to conceptualize and produce the racial representations had *less* insight as to their meanings than those who were acted upon and implicitly had to "figure out" what those formations meant.

Some students in our classes said it was stressful to be the facilitators. Others experienced stress being moved around at the whims of the facilitators and felt vulnerable to their power, and some even resented their powerlessness. However, the overwhelming reaction to the exercise was a positive one because of the insights it afforded them about race.

When asked to make a comparison between how they were positioned in the class and racial positioning in U.S. society, some compared the "chosen ones" who moved others to "White men" because they have the power to represent the world and ask people to move without having to explain anything. Some students noted some facilitators seemed to take up their role of power with relish, while others seemed more reluctant. These comments can lead into a discussion about voice, power, powerlessness, representation, collaboration, and competitiveness.

Now shift the discussion to yourself as the teacher conducting this exercise. It is likely that your position in the class and exercise has not been discussed or even noticed up to this point. Focus on the fact that you were orchestrating the whole exercise without even being "visible" within it. Relate that to whiteness and how it functions—commenting, for example, that whiteness is normative and functions through its invisibility. Some students in our classes noticed this quickly. Others made the analogy to the white educational system and how it reproduces relations of power.

Next, discuss how the different facilitators were really "modeling" you in the exercise, after having being chosen by you to embody that place of power and privilege. Move the discussion to the relationship between whiteness and the model minority. In one class, students saw the lead pairs as "White women" in relation to the instructor who represented "White men" because she was orchestrating the whole exercise and they were acting from her unseen command. From this perspective, they also saw the model minority as assimilated people of color who were willing to do the work of whiteness.

One way to further clarify the relationship between whiteness and the model minority is to deconstruct the linguistic assumptions of being a model minority:

- What does it mean to be a model?
- What are they supposed to be "modeling"?
- For whom are they a model?

- What are the benefits of being a "model"?
- What are the costs of being a "model"? To oneself, one's community, other communities of color?

Finally, get students to reflect on their own identity and how it is positioned within whiteness. Discuss in particular the points of similarity and departure for Asian Americans or other minority groups who get positioned as a "model minority." End by discussing possible ways for resisting these constructions.

Have students engage in a "free write" for five minutes at the end of class to capture their experiences of this exercise. Ask them to write creatively about the issues brought up in the exercise and particularly about their reflections on their own positioning within the exercise and within race in U.S. society.

Take-home Assignment

Following this assignment, tell students to develop the free-write exercise into a "reaction paper" (three-to-five pages) and turn it in for a grade. They must use at least one outside source and analyze the class exercise using the readings on whiteness, race, and the model minority. Most important, they must reflect on their own positionality in relation to whiteness and race and explain how they can change into being anti-racist.

Notes

1. E. Martinez, "Seeing More Than Black and White: Latinos, Racism, and the Cultural Divide," in *Race, Class and Gender. An Anthology*, eds. M. L. Andersen and P. H. Collins (Belmont, CA: Wadsworth, 2001): 108-14.

2. Ruth Frankenberg, *White Women, Race Matters: The Social Construction of Whiteness* (Minneapolis: University of Minnesota, 1993).

3. Paula Gunn Allen, "When Women Throw Down Bundles: Angry Women Are Building," in *Race, Class and Gender*.

4. Peggy McIntosh, "White Privilege and Male Privilege," in *Race, Class and Gender*.

5. Lee Mun Wah, *The Color of Fear* (Oakland, CA: Stir Fry Productions, 1994), videorecording.

Recommended Resources

Richard Dyer, *White* (London: Routledge, 1997).
George Lipsitz, "The Possessive Investment in Whiteness: Racialized Social Democracy and the 'White' Problem in American Studies." *American Quarterly* 47:3 (1995), 369-87.

Part V

Resources

Chapter 28

Web Resources for Teaching Asian American Studies

Glenn Omatsu

The Internet is expanding ways we teach and ways we can think about our teaching. In this chapter, I provide a list of websites that can serve as teaching resources. These websites are not simply resources for subject matter but can serve as teaching tools that expand our horizons about pedagogy.

Generally, most educators use the Internet to gain access to information for the content of their instruction. A smaller number experiment with the web's interactive capabilities by introducing hypernews assignments, discussion boards, e-mail listserves, and chat rooms into their classrooms. Still others use the technology to share insights with others by documenting and archiving class accomplishments. Perhaps not surprising, students and youth are at the vanguard in exploring the pedagogical capabilities of the Internet through web-based projects. Thus, in the list of resources below, I highlight web projects created by students on topics ranging from history and literature to popular culture and community mobilizations for social justice. I compiled this list of websites from resources from previous classes as well as lists created by advanced webmasters Wataru Ebihara, Loren Javier, C. N. Le, Mimi Nguyen, Tony Osumi, and Daniel Tsang.

The Internet is dynamic, and by the time this book is in print the list of resources will be out of date. However, my main goal in creating this list is not to be comprehensive but to encourage educators to use the Internet as a teaching resource. Especially as the "teaching tools" and class projects sections below demonstrate, the Internet can help us reconceptualize pedagogy as an interactive process linking teaching and learning.

Aside from being outdated and non-comprehensive, the list below is also selective. Omitted are the numerous websites created by new Asian Pacific immigrants that are in languages other than English. Since the great majority of Asian Americans and Pacific Islanders today are immigrants, this is a serious limitation. Those educators with language expertise beyond English should explore ways to incorporate immigrant language websites into their classrooms. Among valuable immigrant language websites are home pages of ethnic media and community organizations.

Finally, it's ironic that I'm writing this chapter. Those who know me know that I'm technologically backward. In other words, technology moves forward, while I lag far behind, driving old cars, not buying a computer until relatively recently, and not owning a cell phone. Yet, in classes I've taught at UCLA during the past seven years, I've experimented with "web magazines" to document student work. Of course, I know nothing about website design, and I've relied entirely on the resources provided by the UCLA Asian American Studies Center and on the expertise and kindness of webmasters such as Tam Nguyen and Steven Masami Ropp.

Why have I embraced web technology in contrast to other technologies? I suspect that I am intrigued by the political implications of the Internet—its capability to promote grassroots education and mobilization over time and space, its capacity to access vast amounts of information that until now was available only to an elite, and its dynamic impact on expanding consciousness, especially our connections to a global community.

Veteran activist Grace Lee Boggs of Detroit was one of the first to recognize the political implications of the Internet for grassroots organizing in this period of globalization. Several years ago, she urged fellow activists to study Margaret Wheatley's *Leadership and the New Science* (San Francisco, 1999) and to apply its insights to political organizing. Wheatley critiques the way we conceptualize social organization and social change. According to Wheatley, we are mired in concepts adopted from Newtonian physics—concepts such as critical mass, inertia, equilibrium, and hierarchical stages of development. Science has moved on; yet, our thinking remains imprisoned in a framework from three hundred years ago. Wheatley explores the ideas from "new science," especially quantum physics, such as chaos, disequilibrium, fields, and interactive processes in complex systems involving webs of relationships. She encourages us to see their relevance for social change in the twenty-first century. Adopting Wheatley's perspective of "new science," Grace Lee Boggs analyzes the significance of global protests—both small and large—against multinational corporations and institutions such as the World Trade Organization. She quotes a passage from Wheatley's book contrasting Newtonian notions of social change to those of the "new science":

> In a web, the potential impact of local actions bears no relationship to their size. When we choose to act locally, we may be wanting to influence the entire system. But we work where we are, with the system that we know, the one we can get our arms around. From a Newtonian perspective, our efforts often seem too small, and we doubt that our actions will make a difference. Or perhaps we hope that our small efforts will contribute incrementally to large-scale change. Step by step, system by system, we aspire to develop enough mass or force to alter the larger system.
>
> But a quantum view explains the success of small efforts quite differently. Acting locally allows us to be inside the movement and flow of the system, participating in all those complex events occurring simultaneously. We are more likely to be sensitive to the dynamics of this system, and thus more effective. However, changes in small places also affect the global system, not through incrementalism, but because every small system participates in an unbroken wholeness. Activities in one part of the whole create effects that appear in distant places. Because of these unseen connections, there is potential value in working anywhere in the system. We

> never know how our small activities will affect others through the invisible fabric of our connectedness. I have learned that in this exquisitely connected world, it's never a question of "critical mass." It's always about *critical connections*.

The Internet helps us grasp the significance of "critical connections" in this period in world history. It helps us understand how our small actions, even in one classroom, can have impact if we take the time to share our insights with others. By conceptualizing the Internet as our connection to a community of colleagues around the world, we can build on each other's insights to grapple with common challenges in our classrooms. Of course, "virtual" communities are no substitutes for face-to-face communities, but in this period of globalization they can help highlight what Wheatley calls our "connectedness" and the crucial role that community-building plays in learning and teaching.

Learning, according to the Russian psychologist Vygotsky, is intrinsically a social activity based on social interaction and mentoring. Yet, paradoxically, in the United States today, teaching is usually described as a solitary activity. Teachers—whether in K-12 schools or in colleges—hunger for community and the opportunity to share ideas about pedagogy with colleagues. Perhaps through new technologies like the Internet, we can rediscover the crucial role that community-building plays in pedagogy.

Asian American Education: General Resources

Asia for Kids
Catalog of children's books relating to Asia and Asian Americans.
www.afk.com

Asian American History and Culture Resources
Web links compiled by the Center for Educational Telecommunications, which develops multimedia programs promoting multiculturalism.
www.cetel.org/res.html

Asian American Literature for Young Adults: A Bibliography
An annotated bibliography for youth, twelve years and older.
http://falcon.jmu.edu/~ramseyil/asian.htm

Children and YA's Books with Asian American Themes
Asian American books from Cynthia Leitich Smith's children's literature list.
www.cynthialeitichsmith.com/AsianAmerican.htm

Race and Ethnicity
Michael C. Kearl's comprehensive directory of websites on racism and stereotypes.
www.trinity.edu/~mkearl/race.html

Asian American Education: Teaching Resources

Ask Asia: Asian American
Lesson plans, readings, and resources from the Asia Society.
www.askasia.org/teachers/Instructional_Resources/Regional/Asian_American.htm

Boggs Center to Nurture Community Leadership
Website promoting the ideas of James Boggs and Grace Lee Boggs; includes essays on Freedom Schooling for this period.
www.boggscenter.org/

Bridge Teaching Demonstration Website
This website explores the special challenges of teaching low-income, underprepared college freshmen who are often the first in their families to attend college.
www.csun.edu/eop//htdocs/bridgedemo/

Educational Leadership
Each issue of this magazine focuses on an issue related to education and teaching.
www.ascd.org

Educators for Social Responsibility
ESR's mission is to "make teaching social responsibility a core practice in education so that young people develop the convictions and skills needed to shape a safe, sustainable, democratic, and just world."
www.esrnational.org

Faculty Mentor Program

Resources from California State University, Northridge, focusing on ways to incorporate the concept of mentoring into teaching and other interactions with students.

www.csun.edu/eop/htdocs/fmp.html

Healthwrights

Website for David Werner, co-author of *Helping Health Workers Learn*, an excellent book applying the ideas of Freire to grassroots education for social change.

www.healthwrights.org

Kathy Shrock's Guide for Educators

An annotated list of teaching resources, lesson plans, and other tools.

www.4j.lane.edu/tilt/tools_teacher/workshop/nehs/nehs.html

Learning and Teaching

Excellent list of links on learning theory; created by James Atherton.

www.dmu.ac.uk/%7Ejamesa/learning/

Mind/Brain Learning Principles

Summary of ideas of Renate Nummela Caine and Geoffrey Caine on implications of latest research on the human brain for teaching in the classroom.

www.newhorizons.org/neuro/caine.htm

A Primer on How Learning Happens

From the National Education Association's "Thriving in Academe" series.

www.nea.org/he/advo02/advo0602/feature.html

Rethinking Schools

Lesson plans and other resources for K-12 teachers interested in social justice.

www.rethinkingschools.org

Teachers' Asian Studies Summer Institute

This website from California State Polytechnic University, Pomona, includes lesson plans on Asia and Asian Americans created by participants in 1996 and 1997.

www.intranet.csupomona.edu/%7Etassi/tassi.htm

Teaching and Learning Strategies

Strategies described include character education, cooperative learning, democratic classroom, learning styles, multicultural education, and service-learning.

www.newhorizons.org/strategies/front_strategies.html

Teaching for Change

Books and other resources for teachers interested in linking classroom education to social change; publisher of the important book, *Beyond Heroes and Holidays: A Practical Guide to K-12 Multicultural, Anti-Racist Education and Staff Development*, which contains numerous lesson plans relating to social justice.

www.teachingforchange.org

Teaching Techniques and Lesson Plans

Extensive list of lesson plans for K-12 classrooms, with special sections on teaching literature and history; created by Dr. Janice Patten and updated regularly.

http://theliterarylink.com/teaching.html

Teaching Tolerance

Educational resources for teachers and students, including classroom exercises.

www.teachingtolerance.org

Visible Knowledge Project

Explores uses of technology to promote college-level teaching at twenty-one campuses.

http://crossroads.georgetown.edu/vkp/

Asian American Studies Class Websites and Student Projects

Asian American Community Education and Youth Empowerment

Explores ways that college students can work with K-12 teachers to respond to educational needs of in an elementary school classroom.

www.sscnet.ucla.edu/aasc/classweb/fall01/aas197j/

Asian American Contemporary Issues

Professor Steven Ropp's online class on Asian American contemporary issues.

www.csun.edu/~smr78195/aas345/

Asian American Movement

Students apply lessons from the Asian American Movement of the early 1970s to issues facing communities today.

www.sscnet.ucla.edu/aasc/mvmt/

Asian American Social Movements: Mobilizing for Peace and Justice

On the eve of the U.S. invasion of Iraq in 2003, students mobilize fellow students around issues relating to peace and justice.

www.sscnet.ucla.edu/aasc/classweb/winter03/aas116/index.html

Asian American Social Movements: The Role of Students in Redefining Asian American Studies

UCLA students redefine the mission of Asian American Studies to serve the needs of communities.

www.sscnet.ucla.edu/99F/asian197j-1/webmag99.htm

Asian American Social Movements: Strategies for Community Education

www.sscnet.ucla.edu/aasc/classweb/winter05/aas116/

Asian American Student Community Activism

Examines the "pivotal role that Asian Pacific Islander students have played in community organizing, both historically and today."

www.sscnet.ucla.edu/aasc/classweb/spring00/webmag_197j/index.html

Asian American Studies & Community Webpage
Professor Eric Mar's homepage contains links to community organizations, current events, and other resources.
http://online.sfsu.edu/~ericmar/

Asian American Studies and Students, "How the West Was Won-Ton"
Professor Ellen Wu's class focuses on issues affecting Asian American youth.
www.sscnet.ucla.edu/aasc/faculty/ellenwu/asian100/

Asian Americans Share Their History
High school students present a workshop on Asian Pacific American history.
www.inform.umd.edu/News/Eclipse/eclipse/4-7-98/4-7-98-history.html

Asian Pacific American Labor Studies
Through participatory research on Asian immigrant labor struggles in Los Angeles, UCLA students help a community organization create a documentary on grassroots labor struggles.
www.sscnet.ucla.edu/aasc/classweb/winter02/aas197a/index.html

Asian Pacific American Labor Studies (community internships)
Students participate in internships in organizing campaigns involving immigrant garment, market, and newspaper workers.
www.sscnet.ucla.edu/aasc/classweb/spring02/aas197b/index.html

Brown from the Sun
Students compile resources relating to Filipino and Filipino American literature.
http://eths.sfsu.edu/aas363s2003/resource.html

Electronic Pedagogy Project
Project bringing together Asian American Studies faculty and students from campuses in the Northeast and Midwest around discussions based on common texts.
http://chnm.gmu.edu/eoc/EP/epindex.html

Feast of Resistance
Educator Tony Osumi's lesson plan using food to teach Asian American history.
www.sscnet.ucla.edu/aasc/classweb/spring00/webmag_197j/tony_fea.html

Field Notes & Photographs from San Francisco Bay Area and Seattle
Professor James Sobredo uses his expertise in photography and research to show students how to do an assignment about visits to historic Asian American communities.
www.csus.edu/aas/aas-faculty/sobredo-fieldnotes-7-99.htm

Information Technology in Teaching
Professor Jerry Kang's website shows how information technology can "help us become better law professors, in our scholarship, teaching, and service."
www1.law.ucla.edu/~kang/Scholarship/Cyberspace/IT_in_Teaching/it_in_teaching.html

Interactive Chinese American History

Professor Sandra Liu's class includes an historical timeline and other resources.

www.itp.berkeley.edu/~asam121/

Investigative Journalism and People of Color: Race Relations in L.A.

Web magazine of student writings examines race relations in Los Angeles.

www.sscnet.ucla.edu/aasc/classweb/fall98/M163/webmag.html

Investigative Journalism and People of Color: Words of Color

Web magazine of student writings examines interethnic conflict and cooperation.

www.sscnet.ucla.edu/aasc/classweb/fall97/M163/index.html

Lesson Plans: Asian American Studies

Lesson plans relating to Asian American history for K-12 classrooms compiled by public television station KQED.

www.kqed.org/topics/education/educators/lessons/asian-american.jsp

Making Murals, Making History

Educator Tony Osumi's guide for mural-making for K-12 teachers.

www.kuidaosumi.com/murals/muralguide.html

Math in Motion: Origami in the Classroom K-8

Barbara Pearl shows how origami can be used to teach math and issues relating to history, the environment, and social responsibility.

www.mathinmotion.com/

Moving Words: Asian Immigration

Four lesson plans on Asian American history by Barbara Kramarz.

www.intranet.csupomona.edu/%7Etassi/moving.htm

Oral Histories

Librarian Jie Tian of California State University, Fullerton, provides a research for Asian American oral histories.

http://guides.library.fullerton.edu/asian/oralhistory.htm

The Oriental Aisle: A Survey of Asian Junk Food

Allan Balangue's exploration of popular Asian snacks and drinks in Asian markets as well as frozen Oriental foods in mainstream supermarkets.

www.geocities.com/grubonrice/

Religious Studies

Professor Amir Hussain's homepage provides links to understanding Islam and other world religions as well as links to his favorite band and poet William Blake.

www.csun.edu/~ah34999/

Teaching to Change L.A.

Online magazine explores the theme "What Does Democracy Look Like?" through lesson plans created for kindergarten, elementary school, and high school classes.

http://tcla.gseis.ucla.edu/democracy/home.html

Teaching with Historic Places

K-12 lesson plans about early Asian immigrant enclaves of Locke and Walnut Grove in California and factors behind the WW II incarceration of Japanese Americans.

www.cr.nps.gov/nr/twhp/may00.htm

Theory

Professor Melinda L. de Jesus' website uses "hypertext amplifications to deepen understanding of theory in Asian America."

http://www.public.asu.edu/~dejesus/330groupprojects.htm

Tufts Chinatown Project

Students respond to the needs of Boston Chinatown through class projects under the supervision of Professor Jean Wu and other faculty.

http://uccps.tufts.edu/04_Community/BridgesChinatown.html

Asian American and Pacific Islander Communities: General Resources

AA Rising

Frequently updated website with extensive links on Asian American entertainment, publications, resources, and topics such as "import culture."

www.aarising.com

Asian American Cybernauts Page

Website created by Wataru Ebihara in 1995 contains links to community groups and cultural expression; last updated in November 2000.

http://janet.org/~ebihara/wataru_aacyber.html

Asian American History Timeline

History timeline created for the PBS documentary *Ancestors in the Americas*.

www.cetel.org/timeline.html

Asian American Resources

Loren Javier's website provides links to history, community groups, and media.

www.lorenjavier.com/asian/index.html

Asian American Movement Ezine

A website for radical and progressive Asian American perspectives with a focus on community organizing.

www.aamovement.net

Asian American Village

Online magazine explores issues relating to Asian American employment, education, politics, and culture.

www.imdiversity.com/villages/asian/village_asian_american.asp

Asian Immigrant Newspapers

New California Media Online provides perspectives from Asian immigrant newspapers; includes some translated articles from Chinese language newspapers.

www.ncmonline.com/asian/

Asian Indian resources

Web resources on history and demographics of Indian Americans.

www.thingsindian.com/history.htm

Asian-Nation: The Landscape of Asian America

Essays and links to history and contemporary issues; created by C. N. Le.

www.asian-nation.org/

Asian Week

Online version of Asian American weekly newspaper, published in San Francisco.

http://news.asianweek.com/news/

East and Southeast Asia: An Annotated Directory of Internet Resources

Extensive list weblinks relating to history, community organizations, and issues affecting Asian Americans, including the Wen Ho Lee controversy.

http://newton.uor.edu/Departments&Programs/AsianStudiesDept/asianam.html

Daniel Tsang's Asian American Studies Resources

Extensive list of created by UC Irvine librarian Daniel Tsang; updated regularly.

http://sun3.lib.uci.edu/~dtsang/aas2.htm

The Diverse Face of Asians and Pacific Islanders: A Demographic Profile of Los Angeles County

Created by Kimiko Kelly for the Asian Pacific American Legal Center.

http://apalc.org

Goldsea Asian American Supersite

Covers issues affecting Asian Americans; includes interactive areas on topics ranging from "Asian American male image" to "eye makeup tips."

www.goldsea.com/

Hawaiian nation

History and information on the movement for Hawaiian self-determination.

http://hawaii-nation.org/

Model Minority: A Guide to Asian American Empowerment

Essays and weblinks on community issues.

http://modelminority.com/

National Asian American Telecommunications Association
Video catalog and resources for community-based filmmakers.
www.naatanet.org/

Pacific Islands Internet Resources
Valuable collection of web links to nations of the Pacific.
http://www2.hawaii.edu/~ogden/piir/index.html

Queer Asian Pacific Resources
Resources relating to AIDS and "coming out"; last updated in 1998.
www.geocities.com/WestHollywood/Heights/5010/resources.html

SAMAR, South Asian Magazine for Action and Reflection
Online version of magazine focusing on social processes and social analyses "drawing energy from activist involvement" in North America and South Asia.
www.samarmagazine.org/

Southeast Asian Archive
Includes a virtual exhibit on the Southeast Asian refugee experience in the U.S.
www.lib.uci.edu/libraries/collections/sea/sasian.html

UCLA Asian American Studies Center
Resources relating to Asian American Studies and communities.
www.sscnet.ucla.edu/aasc

U.S. Census Bureau Reports on Asian Americans and Pacific Islanders
Downloadable files (PDF) based on the 2000 U.S. Census.
www.census.gov

Vietspace
Virtual community for Vietnamese Americans.
www.kicon.com/

Yellowworld.org
Promotes the "cultivation of a social and political Asian consciousness."
www.yellowworld.org

Index

About the Contributors

Editors

Edith Wen-Chu Chen (Ph.D. sociology, UCLA) is an associate professor in the Asian American Studies department at California State University, Northridge (CSUN). She has taught at University of Hawai'i, Kapiolani Community College, UCLA, and Harvey Mudd College. Her interests include race and ethnicity, Asian American women, intercultural communication, and Asians in the Americas. Her work, "Constructing a Non-Asian Identity: Asian American Sisters in 'White' Sororities," will appear in *Living in the Light: Multicultural Communication and Asian American Women*.

Glenn Omatsu (glenn.omatsu@csun.edu) is a lecturer in Asian American Studies and the Educational Opportunity Program at California State University, Northridge (CSUN) and also teaches classes at Pasadena City College and UCLA. He is co-editor (with Steve Louie) of *Asian Americans: The Movement and Moment* and has written articles on freedom schooling, immigrant labor campaigns, and other social movements for justice.

Contributors

Allan Aquino is a lecturer specializing in Filipino American history and literature. He has taught courses at California State University, Northridge, Loyola Marymount University, and UCLA. An oral historian, journalist, and poet, Aquino is an active member of the Los Angeles chapter of the Filipino American National Historical Society (FANHS-L.A.) and the L.A. Enkanto Kollective, a verbal arts performance group.

Asian Pacific American Legal Center (APALC) is the largest organization in Southern California that provides Asian and Pacific Islander and other communities with multi-lingual, culturally sensitive services and legal education in the areas of immigration and naturalization, workers' rights, family law and domestic violence, immigrant welfare, and voting rights and anti-discrimination. Has also worked toward building interethnic relations.

Wayne Au is attending the doctoral program in the department of curriculum and instruction at the University of Wisconsin, Madison. He has been a high school teacher in history,

English, Ethnic Studies, and Asian American Studies. His work has appeared in *Rethinking Schools, Resistance in Paradise,* and *Beyond Heroes and Holiday.*

Christina Ayala-Alcantar (Ph.D. ecological-community psychology, Michigan State University) is a faculty member in the Chicano/a Studies Department at California State University, Northridge. Her areas of interest are K-12 teacher training and multiracial feminism. She shares her life with husband, Alex, 2-year-old daughter Maya Guadalupe, and Luna the cat.

Eiichiro Azuma is assistant professor of history and Asian American Studies at the University of Pennsylvania. His research focuses on Japanese American history, immigration history, and transnational dimensions of Asian American experiences.

Carl L. Bankston, III, is professor of sociology, director of graduate studies in sociology, and director of the Asian Studies program at Tulane University. He spent two years in Thailand as a U.S. Peace Corps volunteer and five years working overseas with refugees from Southeast Asia. He is co-author, with Min Zhou, of *Growing Up American: How Vietnamese Children Adapt to Life in the United States.* He is also author of three additional books and editor of six books, as well as author of more than ninety journal articles and book chapters.

Dharm P. S. Bhawuk (Ph.D. Illinois), a citizen of Nepal, is professor of management and culture and community psychology at the University of Hawai'i at Manoa. His research interests include indigenous psychology and management, including cross-cultural training, diversity management, and individualism and collectivism. He has published more than thirty articles and book chapters and is a co-editor of the book *Asian Contributions to Cross-Cultural Psychology.* He is a founding fellow of the International Academy of Intercultural Research.

Michi Fu (Ph.D., Clinical Psychology, California School of Professional Psychology at Los Angeles, 2002) is a licensed psychologist in the states of Hawai'i and California. She is a supervising psychologist at the Asian Pacific Family Center of Pacific Clinics in Rosemead, California. She also teaches at Claremont McKenna College and Alliant International University and has a part-time private practice in Southern California. Her research interests are: ethnic identity, acculturation, family conflict, interracial relationships, and Asian American females. She has served two terms as board member of the Asian American Psychological Association (1998-2000 and 2003-2005) and is an Okura Mental Health Leadership Fellow (2002).

Joseph A. Galura is a faculty associate in the Asian/Pacific Islander American Studies program, co-director of the Lives of Urban Children and Youth Initiative, and director of the Project Community at the University of Michigan. His latest books are *Praxis IV: Engaging the Whole of Service-Learning, Diversity and Learning Communities* (lead editor) and *Tapestry: Filipinos in Michigan, 1900-1950,* his second book with Emily Porcincula Lawsin.

Amir Hussain is Associate Professor of Theological Studies at Loyola Marymount University, where he teaches courses in world religions. His speciality is the study of Islam, focussing on contemporary Muslim societies in North America. Although born in Pakistan, he emigrated to Canada with his family when he was four. His academic degrees (B.Sc., M.A., Ph.D.) are all from the University of Toronto.

Kimiko Kelly is a research analyst in the demographic research unit at the Asian Pacific American Legal Center. Her current projects include compiling demographic profiles of Asians and Pacific Islanders in Southern California. She also helps conduct Census 2000 trainings for the community in coalition with local Census Information Centers. She received her masters in public policy from UCLA.

James Lam is currently a nonprofit sector consultant and a graduate student at Claremont Graduate University's Peter F. Drucker School of Management. He has worked in the areas of nonprofit management, health care philanthropy, and affordable housing development and finance, and was formerly the associate director of the Orange County Asian and Pacific Islander Community Alliance. Lam is a graduate of Orange County public schools, the UC Irvine, and Harvard University's John F. Kennedy School of Government, where he received a masters in public policy.

Mariam Beevi Lam (Ph.D. UC Irvine) is assistant professor of comparative literature and Southeast Asian Studies at the UC Riverside, with emphases in Asian American studies and women's studies. Her research and teaching areas of specialization include the Vietnamese American community, Vietnam studies, the French Vietnamese, and comparative diasporic studies.

Emily Porcincula Lawsin is a trustee of the Filipino American National Historical Society and a lecturer in Asian/Pacific Islander American studies, American culture, and women's studies at the University of Michigan. She is the co-author (with Joseph A. Galura) of *Filipino Women in Detroit: 1945-1955, Oral Histories from the Filipino American Oral History Project of Michigan*. A spoken word performance poet originally from "She-attle," Washington, she has performed on radio and stage throughout the United States and Manila.

Andrew Leong is associate professor at the College of Public and Community Service at the University of Massachusetts in Boston. His specialty is law, justice, and equality pertaining to disenfranchised communities, with a particular focus on the Asian American community. He has served in many capacities in the struggle against institutional expansion and environmental racism in Boston's Chinatown. He is the chair of the Campaign to Protect Chinatown. He has also provided technical assistance to victims of anti-Asian violence and has written on issues pertaining to welfare and immigration reform, hate crimes, and environmental justice.

Sin Yen Ling is a staff attorney at the Asian American Legal Defense and Education Fund (AALDEF), where she has done litigation and advocacy in the areas of anti-Asian violence, racial profiling, and 9/11 detentions. She has received numerous awards, and was selected as one of the Top 25 Lawyers Under 40 by the National Asian Pacific American Bar Association in 2002. A native New Yorker, she was born in Manhattan's Chinatown to immigrant parents who worked in garment factories and restaurants.

Sheena Malhotra (Ph.D. communication studies, University of New Mexico) is an associate professor in the women's studies department at California State University, Northridge. She has been involved with film, television, and documentary work in India and the United States. Her research focuses on constructions of the nation in postcolonial mediated contexts, and performances of whiteness and diasporic South Asian communities. Her recent writing appears in *Globalization, Media Hegemony and Social Class*.

Gina Masequesmay is a 1.5 generation, Vietnamese American, lesbian sociologist. She earned her doctorate degree in sociology at UCLA. She is currently an associate professor in Asian American studies at California State University, Northridge. Her research interests include Vietnamese Americans, sexualities, negotiating multiple identities, race and ethnicity, and immigrant adaptation.

Michael Matsuda (M.P.P., University of Southern California) works as a coordinator for the Anaheim Union High School District Beginning Teacher Support and Assessment Program. He also teaches multicultural education in the teacher education programs at California State University, Fullerton, and Chapman University. He is a two-time "Teacher of the Year," an Orange County Human Relations Award recipient, and a founding board member and current chairperson of the Orange County Asian and Pacific Islander Community Alliance.

Vijayan P Munusamy, a Malaysian citizen, is an East-West Center degree fellow pursuing a Ph.D. in international management at University of Hawai'i at Manoa. His research interests include cross-cultural management, cultural intelligence and cross-cultural training. He is the recipient of a number of awards including the The Wall Street Journal Student Achievement Award, and Asian Development Bank-Japan Government Scholarship Award.

Ajay T. Nair (atnair@sas.upenn.edu) is the director of the Pan-Asian American Community House and assistant director of the Asian American studies program at the University of Pennsylvania. He received his Ph.D. from the Pennsylvania State University's College of Education. At the University of Pennsylvania, he teaches service-learning courses in Asian American studies and urban studies.

National Asian Pacific American Legal Consortium (NAPALC) works to advance the human and civil rights of Asian Americans through advocacy, public policy, public education, and litigation. Founded in 1991, NAPALC includes some of the nation's leading experts on issues of importance to the Asian American community including affirmative action, anti-Asian violence prevention/race relations, census, immigrant rights, language access, and voting rights.

Orange County Asian and Pacific Islander Community Alliance (OCAPICA) was established in 1997 to build a healthier and stronger community by enhancing the well-being of Asians and Pacific Islanders through inclusive partnerships in the areas of service, education, advocacy, organizing, and research. OCAPICA also facilitates partnerships among organizations serving or representing the various Asian and Pacific Islander communities in Orange County, California, to collaborate on policy and advocacy issues important to the community.

Tony Osumi (tosumi@lausd.k12.ca.us, www.kuidaosumi.com) has taught elementary school at UCLA and now teaches at Central High School/All Peoples Branch in Los Angeles Unified School District. He received his M.A. in Asian American Studies at UCLA and is a member of Nikkei for Civil Rights and Redress (NCRR) and the Little Tokyo-based J-Town Voice!. He has written articles and poems and created artwork for numerous community issues.

Steven Masami Ropp (Ph.D. anthropology, UCLA) is a cultural anthropologist and community activist whose research focuses on the intersections of race, ethnicity, and nationalism for people of Asian descent in the Americas. He has conducted research on subjects such as political empowerment, ethnic conflict, and economic development in Belize, Los Angeles, and Peru. He is particularly interested in translating political economy themes into grassroots action through popular education techniques such as Forum Theater. Currently he is an Assistant Professor in the Asian American Studies Department at California State University, Northridge.

Aimee Carrillo Rowe (Ph.D. communication studies, University of Washington) is assistant professor of rhetoric at the University of Iowa. Her research and teaching focus on third world feminisms, whiteness and antiracism studies, critical pedagogy, and the politics of spirituality and justice. Her recent writing appears in *Feminist Media Studies* and *Radical History Review* (forthcoming).

Sweatshop Watch is a coalition of over thirty labor, community, civil rights, immigrant rights, women's, religious, and student organizations, as well as many individuals, committed to eliminating the exploitation that occurs in sweatshops. It serves low-wage workers nationally and globally, with a focus on garment workers in California. Its supporters believe that workers should earn a living wage in a safe, decent work environment and that those responsible for the exploitation of sweatshop workers must be held accountable.

Daniel Hiroyuki Teraguchi received his Ed.D. in educational leadership and higher educational administration from Idaho State University. In addition to being a program and research associate at the Association of American Colleges and Universities, he has been an adjunct faculty in the Asian American studies program at the University of Maryland College Park. His research interests include pedagogy and voice in the classroom and the use of organizational theory to sustain ethnic studies programs.

Masaru Torito was raised in Colorado by a Japanese father and a Panamanian mother. He recently graduated from the University of Colorado with a degree in communications. At the University of Colorado, he helped establish the multiracial/ethnic/cultural student organization. He also helped establish a politically motivated Asian American campus group called CAPSA (Colorado Asian Pacific Student Alliance).

Diep Tran is a program coordinator at the Orange County Asian and Pacific Islander Alliance. Besides her post-production administrative work on the curriculum project, she helps coordinate a regional research, education, and outreach program promoting the prevention of breast and cervical cancers among Vietnamese American women. She earned a B.A. in psychology and international studies from UC Irvine.

Haunani-Kay Trask is former head of the Center for Hawaiian Studies at the University of Hawai'i, Manoa campus and is currently a professor there. Both her poetry and prose have been published widely, and as a Native Hawaiian activist, she has been on the forefront of the fight for Native Hawaiian sovereignty and justice.

Vivian Tseng is a Postdoctoral Fellow and Program Associate at the William T. Grant Foundation. She received her Ph.D. at New York University in community and developmental psychology. The overarching goal of her work is to facilitate social justice through research, teaching, and activism. Her teaching and research examines race, culture, and immigration in the lives of children, young adults, and their families. Her work has been published in a number of journals including *Child Development* and *Community Psychology*.

Maria Mami Turnmeyer is a lecturer at California State University, Northridge, in the department of Asian American studies. She teaches courses in Asian American literature and Asian American women. Aside from teaching, she is active in community performance art and is a published writer of fiction and poetry.

George Uba is joint professor of English and Asian American studies at California State University, Northridge. He was on the executive committee of the Asian American Literature Discussion Group of the Modern Language Association, and from 1998-2000 served as chair of the department of Asian American Studies at CSUN. Currently, he directs the Honors Program for the department of English. His scholarship has centered on Asian American literature, nineteenth and early twentieth-century American fiction, and composition and literary pedagogy.

Laura Uba, Ph.D., has written *Asian Americans: Personality Patterns, Identity, and Mental Health*; senior authored *Psychology* ; and written *A Postmodern Psychology of Asian Americans: Creating Knowledge of a Racial Minority* during the almost twenty years she has been teaching Asian American studies. Currently she is a lecturer at the Asian American studies department at California State University, Northridge.

W. David Wakefield is an associate professor in the department of child and adolescent development at California State University, Northridge. He received his Ph.D. in educational psychology from UC Santa Barbara. He has developed and taught innovative university courses exploring race, culture, and ethnicity in children's development for prospective practitioners working with children, families, and youth and facilitated diversity training seminars. He is of mixed heritage (African American/white).

Grace J. Yoo is an associate professor of Asian American studies at San Francisco State University. She received her Ph.D. in sociology from UC San Francisco. She has worked previously with National Asian Pacific Islander American Health Forum and National Asian Pacific Center on Aging. Her teaching and research interests are in the areas of Asian Americans and health and aging.

Min Zhou, Ph.D., is professor of sociology and chair of the Asian American Studies Interdepartmental Degree Program at UCLA. Her main areas of research are immigration, race/ethnicity, and urban sociology. She has written a number of articles, chapters, and books relating to Asian American experiences, including co-authoring with Carl L. Bankston III *Growing up American: How Vietnamese Children Adapt to Life in the United States*.